Italian Communism: The Escape from Leninism

An Anthropological Perspective

CRIS SHORE

PLUTO PRESS
London • Concord, Mass

To Fiona Graham
with my love

First published 1990 by Pluto Press
345 Archway Road, London N6 5AA
and 141 Old Bedford Road,
Concord, MA 01742, USA

British Library Cataloguing in Publication Data
Shore, Cris
Italian communism: the escape from Leninism
1. Italy. Political parties. Partito communista italiano
I. Title
324.245'075'09

ISBN 0–7453–0334–X
ISBN 0–7453–0554–7 pb

Library of Congress Cataloging in Publication Data
Shore, Cris, 1959-
Italian communism: the escape from
Leninism / Cris Shore
Includes bibliographical references.
ISBN 0–7453–0334–X
ISBN 0–7453–0554–7 pb
1. Partito comunista italiano. 2. Communism–Italy–History–20th
century. I. Title.
JN5657.C63S56 1990
320.5'32'0945–dc20 90–35659
CIP

Typeset by Stanford Desktop Publishing Services, Milton Keynes
Printed in Great Britain by Billing and Sons Ltd, Worcester

Contents

Abbreviations iv
Preface and Acknowledgements v
Figures 1 and 2 viii–ix

Introduction: Communism in Crisis – the Search for a Way Forward 1

Part I: The PCI's Approach to Power: Society, State and the Role of the Party

1: History, Identity and Political Socialisation in the PCI 25

2: Construction of Communist Identity in Italy 52

3: Theory and Practice of Italian Communism: PCI Hegemony, World-view and Myth 70

4: Italian Communism and the Problem of Organisation 88

5: The PCI–Soviet Rift and the Internal Party Debates of 1983 110

Part II: Communism and the Question of Democracy
Introduction 127

6: Party Democracy and the Structure of Power Relations 128

7: Communist Identity Versus Legitimacy: PCI's Awkward Leninist Legacy 145

8: Democratic or Bureaucratic Centralism? Ideology, Organisation and the Crisis in Communism 164

Conclusion: End of the Road for Leninism 185

Notes and References 196
Bibliography 223
Index 242

Abbreviations

ACLI	(Associazione Cristiana dei Lavoratori Italiani) Association of Italian Christian Workers
AKEL	Communist Party of Cyprus
ANPPI	Italian Ex-partisans' Association
CCP	Chinese Communist Party
CGIL	(Confederazione Generale del Lavoro) – General Confederation of Italian Workers (communist and socialist)
CGL	(Confederazione Generale del Lavoro) General Workers' Confederation (recast as CGIL during the partisan struggle)
CISL	(Confederazione Italiana dei Sindacati dei Lavoratori) Italian Confederation of Workers' Trade-Unions (Christian Democrat and Catholic in origin)
CND	Campaign for Nuclear Disarmament
CPGB	Communist Party of Great Britain
CPSU	Communist Party of the Soviet Union
DC	(Democrazia Cristiana) Christian Democrat Party
EEC	European Economic Community
ENI	(Ente Nazionale Idrocarburi) state-owned National Hydrocarbons Corporation
FGCI	(Federazione dei Giovani Comunisti Italiani) Federation of Young Italian Communists
HSWP	Hungarian Socialist-Workers' Party (communist)
IRI	(Istituto per la Ricostruzione Industriale) state-owned Institute for Industrial Reconstruction
KGB	USSR secret police
KKE-Exterior	Communist Party of Greece (pro-Soviet)
KKE-Interior	Communist Party of Greece (Eurocommunist)
MSI	(Movimento Sociale Italiano) Italian Social Movement (neo-Fascist)
NUM	National Union of Mineworkers
OECD	Organisation for Economic Cooperation and Development
OPEC	Organisation of Petroleum-Exporting Countries
PCd'I	(Partito Comunista d'Italia) Communist Party of Italy (changed to PCI in 1943)
PCE	Spanish Communist Party
PCF	(Parti Communiste Française) French Communist Party
PCI	(Partito Comunista Italiano) Italian Communist Party
PCP	Portuguese Communist Party
PdUP	(Partito d'Unità Proletaria) Party of Proletarian Unity
PSI	Italian Socialist Party
PUWP	Polish United Workers' Party (communist)
SED	Socialist Unity Party (East German communist party)
SPD	Social Democratic Party of West Germany
UIL	(Unione Italiana del Lavoro) Italian Union of Labour (Social Democrat, Republican and Socialist)

Billion is used throughout as 1,000 million.

Preface and Acknowledgements

This book is a study of one of Europe's largest and most important left-wing political parties, the Italian Communist Party (PCI).

Created in 1921 after a schism in the Socialist Party, the PCI has had a peculiar history, from which has emerged a party unique in the communist world. It has been the pioneer of a novel form of Marxism, and architect of many ground-breaking concepts in political theory and strategy, including hegemony, polycentrism, Eurocommunism and Historic Compromise. The PCI continues to rank among the world's most creative and intellectually robust parties of the Left, and it is, without doubt, one of the few outstanding success stories in world communism. These are just some of the reasons that make the PCI an essential focus of study for any serious student of political anthropology and European party politics. The PCI's successful adaptation of Marxism also provides some particularly valuable lessons for socialists and left-wing organisations in general, both in Europe and beyond.

My interest in Italian communism began in 1981 when, as a student of social anthropology inspired by reading Gramsci, I embarked on a doctoral study of communism and Catholicism in an inner-city neighbourhood of Perugia, a communist-governed city in central Italy. That study developed into a more detailed analysis of the political culture of Italian communism as I became more intimately acquainted with several local Party sections and the lives of their members. For 18 months I carried out intensive anthropological fieldwork in Perugia during which I was fully involved, both as participant and observer, in local politics. This was complemented by research into local section and federation archives, a period of study at the PCI's national school in Rome, and countless interviews and conversations with ordinary Party members and leaders. I returned to Perugia for a further year in 1986 to take up a teaching post at the university, which enabled me to consolidate this research and deepen my understanding of Italian politics and society.

This book developed partly out of those years in Italy, but partly too from a long-standing interest in Marxism and the state of British and European socialism. However, though political in orientation, the study remains firmly grounded in the anthropological tradition of empirical analysis derived from first-hand experience and close personal contact with the subjects of this book – the Italian communists themselves. It is not, strictly speaking, a work of political science, sociology or history. Neither is it a study of 'Eurocommunism' *per se*, nor a small-community study of the kind typically portrayed in the standard anthropological monograph – though it straddles all of these disciplines. Instead, it combines anthropological insights into the structure and culture of communism with an analysis of communist theory and ideology and their development in Italy and elsewhere. Above all, by focusing on 'communist identity' it tries to explain what it *means* to be communist in Italy, and to show why this sense of identity is fundamental to the PCI's success and its strategy for the conquest of power in Italy.

The local Party in Perugia, though convenient as a locus for anthropological study, proved inadequate as a unit of analysis. A deeper understanding of Italian communism requires a broader perspective of the Party as a whole, one that is able to locate PCI politics in their wider social and historical context. At the same time, however, it is important not to lose sight of the subjective and emotional dimension of politics, or forget that political actors are individuals who experience the world in complex, personal ways. Much of the book therefore adopts a neighbourhood-outward perspective: a view of the PCI from the bottom looking upwards; from the inside looking outwards, and from the subjective aspect of communist identity to its more structural and historical dimensions.

Part I of the book explores key elements in the political culture of the PCI. It focuses on communist identity, political socialisation, the construction of Party history, and the theory and practice of Italian communism. Part II develops these themes by addressing questions concerning Marxist-Leninist theory and ideology that are of major significance to the PCI and to communist parties in general. The key problem addressed is, why have the Italian communists succeeded where most other European communist parties have so conspicuously failed? The main argument of the book, as suggested by its title, is that the answer lies not only in the PCI's critique of Soviet communism but also in its rejection of Leninist theory. To explain Stalinism and the degeneration of communist systems into ossified and repressive party bureaucracies it is not enough to examine Bolshevik history or the personalities of Stalin or Brezhnev. Nor is it sufficient to look for the roots of the problem in the corrupt and 'distorted' practices adopted by Stalinist parties in power. Any serious study is forced, instead, to consider Leninism itself: the principles of ideology and organisation that Lenin claimed are fundamental to the structure and function of the communist party. The PCI long ago embarked upon a road that would distance itself from the Soviet model of communism, but the question of relevance to all communist parties is whether the 'retreat from Moscow' must eventually lead to a repudiation of Leninism itself. The PCI has, in effect, already answered this question, though it has yet to match its practical revisionism with a more thorough-going and coherent theoretical critique.

The upheavals that swept the Soviet bloc at the end of 1989 have brought to an end an era of communist party rule in Eastern Europe. The political map of post-war Europe is being redrawn, and as a result the stability of the Soviet Union, the survival of Gorbachev and the future of the CPSU itself hang in the balance. Against this tumultuous background of events communist parties everywhere have been forced to rethink not only their future role in society – if indeed they still have one – but also their theory of themselves. In short, they must now grasp the nettle and ask what is perhaps the most difficult question of all: has Leninism succeeded in achieving the ideals of socialism, including the emancipation of the oppressed and the socialist transformation of society, or has it instead crushed those ideals and condemned communist society to a culture of repression and tyranny?

Seen in this broader context, the study of Italian communism becomes all the more topical and relevant to the problems of communism at large. The PCI's attempt to reconcile itself to its past provides an important case-study of how one communist party in Europe has confronted the problems common to most communist parties today. Whether the PCI's adaptation of Marxism holds any immediate answer to some of the dilemmas currently facing other parties of the European Left is debatable, but there are undoubtedly important lessons to be learned here that have ramifications beyond Italy. This book will therefore be of interest to students of the Left, political scientists and those involved in European politics. It will also be of particular relevance to students of anthropology and sociology, and to the general reader with an interest in contemporary Italian culture and society.

Those who helped make this book a reality and to whom I am indebted for their friendship and support during my years in Italy include: Primo Tenca, Alberto Stramaccioni, Cinzia Falaschi, Salvatore Cusenza, Daniela Evangelisti, Enzo Forini, Franco Morrone and the members of the PCI section, 'Piazza Grimana'. I would like to thank Jeff Pratt and Ralph Grillo of Sussex University for their constructive comments on my doctoral thesis, from which the initial idea for this book developed, and the Economic and Social Research Council, which sponsored my D.Phil. at Sussex University. Finally, I am particularly grateful to my parents, Peter and Liz, and to Fiona Graham, Steven Roberts and Derek Boothman for their critical feedback on earlier drafts of this manuscript.

Cris Shore,
London, March 1990

Fig. 1: Votes for Major Parties at Italian General Elections 1946–87

	Votes cast (thousands)				*Percentages*		
	PCI	PSI	DC	Total	PCI	PSI	DC
1946	4,358.2	4,765.7	8,102.8	23,016.5	18.9	20.7	35.2
1948	8,137.0	(a)	12,741.3	26,268.9	31.0	(a)	48.5
1953	6,121.9	3,441.3	10,864.3	27,092.7	22.6	12.7	40.1
1958	6,704.5	4,206.7	12,520.2	29,560.3	22.7	14.2	42.4
1963	7,768.2	4,257.3	11,745.3	30,758.0	25.3	13.8	38.2
1968	8,557.4	4,605.8(b)	12,407.2	31,803.3	26.9	14.5(b)	39.0
1972	9,069.8	3,208.3	12,913.9	33,402.2	27.2	9.6	38.7
1976	12,620.8	3,541.4	14,213.7	36,718.5	34.4	9.6	38.7
1979	11,139.2	3,596.8	14,046.3	36,671.3	30.4	9.8	38.3
1983	11,032.3	4,223.4	12,153.1	36,906.0	29.9	11.4	32.9
1987	10,285.0	5,510.6	13,252.9	38,652.5	26.6	14.3	34.3

(a) The PCI and PSI formed an alliance, the Fronte Democratico Populare
(b) The PSI and PDSI (Social Democrats) merged from 1966 to 1969 to form the Partito Socialista Unificato

Sources: T.T. Mackie and R. Rose, The International Almanac of Electoral History 2nd Edition Tables 13.7, 13.8
Annuario Statistico Italiano 1988 Table 5.26

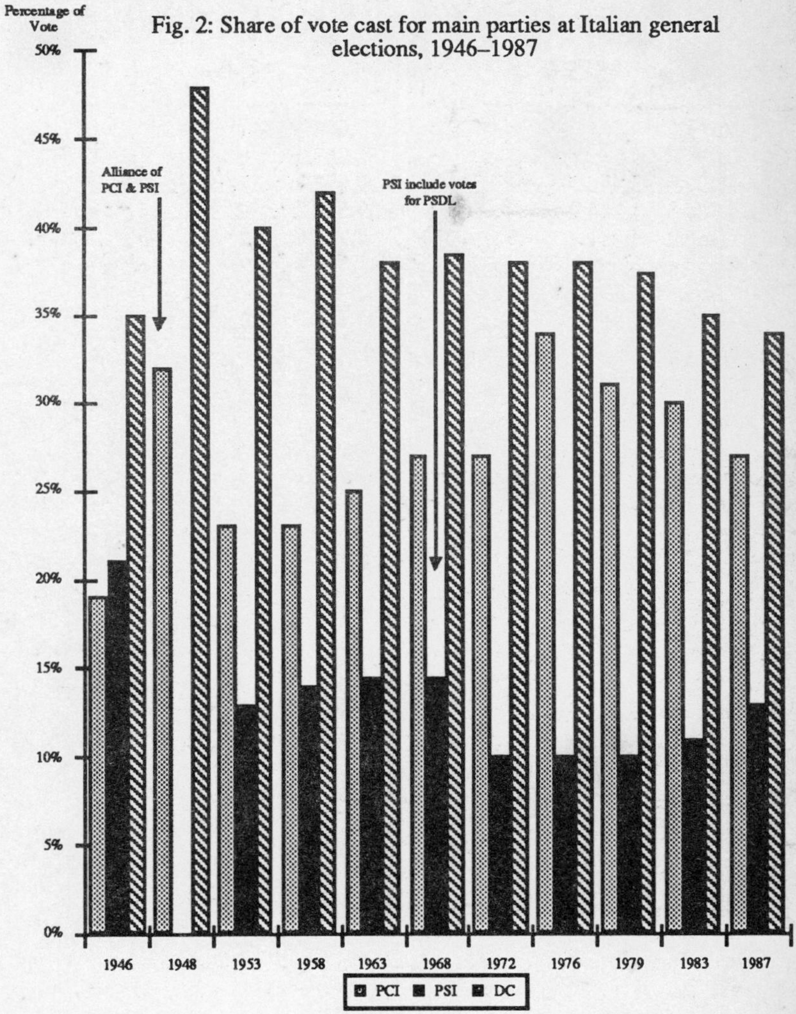

Fig. 2: Share of vote cast for main parties at Italian general elections, 1946–1987

To Fiona Graham
with my love

Introduction:

Communism in Crisis – the Search for a Way Forward

Italian Communism in Political Context

In 1945, following the defeat of Nazi Germany there was an upsurge of support for the parties of the Left throughout Europe – particularly the communist parties. In Italy alone membership of the Communist Party (PCI) soared to over 2 million, and with successive electoral gains – which brought its share of the vote up from 19 per cent in 1946 to 34.4 per cent in 1976 – it seemed poised on the threshold of power. Today, despite recent setbacks in the 1987 and 1989 elections, where its vote dropped to 26.6 per cent, the PCI is as strong as, if not stronger than, it was over 40 years ago. Not only has it maintained itself intact – while virtually all other European communist parties have splintered or declined – but it has also broadened its influence in society. In an age where allegiance to political parties is increasingly on the wane, the PCI almost alone continues to be the embodiment of a true 'mass party' – and it is still the largest communist party in the Western world.

This book tells the story of Italian communism from its birth in 1921 to the announcement of its 'death', or rather, its leadership's declaration in November 1989 that the Party is considering changing its name and dropping the title 'communist'.[1] In some respects, this book is an account of the 'last days' of Italian communism as we have known it. But to understand the present we must also study the past and the steps that have led up to the current sequence of events that is transforming communism both in Italy and in Europe at large. This study analyses the PCI from various perspectives, but tries, above all, to place Italian communism in its broader political and cultural context in order to fathom what it is that has made Italian communism so distinctive and so successful.

The 'success' of the PCI is, of course, a relative term for it has not held government office since 1947, nor does it look likely to at present, given the Party's current difficulties and the continuing refusal by the ruling coalition parties to concede it any share of governmental power. However, political success and influence cannot be measured purely in terms of parliamentary seats or the capture of government office – particularly in Italy where governments and prime ministers are notoriously short-lived and likely to be brought down at almost any moment by crisis, scandal, intraparty conflict, or political sabotage. The source of this apparent instability is often attributed to the post-war Italian constitution, which created a strong parliament but a weak executive, but it also lies, as we shall see, in the Italian party system, which was also developed after the war.[2]

Giulio Andreotti's appointment as prime minister in 1989 marked Italy's 49th (and Andreotti's fifth) government since the founding of the Republic in 1947 – an average of less than one per year. The problem, according to Italian politicians, is simply that Italy is 'ungovernable'. This claim, however, is something of an illusion for despite the political turmoil and repeated use of the word 'crisis' in Italian political discourse, modern political life in Italy has been characterised by remarkable continuity. Prime ministers may come and go, but the new governments tend to be replicas of their predecessors, with the same coalition partners and the same politicians as before, only reshuffled to suit their shifting electoral fortunes. With a sustained vote of around 40 per cent the Christian Democrat Party (DC), the largest coalition partner, has effectively ruled Italy for the past 42 years, while the PCI has remained in almost permanent opposition (see Figures 1 and 2). Christian Democrat domination of the Italian state has probably been the most important single factor in shaping post-war Italian politics. Only against this background can one begin to understand the nature of Italian communism, its strategy, and its critique of the state and society in Italy.

Furthermore, since 1970, and in accordance with the Italian constitution, many of the powers of central government have been decentralised in the regions, thus strengthening the already strongly established differences in character and culture between the regions of Italy. The result has been a geographical division of the country into marked political zones, including a communist 'Red Belt' area across central Italy (developing out of a long-established socialist sub-culture), and a 'white' zone (i.e. strongly Christian Democrat) based upon a Catholic sub-culture that has developed most conspicuously in the provinces of the Veneto-Giulia region of the northeast.[3]

It would be hard to underestimate the influence of Christian Democracy on post-war Italy, but, equally, one cannot fail to acknowledge the major contribution made by Italian communists. It was they, for example, who led the Resistance and the War of Independence; who restored democracy to Italy and helped found the modern republic; and who were among the foremost architects of Italy's new constitution and its institutions. It was a communist, Terracini, who became the first president of Italy's Constituent Assembly which presided over Italy's transition to democracy after 1945. In the decades that have elapsed since then, the PCI has become a powerfully entrenched force in community life and in local government. Within the Italian parliament too, the PCI has for years been the focus of political dissent and serious opposition to government policies. From a clandestine coterie in 1944, the PCI has developed into one of Europe's most formidable mass socialist parties with prestige both at home and abroad.

Communism in Western Europe: the Rise and Fall of Eurocommunism

Elsewhere in Europe, by contrast, the Left in general and communism in particular have fared less well. In the 1970s the prospects for European communists were, if not exciting, at least reasonably promising, particularly in Spain, Portugal and France. In 1979, 16 of Western Europe's 24 communist parties enjoyed parliamentary representation. The highest percentages were in Italy, where communists held just under one-third of the parliamentary seats (201 out of 630), and Cyprus (25.7 per cent), followed by Iceland (23.3 per cent), Portugal (18.8 per cent), France (17.5 per cent) and Finland (17.5 per cent).[4] In Spain the PCE had increased its vote by 14 per cent, bringing its share to 23 out of 350 seats in the Cortes. More importantly, the 1970s saw the emergence of a serious challenge to Moscow's authority within the pan-European communist movement.

By the 1980s all this had changed: cohesion had been replaced by inter-party conflict, the idea of a pan-European communist movement was in terminal decline, and what had been a challenge to the West became increasingly a challenge to the parties themselves as to what role they might conceivably play in the future. In 1988, by contrast, only twelve of Western Europe's communist parties were represented in their respective parliaments, and most of these had registered electoral decline. The communists in Italy remained highest with just below 30 per cent; then came Cyprus (27.4 per cent), Iceland (13.2 per cent), Portugal (11 per cent), Greece (9.9 per cent), France (9.8 per cent), Finland (9.4 per cent) and Sweden (4.9 per cent). But even in most of these countries the impact of communism on political life was small and still waning.

By the late 1980s, the prospects for socialism in Europe looked decidedly bleak. Once a mass movement at the forefront of political change, it has steadily lost its prestige and popularity. In the past 'socialism' as a concept was associated with 'progress', 'mass movement', 'optimism' and 'transformation'; today, instead, the adjectives most frequently used to describe it are 'crisis', 'dilemma' and 'defeat', and socialists have been described, even by themselves, as an endangered species.

Toward the latter half of the 1970s the idea of 'Eurocommunism' – the convergence of Western Europe's leading communist parties on a series of major points of theoretical and strategic concern – became a beacon for the European Left. Not only did it appear to offer a new strategy for communist parties to win power within the constitutional framework of Western democracies, but it also seemed to resolve many of the seemingly intractable problems of orthodox communism itself. In fact, 'Eurocommunism' was simply an ambiguous code word for a group of parties – the Italian, French, and Spanish – whose common denominator was simply a commitment to constitutional and democratic principles in the quest for an independent and national road to socialism (Urban, 1980: 100). There was no standard text setting out the principles of Eurocommunism, apart from Santiago Carrillo's brief exposition of 1976 – and even Carrillo admitted that 'Eurocommunism does not exist.'[5] Apart from its assertion of the need for greater autonomy, more open discussion and an 'ever broader system of alliances' (Cammett, 1980: x), the leaders of Eurocommunism offered little criticism of Leninism.

Nevertheless, Eurocommunism was hailed as a step toward a new strategy for the parties of Western Europe; a 'third way', or alternative road to socialism – independent of Moscow and aware of the faults and failures of 'achieved socialism' in Eastern Europe. Inevitably, the shadow of Eurocommunism – however ephemeral the reality – became a focus of excitement for the European Left, and alarm for its opponents, who saw Eurocommunism as a guise designed to make the communist parties of Europe more respectable and palatable to the electorate, when in reality they remained totalitarian and subservient to Soviet interests.[6]

Emotions were particularly aroused in 1976 when the Italian Communist Party, the pioneer of Eurocommunism, captured 34.4 per cent of the vote and seemed to be on the brink of taking office. The Spanish and Portuguese communist parties were also doing well. Both had been the best-organised opposition force in their respective countries during the years of Fascist dictatorship under Franco and Salazar. Similarly, both had emerged in the mid-1970s as champions of the resistance to Fascism, and it was widely assumed that this popularity would soon be translated into electoral strength. Then in France the Communist Party (PCF), which had formed a coalition with the socialists, was swept into office in the elections of 1981, gaining four ministerial posts in the Mitterrand government. This event was greeted throughout the communist parties of Western Europe with a wave of euphoria, prompting the *World Marxist Review* to conclude a year later that 'the ideas advanced by Europe's communists meet the innermost interests of the people' (Starr, 1988: 471).

By 1984, however, the cohesion and optimism of Europe's communist parties had deteriorated dramatically, and while they continued to fare reasonably well in elections, a series of internal conflicts began that were soon to focus on the future of communism itself. The decline of Eurocommunism can be traced to a combination of domestic factors, including the revival of the socialist parties in Portugal, Spain and France – which occurred largely at the expense of the communists – and international events, particularly the deterioration of East–West relations. The election in 1979 of President Reagan in America and Mrs Thatcher in Britain, followed by that of Chancellor Helmut Kohl in West Germany, brought a new era in international affairs. Detente gave way to a resumption of hostility and tension between the superpowers not seen since the early days of the first Cold War.[7] These events intensified pressure on Europe's communist parties either to demonstrate their loyalty to the USSR, or to distance themselves from it. Either way the outcome brought a spate of internal divisions and electoral troubles. More damaging still was the Soviet invasion of Afghanistan in 1979 and its deployment of SS-20 missiles targeted on sites in Europe. It was the former of these two events that really brought the divisions to a head. While the Italian and Spanish communists moved swiftly to condemn the Soviet invasion, the PCF did not, and began instead to manoeuvre itself back into the Soviet fold.

Further setbacks for Eurocommunism ensued. In 1984 the French communists resigned from the coalition government when Mitterrand began to reverse the left-wing programme he had been elected to carry out, thus ending the popular-front strategy the PCF had pursued for over a quarter of a century. In Italy, the PCI leadership changed hands for the first time since 1972 when its most respected and intellectually agile leader, Enrico Berlinguer, died suddenly of a brain haemorrhage. After electing Alexander Natta (aged 66) as his successor, the PCI seemed directionless and unable to design any clear programme for the future. Meanwhile, the Spanish Communist Party had been rent apart by ideological conflicts and intraparty factionalism. Its veteran leader, Carrillo, had antagonised many Party members by his style of leadership and his imposition of Eurocommunist policies.[8] In 1982 he was therefore ousted from the post of Party secretary-general and replaced by 37-year-old Gerardo Iglesias. But Iglesias's attempts to heal these Party divisions failed, and the PCE subsequently fragmented into three main parties and several regional parties after the withdrawal first of the Carrillo-led Eurocommunists, and then, in 1983, of the pro-Moscow dissidents led by Ignacio Gellago.

In most other Western European communist parties, rifts of varying magnitude and along similar lines have increased since 1981. The participants in the debate fell broadly into two camps: on the one hand were the Eurocommunists, who argued for major reforms in Party theory and practice and greater independence from the USSR; on the other hand, the more orthodox, pro-Soviet faction, who denounced Eurocommunism as 'anti-Soviet revisionism' or worse, a slide towards social democracy and capitalism. Their solution to the crisis in communism was a return to traditional Party unity by strengthening discipline and by 'greater adherence to Marxism-Leninism'.

These internal conflicts had disastrous consequences for the communist parties of Western Europe. This was borne out most vividly in the case of the PCF, whose history over the last ten years has been one of incessant wrangles, purges and electoral decline. Having flirted briefly with Eurocommunism in the late 1970s but without gaining any immediate electoral dividends, the PCF's orthodox leadership changed its tactics, purged most of the reformers from the Party, and returned to its former orthodoxy and unqualified allegiance to Soviet communism. This backslide reached its peak when the PCF secretary-general, Georges Marchais, went on French television from a Moscow studio to approve the Soviet invasion of Afghanistan (Friend, 1986: 56). These events, however, were accompanied by the most dramatic decline in the Party's electoral standing ever witnessed. From a mass party that regularly won over 20 per cent at the polls, the PCF progressively lost members and supporters until, in the European elections of June 1984, it sank to just 11 per cent. This deteriorated to 9.79 per cent in the parliamentary elections of March 1986 – its lowest vote since 1928 and one below that of even the neo-Fascist National Front.

Similar declines occurred in the other major communist parties. The Spanish Communist Party, for example, dropped to a mere 3.8 per cent of the vote in the 1982 elections. Its public rift with the Soviet Union was not enough, it seems, to wipe out memories of the Spanish Civil War and overcome the distrust of the PCE still felt by many Spaniards. After the 1982 election the PCE began to turn away from Eurocommunism and confrontation with the USSR, but this failed to prevent the splits from destroying the Party's credibility still further. As for the other communist parties of Western Europe, few have recorded any success since 1985. The AKEL, once the largest party in Cyprus, fell to third place in the elections of December 1985. The KKE, the larger of Greece's two communist parties, dropped to below 10 per cent of the vote in 1985 and lost its status as a major parliamentary party. The Portuguese Communist Party (PCP), the most orthodox, pro-Soviet and anti-Eurocommunist of them all, has likewise been marginalised. Its ideological rigidity has rendered it increasingly obsolete; it is stuck in the anachronistic policies of the 1940s.[9] As a result it has been pushed aside by its rivals in the socialist party. In the Belgian election of 1985 the Communist Party lost its parliamentary representation altogether. In Britain the CPGB, which has had no seats in the House of Commons since 1950, was similarly riven by internal power struggles between its Eurocommunist leadership and pro-Moscow wing. The latter, having succeeded in gaining control of the Party's daily, *The Morning Star*, eventually split off to form their own party.

Collapse of Communism in Eastern Europe and China

The issue of subordination to Soviet communism versus greater independence, which dominated communist politics in Western Europe throughout the 1970s, also caused rumblings within the Soviet bloc. What began as a 'Eurocommunist' challenge to the West might have become a challenge to the East, but the communist authorities used repressive means to ensure that it did not. Throughout the early 1980s the hardline Stalinist regimes in Czechoslovakia, Bulgaria, Romania, Hungary and East Germany showed little sign of the impending crisis that was soon to engulf them. Only in Poland was the Party in serious trouble. Following the Solidarity-led revolt in 1980, martial law was imposed by General Jaruzelski, the man chosen by the Soviet Union to restore order. The Polish Communist Party (PUWP), however, had lost credibility and seemed unable to regain any real legitimacy. It reasserted control, but only by the most repressive of measures, and its failure to solve the problems of Poland's sluggish and backward economy was bringing mounting hardship and discontent that could serve only to undermine its precarious position still further.

It was not, therefore, the intellectual challenge of Eurocommunism that eventually shook the communist parties of Eastern Europe from their torpor, but rather the very opposite: the lack of innovation, the suppression of internal debate, and the failure of these ruling parties to satisfy the economic demands of their people. In short, the communist regimes of Eastern Europe appeared stagnant, out of touch, and run by old men from the bygone Brezhnev/Stalin era. The real catalyst for change, however, came after a series of successions within the Kremlin. First Leonid Brezhnev, who had been Soviet leader since 1964, died on 10 November 1982, and was succeeded by Yuri Andropov, a former head of the KGB. Then Andropov, who had been in office for barely 14 months, died on 9 February 1984, and was succeeded by the elderly Brezhnev protégé, Konstantin Chernenko. Yet Chernenko's presidency was shorter still, and on 8 March 1985 he also died and was replaced by Mikhail Gorbachev. Gorbachev's presidency, however, marked the beginning of a new era of sweeping liberalisation and reform in Soviet politics which has sounded the death knell for the Stalinist regimes of Eastern Europe.

The year 1989 marked a turning point in post-war history. It will probably also be remembered as a watershed in the history of communism. No one could have predicted the dramatic sequence of events. Stirrings of revolt in China between March and June provided a vivid warning of just how degenerate and out of touch some of the ruling communist parties had become. Demonstrations first started in Beijing in April, after the death of the former Chinese Communist Party (CCP) premier, Hu Yabang – organised mainly by students demanding greater democracy. By May, support for the demonstrators had grown so widespread that commentators were comparing the event with the revolution of 1949. Indeed, a march in Beijing on 17 May had brought over 1 million people and had included organised groups of workers and government officials. The students staging a sit-in in Tienanmen Square then went on hunger strike to dramatise their call for 'genuine dialogue' with the Chinese leadership. At the same time, over 1,000 Chinese journalists delivered a petition demanding talks with CCP officials to liberalise the news-reporting system. These demonstrations precipitated a major power struggle within the CCP, which subsequently divided into two factions: one generally sympathetic to the student demands (supported by the CCP general-secretary, Zhao Ziyang); the other favouring a hardline military response to the unrest (led by Premier Li Peng, CCP President Yang Shangkun, and China's 'elder statesman' Deng Xiaoping).

Ironically, on the same day of the Sino-Soviet summit which concluded a formal reconciliation between the world's two communist superpowers (16 May), over 10,000 journalists, as well as miners, doctors, lawyers, civil servants and police, joined the groundswell of student protest against the Chinese communist regime. But in a few days it became clear that the hardline elements had gained the upper hand. On 20 May, Li Peng and Yang Shangkun declared martial law, while the students continued their sit-in. By the end of May over 150,000 troops were surrounding Beijing, but the military crackdown provoked an even stronger antigovernment outburst. Rumours began to spread that a full-scale civil war was about to break out, with rival armies supposedly preparing for battle on the outskirts of the capital. But this did not happen, and the prodemocracy movement was brought to an abrupt end when the People's Liberation Army, armed with automatic weapons, entered Tienanmen Square and opened fire on the crowd. The massacre at Tienanmen Square was followed by a military crackdown and a purge within the CCP leading to the dismissal of Zhao Ziyang. The Party leadership in China had survived, but, in the words of one British communist, 'only by mass murder'.[10] In the process it had turned itself, in the words of Gareth Steadman Jones, 'into a form of *ancien regime*'.[11]

Disintegration of Communism in Poland, Hungary, East Germany and Czechoslovakia

Gorbachev's reforms in the USSR had isolated the hardline communist regimes of Eastern Europe and given impetus to growing public demand for liberalisation and political change. Evidence of this was seen most vividly in Czechoslovakia at the beginning of 1989 when the official May Day parade was disrupted by protestors carrying banners demanding the release of civil-rights activists and calling for Soviet-style political reforms. In Hungary the following month a mass rally was held at which Imre Nagy, the Hungarian prime minister at the time of the 1956 uprising who had been convicted of treason and hanged, was formally rehabilitated and reburied. More dramatic still, the new Politburo of the ruling Hungarian Socialist Worker's Party (HSWP) also issued a statement that Nagy's trial had been an illegal show-trial' – a statement which was tantamount to a public repudiation of the legality of the Communist Party regime installed after 1956. Furthermore, in a surprising gesture of support, all of the Warsaw Pact countries, except Romania, sent delegates. Following this, the Hungarian communist leadership began to discuss reform of the Party's leadership structure and called for free, multiparty elections for March 1990. Moreover, they also held several televised discussions with opposition political groups. According to Rezs Nyers, the new HSWP chairman, Hungary had become the first Eastern European state to recognise Western concepts of freedom.[12] Shortly afterwards the HSWP was officially dissolved and reformed as a social democratic party.

These events were superseded by more dramatic changes in Poland. Loss of confidence in the government and the crisis in the economy had forced the ruling PUWP to enter into dialogue with their political opponents, including the previously banned Solidarity trade union. General Jaruzelski had tried to preserve the PUWP's monopoly of power through a communist-led coalition, but without the support of Solidarity this was doomed to fail. The Solidarity leader, Lech Walesa, refused to join, saying that the trade union's role in a PUWP-dominated coalition would be simply decorative.[13] Thus, on 24 August 1989, 45 years of PUWP rule ended when the *Sejm*, the lower house of the Polish national assembly, elected as its prime minister Tadeusz Mazowiecki – a leading member of Solidarity – mandating him to form a Solidarity-led coalition government.

These events had major repercussions in the German Democratic Republic, from which between August and October 1989, over 30,000 refugees had migrated to West Germany – most of them via Hungary, which had begun to dismantle fences along its border with Austria. Though relatively small in number compared with the floods of refugees who had escaped across the border before the establishment of the Berlin Wall in 1961, this exodus was a serious threat to the stability of the East German regime. Paralysed by indecision and by the illness of its 77-year-old leader, Erich Honecker, the ruling Socialist Unity Party (SED) was unable to cope. Mass demonstrations then began in September in Leipzig and East Berlin, organised mainly by civil-rights and Church activists, and members of the New Forum opposition group. When it became clear that the Soviet Union would not intervene to restore order and that Honecker did not have support within the Politburo for a military 'Tienanmen-Square solution' to the public disorder, the government collapsed. Shortly afterwards came the shattering announcement from the new SED leader, Krenz (who was also removed from office a few weeks later), that the Berlin Wall was to be dismantled and that Article One of the East German constitution, which enshrines the Communist Party's 'leading role' and right to rule, would be abolished. The culmination of this dramatic process in December saw not only the dismantling of the Berlin Wall – the most potent symbol of the Cold War and the post-1945 division of Europe – but also the dismantling of the SED itself, the arrest of Honecker and several high-ranking ex-Politburo members on charges of corruption and treason, and the resignation of over 300,000 Party members.[14]

Meanwhile, Bulgaria's leader, Todor Zhivkov, was toppled from power on 10 November, and a mounting tide of protest and strikes in Czechoslovakia led to the fall of Milos Jakes and his government. As in East Germany, the new Czech government renounced the Communist Party's monopoly on power and promised free elections and the introduction of multiparty pluralism in the new year. By early December, orthodox communist regimes had fallen in five out of the six countries that used to be called the 'Soviet satellites'. Only the Ceauşescu regime in Romania remained apparently unshaken, but the revolt had started here too. On 17 December government troops crushed a demonstration in the Romanian city of Timişoara, and thousands were reported to have been killed in the incident. But instead of quelling the revolt, this massacre precipitated a bloody civil war as the army joined demonstrators to fight Ceauşescu's secret police and proclaim a new government. The street battles lasted only a few days before the regime collapsed, and on 25 December Ceauşescu and his wife Elena, who had been caught trying to flee the country, were condemned to death and executed.

Throughout these turbulent events, what surprised people in Eastern Europe, perhaps even more than observers in the West, was that each successive step in the collapse of these Soviet-style regimes was encouraged by the USSR – even the destruction of the Berlin Wall which suggested the possibility that the USSR's frontline state and the second most important member of the Warsaw Pact could be reunited with West Germany. The full implications of these events for East–West relations and for the future of Europe are still far from clear. What is certain, however, is that the old model of communism in Eastern Europe is finished. Stalinism may be dead, and Leninism may well be in terminal decline, but what of the future of socialism and the democratic Left in Europe? While Eastern Europe and the Soviet Union are opening themselves up to Western investors and abandoning not only the concept of the command economy, but the very idea of 'economic planning' itself, what answers, if any, do the European socialists have?

Explaining the Success of the PCI

Against this background of European communist parties in decline and disarray the PCI – virtually alone among the old parties of the Third International – has survived intact. But how have the Italian communists achieved this and what lessons are there here for the Left – communist or socialist – in Europe and elsewhere?

Three factors help to explain the success of the PCI: first, its early disengagement from the tutelage of the Soviet Union and its break with the strictures of Marxist-Leninist orthodoxy; second, the development of its unique, popular, independent and national road to socialism (the so-called *via italiano al socialismo*); and third, and most important of all, the prolific social role that it has created for itself within Italian society. The PCI's survival and expansion in post-war Italy is owing above all to its success in establishing itself as an entrenched part of the fabric of community life. This has been achieved largely by creating a 'communist culture' in Italy: a powerful social movement based around the Party itself, one that in many respects rivals the Catholic Church in strength and influence. The comparison with the Church is significant, for the PCI has borrowed much from traditional Catholicism – particularly in terms of its structure, its territorial network, its methods of recruitment, and its role in community life.[15] In short, the PCI has developed itself as a major social force in contemporary Italian society. This is no accident of history but the result of a conscious political strategy aimed at penetrating society in all its cultural manifestations: what Gramsci called 'hegemony in civil society'.[16]

One important element of the PCI's original notion of hegemony was the novel way that it conceived of the problematic relationship between party, state, and society. Most orthodox communist parties traditionally divided the social world into a simple set of conceptual categories which distinguished between 'us' and 'them', and between 'party' and 'society' (or 'the masses'). The argument behind this conceptualisation, developed most explicitly by Lenin and Trotsky, followed from a logical premise. In order to change society, communists must be strategically placed *outside* it; ideologically and symbolically detached from the corrupting influence of bourgeois ideology and trade-union mentality. But to lead the working class in its historical mission the party has to be physically present among the masses, mobilised and ready to assume command. Classical communist theory therefore rests on a dualism between 'party' and 'society', the former seeing itself as the motor of history leading the latter in a global project of social transformation. The revolutionary party, according to this dichotomy, is therefore placed strategically 'outside' society, but simultaneously agitates 'within' society – a philosophical position somewhat akin to that of some Christian groups who argue that the righteous should be 'of' this world, but not 'in' it.

Following Gramsci's writings, the PCI became one of the first communist parties seriously to challenge this perspective and attempt to formulate a different conception of the relationship between party and society. However, disengaging from its old Leninist world-view has not been an easy task, and echoes of its ideological legacy have continued to permeate the culture and mentality of the PCI, even in the 1980s. This was reflected, for example, in the PCI's definition of itself given in the preamble to the 1983 Party statutes:

> The Italian Communist Party organises proletarians, workers, intellectuals and citizens ... for the transformation of Italy into a socialist state.[17]

Many parties of Marxist inspiration make similar claims about transforming society in a socialist direction, but few have succeeded in penetrating society and in shaping national politics on anything like the same scale. With over 1.5 million members the PCI is the largest communist party in the Western world. It has a local-based network of over 9,000 territorial, factory and workplace sections throughout the country and amongst Italian immigrant communities abroad, and it commands the support of nearly 10 million voters (26.6 per cent of the Italian electorate). Under its tutelage is an elaborate network of auxiliary organisations (including the Italian Communist Youth Federation [FGCI], and the National League of Cooperatives), which enables it to mobilise hundreds of thousands of people for marches, demonstrations, Party rallies and festivals. It has a core of thousands of activists (*militanti di base*) who dedicate large amounts of time and energy to Party affairs, and an army of salaried full-time Party officials – not to mention the thousands of elected Party representatives in the various tiers of government. Moreover, in those areas that the PCI now governs, the Party commands substantial resources, including power and patronage over jobs, appointments, and the allocation of public money.

The PCI's membership includes not only large numbers of pensioners, proletarians and public-sector workers, but also the middle and upper-middle classes – professionals, writers, many of Italy's leading academics and scientists, and even industrialists and small capitalists. It produces one of Italy's most widely read daily newspapers (*L'Unità*); a weekly journal (*Rinascita*); a bimonthly theoretical journal (*Critica Marxista*); and various other important political, economic, and historical publications, including *Studi Storici*, *Politica ed Economia*, *Donne e Polita*, *Democrazia e Diritto*, *Riforma della Scuola*, and *Nuova Rivista_Internazionale*, (Urban, 1988: 514). The PCI also organises national and regional Party schools, 'Gramsci Institutes', agricultural and industrial cooperatives, and recreational centres and community bars. Its host of satellite organisations range from peace committees and ecology groups to pensioners' associations, debating circles and women's associations. For several years, following the spectacular political gains it made in 1975, PCI-led coalitions governed Venice, Rome, Bologna, Florence, Turin, and most of Italy's other major cities north of Naples. Furthermore, the PCI has a powerful presence in Italy's largest confederation of trade unions, the CIGL. Outside Italy, too, PCI theoreticians rank amongst the most important contributors to Marxist thought since Lenin and Rosa Luxemburg, and the writings of the PCI's most renowned leader and theorist, Antonio Gramsci, continue to command the attention of the European Left (cf. Boggs, 1976; Femia, 1979; Mouffe, 1979).

In creating a cultural movement based around the body of the Party, the PCI pioneered one of the most interesting and novel developments ever conceived in communist political strategy. PCI sympathisers see it as the harbinger of a new kind of communism; a specifically 'European' road to socialism founded upon democratic principles and Gramscian theory which, they claim, offers a way out of the theoretical cul-de-sac of traditional Marxism-Leninism and its approach to power. Others, hostile to communism in any form, see the PCI as a dangerous new breed of communism; a sinister force trying to perpetuate a Marxist culture in Italy, a force which, however seemingly benign, still poses a potential threat to Western democracy and to the security of the Atlantic Alliance.[18]

Perspectives on Italian Communism: the Anthropological Approach

Whatever the interpretation, the PCI's impact on Italian society has been extraordinary and has attracted widespread attention from social scientists and writers on modern Italy. Much of this attention has focused on the cultural politics of Italian communism. Little, however, has been written about the actual culture of Italian communism, or about what is meant by this notion of a 'Marxist culture' that repels some and excites others. Nor has there been much written that adequately explains the success of Italian communism. Several schools of thought have attempted to provide an answer, but most have failed to give a satisfactory explanation. Some, including the post-war American school of political science, have failed because of flaws in method;[19] some, because of too narrow a focus;[20] others, somewhat paradoxically, because of too broad a perspective.[21] Whatever the verdict, the sheer diversity of approaches highlights the fact that all interpretation tends to be problematic and partial. This is perhaps inevitable given the multifaceted nature of the PCI and its organisational complexity. Like many political organisations, the PCI is far from monolithic. Though it can be viewed as a formal institution it is also a loose coalition of individuals with differing attitudes and perceptions of the world. It is an ideological as well as social entity; an organisation shaped by its own history and cast within a specific cultural and historical setting. To understand the PCI in all its dimensions one should, ideally, consider all of these aspects. This, however, would be a formidable, if not impossible, task. None the less, this book tries to incorporate a variety of different perspectives and is unashamedly eclectic and multidisciplinary. Where this study differs from most others is that many of the insights into the character of the PCI are derived from an anthropological approach. To explain this approach requires a brief note on the methods and perspective of social anthropology.

Social anthropology attempts to penetrate within the mind and rationale of another culture; to see a group of people as they see themselves and to view the world as they view it. This involves recording and then analysing the social behaviour of the group or people under study – the aim being to understand both the meaning people attach to their lives and the social consequences of their beliefs and actions. Anthropology therefore oscillates between two cultural perspectives; the outsider or analyst's (the 'etic' view) and the insider or participant's (the 'emic' view). One of its premises is that society – or in this case a political party – may be conceived of as a system of social relations or a set of cultural rules. In so far as it is possible, anthropology seeks to discover those rules, explain the pattern of social organisation, and reveal the principles which govern them both. To do this, anthropologists adopt a multidisciplinary approach, but their starting point is the empirical and inductive method based on intensive fieldwork as participant-observer in the culture or community under study.[22] The primary 'ethnographic' information generated by this kind of research therefore tends to be more qualitative and subjective than quantitative.

Finally, anthropology is concerned with symbols and the symbolic order of any group or society; that is, the words, objects and signals people use to convey meaning and represent other things. All societies have, and are organised around, a structured system of symbols, though the structure of our own symbolic world is often invisible to us. As Kertzer (1988: 4) puts it, 'People are not generally aware that they themselves endow the world with their own symbolically constructed version of reality.' Not only do we construct reality through symbols, but we also tend to objectify these constructs so that we come to see them, not as arbitrary creations of human invention, but as objective, *a priori* facts and part of the natural order. The concepts 'state', 'nation', 'society' or 'communist movement' are all examples of this. Each is a cultural entity which, for most people, becomes a tangible reality only when expressed in symbolic form. One cannot, for example, see or meet a state or a nation, but only their symbolic expressions, such as the queen or president, the flag or national anthem, and a bust of Lenin or the hammer and sickle emblem.

These symbols are part of a culturally specific system of classification through which each society imposes order and meaning on an otherwise chaotic universe. Symbolic classification provides us with the conceptual framework through which we interpret the world and our place within it: it is the medium through which we construct our cognitive world. Moreover, it is something we learn as members of a society through the process of socialisation. The study of symbol systems is therefore integral to understanding other cultures and forms of political organisation. It is particularly important for political analysis for politics is expressed primarily through symbols. For example, effective 'leadership' is predicated upon the successful appropriation of the symbols of authority, legitimacy, and status, and political domination rests on the ability to master the mechanisms of consent and control. It is impossible, therefore, to have political relations without symbolic acts.[23] It is this dimension above all which gives anthropology its unique perspective on political behaviour and organisation: namely, its focus on the cultural dimension of politics, the insider's perspective or world-view, and the symbolic order that gives meaning and structure to that world-view. From this perspective one can begin to understand Italian communism in its wider social context.

Identity, Ideology, Organisation: Key Concepts in the Study of PCI Culture

The development of PCI politics since its foundation in 1921 has been shaped largely by three forces and the tension between them: identity, ideology, and organisation. The first of these, 'identity', perhaps holds the key to understanding the success of communism in Italy. However, defining 'political identity' as an analytical category is problematic. According to some authors, it is an overworked cliché, too vague to be of any analytical value (cf. McKenzie, 1986). Anthropologists would dispute this, though distinctions must be drawn between its anthropological significance and its more journalistic or propagandist usage.[24]

As an anthropological concept, 'identity' is simple but profound. At its most basic, identity represents the way an individual or group sees itself: that is, self-image and the features that characterise distinctiveness. But identity also includes the way a group or individual is defined by others – and how these definitions, self-definitions and counterdefinitions interact and affect each other.[25] Essentially, therefore, identity construction can be conceived of as a process involving the classification and labelling of 'self' in relation to others, and vice versa. This process has both a psychological and a social dimension, and embraces the most elementary force involved in group cohesion: that 'consciousness of kind' which leads people to create stable social networks and to engage in collective action. Identity is therefore concerned with the way people acquire a *sense* of community (albeit real or imagined), and the feelings of belonging upon which that community is based.[26]

Political parties, like ethnic groups or religious sects, have a strong sense of their own identity and undoubtedly constitute a self-recognising community. Like any group, clique or minority, parties have their rules of organisation, their own peculiar 'cosmology' and a distinctive social identity. The question is how are political identities created?

At its simplest, identity construction presupposes defining a community and establishing boundaries that distinguish between categories of 'us' and 'them'.[27] It is a two-way process that often begins with the labelling and pigeonholing of others, but, invariably, in defining others one also defines oneself. For example, the label 'foreigner' identifies all those who do not belong to a particular national community but simultaneously reminds those who are 'citizens' or 'free-born Englishmen' of their shared heritage, or 'ethnic affiliation', and their rights and obligations to each other. But such labels that serve to define the boundaries of identity are seldom neutral or free from ideological constraints. For example, the nationalist identity constructed in Germany during the period of Nazi rule was based on the myth of the Aryan master race.[28] Defining the Aryan 'We' was, in effect, an assertion of Nazi beliefs about German superiority – which presupposed the inferiority of other races and served to justify Nazi treatment of others as sub-human, fit only to be enslaved.

But identity construction is complicated by the fact that individuals tend to possess not just one, but a whole series of social identities, which shift according to the position of the actor. The result is usually a stratified pattern of loyalties that 'nest' within each other, each corresponding to different levels of perceived community (Epstein, 1977: 113). For example, an inhabitant of Londonderry might be at the same time a 'Londonderryman', an 'Ulsterman', 'Northern Irish', 'a Protestant' and a 'citizen of the United Kingdom'. Alternatively, he might be a 'Derryman', 'Northern Irish', 'Catholic', 'Fenian' and 'Nationalist'. The contrasting identities in this case highlight precisely the social cleavage dividing people in Northern Ireland.

This process of stratifying loyalties has been commented upon many times since its political importance was first made clear by Evans-Pritchard's work (1940) on the Nuer herdsmen of Sudan and the 'fission–fusion' principle which governs the kinship and territorial cleavages among them. But its political significance applies as much to complex societies as it does to tribal and nomadic peoples. Such principles have long been the cornerstone of private education and military organisation in Britain and elsewhere.[29]

In Italy the political party most successful in forging a distinctive identity and symbol-system for itself has been the PCI. '*Cambia L'Italia Con Noi*' ('Change Italy With Us') runs the slogan of a 1981 recruitment leaflet, for, joining the Party is said to be 'a great act of freedom'. The leaflet goes on:

> To be a Communist militant is to enrich one's humanity and one's individuality. It means to be oneself, not a passenger or a spectator, but at the centre of a great collective movement.[30]

The basis of that identity is the sense of being 'We Communists' ('*noi comunisti*'), a phrase heard frequently in Party discourse; it means being 'One of us', working to transform Italy and the world.

This identity has achieved a tremendous capacity to mobilize others for tasks that are not simply political. Viewed from a distance communist identity appears monolithic and homogeneous, but seen from the inside it consists of a complex arrangement of different, compounded and stratified sub-identities. In part, these correspond to different levels of involvement. For example, the distinctions between Party members (*compagni*) and non-members; between 'the Left' (*gente della sinistra*), and the 'Right' and 'Centre'; between sympathisers, voters, supporters and opponents; between 'comrades' who are 'fellow members' (*compagni di sezione*), and those who are 'rank-and-file activists' (*militanti di base*); between those who are ex-partisans, (*partigiani*), 'cadres' (*quadri*), 'leaders' (*dirigente*), and so on. In part, too, these identities also correspond to the local–provincial–regional structure upon which the Party is organised (i.e. *i comunisti della Sezione di Piazza Grimana, i comunisti perugini, i comunisti umbri*). This particular hierarchy of loyalties may often merge with older identities related to attachments to place and the pronounced local chauvinism (or *campanilismo*) that exists throughout Italy.[31] In addition to each individual Party section and federation, identities also exist for the Federation of Young Communists (the FGCI – *noi giovani comunisti*), the PCI women's organisations (*le donne comuniste*), its partisans' association (ANPPI), its organisation of sharecroppers (*i comunisti mezzadri*), and so on.

The PCI has won mass support by appealing to a variety of social groups, an appeal which it has achieved by creating a vast collective identity built on a pyramid of ties of feeling and attachment to community, place and peer group. In many respects this Party loyalty is comparable to nationalism. Both are forms of collective identity; both are symbol systems based upon an *idea* of community, albeit real or imagined.[32] Finally, just as nationalism acted as a revolutionary force in nineteenth-century Europe, so communist identity may well have a revolutionary potential in Italy today.[33]

Intentional or otherwise, this communist identity is a powerful tool in reconciling some of the fundamental problems of communism since it helps to channel loyalties and thereby ensures the preservation of Party unity. 'Unity' has therefore become a crucial component of PCI identity, as well as another area where ideology, organisation and identity converge. Political unity is ever present in PCI thinking. This is epitomised in the Party statutes of 1983:

> The unity of the party is essential for the realisation of its programme ... Every organisation and every comrade is called upon to defend it against any attempt towards disintegration or factional activity.[34]

In a functional sense identity has a crucial effect upon internal Party cohesion and consensus. Within the PCI there prevails what might be called an 'ideology of Unity'. This is worth emphasising, for 'unity' and 'Party discipline' are not just formal or external aspects of Party organisation imposed from above or simply laid down in Party statutes; they are internalised and socially conditioned principles woven into the fabric of Party ideology and at the forefront of Party practice. Political unity is the buckle that fastens the theory and practice of Italian communism.

While identity and unity act as cohesive forces, PCI organisation and ideology are a continual source of tension and conflict, for they have not moved in step with each other. The PCI has established its modern identity as a democratic, 'secular', 'nonideological' and parliamentary party, but until very recently it was still basically Leninist in much of its organisation and its ideology.

'Ideology' as defined here concerns patterns of belief, or those constellations of values and concepts that purport to explain complex social phenomena, with a view to directing action towards specific goals.[35] Ideology has two components; the formal matters such as doctrine, statutes, strategy and the Party line, and also the less formal aspects such as popular beliefs and private attitudes of rank-and-file members. It extends to individual and collective perceptions about society, the goals and motivations of Party members, and a set of uncritical, largely unconscious perceptions of the world – or common-sense knowledge – all of which, according to Gramsci and many modern PCI intellectuals, has potentially revolutionary implications.[36] But ideologies and their component values cannot be understood without understanding the social institutions and material conditions in which they are located. Beliefs do not develop in a vacuum. Marx's position on this was eloquently stated: 'It is not the consciousness of men that determines their being, but, on the contrary, their social being that determines their consciousness.'[37] There is room for argument about the degree of social causation and determination. Certainly, ideologies have their origins in social formations and historical epochs, but it is oversimplifying to say that ideology is determined by material conditions and leave it at that. The relationship between consciousness and being is infinitely more complex. As Gramsci argued, it is a dangerous analytical misconception to separate ideology from structure in order to assert the primacy of the latter. Like Gramsci, I would echo Marx and stress that an idea can become a material force.[38]

This is why Leninist ideology poses such a problem for the PCI. Party organisation, or 'organisation' in general, may be regarded as a repository of given values; it is 'ideology made flesh', so to speak. But ideologies are also repositories of given values and though formulated in specific social settings they often survive long after those original social conditions have changed or disappeared. Similarly, if they retain their momentum, or even gain in power and influence, they obtain a measure of independence from current material conditions. For example, Judaism and Christianity, the oldest of the 'desert religions', are two cases in point; the pastoralists, prophets and patriarchs of biblical days created these religions, but history has given them their autonomy from the social world of the Old Testament. While social conditions may shift rapidly with economic change, ideology is usually far slower to adapt, far more resilient than changing social forms, and often armed with in-built mechanisms for conservatism. This is as true for political parties as it is for many of the world's religions – and the PCI is no exception.

The PCI: Half-way Between Leninism and Social Democracy?

If 'identity' helps us to understand what it means to be communist in Italy, the question of 'ideology' illustrates some of the problems that continue to hinder the PCI in its quest for power. The great dilemma for the PCI, and perhaps for all Western European communist parties, is the seemingly irreconcilable conflict between their 'communist' identity and their search for legitimacy within the democratic parliamentary systems within which they operate. The question now is, can European communism succeed without 'renouncing itself'? To put it another way, can the PCI or its European counterparts win power legitimately without jettisoning those parts of their ideology and organisation that have until now distinguished them as 'communist' parties?

Throughout its post-war history the PCI has laboured under the weight of a major contradiction between its ideology, its organisation, and its identity. Founded in 1921 as a revolutionary Marxist-Leninist party, the PCI was armed from the outset with a strategy for insurrection, a structure based on Leninist principles of organisation, and an ideology that was explicitly Marxist-Leninist. Nearly 70 years and three generations have passed since then, during which Italian society has undergone colossal changes. From a largely underdeveloped, agricultural economy, it has become one of the world's leading industrial nations. Politically, it has changed from Fascist autocracy to Parliamentary democracy, becoming a founder member of both the EEC and NATO. More specifically, the PCI has become accepted as a legitimate, constitutional part of the post-war Italian political establishment. Given these and other changes, how feasible today is Marxist-Leninist ideology for the PCI or any of the constitutional communist parties of Western Europe? If it is no longer relevant, as many argue, what has the PCI done about its ideological heritage, and what problems have emerged as a result?

The question of ideology strikes at the core of communist party identity. Like all former parties of the Third International, the PCI originally held to a strict Marxist and class definition of itself. However, Leninist ideology took the Marxist conception of party one step further than had hitherto been Marx's view. For Lenin, the Party was not simply an expression of the organised working class, but its natural *leader* and 'historical vanguard'. According to Lenin's definition, all true communist parties were to be modelled on the Russian Bolshevik Party. They were to be cadre parties composed of dedicated, professional revolutionaries; class fighters recruited from the 'most advanced' and 'most politically conscious' sections of the working class.[39] The role envisaged for the Communist Party by Lenin was that of a disciplined, centralised body; a military-like general staff leading the workers of all countries toward emancipation through class war. The Communist Party was thus the instrument and 'protagonist of history'; its mission, to lead and inject 'revolutionary consciousness' into the masses in order to destabilise the bourgeois state. As this revolutionary process gathered momentum, the capitalist system would collapse, the Party would seize power and impose a dictatorship of the proletariat, and this would eventually pave the way for a unified, one-party workers' state.

Justification for the one-party state and the Communist Party's monopoly of power – which even to many Marxists sounded authoritarian and a far cry from true socialist ideals of human emancipation – lay precisely in this class definition of party.[40] According to Lenin, parties are articulations of class and class interest.[41] Marx had identified only two determining classes in the dialectic of history: proletarians and bourgeoisie. His prediction, based on the supposed 'laws of capitalism', was that the bourgeoisie would shrink as the working class expanded, and become progressively more abject and miserable. Eventually the working class would absorb all but a tiny percentage of the population into its ranks – only the capitalist exploiters would remain outside in this inevitable process of polarisation. As leader of the proletariat (whom history had proclaimed the most advanced core of the working class), the communist party claimed to be the representative of the whole working class and its interests. Since, 'historically speaking', no other classes really mattered except for the bourgeoisie – who were the enemy to be suppressed after the revolution anyway – other parties were unnecessary. Liberal pluralist democracy was a sham; it was a subterfuge used by the enemies of socialism to drive a wedge into the essential unity of the masses and exploit its divisions for capitalist gain.

Most orthodox communist parties still subscribe to this line of reasoning – not least because it provides a solution to the vexed problem of political legitimacy in many communist party regimes.[42] The PCI, however, does not, for it has basically accepted the parliamentary and legal norms of 'bourgeois democracy'. Moreover, it has tried to redefine Marxism in order to create a more independent, democratic, and pluralist form of communism. But this has not been an easy task. The history of the PCI's 'Italian road to socialism' is fraught with contradictions and conflicts. These have emerged particularly between the PCI's Leninist ideology and structure and its identity as a mass, democratic socialist party. According to its critics – and in the eyes of many Italian electors – these contradictions have not been properly resolved.

The root of the problem lies in the PCI's Leninist heritage, which has never been compatible with the 'bourgeois democracy' of the Italian parliamentary multiparty system. Thus, critics argue that the PCI's commitment to democracy is ambiguous, and say that it was only as recently as 1979 that the term 'Marxism-Leninism' was dropped from the Party statutes. In reality, however, the PCI began seriously to distance itself from Marxism-Leninism even before the mid-1970s.[43] But how far, one might ask, is the PCI, or any political organisation, a prisoner of its own history? Is Leninism a relic of little significance, or is it, instead, a set of practices and structures that are still deeply embedded in the organisation and culture of the PCI? Marx and Engels once wrote that communism was the 'spectre haunting Europe'. The question now perhaps is, has Leninism become the spectre that is haunting Europe's communist parties as they struggle for survival?[44]

The core of that Leninist legacy identified in this book is the theory and practice of 'democratic centralism': that method of Communist Party organisation that was formulated by Lenin for the Bolshevik Party, but which subsequently became the organisational linchpin of all those parties belonging to the Third International. Though modified by each of these parties, democratic centralism has remained the key mechanism for regulating internal Party life in all of them. It is the backbone of Communist Party organisation; the *éminence grise* behind the formation of Party elites, the formulation of Party policy, and the structure of internal Party power relations.

But there are some awkward and unanswered questions surrounding Lenin's principle of democratic centralism – not least, its link with the rise of authoritarianism in all of those ruling parties that have practiced it. The obvious question this raises is one that most Leninist parties have failed to address convincingly or with sufficient intellectual honesty because of the uncomfortable implications it has for them; namely, how far do the faults lie in Leninist theory itself – and not simply in its application or misapplication? In other words, were the 'Stalinist' regimes of the USSR and Eastern Europe the unfortunate result of a peculiar set of very specific, historical circumstances, or were they a by-product of Lenin's theories combined with his rigid principles of Party organisation? And under what circumstances is

Leninism likely to become a formula for tyranny elsewhere? If the theory is blameless, then how do we explain the authoritarianism that has been the fate of virtually all Leninist parties in power? The PCI may not have all the answers to these questions, but it has certainly gone further than most communist parties in addressing them, and in trying to come to terms with its ideological heritage. Hopefully, that experience will provide, if not a model for others to emulate, then at least some salutary lessons for other parties of the Left to think about.

Part I

The PCI's Approach to Power: Society, State and the Role of the Party

1

History, Identity and Political Socialisation in the PCI

All the world's a stage,
And all the men and women merely players;
They have their exits and their entrances;
And one man in his time plays many parts,
His acts being seven ages.

(Shakespeare, *As You Like It*, Act II, scene vii)

Joining the Party: Recruitment and Socialisation

Italian political parties are not like their British or American counterparts. Generally speaking, they tend to be more active and more explicitly ideological, and they make much greater demands on their membership. Furthermore, since the beginning of the post-war period they have played an increasingly major role as dominant institutions in Italian public life – so much so that it is sometimes suggested that the parties have 'colonised' Italian society (Sassoon, 1986: xii).

To join a political party in Italy, therefore, though it may be regarded as the culmination of a much longer process of political socialisation, is none the less an extremely important social and symbolic act. It is a personal and public statement that represents a turning point in the life of both individual and party. In many respects it is akin to what the Belgian anthropologist Arnold Van Gennep (1908) described as a 'rite de passage' in that recruitment can be seen as part of a ritual process whose goal is to initiate newcomers into the body of the party. The act or moment of joining is a vital event to all concerned. For the individual it may represent personal commitment, an expression of loyalty and perhaps even an act of faith. For the party, on the other hand, it is a mark of vigour and political strength, the most visible sign of its relationship with the public, and a concrete expression of its all-important 'presence' in society. Furthermore, it is through recruitment that a party reproduces itself, and in so doing, symbolically defines itself and its political boundaries. As a prelude to studying the broader theme of communist political socialisation, this chapter focuses on recruitment to the PCI: the way ordinary Party members interpret it and the contexts in which it occurs.

The issue of political socialisation is complex, but the core of the problem can be framed in one simple question, why do people join the PCI? Reduced to this level, the question appears relatively uncomplicated. This apparent simplicity is misleading, however, for it begs the vastly more complex questions of what it *means* to be communist in Italy today, how that meaning varies among different generations of Party activists, and how PCI members who joined the Party in different periods vary in their conceptions of such fundamental notions as 'communism', 'the State', the role of the Soviet Union, and the function of the Party. To answer these, one must begin by addressing a supplementary set of questions concerning *who* joins the PCI. In other words, what social categories are drawn towards Italian communism? What is its appeal? How does this appeal affect the social composition of the Party, and how has this composition changed over the years?

As a social anthropologist doing research into communist culture in central Italy, and as a participant-observer actively involved in daily Party life at the local level, I frequently put these questions to members themselves. Their explanations of why they had joined varied considerably. For some the answer lay in the experience of the war, the Resistance, and Fascism; for others it was the prestige of the Soviet Union and the alluring vision of a new society that socialism offered; still others stressed the influence of friends and mentors, the Party itself, and the experience of exposure at a young age to socialist ideas – and of being able to interpret their own social reality in terms of those ideas. Generally speaking, few members had difficulty pinpointing the key influences and moments that had been critical to their political formation. Furthermore, these responses were usually articulated with extraordinary clarity, detail and insight – suggesting that joining, from their point of view, had been of profound importance to their lives.

Significantly, these explanations were seldom given in terms of an abstract or disembodied set of 'reasons', but rather, as part of a complicated and detailed autobiography. If particular reasons were emphasised they were always specific to historical and social situations – which, in turn, were firmly rooted in the broader context of each personal life history. In other words, the explanations for joining the PCI given by ordinary Party members invariably tended to be cast within the same kind of historical/materialist perspective that characterises the culture and outlook one finds throughout the PCI. To see oneself as part of a political group, or part of a movement and historical process is a fundamental element of what may be called the 'PCI world-view'. However, the way PCI members explain their own behaviour also echoes the 'holistic' approach favoured by social anthropologists; one that tries to understand social behaviour not by any single or objective set of facts, but rather in its broader social and cultural context.

The following chapters set out to analyse the PCI from precisely this kind of approach. To understand political socialisation, one must explore not only historical, sociological and political factors in themselves, but also how these factors are subjectively experienced and interpreted. From this empirical and autobiographical data, together with evidence from more substantive, historical and sociological sources, some of the common threads that help us to understand the nature of Party membership can be isolated.

An approach of this kind, which is neither strictly historical nor purely sociological, invariably risks being charged with lack of methodological rigour, and with blending, or conflating, different levels of analysis (for example, subjective and objective) which, in principle, should be kept separate. Certainly, there are problems involved in trying to incorporate these different approaches, and one must recognise the limitations this imposes. However, the principle of an holistic perspective demands an interdisciplinary approach, for anthropological explanation lies neither at the level of individual experience nor at the level of sociological abstraction or historical reconstruction, but somewhere between; i.e., in the complex interplay between subjective reality and the social–cultural construction of reality.

Seven 'Ages' of Communist Man: A Model for Studying PCI Culture

If one looks therefore, at recruitment in its anthropological context, five factors, above all others, stand out among the most important influences determining choice of party and the initial decision to become politically involved: family, friendship, the work experience, the Party itself (in the sense of propaganda and social presence), and major historical events. Of these, the last-named appears to have played the most critical role. For many PCI activists, it seems, a certain view of the world, and a particular attitude towards the Party became crystallised at a precise historical moment. The general pattern of recruitment and participation in the PCI correlates closely with major national and international developments. In other words, distinctive groupings in the membership arising from specific epochs and events can be quite clearly identified: what we might call 'generations of political activists'. Shakespeare's 'Seven Ages of Man' is, perhaps, analogous to the seven ages of 'Communist Man'; that is, the key historical 'epochs' through which the PCI has progressed.[1]

From the combined perspectives of history and anthropology, one can discern at least seven distinct phases in the history of Italian communism, from which seven fairly discrete cohorts of Party militants have emerged. The following pages describe and then analyse these different political generations. This 'cohort' model, it should be stressed, is only an arbitrary schema of heuristic value, not a definitive classification of the different types of Party activist. Its purpose is to provide a conceptual tool for studying some of the social and ideological divisions that have developed within the Party. However, this is not simply an observer's model or a sociological construct either, but rather it is part of the folk model, or actors' frame of reference. In other words, PCI members perceive *themselves* as falling into generational groupings whose political formation can be explained by reference to the events of these different historical epochs. Those political 'generations' that are identified, therefore, are, by and large, self-identifying groups. However, there is no consensus among Party activists as to exactly where the boundaries of each generation begin or end – nor even about how many generations actually exist within the Party at any one time. These factors tend to shift according to the perspective of different individuals. Some argue that there are really only four generations (pre-war, pre-1968, pre-1980 and post-1980); others can point to at least twelve.[2] The problem is what one means by 'generation'. According to some of those I interviewed, a political generation represents a fundamental break with the cultural and political tradition of the generation that preceded it. However, this definition fails to recognise that generations are as much concerned with socialisation and continuity as they are with rupture and change.

The conclusion seems to be that the concept of 'political generation' is too vague and too ephemeral to be of much analytical use other than as a kind of metaphor or loose framework.[3] None the less, the fact remains that there is a common perception among PCI members of key differences relating to age and experience, and it is on the basis of these 'key events' that a periodisation of PCI history can be constructed. Such an historical framework serves two purposes: first, it provides a brief, contextualised overview for understanding the evolution of the PCI against the backcloth of twentieth-century Italian history; second, it indicates something of the spirit of the times in which Party members were politicised, and the kinds of social and ideological influences they were exposed to. From this historical portrait one can begin to understand something of the mental make-up and value system characteristic of the generational groupings that currently coexist within the PCI. And by understanding that mental make-up, one can begin to see some of the internal divisions and ideological problems which will determine the future of Italian communism.

Much of the data for the analysis which follows is drawn from fieldwork observations in the central Italian region of Umbria. Interviews and eyewitness accounts were collected from a small sample of some 40 Party activists and officials throughout the age ladder.[4] The sample's size and geographical focus are inevitably too limited to permit the sort of major sociological generalisations that a large, statistics-based questionnaire survey might allow – though any conclusions drawn are corroborated by evidence from other surveys. But these interviews do reveal something about the mood, the experience of communism and the subjective meaning of Party allegiance that statistics singularly fail to show. They also provide sharper and more qualitative insights into attitudes and behaviour which can be verified but seldom generated by quantitative methods.

What follows is a twentieth-century history of events particularly significant to the PCI. This is not a standard political history of Italy but a highly selective one based on key events deemed important to the Party and, more specifically, to the political socialisation of Party members.

First Generation: Formation of the PCd'I;* Factory Occupations; Birth of Fascism (1921–3)[5]

World War I had left Italy's unstable economic and political structure badly shaken: the war had cost the country half a million lives, another half a million people were mutilated and over a million were less seriously wounded. The budgetary deficit was enormous, and the cost of living between 1913 and 1920 had climbed from 100 to 624.[6] The government had regularly promised the troops rich rewards for their labours and land to the peasants, but nothing was actually done: unemployment remained high, the economy was depressed and political tensions threatened major instability. Much of Europe appeared to be charged with revolution. Army veterans returning from the war carried home with them advanced democratic, if not socialist, ideas. In Italy, peasants began to demand a redistribution of land, and the number of workers enrolled in the Confederation of Italian Workers (CGL) increased from 250,000 in 1918 to 1,000,000 in 1919. Within the Socialist Party (PSI) there coexisted revolutionary and gradualist elements, but by 1919 most of the PSI had abandoned all half-way reformist measures. At a Party directorate meeting in December 1918, Serrati, director of the Socialist Party newspaper *Avanti*, declared himself against a constitutional assembly and in favour of a dictatorship of the proletariat – a declaration which was adopted as the PSI's official party line. By a vote of ten to three, the PSI leadership subsequently decided to abandon the Second International and join the Comintern, founded in Moscow less than two weeks earlier.[7] An international general strike was proclaimed on 20–21 July 1919, in protest against Allied military intervention in the Soviet Republic, but, significantly, among Europe's socialist parties only the Italians participated.

On 3 September 1919, embittered nationalists led by Gabriele D'Annunzio occupied Fiume in an act of political adventurism which stirred Italian super-patriots. But Prime Minister Giolitti, then aged 78, tried to remain neutral in domestic conflicts and did nothing to deal with the climate of growing social unrest. Law and order were further weakened, and the liberal state was rapidly disintegrating. During September 1920 the crisis took a new turn with the occupation of the factories by workers in Turin and Milan. At the 16th PSI Congress in 1919 the Party's 'maximalist wing' (i.e. those favouring immediate Bolshevik-style extraparliamentary action) emerged victorious, drawing both Italy and the PSI still closer to revolution. Against this background of events, the 'antielectoral' communist splinter group associated with Amadeo Bordiga and Antonio Gramsci's paper, *Ordine Nuovo*, organised themselves on the Left of the 'maximalists'. Disenchanted with its weak and 'revisionist' leadership and fired by the Bolshevik example, they finally split from the PSI at its Livorno Congress in 1921.[8]

* The 'Partito Comunista d'Italia' (PCd'I) – the Italian section of the Communist International – changed its name to 'Partito Comunista Italiano' (PCI) in 1943 with the dissolution of the Communist International (cf. Chapter 7, pp. 146–52).

Italy was swept by rapid inflation, while production fell, industrial strikes spread and unemployment increased. For the salaried middle classes this inflation proved ruinous – a situation which helped their adherence to Fascism (Cammett, 1967: 96). But this wave of unrest was uncoordinated, receiving only hesitant support from the labour organisations and Socialist Party leaders. Mussolini's Fascist movement, launched in Milan on 23 March 1919, gained support as hostility to socialism and street violence grew. Initially it had no comprehensive ideology other than a general programme stressing opposition to socialism and Bolshevism, and collaboration between management and labour in production in order to further the interests of the 'nation'. But it exploited all the discontent that prevailed in the country; from the nation's economic problems and parliamentary ineffectiveness, to management's anxiety about the growth of trade unionism, the middle classes' fear of socialism, and the state's inability to govern.

From the early 1920s onwards, Fascist paramilitary *squadristi* groups organised punitive expeditions against working-class organisations. The socialist and trade-union movement were thrown into disorder. A further schism in 1922 saw the expulsion of the 'reformists' from the PSI. The hour of the Fascist Party was at hand, and, having gained 35 parliamentary seats and a membership now well over 300,000, it set out to wrest power from a crumbling liberal government. A general strike was proclaimed on 31 July 1922 in a last-ditch attempt to block Mussolini, but this backfired disastrously. Mussolini led the so-called 'march on Rome' (28 October 1922), and was finally asked by the king to form a new government. Once in office, the Fascists set about destroying the old constitutional order and in its place established a totalitarian regime.

Most of those who joined the Communist Party of Italy (PCd'I) at its inception in 1921 came from the left-wing and youth elements of the PSI. Foremost among the influences on their political formation was the pervading social unrest and sense of imminent revolution. For many, it really seemed as though the dawn of a new age had begun and that revolutionary socialism would sweep away the old social order. The mood of optimism was summed up by the PSI's most famous leader, Nenni:

> All the extraordinary and clamorous events at the end of 1918 and the beginning of 1919 fired the imagination, and inspired the hope that the old world was about to collapse and that humanity was on the threshold of a new era and a new social order. [9]

Even the leaders of the Third International were persuaded during the struggle in Turin that a proletarian revolution was imminent in Italy.[10] The Red Army was advancing towards Warsaw. Revolutionary prospects looked good. The immediate task to bring about the revolution was to expel the reformists and forge communist parties. As Hoare and Nowell-Smith (1971: lxii) put it: 'Right-wing opportunism was the enemy – left-wing communism merely an infantile disorder to be outgrown.'

Secondly, there was widespread disillusionment with the PSI leadership, which had been manifestly weak and indecisive. The attitude was summed up by Mario Sambuccari, former Socialist Youth Federation member and founder member of the PCd'I:

> Yes, they [PSI leaders] spoke much about 'revolution', but when it came to real conflict – and these clashes were weekly affairs – they did everything possible to avoid revolution. When the moment for action came they turned traitor. That was one reason for the schism and the birth of the PCI. That and the October Revolution ... About 90% of us youngsters crossed over from the PSI at that time.[11]

A further characteristic of this generation's world-view was its image of the state as weak, dithering and corrupt. Industrialists and communists alike were convinced that the government could no longer protect their interests.[12] To young socialists the liberal state appeared as a thinly disguised instrument of class rule. Bolshevism, and the hope that its revolution could be repeated in Italy, had fired their imagination.

Second Generation: Italian Communism under Fascism (1924–43)

For Italian communists these were years of clandestineness, anti-Fascist resistance, repression, imprisonment and exile. The PCd'I in 1924 had some 12,000 members and its youth organisation a further 5,000, and the communist trade-union committee controlled about a sixth of the 120,000 members who remained in the Confederation of Italian Workers (CGL).[13] A small party, the PCd'I was moderately successful in the elections of 1924, gaining 19 parliamentary seats. But following the violent electoral campaign of 1924, further Fascist gains and the murder of the socialist parliamentary deputy Matteotti, Mussolini abandoned democracy altogether. Between 1925 and 1926 Italy was transformed progressively into a police state. The PCd'I, its activists facing daily arrest and its leaders mostly in prison or exile, was driven underground. Gramsci, who had replaced Bordiga as Party leader, introduced changes aimed at bringing about the complete 'Bolshevisation' of the PCd'I.[14] The Comintern's position spelt out by Zinoviev (and the line the PCd'I leadership under Gramsci followed for the next two years) was that social democracy was the left wing of Fascism; historically, these were the right and left hands of modern capitalism. Both were equally enemies of the revolutionary proletariat, and whether a Mussolini in Italy followed the path of Fascism, or a MacDonald in Britain took the road of democracy, was of little consequence.[15]

The Comintern became progressively entangled in internal power struggles between Bukharin, Kamenev, Zinoviev, Stalin and Trotsky – events which had major consequences for Italian communism.[16] Although communist leaders still viewed socialists as 'social Fascists', the Comintern now began to persuade them to follow a united-front strategy, though it was not until 1935 that the notion of a 'popular front' against Fascism came to fruition. By the end of 1926 the Communist Party in Italy had some 27,000 members, recruited mostly from factory workers in the North and peasants in central Italy, and organised into cells. Most Party activity after this date was directed toward efforts to foment strikes and infiltrate Fascist mass organisations. Following Gramsci's arrest in 1926, direction of the PCd'I was assumed by its leaders abroad, and what remained of the clandestine Party was financed mainly from Moscow. The PCd'I lost rather than gained members during most of this period. Only toward the end of the 1930s, with increasing opposition to Fascism, were new supporters drawn into the communist camp.

For Party recruits in this period, arriving at communism was often a logical progression in a process which began with the decision to oppose Fascism – hence, the Communist Party also recruited many non-Marxists. As former partisan and PCI senator Ilvano Rasimelli, who joined the PCd'I in 1941, described his decision:

> The reason I joined the Party was because I was anti-Fascist. Membership for each one of us had libertarian roots. We took our ideology from the *Communist Manifesto* which provided answers to the vexed problems of the war. Very probably, the war facilitated my acceptance of the Party – and a Party that, quite frankly was still Stalinist. Once someone had arrived at the criticism of Fascism he needed some means of fighting it, or of being able to be a fighter. The communists here provided the main reference point.[17]

Two key experiences that influenced this generation were the Spanish Civil War and the Popular Front experience. Both were heroic causes that epitomised proletarian internationalism and symbolically united the Left against a common enemy. Whereas the previous generation had consciously striven to differentiate itself from the noncommunist Left, these experiences, for a while, helped forge a spirit of interparty unity. Tolerance and cooperation, rather than sectarian exclusivity, was the officially sanctioned outlook, however much the Comintern may have perceived this as a mere tactical expedient.

Another influence was the enormous prestige of Stalin – which grew progressively following Germany's invasion of Russia in 1941. Italy's own entry into the war in 1940 and its subsequent military defeats were also significant in recruiting people to communism. Despite its own heavy losses through imprisonment, execution and exile, the PCd'I slowly came to lead the Resistance – a policy which helped lay foundations for its massive expansion immediately after the war.

One salient aspect of the world-view of this generation was a powerful sense of solidarity with the Soviet Union. Other characteristics grew out of the formative political experiences of clandestineness and armed struggle; a readiness to take up arms for the communist cause, combat the state, and sacrifice oneself for the Party. This included an adherence to a Leninist concept of party; namely, a necessarily disciplined, subversive organisation requiring total commitment and obedience. Significantly, there is a prevalent attitude in this and subsequent generations that sees moral rectitude and rigorous adherence to the party line as being among the highest virtues of the ideal Party activist (Sebastiani, 1983: 144).[18] During this period the Party membership was overwhelmingly working-class. Furthermore, the Party was convinced that history was on its side and that the world-wide defeat of capitalism was imminent – thus, every strengthening of repression was widely misconceived as a sign of the growing weakness of the ruling class.[19]

As Fascist rule continued, these members looked increasingly to the Soviet Union for deliverance. Mussolini confirmed for them the Marxist view of capitalist democracy as a mere stage toward Fascist dictatorship. In addition, though, there was prestige in being communist for this generation, for they were engaged in an heroic struggle against all the odds, though they never doubted that progress was on their side.

Third Generation: Return to Legality; National Unity; Communists in Government (1944–7)

The Allied landings in Sicily in July 1943, and then at Salerno, heralded the beginning of the end of Fascism. The front line had cut Italy in two: the South under the Allies and the North under the Germans. The anti-Fascist parties formed clandestinely during the war emerged to form committees of national liberation. All joined the king's government in Salerno after the surprising switch in Communist Party policy, announced by Togliatti, and together they started a partisan struggle to speed the liberation of the North. Of the six anti-Fascist parties, three had mass support: the Christian Democrats, led by De Gasperi, a party formed of various Catholic groups and supported by the Church; the Socialist Party, led by Nenni, formed from a merger between various socialist groups; and the Communist Party, led by Togliatti, and supported by a combination of workers, peasants, anti-Fascists and intellectuals. Significantly, of all the parties, only the communists had remained active throughout the Fascist period, and this gave communism a national prestige that was to prove vital to its survival and development in later years.[20]

Following Italy's liberation a new government was formed, led by ex-partisan leader Parri (leader of the non-Marxist, radical Party of Action). But despite popular hopes that this would fulfil the general desire for political and social renewal, the Parri government collapsed after only six months. Deep disagreements between the leaders of the Resistance had undermined their precarious unity, and these now set the pattern for post-war Italian politics for almost the next 30 years (Allum, 1978: 264). In this tense political atmosphere two alternative concepts of democracy emerged, polarising the forces of conservatism and socialism.[21] As Allum (ibid.) described it:

> On the one hand stood the Communists and Socialists, whose mass support came from the industrial proletariat of the north and the sharecroppers of central Italy, and who wanted a progressive, popular democracy and a programme of social transformation (workers' management committees, land reform, etc.). On the other hand stood the Christian Democrats, whose support came from the peasants and the urban petty bourgeoise, who feared a Communist take-over and wished to reconstruct a liberal market economy.

Italy after the war was in a state of economic catastrophe: the gold value of the lira had plummeted; national income had dropped to less than half its 1938 level and one-fifth of the nation's assets had been destroyed; 40 per cent of railway property had been demolished, and so had 90 per cent of dock equipment and 60 per cent of the state road system (Galli and Prandi, 1970: 4).[22] The country was wracked by problems of banditry, black-marketeering and food shortages. Post-war reconstruction took place therefore in an atmosphere of hunger, bereavement, uncertainty, and increasingly inflamed social tensions as anti-Fascist vendettas, strikes, and demonstrations continued. By joining the government of national unity the PCI had formally allied itself to the legal constitutional process – rejecting, so it seemed, the immediate Bolshevik strategy for the revolutionary seizure of power. Insurrection and socialist transformation would have to wait until the last roots of Fascism had been completely eradicated.[23] Communist partisans now found themselves in the paradoxical position of vigorously proclaiming such bourgeoise notions as constitutionalism, law and order, and parliamentary democracy.

During this period the PCI had an extraordinary revival: from a membership of some 6,000 in 1943, it had risen to 400,000 by 1945. Skilfully organised and adequately financed, it rapidly established a system of sections and cells throughout the country. Within a few years this communications network had recruited over 2 million members. This was the PCI's second major innovation and departure from orthodox Marxism–Leninism: the creation of a new kind of political party – Togliatti's concept of the *Partito Nuovo*.[24] It was a totally unorthodox strategy, which no communist party hitherto had embarked upon. Instead of the traditional Leninist party model of a small, revolutionary elite, the PCI opened its doors to everyone – even 'honest capitalists' – in a move designed to capture the active support of the masses, 'irrespective of ideology, religion or philosophical disposition', (Amendola et al., 1981: 6). The result was a period of unprecedented rapid growth as the Party absorbed hordes of inexperienced recruits.

For many of those new recruits the *Zeitgeist* of this period (at least for left-wing intellectuals) was akin to that of the 1930s in Britain: communism was not only respectable but also highly fashionable. Monarchism, liberalism and social democracy, by contrast, had all been tainted by compromise with

Fascism (Blackmer, 1968: 28). The Soviet Union – its prestige enhanced still further by its victory over Hitler – appeared to many as a 'New Heaven' and 'New Earth'. As the former PCI deputy Alfio Caponi (who joined the Party in 1943) described it:

> The light of Russia, the Russian experience and the realization of socialism stood before us. The only reference point was the communist party; communism, not socialism. It was in the communist party that hope lay, above all for us youngsters.[25]

A major influence on Party recruits was the PCI's prestige gained during the partisan struggle. Anti-Fascism was the great appeal of communist identity. Communism, it seemed, was the only force in Italy that had stood up to Mussolini and liberated the nation from the yoke of dictatorship. In fact, the real liberators were the Allied armies, but traditional PCI textbooks and official histories seldom portray them as such. Higher accolades, instead, were given to the Soviet Union and to the communist Garibaldi Brigades. The message of this selective history was clear: communists did not see liberation solely in terms of overthrowing Fascism and driving German troops from Italy. Their concept of liberation was the overthrow of the capitalist system and its replacement by socialism.

The world-view characteristic of this generation is linked to the high prestige of being communist: anti-Fascists were the heroes of the hour and the making of a popular politician lay in his sacrifice to the struggle against Fascism (hence the virtual canonisation of Antonio Gramsci and the enormous respect for the Soviet Union). It was possible, therefore, to be 'liberal', patriotic *and* communist. On the other hand, many were also dogmatically Stalinist. Cannavota, a local activist who joined the PCI in 1944, exemplifies the Stalinist outlook typical of most of these recruits; one characterised by a powerful belief in class war, in the need for political subversion or armed struggle against capitalism, and in the Bolshevisation of Italian society. On joining the Party, he adds,

> Like everyone else I was in the Fascist Party, or rather the Fascist Youth Organisation – if you weren't a member you couldn't attend school; it was compulsory. I joined the PCI because the communists were closer to me. Youngsters are always a bit extremist perhaps, but the communist party was also better organised than the others, and what it was saying was closer to my ideas and intentions: also because of the Party's doctrine at that time – which I wanted to see put into effect.[26]

Despite the powerful Soviet link, Italian communism assumed, for the first time, a distinctive national character, and the PCI established its reputation as a truly patriotic (as well as revolutionary Marxist) party struggling to create a new social order – a factor which helps explain its strong appeal amongst intellectuals.[27] Significantly, it then changed its name: prior to 1944 it had been the 'Communist Party of Italy' (*Partito Comunista d'Italia*, or PCd'I) – a definition which reflected the Party's view of itself as merely the Italian section of the Communist International. After 1944 it became the 'Italian Communist Party' (*Partito Comunista Italiano*, or PCI), a name change that symbolised the beginnings of a new identity as the PCI began to acquire a more national and autonomous perception of itself, increasingly independent of the Soviet Union and the Soviet model of communism.

Fourth Generation: Cold War, Containment and the 'Hard Years' of Persecution (1947–55)

By 1947 the political climate in Italy had begun to change dramatically. Post-war unity and cooperation gave way to political tensions which largely echoed events occurring at the international level. East–West relations were deteriorating rapidly. Churchill, in his Fulton speech of March 1946, captured the mood memorably when he spoke of an 'iron curtain' fallen across Eastern Europe.[28] The polarisation of Europe had serious repercussions within Italy as conflict intensified over the shape of post-war reconstruction. In June 1947 the communists and socialists were unceremoniously expelled (some maintained illegally) from government by the Christian Democrat prime minister, De Gasperi – largely at the behest of the United States (Kogan, 1983: 35).[29] The PCI and the Nenni wing of the PSI, both emphatically Marxist parties at that time, had already combined in 1946 to form a 'Pact of Unity' and to present a joint list of candidates at the next election.[30] Meanwhile massive economic aid had started to arrive from the USA (the result of the Marshall Plan and the Organisation for Economic Cooperation and Development [OECD]), but this was fiercely opposed by the communists, who saw it as part of the Truman Doctrine and other American designs toward global hegemony (Amendola et al., 1981: 50).

The first parliamentary election under the new constitution was scheduled for 18 April 1948. In the early spring of 1948, tensions mounted as the electoral campaign got underway, but the event which brought things to a climax occurred outside Italy: the communist *coup d'état* in Czechoslovakia in February 1948. Overnight, 'Red' scaremongering and anti-communism rose to a frenzy. The Italian election campaign was immediately transformed 'into a struggle of apocalyptic proportions and the vote depicted as a battle between Christ and Antichrist, between Rome and Moscow' (Kogan, 1983: 39). The full resources of the Catholic Church were mobilised behind the Christian Democrat Party, and the United States contributed to the assault on Marxism with economic weapons, announcing that economic aid would be cut off if the Communist–Socialist slate won. The result of the election was a resounding defeat for the Left (who polled only 31 per cent of the vote to the Christian Democrats' 48.5 per cent), and a 'Centrist' coalition government of four parties was subsequently formed by De Gasperi.

But electoral defeat did nothing to ease the tension, which was exacerbated still further in July 1948, following the massive airlift that was launched when Soviet and East German forces blockaded Berlin. In Italy, however, the final straw occurred that same month when an attempt was made on the life of the Party leader, Palmiro Togliatti. The effect of this was devastating; the closest Italy has come to civil war in the post-war period.[31] As soon as news of the attempt became known, the Rome Trades Council declared a general strike which practically paralysed the capital. Thousands of workers marched to the centre of Rome, and clashes occurred at various points with the police, who were compelled to fire in the air to check repeated assaults on the Parliament Building. Wild scenes occurred in the Senate. Meanwhile serious public disorder had also broken out in some of the larger cities. In Genoa, armed workers occupied the telephone exchange and an electric power plant, installed machine guns on the roofs of strategic buildings, attacked the police barracks, erected roadblocks, overturned vehicles, cut railway lines, and disarmed *carabinieri* at various places. In Turin, workers arrested the entire managements of some 30 large industrial establishments, including the Fiat works, and took over management of the factories themselves (Keesing's, 1948: 9442).

Further riots resulting in death and injury also occurred in Florence, Naples, and Livorno. Throughout the country, armed 'revolutionary forces' went into action: a nationwide general strike was called by the CGL; in Rome Province, Umbria and Tuscany, stretches of railway track were blown up by rebel bands, and main telephone exchanges linking northern and central Italy were attacked. The PCI appeared to be in a state of general alert; ex-partisans took command, and 'machine guns and bazookas once used against the Germans were taken out of their hiding places, cleaned of their protective grease, and mounted on buildings facing police and carabinieri headquarters' (Marzani, 1980: 94).

For many Party activists it seemed as though the revolution had begun. As one local activist described it: 'It was an explosive moment. In Perugia the headquarters of the other parties were burnt down. We also destroyed the offices of the Fascists and the Monarchists.'[32] Party militants were ready to move; all they needed was the signal from their leaders – but the word never came. The Central Committee of the PCI decided instead that insurrection was not possible, and the order went out to quell the tension and end the strike.

For PCI members in the wake of this upheaval, it was a period of hardship and conflict, intensified still further in March 1949 when the cabinet announced Italy's membership of the Atlantic Alliance. Then in 1949/50 revolution brought communism to power in China, and in June 1950, the North Korean army invaded the South. In response to these developments the United States developed its policy of 'containment' of communism.[33] Similarly, in Italy, the government embarked upon a campaign aimed at 'isolating' the Communist Party. Known Party members and sympathisers were blacklisted, persecuted at work, openly discriminated against by employers and fired from their jobs. The Catholic Church contributed to this attack by excommunicating all communists in Pope Pius XII's famous *Avvisso saccro* declaration of 1949.

PCI membership fell during this period, but by surprisingly little; from 2,115,327 in 1948, to 2,027,271 in 1949. Furthermore, by 1950 it had increased again to 2,112,593 (Ghini, 1981: 263). But to survive this assault the PCI was forced to implement major tactical and organisational manoeuvres, dividing membership up into small protective cells and nuclei.[34] It also responded by stepping up its campaign for agricultural reform, organising the peasant movement and occupations of the land, particularly in the South where it gained considerable new support as a result.[35]

This cohort of PCI members is difficult to characterise, given the massive social upheavals and differential patterns across the country. The Cold War stereotype (see Chapter 2), portrayed them as pathological fanatics characterised by a dogmatic, narrow-minded and sectarian mentality. Given the climate of tension and isolation, it would not be unrealistic to characterise their world-view as, at least, 'sectarian'. Significantly, the recruitment in this period dropped from half a million in 1947 to 160,000 in 1955 (Ghini, 1983: 280). Many of these new recruits were peasants in the South and sharecroppers from central Italy, both of which groups increasingly came to identify the PCI, rather than the PSI, as their major ally in their struggle against the landowners and the semifeudal *mezzadria* and *latifundia* systems of land tenure. Generally speaking, the primary appeal of the PCI for them was its record of combat and active opposition to the old system of land tenure upon which the old, semifeudal social order had continued to survive in much of rural Italy.

Fifth Generation: Krushchev, Hungary, the 'Economic Miracle' and the New Left (1956–66)

By the mid-1950s the intensity of the Cold War had been moderated by a growing atmosphere of detente which finally led to the Geneva agreement of 1955. During this period the PSI changed its strategy, distanced itself from the communists, conditionally accepted the Atlantic Alliance, and made overtures to the Christian Democrats, hinting that it was willing to enter a new Centre–Left coalition. The PCI, in contrast, was still fervently pro-Moscow and still seen by many as the instrument of Soviet foreign policy. It had survived the early 1950s intact, but had become heavily bureaucratic and closed. However, it still retained its prestige as champion of anti-Fascism and land reform, and its strong Soviet links were still a source of widespread popularity amongst the Italian working class. But in February 1956, the entire Communist movement was plunged into turmoil by Khrushchev's speech to the 20th Congress of the Soviet Communist Party. In his report

Khrushchev documented the many atrocities of Stalin's rule, from the military blunders committed in World War II, to the staged trials, torture and periodic purges carried out against innocent Soviet citizens, including many of the heroes of the Bolshevik Revolution itself.[36]

The news, when it eventually broke, had a devastating effect on the Italian Left. The heroic myth of Stalin, so assiduously cultivated in all the parties of the Third International, was shattered.[37] Throughout Europe large numbers of leading communists, particularly intellectuals, abandoned their parties. Interestingly, the PCI was not as badly affected by this as were other communist parties: membership fell by approximately 200,000 (less than one-tenth of its strength). But the revelations were traumatic and threw up some uncomfortable questions that PCI leaders were compelled to address. In a sense, what later came to be termed 'Eurocommunism' was born at this watershed in Communist history for it led to serious soul-searching and 'revisionism' in PCI strategy. Indeed, shortly after this Togliatti seized upon Khrushchev's assertion of the legitimacy of 'various paths to socialism' as an endorsement of the actual policy of the Italian Communists, who now proclaimed their own independent 'Italian' road to socialism. This became the rallying slogan of the PCI's 13th Congress – the first time PCI leaders began to speak publicly of the *via italiana al socialismo*. Hereafter the PCI openly asserted the doctrine that the Soviet Union and the Soviet Party were no longer the 'leading state' and 'leading party' for the world communist movement.[38]

But the trauma for the Italian Left was compounded still further in November 1956, following the Soviet suppression of the uprising in Hungary. Whilst its leadership half-heartedly echoed the Moscow line that this was a counterrevolution organised by foreign and domestic reactionaries, the communist leadership of the CGL and many communist intellectuals openly sided with the Hungarian insurrectionaries.

In the same period that the *via italiana al socialismo* was born, Italy was undergoing a period of phenomenally accelerated industrial growth (the so-called 'Economic Miracle'), which reached its peak between 1950 and 1962. During this period Italy was transformed from a predominantly agricultural nation to a leading industrial state: its GNP doubled (Allum, 1973: 25), and its growth rate between 1958 and 1962 rose to an unprecedented 6.6 per cent.[39] But despite the massive social transformation and the creation of a vast new proletariat, the PCI was doing badly: it had lost one-quarter of a million members by 1959, and it was conspicuously failing to recruit from the new industrial working class. The Socialist Party had broken the Pact of Unity and was seeking coalition with the government parties. Aldo Moro's election as DC Party secretary-general accelerated this *rapprochement* and initiated the era of the so-called 'opening to the Left' (*appertura a sinistra*), paving the way for the first Centre–Left government in 1962.

The 'Containment' policy had succeeded in isolating communism, and the PCI was in serious danger of becoming irreparably marginalised, when, by a stroke of good fortune, an event occurred which enabled the Party to break out of the political cul-de-sac into which the Cold War had pushed it. In 1960 a new wave of anti-Fascist sentiment swept through Italy following a series of blunders by the right-wing Christian Democrat prime minister, Fernando Tambroni. Following the formation of his DC-led minority government, Tambroni tried to carry through unpopular parliamentary legislation and won a vote of confidence only through the support of neo-Fascist Movimento Sociale Italiano (MSI) votes. But his plan for a 'government of order' misfired badly, resulting in violent mass demonstrations and a surge of anti-Fascist and anti-government animosity. The decision of the neo-Fascist MSI to hold its sixth Congress in the centre of Genoa, only yards from a memorial dedicated to partisans executed during the Resistance by Fascists, caused widespread riots in the city. A violent demonstration erupted in Genoa on 30 June, which was eventually broken up by police using tear gas and water hoses. Protest rapidly spread throughout Italy. In Bologna, Rome, Reggio-Emilia and Catania, further clashes broke out between anti-Fascist demonstrators and the police, resulting in several deaths and injuries. The June 1960 wave of protest culminated in a general strike in northern of Italy on 8 July which brought transport and industry almost to a standstill and forced Tambroni to resign (Ferrarotti, 1978; Keesing's, 1960: 17713–14).

For many young PCI activists this event was the formative incident of the decade. As Enzo Forini (a 45-year-old former Party cadre), who joined the PCI in 1960, described it:

> The Genoese refused to hold the MSI congress. They took it as an offence and provocation against their history. Throughout Italy ex-Partisans and anti-Fascists were arriving at Genoa in protest. Even though I wasn't personally involved in all this I lived it all ideally and ideologically. The real explosion of protest lasted only a few days, but the results and consequences continued for a long time after. A whole generation of militants was forged in those days of July 1960.[40]

For the 'generation of 1960' this was the most compelling reason for joining the PCI; communism seemed to epitomise the organised struggle against Fascism and colonialism. In Italy, France, the United States and elsewhere, the struggle for national independence in the former colonies of Africa, Asia and the Middle East had major repercussions on the emerging 'New Left'. In Italy it gave rise to a host of spontaneous, revolutionary, Marxist movements – most of them avidly anti-imperialist, but equally anti-Stalinist and hostile to the Soviet Union and its repressive style of communism.

Three other events were of major significance in the world-view of this political generation. First, the growing threat of nuclear war led to the beginnings of a serious campaign for nuclear disarmament both inside and outside of the PCI.[41] Secondly, the papacy of the new 'liberal' pope, John XXIII (Autumn 1958), came to fruition with two major encyclicals, *Mater et magistra* (1961) and *Pacem in terris* (1963), which heralded a new era of dialogue between Catholicism and Marxism – and what seemed to be the end of the first Cold War.[42] Thirdly, the success of the PCI's campaign for land reform drew many new recruits into the Party from the peasantry, particularly from the sharecroppers of central Italy where the PCI had successfully carried out a series of 'reverse' strikes in which peasants undertook needed improvements on neglected estates, calculated the value of landlords' incomes, and showed how they could be used for investment and improvement. As a result, the social composition of the PCI, particularly in the central 'Red Belt' regions, came to be dominated by *mezzadri* sharecroppers for much of this decade (Amyot, 1981: 106).

Sixth Generation: May '68, the 'Movimento', Electoral Advance and Terrorism (1967–76)

The 'opening to the Left' of the Aldo Moro governments of 1964–68 had aimed to carry out a programme of democratic reforms, both to satisfy industry and benefit the working class. It failed on both counts. One reason for this, apart from the half-hearted support of industry, was that any reform that seemed to threaten the interests of the middle classes was vetoed in parliament by the same bloc of provincial party bosses who owed their position of power to the earlier clientelist strategy of the Christian Democrats (Allum, 1978: 265). This failure is often cited as the main cause of the subsequent crisis that endured for the next decade (Allum, ibid.). As private investment dried up, public investment was increased almost as a panacea, but much of this spending went towards funding an ever-expanding, parasitical and corrupt state bureaucracy. Economic recession was prolonged, and the growth of the previous two decades came to a grinding halt.

What followed from 1968 to 1976 was a period of intense social and political unrest in Italy. A generation of politicised activists was formed against a background of turbulent world events. In the USA, the 'Black Power' and anti-Vietnam movements were growing in influence. Martin Luther King, Jr, was assassinated on 4 April 1968; a month later, Senator Robert Kennedy. Then on 10 May 1968, barricades went up in the Latin Quarter of Paris, heralding the beginning of the 'May '68 Student Movement'. In August the Czechoslovak Communist Party's initiative toward political reform and democratisation (Dubček's 'New Course') was pronounced by Moscow a threat to the security of the Warsaw Pact and a danger that was impermissible to the 'Socialist Community'. Orders were issued to the Czechoslovak communists to close Party ranks on the basis of the principles of Marxism-Leninism and democratic centralism, and having accused the dissidents of subverting the socialist system by attempting to abolish the 'leading role of the Party', Soviet troops and tanks invaded the country (the 'Prague Spring'), Prime Minister Dubček was put in chains, and martial law was imposed (Keesing's, 1968: 22996).

The PCI's National Executive issued a statement on 21 August 1968 sharply condemning the Soviet invasion as a violation of the 'principles of autonomy and independence of every Communist Party and Socialist State'.[43] These events had a deep influence on the formation of the Italian New Left – as did the election in November of Nixon to the American presidency, and his immediate violation of election promises not to step up US involvement in Vietnam.

In Italy an explosion of revolt took place, far more intense than anything in Britain or the USA, and far longer-lasting than in France. Spontaneous protest developed against low wages, lack of trade-union rights, and 'established' forms of authority (which now included the PCI). A wave of industrial militancy swept the country during the 'Hot Autumn' of 1969, culminating in a general strike in November 1969, called by all three trade-union confederations. As in France, social unrest and industrial militancy spread throughout the universities and colleges; students occupied buildings, fought with the police and organised revolutionary committees. Varieties of Marxist-Leninist groupings (most notably *Avanguardia Operaia* and *Lotta Continua*) sprang up spontaneously in all major Italian cities. Following the expulsion of the left-wing intellectual group associated with the newspaper *Il Manifesto*, many young PCI members abandoned the Party in favour of the *movimento*.[44] Marx, Lenin, Che Guevara and Mao became the staple literary diet of the student generation and the New Left – an influence which soon spread into many Italian high schools. The '68 Left developed a distinctive political style – even a particular style of dress. To be recognised by members of that generation as a political militant was to achieve status, but this recognition rested on fashion as well as behaviour; for example, on wearing the obligatory 'Loden' coat or 'Eskimo' combat jacket and jeans.[45] It also meant campaigning for reform, and attending lengthy political assemblies – which characterised student life throughout Italy.

The Italian Communist Party was caught unprepared: students and workers were taking to the streets, but it had failed to provide leadership. Worse still, in condemning the violence of the extraparliamentary Left, it found itself identified with the political Right. During the late 1960s Italy was threatened with serious political instability as clashes between communist students and neo-Fascists increased throughout the country.[46] This culminated in 1969 with the Piazza Fontana bomb incident in Milan, which was to become a symbol of neo-Fascist outrage and government complicity.[47] There was even an abortive military coup in Rome in December 1971 led by the ex-military commander, Valerio Borghese, in what was yet another sign of Italy's growing destabilisation.[48]

Terrorist activity increased throughout the early 1970s with a series of bombings, kidnappings and assassinations perpetrated by the Red Brigades, the Fascist group *Ordine Nuovo*, and dozens of smaller political organisations. In the May elections of 1972 the PCI made minor electoral gains, winning 27.7 per cent of the vote (up only 0.3 per cent from the previous elections in 1968). The replacement of Longo and the election of Enrico Berlinguer as the new Party general-secretary in 1972, heralded a new period in the development of the Italian road to socialism.

The PCI was becoming less radical and more pessimistic. It was apparent in the early 1970s that the Christian Democrats still commanded mass popular support and that little had been achieved in the attempt to split the DC from the Catholic masses. If the PCI was to be successful it had to appeal to progressive Catholics. Once again a major political crisis in the communist movement spurred a dramatic change in PCI policy: the CIA-backed coup in Chile in September 1973. The first democratically elected Marxist government was violently overthrown by the forces of reaction. If this could happen in Chile, the PCI asked, what would happen if a communist government were elected in Italy? Extraparliamentary groups insisted that the fate of Allende proved the impossibility of a peaceful way to socialism. The PCI leadership thought otherwise, and in a series of articles reflecting on the events of Chile, and drawing upon the Party's own lessons of 1921–2 and the Fascist seizure of power, Berlinguer concluded that US intervention was not the issue.[49] Rather, the destabilisation of the situation by extremist elements in Allende's camp had driven the moderate Centre into the arms of the Right. The lesson for Italy was obvious: any PCI government would need the support of that large moderate centre if it was to survive the potential military backlash. An 'Historic Compromise' was thus proposed between Marxist and Catholic camps; between PCI and DC as a whole. A Left-coalition government – even were it to gain 51 per cent of the vote – would not survive a frontal assault by the frightened remaining 49 per cent of voters.[50]

The 'historic compromise' strategy seemed to win major support with the electorate; first in the municipal elections of 1975 (in which most of the major cities from Naples northward were taken by the PCI or Left-coalitions), and then in the 1976 political elections, when the PCI leapt forward to its electoral high-water mark of 34.4 per cent (13 million votes). The PCI therefore continued its line of seeking agreements with the DC and dialogue with Catholicism, and it publicly advocated its Eurocommunist principles. On 12 July 1975, the Italian and Spanish communist parties issued a joint proclamation of Eurocommunist commitment to parliamentary democracy. Four months later Berlinguer and Georges Marchais, secretary-general of the French Communist Party, proclaimed their commitment to democratic socialism. Following this, both parties quietly dropped the term 'proletarian dictatorship' from their statutes. The Soviet Union, for its part, condemned Eurocommunism as erroneous.[51]

To characterise the world-view of members of the generation of '68 (or *gli sessantottini* as they are often called in Italy) is extremely difficult, not least because the '68 movement was so complex and fragmented, and because most of those who were politically active on the Left belligerently rejected the PCI for its compromised, nonrevolutionary stance. Outflanked on the Left by a plethora of radical groups, the PCI lost much of its prestige, particularly among intellectuals, radicals and the young. Even some of its own leaders left, in order, as they put it, 'to join the movement'. Indeed, PCI leaders often refer to the '68 Left as 'our lost generation'.[52] However, those on the '68 Left outside the PCI were nevertheless regarded by most PCI members as 'comrades' (*compagni*), and therefore allies. According to the *sessantottini*, the PCI had become bureaucratic and Stalinist, and many felt that it had not gone far enough in condemning the Soviet invasion of Czechoslovakia – a revolt against Soviet-style communism with which, no doubt, many Italians identified. The PCI's decline in this period is reflected in the pattern of recruitment: whilst there was little drop in the overall numerical balance of membership and recruitment, the Party's youth sector (FGCI) plummeted from 135,000 members in 1967 to below 67,000 by 1970 (Penniman, 1977: 162). Strangely, the broader trend in membership recruitment between 1966 and 1975 was quite the reverse: between 1965 and 1968 new recruitment fell slightly from 121,771 to 102,340, and then rose again to 134,926 in 1972. (Ghini, 1982: 273).

Typically, this generation saw the PCI as a party on the defensive; a party consumed in the practical task of winning regional government elections and manning its newly won offices. The long-awaited establishment of regional government (1970) opened up a vast new avenue for party patronage. Party bureaucrats and administrators were needed urgently. This fact, members claim, combined with the abandonment of Party offices by its more radical militants, paved the way for a very different kind of party cadre: one with little of the integrity, independence or class consciousness of their predecessors. Amyot (1981: 24) confirms this view:

> Many of these new recruits have no clear commitment to revolution, and some, certainly, seem to have been attracted to the Party in part because of their desire for gainful employment; most of these come from the intellectual petty bourgeoisie.

But while communism might have lost much of its appeal to radical students and intellectuals, the first recession precipitated by the OPEC oil cartel of 1973 – which led to major plant closures in Italy – undoubtedly encouraged workers to rally to the PCI for fear of losing their jobs.

Seventh Generation: Terrorism, Aldo Moro, Poland and the PCI–Moscow Rift (1977–89)

The present 'epoch' is equally difficult to characterise. Despite massive electoral gains the PCI was still excluded from participation in government, but with so large a percentage of the vote it could no longer return to its traditional role of opposition. After 1976 no party could govern Italy without the PCI's active consent. A new slogan was thus coined: the PCI was a 'Party of Government *and* a Party of Struggle' (*un partito di lotta e di governo*). Italy was still gripped by social unrest.[53] The elections of 1976 simultaneously marked the zenith and decline of the Italian Left. The word commonly used to describe the post-1976 period is *il riflusso* (the ebb). Thereafter, what cohesion there had been among the various groups that comprised the '68 *movimento* collapsed, many turning to terrorism or simply apathy. There followed a period of short-lived governments and national scandals (including the Seveso disaster, the Lockheed scandal, the Banco Ambrosiano collapse, and the P2 Masonic Lodge scandal). But the single most important event of the late 1970s was the kidnap by the Red Brigades of the former prime minister and president of the Christian Democrat Party, Aldo Moro. On 16 March 1978 Moro's convoy, en route to the official opening of parliament, was ambushed. Five armed bodyguards were killed in the machine-gun attack that followed. Moro was probably Italy's most senior politician, and had been the DC's principal architect of the 'Historic Compromise'. His abduction was therefore interpreted not only as an assault against the Italian republic, but also as a direct attack against the Italian communists.

The government, backed by the PCI, refused to negotiate with Moro's kidnappers. Consequently, on 9 May 1978, Moro's body was symbolically dumped in the boot of a red Renault 4, strategically parked exactly half-way between the respective Rome headquarters of the PCI and the DC. In the state of emergency that followed, the PCI adopted a programme of 'democratic solidarity', giving full support to the Centre–Left coalition government of Prime Minister Andreotti.

This incident, coupled with Pope Paul VI's death and succession by the far more anticommunist popes, John Paul I and Wojtyla (John Paul II), spelt the end of the 'Historic Compromise'. The PCI's support for the emergency government undermined rather than enhanced its credibility, for it was now identified with a right-wing government on the one hand, and (in many people's eyes) the terrorist Left on the other. In the 1979 elections the PCI vote fell by four points to 30 per cent – a fall which augured badly for Eurocommunism.

Once again events *outside* Italy profoundly altered the PCI's position: first the Soviet invasion of Afghanistan in 1979; then the crisis in Poland that exploded in August 1980 following the revolt in the Lenin Shipyard in Gdańsk. This latter event brought major condemnation from the PCI, precipitating a full-scale critique of Soviet communism and a heated row between Moscow and the PCI. Henceforth began the most serious rift ever between the two parties. This rift, the tensions it caused and the debate it generated, raged through the PCI sections throughout 1982–3, threatening to split the Party. The conflict was finally concluded at the 1983 PCI Congress where the pro-Soviet wing of the Party was resoundingly defeated. Thereafter the PCI leadership was free to move forward with its interpretation of the 'Italian road to socialism', to which Berlinguer had added several new concepts – including the 'transformation of Italy', the 'third way' (*la terza via*) and the 'new internationalism'.[54]

Only brief and sketchy points can be made to characterise the outlook of

PCI recruits in this period. Berlinguer's full-scale condemnation of Soviet communism and the Party's declaration of war against terrorism were among the formative events on the generation of new recruits. So too was the PCI's declaration of war against the Mafia – particularly for Party members in Sicily and Calabria. In May 1982, the government appointed the deputy commander of the *carabinieri*, General Carlo Alberto Dalla Chiesa, as prefect of Palermo with special responsibility for fighting the Mafia. His appointment came shortly after the murder, in an ambush in Sicily in April, of Pio La Torre, former PCI regional secretary for Sicily and member of the chamber of deputies. However, Dalla Chiesa was himself ambushed and killed in Palermo on 3 September 1982 – as were hundreds of people in western Sicily during the Mafia wars for control over the heroin market in the early 1980s. Following a wave of public outrage, the PCI began a full-scale mobilisation of opinion against the Mafia. This was not so much because of Mafia victimisation of communists, as because the struggle against the Mafia is, as the PCI perceives it, also a critique of Christian Democrat corruption and clientelism in Italy (cf. Buxton, 1984; Arlacchi, 1979 and 1986). Thus, communist recruits in Sicily today have perhaps more in common with the generation of the first Cold War than with their contemporaries in northern Italy, for they too are a persecuted political minority, and the dangers they face are very real indeed.

Another difference in the outlook of the new generation, as compared to that of their predecessors, was their detatched attitude toward the Soviet Union. Gone are the old emotional ties that once bound Party members in a Soviet-inspired global vision of communism. Many indeed are as positively anti-Soviet as they are anti-American. As Forini (who rejoined the Party in 1980) remarked, 'I joined the PCI when I realised that you could be Communist *and* anti-Soviet.'[55]

The activities of the Soviet Union and the deterioration of international relations no longer damage the PCI as they used to. With the passing of older generations of Party activists the PCI's extrication from Soviet influence may even be a source of credit to it. Many new recruits come from traditionally communist families. Some of these received their principal political education at school, where the repercussions of the *movimento* were still very much in evidence. As Sereni (Interviews, 1983) described it:

> The state of mobilisation was still very much alive. My personal encounter with politics came about substantially through this. I'm not exaggerating when I say that probably some 80 per cent of the students at school at that period were politically aligned in some way or another, and regularly attended meetings, assemblies, open-discussions and such like. It was obvious that someone like myself – coming from a house where politics had always been openly discussed – should have felt drawn towards an organisation like the PCI.

Evidence of a widening generation gap between older PCI members and younger cohorts was also apparent, particularly in the provincial level leadership. By the late 1970s this was, in the words of Emanuele Macaluso, a mix of older, working-class members with strong peasant roots; an educated cadre formed during the War of Liberation; a younger cadre formed during the years of capitalist reconstruction in the trade-union movement, in local government and in the campaigns against the Scelba government; and a new cohort whose formative experiences had been in the student, civil-rights, women's and feminist movements.[56] Marco Fumagalli, then secretary of the Communist Youth Federation (FGCI), which in the past had been closely aligned with the Party, was interviewed about the FGCI's previous congress, where a motion critical of *L'Unità* had been approved with a standing ovation. Commenting on this, Fumagalli explained that the Communist youth of today had doubts

> on many aspects of Communist culture, of the culture of the workers, of the PCI itself ... There are new issues, such as a different relationship with politics, a different conception of sexuality, of music, and of the environment ... and we ask that these issues be discussed. The Party is having considerable difficulties in quickly taking hold of these new ideas. The society we live in is much more complex than many of our older comrades perceive it to be. Perhaps more important than a job to us Young Communists today is the guarantee of a satisfying quality of life. But try to tell this to an old worker who has spent his entire life on the job ... We are the first generation without myths. We grew up in the era of Vietnam, Cambodia, Afghanistan, and Poland. The experiences of those governments have nothing whatsoever to do with the socialism in which young people believe. In fact, from our viewpoint, there are no models for our socialism, not even that of the 'third way'.[57]

Between 1984 and 1989 the fortunes of the PCI continued to decline. On 11 June 1984 Enrico Berlinguer, who had shaped PCI policies since the beginning of the 1970s, died of a cerebral haemorrhage. In the European elections that followed only days later, the PCI received an extraordinary 34.4 per cent of the vote – making it the largest single party in the European Parliament. But this success (which many attributed to a sympathy vote for Berlinguer) represented little more that a momentary blip in an otherwise steady electoral fall. Alesandro Natta, who succeeded Berlinguer, was widely seen as a caretaker leader who would continue the Berlinguer line until a new strategy could be elaborated. This the PCI attempted to do at its 17th Congress in Florence in April 1987. Significantly, this was the first time that a congress had been called before the normal four-year interval had elapsed. The congress, which re-elected Natta as general-secretary and Achille Occhetto as his deputy, presented a new image of the PCI as part of the 'European Left' which was increasingly differentiating itself from the Soviet model. Natta's congress speech referred to the possibility of a coalition government of left-wing reformist forces, and Giorgio Napolitano (then leader of the PCI's parliamentary group) described the PCI as a 'modern reformist party ... an integral part of the European Left which is moving towards dialogue and convergence with the major European socialist and social democratic parties' (Keesing's, 1987: 34955).

Eurocommunism, no longer on the political agenda, had been replaced by the notion of Eurosocialism. But this brought the PCI little tangible success: the PSI under the leadership of Bettino Craxi consistently refused to enter a left-wing government coalition – which the PSI feared (perhaps correctly) would be dominated by the communists – and in the 1987 elections the PCI's share of the vote fell from 29.9 to 26.6 per cent. Following a heart attack, Natta resigned as PCI general-secretary on 13 June 1988 and was succeeded by Occhetto, whose position was officially ratified at the PCI's 18th Congress in March 1989.

Yet despite electoral decline the PCI has continued to attract large numbers of new recruits, with over 375,000 new members (25.8 per cent of its total membership) joining the Party since 1980, and 143,000 (9.5 per cent) since 1986.[58] Many of those entering the PCI in this period were politicised during the late 1970s and early '80s, the years of 'terrorism and alienation', as many of this cohort describe them. If the views of young delegates to the 1989 Congress are taken as representative, many were politicised at school or university; became politically active over major issues such as abortion, divorce, nuclear power and the environment (in all of which there have been national referenda); and finally joined the PCI as a logical continuation of these single-issue campaigns. Similarly, many have been drawn to the PCI through the ecology and women's movements, which the PCI has (somewhat belatedly) come to represent. Peace, nonviolence and protection of the environment are but the latest in a series of campaigns to be subsumed under the PCI's banner. But appealing to the last-named of these movements has required a monumental shift in traditional communist ideology. One example of this was the economic programme sketched in the 1989 Congress theses; 'ecological restructuring of the economy', and a stress on consumption rather than production marked two of these innovations. Another was the PCI's confession of 'patriarchal tendencies' within the Party that need to be eradicated and its emphasis on overcoming the traditional sexual division of labour.[59] With its stress on these new themes, the PCI is perceived by many of its new and younger recruits as 'less ideological' and 'more emotional'.

Throughout this analysis of political socialisation, the emphasis has been on key events and active politicisation, but a word should be said about a different kind of PCI member and a more passive form of socialisation: those who join the PCI out of habit or tradition. In a large number of cases the explanation given by people as to why they joined the PCI was simply that their parents were communists, or that they grew up in a communist area and it seemed somehow natural to be in the PCI rather than any other party. For many it is also of some economic and political advantage to belong to the PCI (particularly where communists control local-government patronage) as the Party may provide a useful source of employment and protection. But, similarly, in areas traditionally dominated by the DC and PSI (such as Sicily, the Veneto and most of southern Italy), the reverse is true, and PCI membership may be considered a statement of defiance. As one young delegate from Catania expressed it (Interviews, 1989), 'Most of my classmates joined one of the coalition parties [because] with a DC or PSI party card it's much easier to get ahead with your career. That's how it is in Italy.'

Seven Generations of Communist Man: a Key to Understanding Internal Party Conflicts?

'Men create their own history, but not always as they please', wrote Marx. Likewise, Marx wrote history that was not always as others pleased. Indeed, it is perhaps one of the universal truths about history that 'histories' are arbitrary constructs continually disputed; or as E.H. Carr (1961: 30) described it, 'an unending dialogue between the present and the past' and 'between the historian and his facts'. In attempting to describe these cohorts of PCI activists, I have not pretended to discover what Engels (1968: 94–5), described as 'the great laws of motion of history'.[60] My aim instead was simply to look at the broad generational patterns and ideological groupings that currently coexist within the PCI and to provide a background and starting point for understanding the way in which PCI members were exposed to politics.

The 'seven generations of communist man' provides a model akin to that of the life cycle itself. The metaphor is perhaps best summed up by applying the Shakespearian analogy to the PCI: at first a 'mewling and puking infant' of a party, composed of disenchanted young socialists, and nursed by visions of Bolshevism. Then a cabal, thrust unwillingly into exile. Next a party of partisan heroes, liberators and patriots favouring progress. Then ostracism; noble class warriors under siege in a climate of Cold War containment. Middle-age crisis follows with the maturing experiences of Khrushchev, Hungary and Italy's capitalist boom; but Party vigour is revived by a wave of anti-Fascist sentiment. 'The sixth age shifts' into tired respectability and cautious compromise; the Party is condemned for its 'reformism', but propelled forward by electoral conquests. 'Last scene of all that ends this strange eventful history', and the Shakespearian analogy either breaks down or ends with the metaphorical death of the PCI. In Shakespeare's seventh age, man slips into doddering senility and 'mere oblivion' – a phrase which could be applied to other European communist parties. The PCI, by contrast, seems to have gained a new lease of life and become, quite literally, 'rejuvenated'. This is borne out in the changing compositions of the Party. By 1976 over 37 per cent of provincial-level cadres were under 35 and had joined the Party after 1969, and the composition of delegates to the 1979 federation congresses revealed that over half were under 30 and roughly three-fifths had joined the PCI after 1970.[61] By the early 1980s well over half of all PCI members had joined the Party since the 1960s, and nearly half of all federation cadres had joined after 1968.[62]

Unlike Shakespeare's metaphor, where the same individual passes through each phase in the life cycle, the phases of PCI history are experienced differently by each age group. These different cohorts are not chronologically discrete but coexist simultaneously. This has serious implications for internal Party politics. As we shall see, the battle lines of ideological conflict and dissent within the Party tend to run along precisely these generational divisions. The split between the pro-Moscow hardliners and Eurocommunist revisionists, and the tensions between the leadership and the rank and file can be traced directly to the socialising influences and ideological differences arising from the experience of these key historical events. While some fundamentals of Party ideology and organisation remain constant across the generations,[63] each generation tends to have a very different identity from its predecessor, one shaped by its own particular world-view and the historical epoch in which it was formed.

Alongside this generational turnover, the 1970s witnessed a major transformation in the class composition of the PCI, particularly among its middle-level cadres. With the creation of regional governments in the early 1970s, many young PCI functionaries were rapidly promoted to new administrative posts or drawn into the Party apparatus to replace those who had taken up elected posts. Members of this new age group differed radically from their predecessors. Many were politicised in the 1968 era, had been temporarily involved in the extraparliamentary Left before entering the PCI, and were from predominantly bourgeois backgrounds (Pridham, 1981: 94). They were less sectarian than the previous generation, had entered a Party that had shed much of what Pridham called its 'trench mentality' of the Cold War, and had experienced little of the political hardship and defeat of their predecessors.[64]

While this turnover was actively encouraged by Berlinguer, who had become general-secretary in 1972 (cf. Urban, 1986: 334, 350), others asked whether this posed a threat to the class identity of the PCI.[65] Critics replied that it did and pointed to the 'Historic Compromise' and the PCI's 'revisionist' policies as proof of this. Thus, several authors, including Covino (1981) and Amyot (1981), see the post-1970s trend towards bureaucratisation and the progressive recruitment of middle-class members to the Party leadership as evidence of its 'deradicalisation' and growing estrangement from the masses.[66] Stripped to its essentials, the argument was basically a variation of the old '*embourgeoisement* thesis'.[67] Against this, however, one should note that decision-making in the PCI has almost always been dominated by middle-class intellectuals. None of the PCI's leaders since Togliatti could be described as proletarian; most have been university-educated, middle-class intellectuals, including Togliatti, who was himself a university lecturer. Working-class hegemony within the PCI has not been 'usurped' by bourgeois intellectuals; it never existed in the first place. More accurately, the middle-class intelligentsia (who traditionally constitute the Party vanguard) have always exercised hegemony over the PCI, however much that hegemony is conducted in the name of the working class. Certainly, the percentage of educated, middle-class functionaries at federation and regional level has risen considerably since 1969, but the correlation between class composition and 'deradicalisation' cannot be easily substantiated. Given the increase in mass further education and the rise in living standards, it is hardly surprising that young recruits are better educated and more middle class than the older activists they replace. Amyot's (1981: 25) disparaging references to the 'petty bourgeois interests and attitudes of this group' is a conjecture that is assumed but insufficiently documented or analysed. Moreover, his concept of 'deradicalisation' is ambiguous and arbitrarily adapted to suit a partisan interpretation of 'class interest'. Thus, the new middle-class cadres provide evidence of the 'growing penetration of bourgeois ideology in the PCI' (because they supported the 'Historic Compromise' strategy), while those cadres who supported the Ingrao Left (equally middle class) remained radical because, unlike their successors, they had somehow 'broken with their class years before' and managed to 'declass' themselves. This idea, as we shall see, is part of the myth of Leninism from which the PCI is trying to extricate itself.

2

Construction of Communist Identity in Italy

Catholic–Communist Division in Italian Society

Spiritual centre of the Roman Catholic Church, seat of the Vatican, home to the largest communist party in the Western world; this disparity explains why Italy is described as a country of contrasts and contradictions. This is neither a trivial division nor a coincidence. In Spain, France and Portugal, where Catholicism is equally entrenched, communism and socialism also developed strong roots in the pre- and post-war periods as the forces most opposed to Church power. In Italy, however, this division marks a major social cleavage which, perhaps more than any other, has dominated the course of Italian history in this century.

The Catholic Church's influence over Italian society goes back to the fourth century, to the Emperor Constantine's conversion and his adoption of Christianity as the official religion of the Roman Empire. The Communist Party, in contrast, has existed only since 1921, yet its growth and social impact in that period have been remarkable. From a conspiratorial coterie before 1944, the PCI has become a massive force permeating Italian society in virtually all its public manifestations. In many local communities, it has come to rival, if not supplant, the traditional role of the Catholic Church as organiser of community events and symbol of local identity. Since the end of World War II in particular, communism and Catholicism have become increasingly antagonistic to each other, not merely as rival organisations but as competitive, polarised and often mutually exclusive cultural systems.

Italy's peculiar party system, combined with the extensive use of political clientelism, has reinforced a tendency for parties to perceive themselves almost as exclusive sub-cultures. This point is often overemphasised, but it is essentially true. Political divisions cut very deeply into Italian society and popular consciousness – so much so that, as Barnes (1967: 27) observed, 'Some parties come close to encompassing the entire existence of many of their adherents.'[1] In a far more ambitious way than their British counterparts, Italian parties compete for the emotional and intellectual support of the masses. This idea is epitomised in the Italian conception of the 'Two Worlds': *il mondo cattolico* and *il mondo comunista* (Riccamboni, 1976).

According to Kertzer (1980: 2), the Catholic Church and PCI try to provide comprehensive systems of belief and behaviour: they are not simply 'segmental institutions calling for limited areas of allegiance', but organisations demanding the individual's total support in a wide variety of roles and situations. In parts of Italy, notably the Red Belt regions of Emilia-Romagna, Tuscany and Umbria, this Church–communist confrontation 'tends to divide people into two hostile, and to an extent, socially autonomous worlds' (ibid.). People drawn into the web of organisations that constitute the Catholic or communist World and who recognise the authority of the Vatican or Party are sometimes presumed to have 'an all-pervading allegiance to the social and political as well as to ritual and ideological edicts of the hierarchy' (ibid: 2–3). According to this conception, Italian society remains fundamentally divided between two competing sub-cultures, one centred on the Catholic Church and the Christian Democrat Party, and the other on the Communist Party and its satellite organisations (Riccamboni, 1976).

The striking extent to which PCI support is concentrated both geographically and socially is often cited as evidence of this division. Despite the demise of the industrial and rural proletariat, the PCI still sees itself primarily as a 'proletarian party'. According to figures from membership returns, over 40 per cent of the Party's 1.5 million members come from 'proletarian' backgrounds.

However, looked at in another way, these figures show that over half the PCI's members – and an even larger number of its electors – do not belong to the industrial working class, and more than three-fifths of this class does not support communism. The traditional image of the PCI as *the* party of the working class is evidently no longer true, and this causes some concern among PCI members. Naturally, that working-class presence is a fundamental component of the PCI's class identity, for it is the *raison d'être* and justification for any communist party's existence. As the 1983 pre-Congress document put it, the working class remains 'the nerve of the Party's strength', and 'this class character must be firmly safeguarded and fortified.'[2] This is qualified by the assertion that the PCI is also a mass, interclass party, the implication being that it must not make the mistake of exaggerating and romanticising its 'proletarian' image.[3] However, that working-class presence diminishes progressively the higher one climbs the PCI's bureaucratic ladder; there are virtually no working-class members in the Central Committee Executive. Thus, Party leaders were forced to admit in 1978 that 'the number of working-class cadres and comrades in production holding high-level leadership positions is still generally inadequate', and that an 'organic cadre policy' for the promotion of working-class and women cadres was needed.[4]

The geographical concentration of communism in Italy is another indication of a communist sub-culture. Over 700,000 members (or 48.4 per cent) come from just four regions, Emilia-Romagna, Tuscany, Umbria and Liguria (PCI, 1989: 9–13). In fact, these are all areas where traditions of socialism and workers' cooperatives were established in the period before the 1920s. Most PCI support within these regions was traditionally concentrated among the male working class (though increasingly the PCI draws support from the middle classes). Only the Christian-Democrat Party traditionally attracted substantial numbers of voters from all classes, most of these coming from the lower-middle classes, independent farmers, the self-employed and professionals. This broad class appeal is derived largely from the DC's association with Catholicism and the Church's ability to cut across class boundaries. Like the Church, too, the DC's largest group of supporters (i.e. voters) are women. As Almond and Verba (1963: 404) stated, somewhat dramatically, it is the DC's appeal to 'uninvolved Catholic women' that has proved the decisive factor in the election of every successive Italian government since the war.

Explaining the emergence of Italy's marked regional divisions is a more complex issue which, for lack of space, is dealt with here only briefly.[5] The origins of these geographic divisions can be traced to social and religious schisms which occurred over a century ago. Italy's two liberating experiences – the Risorgimento and the Resistance were both incomplete and deeply divisive in their effects, as was early industrialisation (cf. Seton-Watson, 1967). Italy's modest industrial boom during the 1880s caused inevitable upheavals, but these coincided with the beginnings of a more serious crisis in agriculture precipitated largely by imports of American and Russian corn. The damage this inflicted on Italy's weak agricultural system was brought to public attention in a parliamentary report on the conditions of life in rural areas.[6] This official inquiry pointed out that in large parts of the countryside, disease and undernourishment were the rule; malaria was rampant; and 'hovels', forced child labour, 'illiteracy and degradation' were the norm (Procacci, 1973: 342). For the victims of this agricultural crisis, emigration to the New World offered the simplest form of escape from the prison of rural poverty. Others preferred to migrate to northern Europe, many on a seasonal basis. The 1880s thus gave rise to the first wave of mass emigration, but they also heralded the beginnings of the Italian peasant movement which emerged in response to popular discontent with economic developments. This was given greater impetus as migrants and itinerant labourers who had been exposed to socialist or anarchist ideas abroad, and who had acquired knowledge about unions and how to strike, began to return home (cf. Procacci, ibid.; White, 1980: 168).

Against this background of economic change the seeds of class consciousness and conflict were sown. Simultaneously, however, an alliance was forged between bourgeois northern businessmen and southern landowners – what Gramsci called the 'agricultural–industrial bloc' of the Italian dominant classes – which dominated Italian history throughout the next century by consolidating and exacerbating these social divisions. Generally speaking, therefore, where these processes of economic upheaval, migration and class formation were not developed to the full, such as the northeastern regions of Friuli, Trentino, Veneto and much of Lombardy, there was little disruption of the established social order. Consequently, socialism made little impact in winning popular support, and the Church remained the most powerful community institution beyond the family.[7] However, in the central regions, including

Emilia-Romagna, Umbria and Tuscany, urbanisation, rapid industrialisation and an extensive division of labour along capitalist lines caused extensive social dislocation. The consequences were class polarisation, the alienation of the Church from the community and a shift in support toward the Left.

More specifically, the predominantly Catholic (or 'White') provinces today include areas which from 1815 to 1866 were under Austro-Hungarian rule. The Church was particularly instrumental here in defending Italian nationalism against a common foreign oppressor, and it became a symbol of continuity and stability during the turbulent period of the Risorgimento (Stern, 1975: 231–2). Simultaneously, however, Austria introduced new fiscal and administrative reforms which made these regions amongst the most advanced and well-governed in Italy. In contrast, the Red Provinces (excluding Tuscany) formed part of the Papal States, formerly ruled by the oppressive and dictatorial Papal legate. Unification in the central regions therefore took the form of a virulent and often rabid anticlericism, and many people turned to socialism as the movement most opposed to the Vatican's power. Furthermore, following the defeat of the Vatican and the confiscation of its property, the clergy became increasingly dependent upon local landlords, a fact which helped to alienate the Church still further from the rural masses in the ensuing struggles for land reform. This anticlerical legacy is reflected superficially in the extraordinary vocabulary of insults against the pope, the Virgin Mary and God which characterises local speech.[8] More importantly, however, it is witnessed in the fact that Catholics and active communists have come to occupy separate social worlds. Contrary to the stereotype portrayed in the popular 'Don Camillo' novels, few communist activists are regularly churchgoing Catholics. The PCI, however, has never defined itself as explicitly anti-Catholic or anticlerical.

Economic factors, particularly class, and land tenure and ownership, also played a major role in shaping political identity and regional politics. In broad terms, independent farmers tend to vote for right-wing parties, particularly the DC, which traditionally claims to represent their interests (though this pattern is complicated by numerous provincial variations).[9] Thus, in the mountainous regions of northern and southern Italy, where owner-operated farms predominate, the DC vote is usually highest and the left-wing vote lowest. As Guizzardi (1976) argues, the small-to-middling farm pattern was actively promoted by the conservative wing of the Church as the basis for its ideology of 'Rural Civilisation'. According to this ideology, the small family farmstead represents the ideal of 'man in nature'; the form of social organisation closest to what Pope Pius XII defined as 'the natural order willed by God' (Guizzardi, 1976: 202). This model incorporates the Church's most cherished values, including private property, the integrated family and the right to land established through honest work. The ideology thus depicted the peasantry as the repository of uncorrupted Christian tradition. This link between patterns of land tenure and Catholic ideology may also help to explain the land-reform programme pioneered by the DC in the 1950s, the aim of which was to create hundreds of thousands of small farm holdings from the break-up of the old great estates in the south.

By contrast, the PCI vote is highest in the lowland provinces of the Po Valley (Bologna, Ferrara, Ravenna, Forli), where better farmland existed, and where until recently most land was held by wealthy landlords employing seasonal labour. It is also concentrated in the prosperous farm regions of central Italy (Tuscany and Umbria), where the characteristic form of land ownership was *mezzadria* sharecropping. This system, while offering some security to the families who till the soil, gave them no hope of ever owning that land. The massive support given by sharecroppers first to the PSI and then to the PCI is usually interpreted as a traditional protest against this pattern of ownership.

If the emergence of communist and Catholic subcultures in Italy stems from much older patterns of land tenure and class conflict, these divisions were strengthened rather than weakened by post-war developments. Until the 1950s, Italy was still a predominantly agrarian society and many present-day attitudes still reflect cultural traditions formed in an agricultural rather than an industrial context. Added to this, political loyalty in Italy often entails loyalty to one's family and community. This is what Almond and Verba's study (1963) revealed, what Barnes's observations (1967) reinforced and what anthropological studies have consequently confirmed.[10] Party allegiance rests largely on affective social ties, and the comments made by Allum (1979: 219) on the PSI might equally apply to many PCI members (though not to the activists): 'The principal reason for membership still appears to be family tradition, son following father, and the chief motive for going along to the Party section is recreation.'

Up until the 1950s, it was the Socialist Party (PSI), and not the PCI, that was the dominant force on the Left. Even in the first post-Resistance elections, the PSI won more votes than the communists. However, all this was to change. The extraordinary rise of communism was matched by the steady decline of the Socialist Party, which it displaced. The PCI, with its traditions of unity and discipline, had emerged from the war far stronger and better organised than the PSI, which continued to be plagued by internal divisions, just as it had been in the 1920s. Furthermore, the PCI was far more successful than the PSI in leading the movement for agricultural reform, a fact which explains the massive support it continues to enjoy in the former sharecropping areas of central Italy and elsewhere. Bearing these social and historical factors in mind, we can now focus more clearly on the evolution of communist identity and what it means to be communist in Italy.

Changing Face of Italian Communism: Pre-war and Post-war

To be communist during the Fascist dictatorship was to be a member of a tiny, close-knit, subversive, isolated and persecuted minority – the very opposite of Party membership today. Many members undoubtedly were convinced Marxist-Leninists, fighting for the communist cause as interpreted by the official party line. Others were simply 'anti-Fascists' who were inspired by the struggle for liberation, rather than ideological converts to Soviet-style communist orthodoxy. The pre-war PCI was by necessity a highly sectarian group of individuals whose links with each other grew steadily firmer, not in spite of the dangers and sacrifices involved, but rather because of them. Autobiographical accounts indicate the extent to which the Party provided for its members an intensive, shared and sometimes total psychological environment. Ignazio Silone, once a prominent PCI leader, describes the nature of Party membership under Fascism:

> To join the party of proletarian revolution was not a simple matter of signing up with a political organisation; it meant a conversion, a complete dedication. Those were the days when to declare oneself a Socialist or a Communist was equivalent to throwing oneself to the winds, and meant breaking with one's parents and not finding a job (Silone, 1950: 104).

For many communists of that era, the Fascist conquest of the state merely confirmed their beliefs about the repressive nature of capitalist democracy and provided the opportunity to create an organisation compatible with the sectarian, vanguard and military mentality outlined in Lenin's Bolshevik Party model (see below). As one old Party secretary in Modena described it: 'We came to the Party with rifles in our hands.'[11] Silone's autobiography again captures the flavour of early Party membership:

> I had to adapt myself, for a number of years, to living like a foreigner in my own country. One had to change one's name, abandon every former link with family and friends, and live a false life to remove any suspicion of conspiratorial activity. The Party became family, school, church, barracks: the world that lay beyond it was to be destroyed and built anew' (Silone, ibid.).

The Communist Party demanded of its members a progressive surrender of the individual to the collective, perhaps to the point where the identity of the group became integral to the conception of one's self.[12] The PCI was never a party of intellectuals – at least, not at the level of the rank and file.[13] Even during the height of its Bolshevik period, it remained plebeian in character. The description given by Amyot (1979) of early PCI members in Bari portrays this clearly: 'Most cadres were ill-educated and had a very schematic political outlook: they saw the major actors in society as "we", "the enemy" and "the Masses".'

This sketch of the PCI's pre-war character and composition is significant for three reasons. Firstly, it indicates something of the degree to which PCI ideology and appeal have developed since the war and since the PCI began progressively to shed its Bolshevik identity. Secondly, it is significant because of the influence this experience and ideological heritage had in shaping the character of the PCI. Despite the fact that some of these early militants were later dismissed from the Party, most remained, and until recently, held influential posts in the Party hierarchy.[14] Thirdly, this sketch is significant because, toward the end of the war, PCI identity changed dramatically. Italy had declared war on Britain and France in June 1940, but after defeats in Greece, East Africa and North Africa, the government was confronted with an Anglo-American landing in Sicily in July 1943. Meanwhile, the partisan movement – led primarily by communists – spread throughout Italy in the final struggle for liberation against the occupying German armies. For the first time communists became true patriots, and the Party could lay claim to many of the emotive symbols of nationalism.

By 1943, it was evident to Party leaders that the PCI would remain ineffectual as long as it continued in the Leninist mould of a small conspiratorial group. Plans were laid for a new kind of party, the *Partito Nuovo* (see chapter 4). This was to be a popular-based, mass organisation represented within parliament. The PCI made its first major break with communist orthodoxy to become, if not reformist, at least 'respectable' in the eyes of its new supporters. To these ends it adopted Togliatti's 'strategy of alliances', the idea being to carry the support of all 'democratic, progressive and anti-Fascist forces' in society and build up the communist movement in the form of a massive social bloc.[15] All 'democratic' elements in society, from peasant landowners and intellectuals to small industrialists, were presumed to have a common interest and to be potential allies of the industrial proletariat and landless farm workers in the fight against monopoly capital.

The *Partito Nuovo* was enormously successful in drawing recruits, and, as noted, PCI membership grew from some 6,000 in 1943, to over 2 million by 1947 (Poggi, 1968: 29, 311). This expansion was the result of excellent Party organisation combined with a spontaneous wave of popular support for the PCI after its leading role in the Resistance. Communism alone had maintained an unblemished war record, whereas liberalism and Catholicism, the competing ideologies, 'were tainted by compromise with Fascism' (Blackmer, 1975: 28). This point is echoed by the former secretary of the Perugia federation:

> We youngsters were critical not only of Fascism but of all the old pre-Fascist parties that had failed to combat Fascism. The communists appeared to us untainted by that responsibility and the effect of continuous Fascist propaganda – the very reason for whose existence was anticommunism – pushed us instinctively towards the view that communism was the most radical anti-Fascist position possible (Rossi, 1977: 63).

More importantly, the PCI had now become identified not only with the international communist movement, but also with the symbols of Italian nationhood. Georgio Napolitano, leading Central Committee member and former head of the PCI's parliamentary group, summed up the meaning of membership for Party recruits of this generation in 1945:

> To those of us who formed the Communist Party in Naples or other regions in the South, the Party meant first of all the most uncompromising force of anti-Fascist struggle ... [and secondly] ... Part of a great world movement, at the head of which stood the Soviet Union (Napolitano in Hobsbawm (ed), 1977: 26).

The main point gleaned from these autobiographical accounts is that the self-image of the PCI in the pre-war and immediate post-war periods was defined primarily in opposition to Fascism and in solidarity with the Soviet Union. Being communist meant above all being pro-Soviet and anti-Fascist, and these factors were welded together into the patriotic cause of the liberation of Italy. However, as the international climate began to change with the onset of the Cold War, all this began to change.

Cold War Construction of Communist Identity

The bulk of writing on communist identity has traditionally come from American psychology and political science, most of it focusing on the 'appeals of communism' and much of it written by behaviourist and functionalist scholars at Princeton and Harvard during the 1950s and 1960s. Though dated, this literature is important because it generated a body of theory that was extremely influential in American social science. This, in turn, played a major role in shaping attitudes towards communism in the West.

This approach characterised communists as activists devoted to a life of self-sacrifice, discipline and fanatical loyalty to the Party. This idea approximated Duverger's model of the 'devotee party' (Duverger, 1954). As an ideal-type, the 'devotee party' differs in structure from the mass or cadre party models, being more closed than the former but more open than the latter.[16] For Duverger, the classic example of this devotee type of party is found in Lenin's Bolshevik Party – which in its strict form includes only the 'advance guard', the fighting wing and the 'most enlightened' sections of the working-class. This represents a change from the conception of the party as class; it is the party conceived as the revolutionary vanguard (Duverger, ibid.: 70).

The devotee party is thus defined as a small, sectarian elite, whose members pledge themselves to their party with an attachment that is irrational, almost religious, in nature; a commitment that admits no distinction between public and private life. Such parties, which, for Duverger, embrace both communism and Fascism, are authoritarian, highly centralised, and specialised in the use of unceasing agitation, propaganda, strikes, sabotage and violence as their primary political strategy.[17] Similar ideas about the nature of communism may be found in Philip Selznick's theory of the 'combat party' (Selznick, 1960: vi), and in Almond's *Appeals of Communism* (Almond, 1954). Each takes Lenin's *What is to Be Done?* as the blueprint for such a party: it is conspiratorial, dogmatic, totalitarian and psychologically adapted for conditions of clandestine warfare.

One variant on the 'devotee party' theme was the attempt to elaborate a general model of communism as a form of 'social pathology'. Caught between the pervasive political climate of McCarthyite anticommunism and an obsession with explaining 'social order' and consensus, American political scientists could only explain communism in terms of its 'dysfunctional' character. Their approach naturally equated communism with deviancy and social abnormality, the roots of which were traced to psychological problems and personality disorders.[18] These ideas are conveyed most explicitly in the work of Almond, but find echoes in Hoffer's *The True Believer* (1951), Daniel's *The Nature of Communism* (1962) and Cantril's *The Politics of Despair* (1958). Each of these depicts communism as the product of pathological socialisation and suggests that where the communist movement thrives it is because Marxist ideology provides a haven for the alienated, the embittered and the rootless. People drawn toward communism are portrayed as perpetually insecure misfits who find security in 'blind devotion' to the communist cause (Hoffer, 1951: 83–4). According to this approach, the communist is an 'outsider': a socially and mentally unbalanced person who, because of neurotic susceptibility or personal inadequacy, gladly surrenders his freedom to a sectarian and subversive creed. The communist is also inherently antisocial. He is a fanatic, a homeless, solitary person who 'hungers for the deep assurance which comes with total surrender – with the wholehearted clinging to a creed and a cause' (ibid.: 85–6). Though his attachment to communism is passionate and absolute, this is only because such single-minded dedication fulfils the fanatic's craving for security. According to Hoffer, therefore (ibid.: 84), 'It is easier for a fanatic Communist to be converted to fascism, chauvinism or Catholicism than to become a sober liberal.'

As has been argued elsewhere (Kertzer, 1980: 240–4), this approach was founded on false assumptions and defective methodologies from the outset. Almond's principal informants were disillusioned ex-communists, never ordinary Communist Party members. To these dubious sources of evidence, Almond added another:

> In order to gain insight into the kinds of psychological problems which may lead to joining the party, we interviewed a group of American psychoanalysts who had had Communists as patients. These analysts provided us with thirty-five clinical case histories of Communists. These case histories suggested hypotheses as to the ways in which emotional disorders of one kind or another may contribute to susceptibility (Almond, 1954: xii–xiv).

Moreover, despite the fact that Almond professes deference to the canons of objective enquiry, the bias latent in the aims of the study – to 'increase our understanding of the vulnerability of the Free World to communist penetration' – hardly permits this. Indeed, Almond later defines communism as 'the greatest evil of the twentieth century' (Almond, ibid.: 370). Reflecting on what he sees as communism's 'ethical vacuum' he asks: 'What ingredients are added to make lives of dedicated ruthlessness bearable?' His answer is that the communist 'has no ethics at all [and is] haunted by the purposeless suffering of his victims and the meaningless distortion of his own character' (ibid.: 370, 376 and 377). Such an analytically sterile and inaccurate model fitted neatly into the American Cold War anticommunist stereotype, giving it a veneer of pseudoscientific respectability.

The interesting point about this work is not that an anticommunist study should produce anticommunist results, but that it should have held such an influential position in American political science. As late as 1964, this book – evidently a popular classic – was republished in its third edition. Such a model clearly has no value in understanding communism today, though it may help us to analyse how communist identity has been construed by American intellectuals and politicians. The vast majority of Italian communists are not activists, let alone devotees, and they are not social misfits. On the contrary, Party membership is a social norm. Far from being socially alienated, the PCI now provides a major focus of community life throughout much of Italy.

'Communism as social pathology' theorists passed out of fashion with the beginnings of detente, but they have not altogether disappeared. As Elliot and Schlesinger (1979) show, echoes of Cold War political science still manifest themselves in the work of contemporary 'containment theorists' and fundamentalist anticommunists, whose writings dominate much of the periodical literature on 'international relations'.[19] Indeed, even in the 1980s, President Reagan still found it opportune to garner support for his presidential campaign by describing the Soviet Union as 'the evil empire'. Whether this rhetoric is still taken at face value is debatable, but certainly the work of these writers has exercised a considerable influence on the style and approach of contemporary and later authors. Thus Kogan (1962: 45–6), for example, in an attempt to counterbalance this jaundiced stereotype, fell into the trap of furnishing another when he described the PCI in the following way:

> The Communist Party is not a vast apparatus of trained professional revolutionaries. Probably no more than twenty or thirty-five thousand could be considered knowledgeable and believing Marxists. The larger mass of the Party membership and the larger mass of the voters comes from the lower income industrial workers, the sharecroppers, the landless peasants, and the unemployed. Many of its supporters have had little or no formal education. Most of these people could not and do not understand Marxism. They consider themselves to be good Catholics and support the Italian Communist Party from the sense of hopelessness with their lot.

Part of the problem with this is the author's stereotypical view of Marxism as a type of ideological credo – a view which reveals little either about the PCI's elaboration of Marxist theory or about the way Italian communists themselves interpreted Marxism in the light of their own experience.[20] The comments about education, the apparatus and the Party's class base were probably correct for 1962, but those concerning members' motivations are more dubious. Far from the supporters of the PCI joining the Party from a 'sense of hopelessness', most empirical evidence suggests the contrary.[21] Furthermore, Galli and Prandi's study (1970), which was based on work carried out in the 1960s, showed that Italian communists exhibit considerably more optimism and enthusiasm about themselves and their Party than do members of other political parties.

The question, then, is not so much how accurate was this general portrait of communism in the 1950s and 1960s, but whose portrait was it and what was its social and political significance? In the main, the communist stereotype arose out of US attitudes, the Cold War and the genuine fear that communism now threatened fundamental US interests – particularly where liberty and the balance of power in Europe were concerned. From a military perspective, US strategists saw the 'free world' becoming increasingly encircled by communist expansionism as, in their view, communist global domination became a reality. Seen in the context of the developing international scene, that view was perhaps understandable (even though it was also unjustifiable). The Russians had developed their own atomic bomb, thanks largely to communist spies such as Fuchs, Kim Philby, Burgess and Maclean. The Chinese revolution had turned most of Asia communist – and with it one-third of all humanity. Britain, over £3,000 million in debt,[22] was reducing its commitments overseas, retreating from empire and giving up its role as international policeman. Eastern Europe had been swallowed by the Soviet empire, and the prospect for the rest of Western Europe appeared grim now that nothing but a group of weak and war-torn nations stood between the Atlantic and the Red Army should it decide to advance across Germany. On the other side of Europe, Turkey and Greece looked particularly vulnerable to communist takeover.

In fact, it was the Greek civil war that became the Cold War flashpoint and prompted President Truman to announce his Doctrine in March 1947, arguably the most succinct expression of American Cold War ideology:

> At the present moment in world history nearly every nation must choose between alternative ways of life.
>
> The choice is too often not a free one. One way of life is based upon the will of the majority, and is distinguished by free institutions, representative government, free elections, guarantees of individual liberty, freedom of speech and religion, and freedom from political oppression.
>
> The second way of life is based upon the will of a minority forcibly imposed upon the majority. It relies upon terror and oppression, a controlled press and radio, fixed election and the suppression of personal freedoms.
>
> I believe that it must be the policy of the United States to support free peoples who are resisting attempted subjugation by armed minorities or by outside pressures (Truman, 1947, cited in Crockatt, 1987: 7).

The Truman Doctrine thus launched an officially sanctioned anticommunist crusade. In order to carry out a more active foreign policy, Truman needed to mobilise the American public against the Soviet threat, and this he achieved with astounding success, perhaps because the crusade itself provided Americans with the opportunity to articulate their sense of identity and moral superiority. As Higgins observed, 'Anti-communism became the hallmark of Americanism.'

One consequence of this was, however, to shift the discourse of international relations away from practical political issues toward moral issues articulated in universal terms of 'good versus evil'. Although the origins of the Cold War are controversial, most authors identify problems of intercultural communication and of ideological and perceptual boundaries as, at least, contributory factors. As Crockatt writes,

> The cloak of secrecy that surrounds decision-making in the Kremlin, the difficulty of constructing a rationale for Soviet policy in terms of traditional diplomacy, has fed the suspicion that the Soviets operate on the basis of a master-plan for world domination, and there are enough statements on the record to lend plausibility to this theory for those predisposed to seek it (Crockatt, 1987: 9).

While Americans believed, perhaps genuinely, that the principles of economic prosperity for all on which their foreign policy was built were devoid of self-interest, the Soviets, from their point of view, saw US foreign policy as little more than a reflection of the interest Americans had in enlarging their prosperity and power by conquering new markets (Kuniholm, 1987: 46 ff.). The Americans, for their part, failed to understand the Soviet view of history and the Soviet need for a sphere of influence in Eastern Europe that flowed quite logically from such a perspective. They also failed to appreciate the differences between Asian and Soviet communism, and they failed to understand the relationship between the Soviet Union and China. As Higgins (1971: 39) observes, the habit of making simplistic judgements about the internal life of other countries, was a phenomenon of American life. The result of this was a foreign policy 'based on ethnocentrism' and 'a world view that other peoples yearned to be like Americans'; if other nations did not act like the United States it was because, from the American perspective, 'something had gone wrong' (Higgins, ibid.).

The anticommunist stereotype, based on an archetypal view of 'the anti-American' and 'fanatic', was therefore both a logical expression of, and a useful political answer to, America's state of uncertainty. It gave form and flesh to an otherwise intangible and unknowable enemy who symbolised all of those fears, and focused them on a convenient scapegoat.[23] In fact, the myth of a diabolical communist threat reflected deeper cultural themes in American society, including the symbolic importance of private property; fear of 'outsiders'; and a rejection of Europe, politics and class conflict – all of which had become values integral to the formation of America's new identity as a nation (Kuniholm, 1987: 51). Communists epitomised the ugly face of all things anomalous – and therefore dangerous and polluting – to the American way of life (cf. Douglas, 1966). The precise forms or personae of the archetypal 'alien fiends' may have changed over time, but the qualities they reflect remain fairly constant. For example, before the 1920s and the emergence of Bolshevism, the figure of the 'Anarchist' was taken to be the epitome of the 'subversive foreigner'.[24] An analogy today is found perhaps in the image of the 'Muslim fundamentalist' or Arab terrorist. In each case, the stereotype embodies all the familiar qualities of ruthlessness, inscrutability and subversion characteristic of the barbaric 'enemy' or 'outsider' whose intention is to destroy civilisation.

Communist Identity and the Cold War in Italy

In Italy, during the Cold War, a similar process of anticommunist containment was underway, one that found inspiration in the American model. As in America, attempts were made to elevate the political struggle onto a universal, moralistic and Manichaean plane. Following Prime Minister De Gaspari's return from a visit to the USA in 1947, the communists and socialists were expelled from government. The electoral campaign that followed in the spring of 1948 is still remembered for the bitterness and acrimony it generated and the crudity of its propaganda. The Christian Democrats, with the help of the Catholic Church, managed to transform the election into the representation of a titanic clash between 'two civilisations, two incommunicable worlds locked in permanent combat' (Gallerano, 1975: 9). The vote was depicted not simply as a ballot for the election of either a DC or Popular Front government, but as a stark choice between freedom and dictatorship; Catholicism and Marxism; good and evil; and Christ and Antichrist (Kogan, 1981: 39). The Catholic Church, because of the Vatican's position in Italy, could not engage publicly in political activity, nor tell people 'officially' which party to vote for. What it did instead was to instruct its supporters to 'vote for the Cross' and support whatever party was closest to Christian and democratic ideals of Italian civilisation. Moreover, the Church's vast network of collateral and satellite organisations was mobilised for the campaign.[25] Centrally coordinated, local action committees (*comitati civili*), which in 1948 numbered over 18,000 (Gallerano, 1975: 9) and which were headed by members of the Church hierarchy, conducted the DC electoral campaign.

As posters from that period show most vividly, religious themes were exploited to the full for electoral propaganda (Romano and Scabello, 1975).[26] The dominant themes of DC propaganda were Catholic unity, the crusade against atheistic Marxism and the salvation of 'Christian Civilisation'. The message to the electorate was blunt: 'If you want to save our civilisation – values of personal liberty, the indissolubility of marriage, family property, Christian education for your children, redemption through work, and private property – vote DC' (Gallerano, ibid.). In mass poster campaigns, communists were variously presented as the alien horde, an infestation of angry insects outside the walled garden of Christian civilisation, the Russian angel of death, a grotesque ape smashing through the monument to the motherland in Rome, and Red Army tanks rolling over Italian babies. By contrast, the DC portrayed itself as the shield, the sword and the Cross keeping the clawed communist demons at bay; the walled city defending the righteous; the defensive dam; or the turreted belfry tower. What is significant about these images is the insight it provides into Christian Democrat ideology. In this interpretation of the apocalyptic struggle, DC identity is defined first negatively as anticommunist, but then positively as the Party of the Church and of Christian values (Pratt, 1974: 215). Just as American identity (the identity of the 'true American patriot') was equated with anticommunism, so, too, this became the dominant expression of Catholic identity in Italy.

Most of this anticommunist symbolism was drawn from the apocalyptic scenes in the Book of Revelation, but it was supplemented by psychological motifs suggesting an association between communism and cannibalism or rape (Pratt, 1984: 229). The dominant motif, however, was simply xenophobia and ethnocentrism, drawing upon old fears and stereotypes associated with the 'outsider'; the DC represented Christian civilisation and all that is Italian, familiar, patriotic and good, while the PCI represented atheistic barbarism and all that is alien, unpatriotic and evil. Hence another poster warned Italians that in the 'communist paradise', workers will become slaves, Italian children will belong to the state, Christians will be deported or executed, and 'domestic peace will be destroyed by divorce and free love' – represented as two hideous, writhing serpents (Romano and Scabello, 1975: 38). Communists were therefore defined explicitly as exponents of an alien creed, agents of Moscow and puppets of Russian despotism bent on destroying the institutions of Christian civilisation – particularly the family, private property and the Church.[27]

This ideological war was also translated into practical political activity, as 'Red-scare' campaigns were organised throughout the country. For example, informants recalled how, as part of the DC electoral campaign in Umbria, buses full of children, guided by their parish priest, were driven from one village to the next, in each of which the children were grouped into circles, each one holding a piece of barbed wire to form an imaginary fence. The DC speaker's message, delivered through a megaphone, was a vivid warning to parents of what would happen to their children 'if the communists took power'.

Despite the crudeness of the propaganda campaign, it proved highly effective.[28] As Ferrarotti states (1978: 48), probably the most important factor behind the Popular Front's heavy defeat was the explicit and vocal support given by the United States and the Catholic Church to the DC. Certainly this was the view of Italian communists, who accused the government of intimidating people. Togliatti declared that the Italian people had not been freely consulted, adding that there had been 'foreign intervention in a brutal manner without precedent, from the threat of starvation to that of using the atomic bomb against certain cities and regions if they had a Popular Front majority'.[29]

Communist identity in the West continued to echo themes of the early Cold War period well into the 1970s. This identity was constructed on the basis of an old stereotype (later couched in the modern pseudoscientific terminology of devotee models and social deviancy) which drew partly from Lenin, but partly, too, upon cultural themes more often at home in Christian eschatology, science fiction and, not least, horror films, with their images of apocalyptic war, evil empires, blood-sucking monsters and the aliens-among-us.[30] What emerges, then, are two rival and starkly contrasting views of PCI identity after 1947: the image of Italian communism projected by the Cold War anticommunist crusade and the heroic self-image held by communists themselves.

PCI Identity and the Modern Party System

Two points are fundamental to understanding communist identity or what it means to be communist in Italy today: firstly, the great extent to which political parties permeate Italian society; and secondly, the peculiarly powerful role played by Italy's largest party, the Christian Democrats. The rise and fall of 49 governments in Italy during the short period from the founding of the republic in 1948 to 1989 gives the impression of profound instability. In fact, Italian politics is remarkably stable, and the Italian state has been dominated for over 40 years by one party, the Christian Democrats, in coalition with the smaller Republican, Liberal, Social Democrat and Socialist parties. Moreover, the basis of that alliance and the cornerstone of its unity is its opposition to the PCI. Thus, anticommunism has provided the foundation of every Italian government since 1948 (Allum, 1979: 135).

However, the fact of more than 40 years of Christian Democrat domination without any alternation of government is widely seen as having brought about administrative inefficiency, political corruption and a series of major public scandals within government bodies. Bureaucratic stagnation and an overidentification of the ruling coalition parties with the state are usually blamed as the primary cause of this.

The second point, the powerful role of parties and their extraordinary penetration of Italian society, stems from the early 1940s. For almost 20 years, Mussolini had outlawed all expressions of democratic life; only the Church and the Fascist Party were allowed to organise freely as mass organisations. When the Fascist state collapsed after 1943, it left a political void in northern and central Italy, and the only forces then capable of leading post-war reconstruction were the Catholic Church, the PCI and the PSI (Galli and Prandi, 1970: 13–14). Political parties thus became the primary architects of constitutional reform, their leading role being subsequently enshrined in the new constitution (which they wrote),[31] and they have dominated the Italian Republic ever since (Pridham, 1981: 4).

The Fascist era also set the agenda for subsequent developments in communist identity and the Italian party system in other ways. Not only did it interrupt the process of democratic development which had been in motion before the 1920s, but it also provided, through the subsequent consensus of anti-Fascism, a basic point of ideological reference for the post-war period. Moreover, the one-party rule of Fascism set a precedent in the concept and practice of the pervasive, capillary party organisation permeating all levels of society and enjoying an intense relationship with the state apparatus (Pridham, 1981: 2). This idea was adapted most conspicuously in the elaborate organisational presence of the PCI and DC in post-war Italian society (Poggi, 1968).

During the 1940s, therefore, the sub-cultural tendencies in Italy were intensified; political affiliations became institutionalised into major social divisions. One effect of this is that political patronage now influences virtually every aspect of Italian social life, from the allocation of jobs and public funds to the composition of most major local and national government bodies. So pervasive is this phenomenon that Italians have invented a word for it: *partitocrazia*, or 'rule by parties'.[32] The term is accurate, for party domination, political patronage and the manipulation of government institutions have become the hallmarks of Italian political culture.[33] Nowhere is this more evident than in the way government patronage is used by the ruling coalition parties in order to place their supporters (*raccomandati*) in positions of power and authority. At every level, the rewards of office are parcelled out among party followers, usually on a basis of party strength at the polls. This division of spoils (or *lottizzazione*) extends throughout government administration and beyond.[34] According to Scalfari (1983), editor of the newspaper *La Repubblica*, the Italian political system has become a 'feudal pyramid' which has 'swallowed public institutions and bodies in relationships of mortifying dependency and forced servility'. Italian parties have reputedly 'clientised millions of people', thereby involving them 'in a web of corruption and blackmail' (Ferrara, 1983: 8). In effect, they have carved up amongst themselves the half of the Italian economy which is under state control. Their 'vassals' are the bankers, industrialists, and managers in the huge public sector who owe their positions and therefore their loyalties to the politicians who got them appointed. According to the journal *L'Espresso* (1983: 6), nothing now escapes from the logic of lottizzazione. Not only the nationalised industries and public corporations but practically everything else rests in the hands of administrators chosen by the parties, 'from the central milk agencies to the small and large banks, from television to hospitals. Some half a million people, placed at the heads of 40,000 public bodies, constitute the real ruling class of the country today.'

Patron–client relations are the bedrock of political life in Italy, and they are used by those with power as a tool to consolidate and extend that power by creating chains of dependency and subordination. To be 'Christian Democrat', 'socialist' or 'communist' in Italy is not, therefore, to carry an arbitrary label, but it is, rather, a fundamental dimension of one's public identity; it means belonging to a clearly defined social and cultural group with clear rules and boundaries.

Although the PCI has traditionally defined itself in contrast to other parties, particularly the DC, structurally all these parties have much in common. Each claims to be heir to a distinctive ideology; each has a highly developed territorial organisation based on a network of local sections, provincial federations, regional secretariats and national leadership, and each tries to promote itself as a 'mass' organisation. Each also has a printing press, a theoretical journal, a weekly or often daily party newspaper, and a large bureaucracy organised at all levels (the PCI's political machine being perhaps the largest of any democratic party in Europe). Furthermore, through control over appointments and public money, each is able to support a host of satellite bodies, including trade unions, schools, youth and pensioners' associations, recreational centres and bars, research institutions, radio and television networks, and publishing houses. Interestingly, it was the PCI (adapting the Bolshevik Party model) that first developed this type of party organisation; the others simply copied it.[35] However, Italy's system of proportional representation, its highly decentralised system of government, its generous state funding for parties (approved in 1974) and its political culture of clientelism are the main factors that have consolidated the pattern of exclusive political sub-cultures.

In each phase of its history, the PCI has been defined by, and primarily in relation to, its principal rivals, Fascism, the Church, and the Christian Democrats – each of whom, in turn, has tried to control the definition of communist identity. As Kertzer described it, the struggle for political domination in Italy has become a battle for ritual supremacy; communist identity has become the battleground on which this ideological conflict is fought. The evolution of communist identity is analogous to the series of campaigns in a war of manoeuvre and position: as one side attacks, the other parries and counterattacks; positive imagery is countered by negative stereotyping; congratulatory self-definition is matched by aggressive counterdefinitions, and so on.

The term 'Eurocommunism' is a recent example of this. The 'Eurocommunist' label, which gained currency in the mid-1970s, was initially coined by anticommunists as a derogatory label. As originally conceived, 'Eurocommunism' was a pejorative title symbolising the fact that the supposed 'new democratic face' of communism in Western Europe was an illusion or, what is worse, a treacherous disguise masking the old Stalinist 'wolf in sheep's clothing'. Most communist parties themselves rejected the label at first. The PCI, however, seeing the potential advantages of this title, accepted it but then appropriated it for its own use, relaunching the concept as a vehicle for uniting those European communist parties like itself which were developing a democratic, national road to socialism and distancing themselves from the Soviet Union. 'Eurocommunism' was thus a contested label which ultimately became an asset rather than a liability to the PCI – particularly when the Communist Party of the Soviet Union denounced it.

The PCI has frequently been castigated by its enemies for being an 'anti-system' party – the implied slur being that it is also 'antiliberal', 'antidemocratic' 'anti-Western' and 'anti-Christian'. To some extent the PCI has always accepted this label but has tried to interpret it in a positive light, vaunting its proud claim to be the party of protest, anticapitalism and progressive social change. In constructing its modern identity, the PCI has consciously sought to lose many of its old Soviet and proletarian credentials. It has abandoned the old language of Communist revolution and class warfare, and has campaigned to broaden Party appeal to a wider social base, particularly the young, the educated and the white-collar classes. Its stress on national themes has helped to put the emphasis on the Party's moral virtues (its uncompromising stance against corruption, the Mafia, and drugs), and on its administrative efficiency (with 'Red Bologna' being the model *par excellence*). The PCI now espouses many causes, including law and order, constitutionalism, defence of the parliamentary system, honest administration and efficiency, which most communists would once have denounced as 'bourgeois' ideology.

For Italian communists today, being communist means opposing corruption and political clientelism. That, by implication, means opposing not only Christian Democrat-led governments but the whole 'system of power' which the latter have created (*il sistema di potere democristiana*). Being excluded from government for 40 years has given the PCI a powerful reputation as the 'party of opposition', for it is the only large party (excluding the neo-Fascist MSI) which has not been drawn into the Christian Democrat-dominated power system. The PCI has made much capital out of this: it alone can claim to be unsullied by collusion with a corrupt system of government, and therefore to offer the possibility of a genuinely alternative government. Once again, therefore, the PCI has claimed for itself the standard of patriotism and has turned the hostile 'antisystem' label to its own advantage – for if the system is, as communists claim, riddled with corruption, then to be 'anti-system' is to be virtuous. Moreover, according to the PCI, institutional reform has real revolutionary implications, as it would 'liberate' Italy from the yoke of political clientelism and, if not from capitalism, at least from some of its more parasitical and corrupt manifestations.

In many respects, to be communist in Italy today has little to do with the communism of the past or communism as understood by orthodox Marxist-Leninists. The PCI does not seek to smash Italian 'bourgeois democracy' or destroy its institutions: on the contrary, it helped to create many of those institutions, it identifies with them, and it has campaigned vigorously to defend them and make them work properly. Yet, significantly, PCI members have by no means abandoned their self-image as the revolutionary vanguard.

3

Theory and Practice of Italian Communism: PCI Hegemony, World-view and Myth

PCI Strategy and the *Partito Nuovo*

Between 1944 and 1947 the links with the Soviet Union posed no problems for the PCI's legitimacy and credibility – indeed, they were a major source of authority and prestige. Nor did they contradict the PCI's strategy of alliances, which was successfully expanding Party membership across class boundaries. However, sooner or later these filial ties with Moscow were bound to conflict with the PCI's new 'national' and independent identity.

Ironically, in the same period that saw communist identity become fossilised by Cold War propaganda into a monolithic conspiracy against the West, the PCI itself was implementing one of the most radical changes in Party ideology and organisation ever undertaken by a communist party. The creation of the *Partito Nuovo* in 1944 and the thinking behind it symbolised this watershed between the PCI's pre-war and post-war identity. This point is summed up by Blackmer (1975: 36):

> The *Partito Nuovo* was to be not merely a mass party in the sense of membership or electoral support, but the centre of a network of semi-autonomous working-class organisations, springing from, and in everyday contact with the masses.

The background to this can be stated briefly. After the war PCI leaders, determined to prevent the rise of another Mussolini, and embarrassed by the way the institutions of the Left had so easily perished during the Fascist repression of the 1920s and '30s, decided to rebuild the Party on firmer foundations. With this goal in mind they abandoned the Leninist model of a small, sectarian elite in favour of a mass party with deep roots in society, one that could survive any amount of persecution and harassment. This necessitated a shift from the old-style revolutionary cadre proclaiming its ideological purity toward a more open and heterogeneous party that would first win the consent of the Italian nation as a prerequisite for winning power and transforming Italy into a socialist society. That identity needed to encourage a sense of unity and elicit feelings of belonging; to project outward a welcoming and all-embracing public image which, viewed from the inside, would fuel sentiments of exclusiveness and intensive party loyalty.

Communist identity would thus be the instrument for attracting new recruits while at the same time resolving the perennial problems of internal cohesion and control endemic to all mass organisations.

The model for the PCI's *Partito Nuovo* ('New Party' – see Chapter 4) launched following the liberation of Italy was unique in the communist world. In fact, the model was a blend of elements taken from the Bolshevik Party and the Catholic Church. The mass, permanently mobilised Party organisation with a visible presence in the heart of every working-class community was clearly inspired by the Bolshevik Soviets. The territorial organisation, based on hierarchically linked sections and federations, on the other hand, paralleled the Catholic parish and diocese. This debt to the Church's organisational model is evident in one of the PCI's slogans of 1945: 'For every church tower a Party section' (*per ogni campanile una sezione comunista!*).

Like parish churches, sections strove to become the focus and sponsor of all local public events. PCI sections housed the cheapest bars in town, card tables, bowling greens, free newspapers, television rooms and much more. The PCI also initiated the *Feste dell'Unità*, local festivals that, in style and structure, were almost mirror images of the traditional saint's-day celebrations: only the symbols and political message differed. Instead of saints, rosaries, crucifixes and candles, the iconography was distinctly communist: red flags, hammer and sickles, clenched fists, banners denouncing imperialism, photographs of communist leaders and speeches paying homage to partisans martyred by Fascists. In short, the PCI consciously constructed a territorial network and symbol-system.

The strategy behind the *Partito Nuovo* followed Gramsci's idea of hegemony[1] in emphasising the need to carry the political struggle onto the cultural front and to spread Party influence into every aspect of Italian society. Hegemony is crucial to understanding Italian communism, not only in discussions concerning political socialisation, but also in the whole debate about Marxist theories of the state. It has become a theoretical cornerstone of 'Eurocommunism', for hegemony offers, in Ferrarotti's words (1978: 59–60), 'the only way – barring armed insurrection or direct intervention by the Red Army – for the communist parties of Western Europe to escape the political ghetto of permanent opposition and to enter eventually into government'.

Hegemony as Revolutionary Strategy

In his prison notebooks Gramsci developed his concept of hegemony. By this he meant a form of class domination understood not only in terms of the political and economic control exercised by a dominant class, but also in that class's success in projecting its own particular way of seeing the world and human relationships, so that this is accepted as 'common sense' and part of the natural order by those who are, in fact, subordinated to it. Consequently, Gramsci saw revolution not only as the transfer of political and economic power but also as the creation of new forms of experience and consciousness.[2] This differs from the more deterministic Marxist position that change in the economic base or relations of production invariably leads to changes in the cultural superstructure, creating new experiences and consciousness. Instead, Gramsci saw the struggle for hegemony as a primary and even decisive factor in radical change (Williams, 1976: 143).[3]

Gramsci was chiefly interested in understanding the mechanisms involved in class domination and the implications of this for revolution in the West. The problem was quite simple: in Tsarist Russia the political system was relatively unsophisticated, power was highly concentrated, and the gulf between the increasingly isolated ruling class and the masses had created an ideal situation for the revolutionary capture of the state. In the West, however, the political system was more complex; there was no Winter Palace to storm, no single locus of power; and revolution was not simply a question of toppling a fragile monarchy. As Gramsci put it in one of his most celebrated remarks,

> In Russia the State was everything, civil society was primordial and gelatinous; in the West, there was a proper relation between State and civil society, and when the State trembled a sturdy structure of civil society was at once revealed. The State was only an outer ditch, behind which there stood a powerful system of fortresses and earthworks (Gramsci, 1971: 238).

Following Machiavelli, Gramsci identified the fundamental categories of political power as force and consensus, arguing that successful class domination rests on a combination of both, for in order to dominate successfully, a group must 'already exercise "leadership" before winning governmental power' – a quality which is a principal condition for the winning of such power (Gramsci, 1971: 57). A ruling class that fails to create its own intellectuals cannot exercise hegemony and is forced to rely on the coercive powers of the state. Effective hegemony, however, is created when a dominant class transcends its immediate corporate interests and unites disparate allies into a unified social bloc of forces (what Gramsci calls 'historic bloc'). This then becomes the basis of consent for the existing social order.[4]

As a political strategy, hegemony incorporates Gramsci's notions of a 'war of position' and a 'passive revolution' precipitated by 'diffusing a proletarian world-view' throughout civil society, in all of its institutional and private manifestations (Gramsci, ibid.: 106–14).[5] The role of interpreter and trustee of that hegemony fell naturally to the Communist Party, which Gramsci, following Machiavelli, called the 'Modern Prince'. The idea of this strategy was to secure mechanisms for consent to a new socialist order, the basis for which lay in the creation of a network of cultural institutions – schools, clubs, newspapers, journals, trade unions, pressure groups, recreational associations and so on. Each of these would act as an agent of socialisation allied to, or under the intellectual and ideological tutelage of, the Party. They would contribute in molecular fashion to the formation of a new social and political consciousness. What it envisaged, in effect, was what Gwyn Williams (1960: 586) calls 'the culmination of the Marxist process as a total cultural reintegration of society'.

This captures the idea of hegemony – a term that has become the keynote of PCI strategy.[6] As the PCI insists, it is neither orthodox Marxism-Leninism nor social democracy, but a new way of applying Marxist analysis in complex Western democracies where electoral politics and public opinion are important. In terms of an applied strategy, the idea of hegemony was to create not simply a revolutionary *party* but a revolutionary counterculture. Whereas Lenin's vanguard-party model stressed the idea of the capture of the bourgeois state by a highly trained group of professional subversives, the PCI's strategy of hegemony would subvert capitalism in a very different way. Through its web of satellite bodies and cultural institutions the PCI would create a powerful communications network, a bloc of social forces through which it could diffuse a Marxist world-view to challenge that of the bourgeoisie. In effect, this strategy envisages not only the creation of a new social order but the instrument for its achievement: the Party itself. According to this view, the PCI is the 'New Society' in embryo, 'growing up inside the womb of the old', in the classic sense of Marx and Engels's metaphor.[7] Membership of the PCI means belonging to this embryonic culture. Becoming a member, as one communist theoretician described it,

> means entering into a life community, sharing a special sort of 'citizenship' and participating with other members in a common existential experience. To militate in such a party means not only assuming organisational duties, but the attempt to spread the proper conception of an associate life, its proper values and styles of life (Baldassari, 1983: 42).

Hegemony and the Appeal of Communism

For some activists the PCI is a way of life. The typical pattern of weekly, often daily Party activities can easily absorb the energies of the most committed militant. Regular Party activities include fund-raising; debates; marches; rallies; demonstrations; canvassing; organising local public events such as festivals, sports tournaments, and round-table discussions on local issues; running the local Party bar/community centre; and an almost endless round of committee meetings. Perhaps the most important of these in terms of the PCI's cultural politics is the *Festa dell'Unità*. Originally this was a casual one- or two-day event held by only a few sections in order to raise money for the Party paper, but, realising its potential as a vehicle for reaching the public as well as generating finance, the PCI encouraged all sections to hold one and to extend the festival for four days or more. Thus, in 1988 the number of Party festivals totalled 5,438 throughout Italy (PCI, 1989: 53). It has also encouraged larger festivals at federation level and nationally, the latter of which has become a megaevent in the PCI calendar, attracting millions of visitors. For example, the 1982 festival held at Tirrenia near Pisa took over six months to prepare and required a volunteer army of no fewer than 5,000 Party activists, volunteering between them over 30,000 hours of work.[8] Furthermore, on the day Berlinguer came to give the Party secretary-general's ritual address, over 2 million people attended the three-and-a-half-hour long speech. The PCI were not the only ones to realise the potential of such venues for reaching the Italian public; Coca-Cola and other companies have since approached the Party to ask for advertising rights at the *festa*.

Another key event in the life of the section is the *diffusione della stampa* – the ritual Sunday door-to-door sale of the Party paper. In the past this often made *L'Unità* the best-selling Sunday newspaper in Italy, but that was not its main function. More significant are the social and political considerations. For the PCI, it is far more important, both strategically and symbolically, to be 'present' and ostentatiously visible; to be seen as a dynamic force working in and for the community. Not only is this good for Party prestige, it also acts as an important mechanism for Party cohesion by keeping members active and mobilised. Similarly, the *festa* with its traditional connotations of celebration and feasting is a powerful symbol of community solidarity. Overt political proselytism and speech-making is unnecessary because the medium is the message, i.e. the event itself is the PCI's most effective self-advertisement.

At another level, membership of a particular section becomes a powerful element in personal identity and social solidarity. From my fieldwork observations in Umbria, it was obvious that social networks among communist activists often centre on fellow comrades and the Party. Close loyalties and friendships were usually politically defined, and many members admitted that they find it difficult to have true friends who are not also 'comrades' or 'on the Left'. Even 'communist funerals' are not uncommon in which the funeral service is carried out entirely by fellow trade-union and Party members. On one occasion, for example, the deceased, a former partisan in the Garibaldi Brigades, was laid out before burial in full battle dress holding a red handkerchief with a tape recorder at the corpse's head playing 'The International' as visitors came to pay their last respects. A large contingent of these were comrades from his section, carrying the unfurled section banner in solemn procession.

Whether or not it has been in the sense that Gramsci intended, the PCI has established a measure of hegemony over Italian society, particularly in the communist-controlled municipalities and provinces of central Italy. The fact that the PCI's central apparatus is dominated by members from this area offers some evidence of this (Sebastiani, 1983: 84–5). Furthermore, the overwhelming majority of activists in the PCI in general come from communist or left-wing families (ibid.). This would seem to confirm the view that there is a clear sub-cultural pattern to Party recruitment. Sub-cultural influences may help to explain why those socialised into the communist world tend to remain there, but the question of why people outside the communist world in the first place join the PCI is more complex. Part of the answer is found once again in hegemony, but for two very different reasons. The first reason is because that hegemony acts as a mechanism for drawing people into the Party's diffuse web of associations which thereby establishes their links with the communist world. Being 'inside' the communist world is of course a precondition for any later political socialisation. This explains the PCI's emphasis on cultivating a social presence, the aim being to convert nonaligned individuals into Party sympathisers; sympathisers into voters; voters into members; and members into activists and perhaps future leaders.

The second reason is that hegemony is widely seen as offering an alternative to the repressive Stalinist Soviet model of socialism. This perhaps helps to explain the appeal of Italian communism to intellectuals, for it offers, in their view, an acceptable way out of the impasse in Marxist-Leninist theory whilst still preserving the essential features of communism. Significant in this respect has been the attempt by PCI theoreticians to disentangle the Party from Leninism, theoretically as well organisationally. Thus, since the mid-1970s various attempts have been carried out by communist intellectuals, including Baldoni (1975), Baggio De Giovanni (1976), Buci-Glucksmann (1976) and Mancini (1977) to tease Gramsci apart from Lenin in order to construct a Gramscian Marxism independent of Lenin.[9]

Much of the structure and character of the Party, however, remains fundamentally Leninist despite the fact that the PCI claims to have become a 'mass', rather than vanguard, party. The PCI's ideal of 'every member a militant', the demands it makes on ordinary members and the traditional 'duties' of membership outlined in successive Party statutes all reflect this Leninist heritage.[10] In reality, however, few ordinary members actually live up to this ideal-type militant, and probably no more than 10 per cent participate regularly in Party events. Nevertheless, most still see themselves as activists and still *feel* deeply committed to the Party. If asked about their involvement they usually say that their political activism is expressed outside traditional Party events; at work, in trade unions and in their personal relationships. To claim that the PCI is permanently mobilised is misleading – better instead to call it a party with a permanent social presence. This distinction is important since 'permanent mobilisation' is more characteristic of a Leninist cadre waiting for the moment to seize power than of a mass party committed to parliamentary democracy, the authority of the ballot box, and consent based upon a strategy of 'social presence' rather than agitation and mobilisation.

Another reason why people join the Party in areas where communism is already the dominant political force is social status. According to Kertzer's (1980: 62) case-study of a working-class community in Bologna, PCI membership is a 'key to in-group status' and a mark of prestige. Indeed, in this case, 'almost all the individuals with the highest prestige are associated with the Party and have either acquired or ratified that prestige through Party activity' (ibid.: 58). In Umbria, not only did most activists have other family members in the Party, but there was also a strong expectation that their children should be, if not in the PCI, then at least 'on the Left' and politically conscious. Joining the Party was sometimes seen as a kind of 'rite of passage'; a coming of age in terms of political maturity. Parents, it seems, provide the main reference point *against* which their children define themselves politically. Significantly, many of those interviewed adopted more extreme political views than had their fathers as adolescents, yet, interestingly, those 'extremes' were usually still within a shared political framework that neither challenged nor opposed the basic left-wing family outlook – just as children of orthodox Jewish or Christian sects sometimes 'rebel' by becoming more devout than their parents. Older Party members often interpreted even this as 'carrying on the family tradition', as they themselves had done this in their youth, a fact they explained as normal, given that 'youngsters are always extremist'.

After family the major social factor influencing early involvement in the PCI appears to be friends and peer-group pressure. For many members, joining the Party was initially a collective act involving others from their neighbourhood or age group. This collectivist aspect of joining is emphasised in a recurrent phrase used at interviews, 'there was a group of us (*eravamo un gruppo*). Party allegiance in most cases appears to have involved adopting a shared political identity in harmony with one's peer group or family. Where this clearly was not the case and joining was an individual act involving a separation from family or peer group, the Party itself often became a substitute for these primary relationships. As one local Party secretary in Umbria put it, 'For me the Party is a family.' For some members the main appeal of communism is that it fulfils a need for companionship and belonging. For others the Party provides an educational environment in which they acquire personal confidence, social skills, responsibility, self-esteem and in some cases even a career.

Another observation is the surprisingly young age at which activists first became involved with the PCI. Many became politicised long before adulthood, often between the ages of 13 and 15. Usually a key, 'trigger' event stimulated their political awareness. In many cases this was related to family circumstances or a shared 'politicising' experience (e.g. Fascism, the Resistance, seeing themselves or their parents exploited as sharecroppers or labourers, and protests at school or university). For younger members it was often a case of a steady progression to the PCI from involvement in the Radical Party, the Young Communists (FGCI), or one of the movements (student, women, environment, anti-Mafia). Others, particularly those from traditional communist families and communities were virtually 'weaned' on communism from birth, and joining the Party appeared a natural and logical step in the life cycle.

Hegemony and the PCI 'World-view'

Most PCI activists clearly share some of the formative experiences of growing up inside the political sub-culture of the communist Red Belt. It would be wrong, however, in explaining PCI membership, to overstate the importance of social factors and ignore ideology. The impression sometimes given (cf. Kertzer, 1980) is that communism in Italy is something contagious: people are either 'infected' by it, or else they are sucked into the Party by some mysterious process analogous to osmosis. Certainly social factors do play a key role in any kind of political socialisation, but, generally speaking, this is a simplistic and innaccurate metaphor for how hegemony works.

Two key elements in the definition of hegemony given earlier were 'new forms of consciousness and experience' and 'the diffusion of a proletarian world-view'. Whether it is accurate to call this 'proletarian' or not, there is undoubtedly a characteristic PCI world-view, or distinctive set of attitudes, which arises from the members' shared political socialisation. In some cases the attempt to instil a communist outlook was carried out far more rigorously and systematically through the institution of a national network of Party schools. The influence of PCI schooling is particularly evident in many of those working-class members from the older generations who had no formal state education beyond primary level. As young Party activists, in fact, many had been obliged to attend courses in 'political formation'. Though these Party schools now encourage a more liberal approach to education, this was not the case during the 1940s and 1950s when the Party was still extremely Stalinist in its outlook. The main aim of these schools then was 'ideological preparation' for future Party leaders (*formazione dei quadri*). Inevitably, much of the older PCI membership retain many of the 'Stalinist' attitudes, language and style once considered necessary for the proper ideological formation of Party leaders.[11] This was expressed most vividly in the comments of members of the PCI old guard; for example, as one 60-year-old interviewee put it, 'Communism means taking all the means of production into the hands of the State: that's what they taught us at the Party School.' Younger members tended to be highly critical even of the idea of Party schooling, which some saw as 'indoctrination'. Others, however, defended it, and, as a PCI senator argued, however dogmatic these schools had been in the past, they had at least 'taught millions of people to look at the world as something that can be changed, and they taught them to become protagonists.'

More important, though, this PCI world-view is reflected in the general attitude of members toward both themselves and the Party. In most cases the socialising experiences referred to earlier helped forge an early, often simple, class conception of the social world. At its crudest, what unified people behind the PCI was a shared hostility to the Italian bourgeoisie. The common perception was that of an unjust, class-ridden society, a world divided between the bosses ('Them') and the workers ('Us')'; between landlords and peasants; or, more simply, between capitalists and workers. As one local activist and former sharecropper explained it, even at the age of 13, 'It had already become clear who was the enemy and who had to be fought, and what side you had to take.'[12] In most instances these perceptions of class and inequality were borne out by a reality that was easily translated into socialist doctrine.[13] In this sense, most older activists (excluding some intellectuals) were emotionally communist long before they had gained any real knowledge of communist party doctrine or theory; the theory simply equipped people with the language and conceptual framework for clarifying and articulating their sentiments. This was summed up by a 30-year-old activist, the son of an Umbrian sharecropper, describing his first major encounter with a communist: 'He knew the answers to all the questions that I also knew the answer to but could never manage to explain.'

The typical world-view among PCI sharecroppers and workers classified society in terms of oppressors and oppressed, class and class conflict, and forces of reaction versus forces of progress. In its broader sense this does reflect elements of what might be called a 'Marxist world-view'. However, members are not required to profess themselves either Marxist-Leninist or Marxist, but must simply accept the Party programme. Indeed, the PCI no longer even defines itself as a Marxist party, but as a party of 'Marxist inspiration'.

PCI World-view and the 'Vanguard' Identity

A revealing observation gained from fieldwork and corroborated by interviews was the large number of Party members that in some way or another saw themselves as 'part of the "vanguard"' and 'different' from the rest of society. Typically, those who joined in areas where PCI membership was unusual saw themselves as somehow set apart from others (intellectually, morally, ideologically) and more enlightened. This was often put down to the fact that 'none of the others developed much consciousness of their situation'. Having one's consciousness raised, being 'politically aware', and being able to see things in a 'concrete historical and economic context' were all elements of the PCI self-image. Though 'ideological formation' is now an outmoded phrase seldom referred to explicitly, there is still inevitably an implicit notion that being communist requires both a raised consciousness of class and a particular understanding of history.

Also significant was the often expressed view that being communist meant belonging to both an historical movement and 'a force that counts' in Italian society. One member summed it up as follows:

> To be communist is to search for a better understanding of the life you lead, to improve that life and the relationships you have with others ... Next are motives regarding some kind of participation in the political programme; it is no small thing to feel yourself a protagonist in social life and in the decisions taken. Being

> communist in Italy is different from being communist in other countries – capitalist or socialist. Ours is a large, powerful party; it has a long tradition, a history rich in experiences and sacrifice which is the patrimony of everyone in Italian society, not only communists. The Party is a force that counts, that has a role ... that enables you to feel like a person who participates in the life of the country.

For others, the appeal of communism lies in its fusion of social involvement with an ideologically fulfilling political role. As one former partisan put it 'being communist means being united with other comrades ... who want to change things.'

Interestingly, the conclusions of Galli and Prandi (1970: 136) concerning the appeal of party involvement for both PCI and DC activists seem to confirm this. Their hypothesis is that the characteristic outlook of party militants depends on the socioeconomic situation of the community they come from. In those where rapid economic change and social upheaval have destroyed the traditional structures, 'political commitment', they argue,

> was a means of identification with an idealized future and of participating in the attempt to direct and control changes taking place. The activists in such communities are likely to be youthful party members, critical of the official party line.

By contrast, in communities that had undergone no marked structural change in the distribution and administration of power, 'active participation in a party meant attempting to benefit from that power to increase one's personal prestige and social position' (Galli and Prandi, ibid.).

There is undoubtedly some truth in these statements, but the conclusions drawn from such a schematic approach are hazardous, not least because the outlook of activists even from similar socioeconomic backgrounds is complicated by other variables, including gender, class, age and family upbringing. These points are exemplified when we examine the comments of PCI members themselves on 'what it means to be communist in Italy today'.

According to a 60-year-old ex-parliamentary deputy, whose views reflect an attitude typical of many from the pro-Soviet old guard, being communist means 'being on the side of progress' in a plan for social change that is 'founded on the principles of scientific Socialism and class'. Another activist (aged 40), who left the PCI in 1968 to join the 'movement' but rejoined in 1980, summed up the meaning of communism for his peer group as 'accepting with conviction that the working class are the protagonists of history ... and that one must stay in close harmony with the working class'. Though claiming that he and his contemporaries reject the idea of 'revolution as the fruit of a vanguard', rather than 'the work of the masses', he adds that when objective conditions are ripe a 'vanguard group is necessary for a vanguard party'. For other members, however, being communist is simply a matter of self-interest articulated as class interest. This view was summed up by one 80-year-old working-class veteran: 'As a worker I saw it as being in the interests of my own kind ... we just wanted to change society – equality!'

These responses indicate the diversity of attitudes towards communism among Party members, yet a recurrent theme throughout them all is the idea of being 'protagonists of history' and part of a 'vanguard' fighting for social progress and leading the struggle against capitalism. It is this 'vanguard mentality' perhaps more than any other factor that seems to characterise the shared PCI world-view. The simple interpretation is that this is a residue of the PCI's Leninist legacy, but the issue is complicated by the question of how one interprets the meaning of 'vanguard'. Commenting on this, one former PCI senator came close to the heart of the problem addressed in this book:

> The problem of how to define what is the spirit of a 'vanguard' is one of the most subtle questions of political analysis, for there is a great difference between a vanguard that helps men to grow and helps 'mass-culture' to have influence in society, and a vanguard of men who want to change society for their own love of power. This [second type] is the root of Stalinism; to imagine that a vanguard can change the people. A vanguard can only stimulate the growth of the people. But Leninism and Stalinism are certainly linked: I am convinced that Stalinism is the 'fruit' of Leninism matured.[14]

What constitutes a 'vanguard' is indeed important for it is the linchpin upon which any communist party claims its legitimacy and proclaims its 'communist identity'. Being a 'revolutionary party' in one sense presupposes that communists see themselves as 'revolutionaries', but the idea of being part of the 'vanguard' suggests more than this. What these subjective interpretations of communism reveal – apart from the depth of thought and feeling members invest in political participation – is the heroic vision many have of the Party and their role within it. The idea of being 'in the van of history', 'part of a great social movement', and 'on the side of progress', which is echoed to a greater or lesser extent by each respondent, is a pleasing self-image. Furthermore, it may also explain the sustained interest and high level of commitment to the Party given by many activists. Hegemony and social appeals provide clues as to why people enter the communist world and why they tend to remain there, but these factors do not explain the degree of involvement and personal sacrifice shown by many activists: to explain this one must also probe into the psychology and the 'myth' of communism.

PCI World-view and Political Myth

What moves people to intense political involvement and what helps sustain their commitment is not only intellectual conviction and strong emotional adherence, but also the reinforcement of these factors by what the French philosopher Sorel (1950: 128) described as the 'myth in which Socialism is wholly comprised'. According to Sorel, all social philosophies involve 'myth', for this is the vision or symbolic expression that unites and inspires participants in their struggle. Indeed, all great social movements have developed through the pursuit of a 'myth'.[15] However, it is unnecessary to analyse the myth or question whether it is true – even to ask whether it is practicable is meaningless. For Sorel, myth was essentially 'an image that can evoke sentiment and that supplies the cohesion and the drive which enables a group to bring its energies into play'.[16]

Political myth can be seen, therefore, assuming a variety of critical social functions, particularly those of sustaining morale and of getting people to demand more of themselves. Significantly, Gramsci (1971: 125–6) also recognised this and referred specifically to Sorel in developing his theory of the Party – a theory which Gramsci referred to euphemistically as Machiavelli's 'Modern Prince':

> The basic thing about *The Prince* is that it is not a systematic treatment, but a 'live' work, in which political ideology and political science are fused in the dramatic form of a 'myth' ... Machiavelli's *Prince* could be studied as an historical exemplification of the Sorelian myth – i.e. of a political ideology expressed neither in the form of a cold utopia nor as a learned theorising, but rather by a creation of concrete phantasy which acts on a dispersed and shattered people to arouse and organise its collective will.

The idea that all social philosophy contains a dimension of 'myth' suggests a definition of myth very close to that of 'ideology'. Both are devices adopted by groups in order to interpret reality, both concern belief, and both provide charters for social action. However, though they share much in common, myth and ideology are not interchangeable terms. Whereas ideology embraces whole sets of ideas that may form the basis of some political or economic system, 'myth', in its proper anthropological sense, refers only to specific events or persons – often purely fictitious – that stand outside ordinary or 'mundane' time (Eliade, 1968: 34).[17] According to Eliade, those who participate in myth are transported temporally from their everyday world onto a plane where time is deemed to be 'sacred', 'concentrated' and of 'heightened intensity'.

Myth, as Sorel suggests, is perhaps best seen as part of ideology; an element woven into ideologies, particularly where visionary speculation is involved. Though Sorel himself was attracted to no one particular political ideology, his ideas about myth became an important part of the revolutionary syndicalism in which Mussolini was for years an agitator and an editor. Interestingly, the Italian translation in 1909 of Sorel's *Reflections on Violence* was reviewed at length by Mussolini. This book evidently had an important influence on the Fascist conception of the nature and purpose of philosophy, a conception which was to become substantially identical to Sorel's conception of myth. This is reflected in Mussolini's own definition of Fascism given in the *Enciclopedia Italiano* (1935: 847):

> Fascism is a religious conception, one in which man is seen in his impending relationship to a superior law, to an objective Will that transcends the individual and elevates him as an aware member of a spiritual society.[18]

Mussolini defined Fascism not only as a political system, but also as a moral philosophy with religious and spiritual overtones. Hence, unlike communism, Fascist philosophy, conceived as myth, offered a vision of life, but not a plan, and still less a theory that depends on reason. For Mussolini, it was, instead, part of the philosophical irrationalist 'revolt against reason', hostile to the 'barren intellectualism' of such philosophies as Marxism and liberalism. Heroism and duty, self-sacrifice and discipline were ends with no rational purpose beyond that of the greater glory of the nation. The Fascist promise was conceived as a release of the profound instincts of the people, inherent in their 'blood' or 'spirit'. Thus, in a speech delivered in Naples in 1922, Mussolini said, in language echoing Sorel:

> We have created our myth. The myth is a faith, it is a passion. It is not necessary that it shall be a reality. It is a reality by the fact that it is a goal, a hope, a faith; that it is courage. Our myth is the greatness of the nation![19]

Part of the Fascist myth was constructed by Italian nationalists such as Alfredo Rocco, who developed the doctrine that Italy was the spiritual heir of the Holy Roman Empire and the intellectual heir of the great 'Latin mind'.

Identity and the Role of Political Myth

Evidently, myth acts as a powerful mobilising force – sometimes even leading its followers to the edge of collective annihilation.[20] Unlike Fascism, however, communism makes no virtue of philosophical irrationalism and claims for itself instead the status of a materialist science. But apart from both communism's claim to be a 'science' and the question of its philosophical validity, *The Communist Manifesto* does, in fact, take up and extend one of the oldest eschatological myths of the Mediterranean world: the redemption of the elect (in this case the proletariat, whose sufferings are invoked to change the ontological status of the world), following an apocalyptic class conflict at the 'end of history'. The Marxian myth of the classless society, the withering away of the state and the disappearance of all historical tensions finds its most exact precedent in the myth of 'the Golden Age' which, typically, lies at the beginning and end of history (and therefore, like all myths, outside ordinary time).

Communism, however, is not unique in casting a 'messianic' role for itself based upon the self-image of heroic engagement in some historical battle against evil. Similar beliefs are also found in movements as far apart from each other as the cargo cults of Melanesia, the Shiites of Iran, or the Protestant fundamentalists in the USA and elsewhere. One explanation is simply that, for whatever motives (be they power, self-glorification, or the search for transcendental experience), people find it necessary to elevate themselves and the movements they belong to onto a higher, extra-historical plane – and this need finds expression in certain kinds of ideology and cosmology.

For the PCI, the myths of the Soviet Union and of the proletariat emancipated by the revolutionary vanguard party are old currency. So is the myth of the Resistance and anti-Fascist struggle – though these once drew large numbers of people into the Party. These particular symbols no longer hold the sentimental appeal they used to – though, clearly, for older generations of Party activists they are still potent. The continuing success of the PCI is perhaps explained by its ability to sustain its myth and create new expressions for it. Class struggle and the revolutionary role of the Party are the two most consistent themes that motivate each generation of political activists. But for each generation, too, there appears to be a particular myth or image that captures the spirit of the times and the idealism of those times. In former years this was the Resistance, the partisan War of Liberation, the 'Progressive Democracy' of post-war reconstruction, the Soviet Union, the peasant movement for land reform, and the movement against imperialism. Nowadays it is the movement for peace and disarmament and those against crime, corruption, the Mafia, drugs, and ecological catastrophe.

For those who joined the PCI and were active in the years prior to the 1970s, 'being communist' was fairly straightforward and involved explicit allegiance to the doctrine and style of a proudly Leninist organisation, clothed in the mantle of the workers' revolutionary vanguard. Though the PCI today is arguably no longer a Leninist party, it, nevertheless, still identifies itself as a vanguard party. This self-image has proved to be one of the most important and enduring aspects of the image members hold of themselves and their Party.

Italian communists are often aware that their politics are idealistic and visionary, but there is almost a pride taken in this, and those lacking in idealism are frequently perceived as somehow lacking in sincerity and commitment. This was summed up by a 40-year-old member:

> If our response in 1960 was to join the PCI, in 1968 it was to leave in order to give strength to another force that was still communist, but that preserved the idealism that had shaped us in the first place. Ours was, let's say, a very different, very beautiful generation. Perhaps it was because we were disillusioned, perhaps it was because we were dreamers. But a communist party – a revolutionary party – needs its dreamers and its illusions of grand idealism.[21]

PCI World-view and the Conception of History

It is a point of sociological significance that the communist view of history commands so much attention and importance in the PCI and that a sense of history features so prominently in the lives of ordinary Party members – as it does, to some extent, throughout Italian intellectual life in general. But history has a special significance for Italian communists. It is both a charter for action and a key political resource; something which all members partake in; a shared outlook which helps reinforce group solidarity. The historical events interpreted in official Party documents provide the coordinates by which Party members locate themselves in time and space. Furthermore, Marxism itself is a theory of history – both a stage theory and a prophecy. The construction of history is, therefore, a key part of the PCI world-view and like a shared language or the close identification one finds between Party members and their local section, it is essential to PCI members' sense of identity and belonging.

Noticeable in this respect is the sensitivity PCI leaders exhibit on matters related to interpreting Party history. This is reflected in the seriousness with which it treats its own historical quarterly, *Studi Storici*, the high profile given to historians and Gramsci Institute conferences, and the severity of disciplinary sanctions brought against Party intellectuals who depart too far from the Party line – as in the case of Bologna historian Salvatore Sechi,[22] or that of Roberto Napoleone, expelled in 1982 for 'propagating embarrassing and hitherto secret historical documents dealing with the attitude of the Party to its members who had been victims of the Stalinist purges in the Soviet Union' (Cornwell, 1982: 5).[23]

The Party leadership has traditionally claimed something of a 'monopoly' on the interpretation of PCI history. The habit of decades has given it a tendency to regard this not only as its patrimony, but often as its private property. Evidence of this is found throughout traditional PCI documents. For example, the 1983 Party statutes explicitly state that it is every member's 'duty' to study the 'history of revolutionary movements' and the Party's 'patrimony of ideas'.[24] Yet despite this exhortation to study history, PCI historiography, until quite recently, was highly circumscribed, concentrating mainly on the pre-war era. Even the five-volume history of the PCI, written by Party historian Paolo Spriano between 1967 and 1975, stopped at the year 1945, thus avoiding the uncomfortable period of the Stalinisation of Eastern Europe. Significantly, this restricted time-frame was seriously questioned for the first time only in 1974 by Berlinguer. In the same speech in which he elucidated the controversial 'Historic Compromise' strategy and affirmed the PCI's acceptance of NATO, Berlinguer also called upon Party historians to explore post-war history – implying that up until then they had not.[25] Two conferences on Soviet history and the Prague Spring were subsequently sponsored by the Gramsci Institute in 1978, the contributions to which were marked by an unusually detached and critical approach to controversial historical issues, including the Leninist roots of Stalinism, the failures of Soviet collectivisation and the abuse of power in the Soviet system (Urban, 1986: 333).

Why the leadership is so sensitive about interpretations of Party history is a question that strikes at the heart of the issue concerning the PCI's image of itself. There are two principal answers, one to do with power, the other with identity. The first can be summed up quite simply in the slogan, 'History is power.' Those who interpret history have a lever of control over both the Party's future and its past and hold one of the most effective keys to political legitimacy and authority. The idea is analogous to the Baconian creed popularised during the Scientific Revolution, 'Knowledge is power.' For Bacon, those who possessed scientific knowledge held a strategic position in the commanding heights of power and authority.[26] From their position of intellectual superiority – or ideological preparation in the canons of Marxism and heightened class consciousness – they alone perceive the course of human history for they alone have mastered its currents and direction. Just as science gave its practitioners a new claim to understanding the laws of nature, so Marxism is seen as a key to unravelling the laws of human history. The historians thus become specialists of a new kind of 'natural knowledge', and symbolic guardians of the Party's past and future.[27] With 'history on their side', the historians assume a critical role as brokers of a vital intellectual resource. The monopoly of historical truth then becomes both an instrument of political orientation and a mechanism of social control.

Bacon's model for the new 'man of science' also parallels Lenin's model of the revolutionary cadre. The noble scientist, like the Party cadre, possessed all those intellectual and ethical virtues required for the discovery of truth in the study of nature (Prior, 1956: 49–50). His humanitarian impulse set him above the state: he could not be confined to local loyalties, for true knowledge, by its nature, transcended time and space. The true scientist, therefore – like the communist – belonged to no country but rather to an 'international freemasonry' (ibid.: 52). Scientists were members of an elite class dedicated to improving man's lot on earth; an educated 'priesthood' whose scientific learning and vision would become the basis for a new intellectual order.[28] Similarly, in the Leninist conception, that educated priesthood is the Party cadre, whose intellectual power-base is historical materialism or 'scientific' socialism.[29] Communist intellectuals are the true leaders of the revolutionary movement. Indeed, according to Gramsci, they are the 'General Staff' who will lead the working class to victory by pioneering a new intellectual order based on socialist principles.[30] The PCI view of history and the Party's exalted role within the historical process therefore unite both the Leninist vanguard conception and the Gramscian idea of hegemony. As creators of hegemony, Party intellectuals become custodians of the most potent of ideological mechanisms for domination and control.[31]

For any Marxist party – or any party or orthodoxy – history is of enormous practical and conceptual importance.[32] It is the process that shapes mankind's past, present and future; that gives ultimate meaning to all political activity. It is not surprising, therefore, that communist parties frequently rewrite history, or that history plays such an important role in internal disputes over power and legitimacy.[33] Soviet historiography provides the best example of this. First, Russian history was reconstructed in order to eradicate the liberal–capitalist slant of 'bourgeois historians'; then, to accommodate Stalin's dogmatism and personality cult; and then, by Khrushchev, in order to undo the distortions of official history perpetrated by Stalin. Significantly, in concluding his speech to the 1956 CPSU Congress, Khrushchev called upon Party historians to

> compile a serious textbook of the history of our Party, which will be edited in accordance with scientific Marxist objectivism; a textbook of the history of Soviet society; and a book pertaining to the events of the Civil War and the Great Patriotic War (Khrushchev, 1956: 28).

Khrushchev however, eased from power and publicly disgraced, was himself written out of Soviet history by his successor Brezhnev, only to be officially 'rehabilitated' much later by Gorbachev. The propaganda section of the CPSU was notorious for rewriting history and 'authenticating' new interpretations of the past by doctoring the official records. Trotsky, Bukharin or any other officially declared 'nonperson' was simply removed from archival photographs with the sweep of an airbrush. Similarly, in Czechoslovakia, after the Soviet government had crushed the Prague Spring of 1968, arrested and imprisoned its leaders, and replaced Prime Minister Dubček with the more dependable Husák, one of the most significant actions of the new government was to dismiss over 145 Czech historians from universities and research institutes. As one of those historians, quoted by Kundera (1980: 159), explained it:

> The first step in liquidating a people is to erase its memory. Destroy its books, its culture, its history. Then have somebody write new books, manufacture a new culture, invent a new history.

In a distorted way this, too, may be conceived of as a version of communist hegemony, though it is a far cry from what Gramsci envisaged: new forms of consciousness generated by intellectuals, but imposed from above; cultural politics and class domination, but domination based on state repression and coercion rather than consent. Of course, there is nothing unusual in all this, for history is constantly being rewritten to suit new policies or new interpretations of the past, and the permutations are seemingly endless. It is perhaps one of the few truths about history that 'histories' are arbitrary constructs continually disputed – 'an unending dialogue between the present and the past' and 'between the historian and his facts', as E.H. Carr (1961: 30) described it. The use of history as an ideological tool merely highlights the politically emotive and partisan nature of all historical reconstruction. This was something that George Orwell commented on long ago. Observing the Spanish Civil War, he noted how 'lies became the official truth', not only in the Fascist war record written after Franco's victory, but equally in the retelling of those lies in the reports of the capitalist and communist press: 'I saw history being written', he wrote, 'not in terms of what happened but of what ought to have happened according to various party lines.'[34] In history, as in the general sphere of culture, the past is frequently invented in order to give legitimacy to present-day institutions, for the simple reason that 'tradition' becomes a major source of authority for those who can appropriate it and know how to wield it.[35]

The second reason for the PCI's sensitivity in interpreting history, closely related to the first, is that history has such direct importance for the political standing of the Party. With many of Italy's foremost historians in the Party, the PCI has been quite successful in projecting its view of history. As a source of pride and prestige, Party history is also a major political asset which the PCI has a vested interest in cultivating. Its reputation for anti-Fascism and partisan struggle, so crucial to the Party's survival during the Cold War and after, has depended upon it. Through the selective interpretation of historical events, the PCI has enhanced that prestige by creating a popular image of Gramsci as hero, martyr, sage and 'patron saint' of the Party.[36] History is thus integral to PCI identity and the process of political socialisation into the communist world; it is how Party members identify themselves, and it symbolises the shared heritage that binds them together. It plays a major role not only in the creation of hegemony, but also in the way the Party articulates its strategy. Thus, justification for any new departure in Party policy is typically accompanied by a new interpretation of history. For example, in 1983 when the PCI began seriously to sever its remaining ties with the Soviet Union, Berlinguer announced the beginning of a 'new phase' – not simply in PCI strategy but in the whole history of the communist movement.[37] But how far the PCI can really shape its own history depends upon its ability to face up to its past – and that, as we shall see, has not been an easy task for any communist party.

4

Italian Communism and the Problem of Organisation

The Party Section in PCI Theory

> A party section exists in almost every village in the land as well as practically every neighbourhood in the towns and cities. Only the network of Catholic parishes is as widespread (Kogan, 1962: 46).

It is the Party section which provides the major point of contact between the Party and the general public. Like the parish network of the Catholic Church, sections are the PCI's roots in civil society and the most visible symbol of its social presence. Like the parish Church, too, each section not only reflects the community from which its members are drawn, but also is a community in its own right, with particular character, its own history, and sense of identity.[1]

Because sections are the elementary units of PCI organisation, they are the basic building-blocks in a massive, hierarchical and territorial based political network through which the Party leadership communicates with its supporters and beyond them to the general public. This network includes 12,340 territorial sections and 1,347 office and factory nuclei organised under 116 federations.[2] It also includes hundreds of PCI 'city committees' and 'zone committees' and over 200 sections located outside Italy in countries such as Germany, Switzerland, Australia and Britain.[3] Each territorial section usually corresponds to a defined geographical area, for example, a village, a small municipality or a number of administrative wards within a city. Immediately above sections are city or zone committees, administrative bodies composed of a cluster of sections within the same municipality. Beyond these are a series of Party executive committees and secretariats, each corresponding both to the hierarchical levels of local government and, in parallel, to levels of Party organisation.

The PCI section is a key link in a chain of organisations that unite, in pyramidal fashion, the Party apparatus with the public. Yet, though sections occupy a central role within this network, they are by no means the locus of power or decision-making. Even decisions concerned with neighbourhood problems are taken by the federal committees or other bodies higher up the Party apparatus. However, sections are more than simply slavish executors of decisions made from above; it is through them that the leadership is brought face-to-face with the Party rank and file, and though it does not aways obey the wishes of its members, the Party hierarchy takes great care in sounding out their views and in presenting its policies in the light of those views. The section is thus the stage upon which any internal conflicts, blood-letting and feuding are played out.

As well as a rallying point and focus for debate, the section is also the level for recruitment into an organisation which aims to be both a party of protest, a community of believers and an alternative government. These contrasting goals, however, raise questions about what sort of party the PCI is, or is striving to become. At different times the Italian Communist Party has been variously described as a 'protest party', a 'cadre party', a 'devotee party', a 'bourgeois party', a 'Marxist party', a 'social democratic party' and a 'catch-all party', each description having very different theoretical implications. According to one of its own frequently used slogans, the PCI is 'a Party of Government and a Party of Struggle'. This self-definition reflects something of a compromise aimed at accommodating both 'Right' and 'Left' within the PCI; the first part of the slogan emphasising governmental alliances and tactical coalitions (a position traditionally associated with Amendola, then Giorgio Napolitano), the second phrase stressing the importance of allying the PCI with popular and progressive movements (such as ecologists, feminists and pacifists – a position associated with Pietro Ingrao). In effect, however, these two positions are by no means incompatible or antagonistic despite the ritual opposition between supporters of each camp. However, the 'Party of struggle/Party of government' dichotomy reflects perhaps another compromise of deeper historical significance; that associated with the PCI's post-war transformation from a Leninist to a mass, democratic party.

PCI after 1944: A 'Mass Bolshevik Party'?

On returning to Italy from exile in Moscow in 1944, Togliatti, who had been *de facto* leader of the Party ever since Gramsci's imprisonment in 1926, introduced two major innovations in the Party. The first, the 'Salerno U-turn' (*Svolta di Salerno*), was a complete reversal of PCI policy through which the communists, contrary to expectations, agreed to join the national government. The second, and more important, was the construction of the *Partito Nuovo*.[4] These two policies together formed the first steps towards transforming the Italian Communist Party from a clandestine army into a democratic political movement.

Though this *volte-face* marked a fundamental strategic change, there is little evidence to suggest that it was inspired by any major ideological revision at this point. Although Togliatti's move toward constitutionalism was consistent with what other communist parties were doing throughout western and southern Europe after the war – except in Greece where the communists were engaged in a bitter civil war – what distinguished the strategy of the Italian communists was the PCI's approach to power and its conception of politics as an all-embracing social activity. The creation of a new type of party organisation (the *Partito Nuovo*) which epitomised this was one of the most revolutionary steps ever taken by a nonruling communist party. It was also a highly unorthodox move, for it entailed abandoning at least two central tenets of Marxism-Leninism: the traditional Leninist model of the vanguard party, and the Bolshevik strategy for the revolutionary seizure of power.[5]

This, at least, is how the PCI interprets its history. Whether in 1944 Togliatti had clearly formulated the strategy that later evolved into a more explicit ideology (the conquest of the Italian state by gradual permeation of society) is uncertain.[6] More likely, Italian communists were anticipating a clear victory in the first post-war elections. This 'Armalite in one hand, ballot-box in the other' type of approach they appeared to adopt was also a practical response to the social and political conditions of the post-war era. Italy's fragile democracy, the widespread poverty and hunger, and the revolutionary political climate that lingered throughout much of the country combined to strengthen their confidence in electoral success. Thus, the Italian communists' initial acceptance of the 'rules of bourgeois democracy' may have been subterfuge, or, alternatively, it may have been conceived of merely as an interim measure. If this was the case, then the PCI's subsequent commitment to parliamentary democracy came about more by accident than design, and in spite of Party ideology rather than because of it.

The expulsion of the communists and socialists from the De Gasperi coalition government in 1947 was justified on the grounds of their hostility to the Marshall Plan. But the communist coup in Czechoslovakia the following year provided De Gasperi and the Christian Democrats with all the excuse they needed to lead an anticommunist crusade. Enemies of communism no longer had to invent charges of treason and treachery; the Czech coup vindicated all their accusations. The pattern of events was a chilling lesson on what could happen in Italy too. Czech communists had helped form a coalition government in which they, as the dominant partner, took control of the Interior Ministry. Once installed, they began to levy a series of false accusations against their coalition partners. From here they proceeded to arrest their political opponents for allegedly planning an armed uprising. Within a few days the communist seizure of power was complete; the border was closed; the opposition leader, Dr Jan Masaryk, had allegedly committed suicide by throwing himself from the window of the Foreign Ministry; and a dictatorship was in place. After the events in Czechoslovakia, the Cold War took on a new intensity. Democratic nations everywhere felt that communists could not be trusted to share power, and the name 'Czechoslovakia' acquired a new meaning: communist perfidy.[7]

Despite the widespread condemnation this provoked in the West, PCI leaders remained noncommittal. Given the polarised political climate at that time it would have been difficult for the PCI to condemn the Czech communists without indicting itself. Furthermore, Togliatti was still deeply committed to Leninism, and despite the PCI's radical innovations in policy and organisation, the *Partito Nuovo* was conceived of as an extension of Leninist theory rather than a repudiation of it. Like the Czechoslovakian Communist Party, the PCI still firmly identified itself with Stalin, the Soviet view of history and the Bolshevik model of revolution. Moreover, like the Socialist Party (PSI), it was still being financed from Moscow.[8]

Significantly, in 1946 – just two years before the Czech coup – Togliatti gave his own definition of the *Partito Nuovo* as a 'mass Bolshevik party' (*un partito di massa bolscevico*).[9] But this definition raises a fundamental question: Is it not a contradiction to speak of a 'mass' yet 'Bolshevik' party? Furthermore, what does it mean to be a 'legal' Bolshevik party? This question is relevant to any communist party operating in a developed Western democracy since the Bolshevik model was specifically formulated as the model most appropriate for an insurrectionary party working within a tsarist police state in a backward peasant society – conditions which hardly apply in Western Europe. It is a contradiction in theoretical terms, and on a practical level many PCI leaders have never considered themselves to be Bolsheviks, though many of the rank and file clearly did and still do.

Togliatti's contradictory conception of the *Partito Nuovo* was bound to have repercussions, particularly at the level of the party's organisational structure, for the PCI, like all political parties, still contains many vestiges of its former values and attitudes, many of which are inconsistent and out of step with current thinking. This is perhaps inevitable, as structures invariably become repositories of the values prevalent at the time of their creation. Thus, the organisation of a party or a trade union will tend to reflect not so much the present as the past in which they were formed. Furthermore, organisations tend to develop in unpredictable ways, for, as Bertrand Russell (1979: 374) wrote, 'organisations have a life of their own, independent of the intentions of their founders.' The PCI is no exception. The Party section still carries many traits that reflect its former years as a clandestine Leninist coterie, even though it now operates as the bottom tier of an open, mass party.

But the question is whether the PCI, or any former party of the Third International, can ever lose its Leninist credentials and become a truly mass and democratic party? According to Lenin, the Communist Party is a 'cadre party' composed of the most advanced elements of the working class and its historical vanguard, the revolutionary proletariat. By definition, it is elitist. Theoretically, therefore, it cannot become a 'mass party' without compromising its class image and its ideological character. For the PCI this poses the question, is it possible for a 'mass communist party' to win power in a pluralist parliamentary system *without* abandoning that which most people understand as its 'communist identity'? In short, can the Italian Communist Party succeed without renouncing communism? This is a question returned to in Part II of this book.

For the present, however, our focus is the structure of the Party section, for this is one of the critical areas where ideology and organisation are welded together most conspicuously. However, that 'welding' is not always successful, and contradictions emerge most visibly at section level between the Party's clandestine Bolshevik heritage and its more democratic, socialist features – i.e. between its antagonistic Second and Third International characteristics. This leads to an interesting debate about the relationship between ideology and political organisation. It is usually assumed that the former precedes the latter; that is, that political ideology is the precursor of forms of organisation – just as a building is developed according to an architectural plan or blueprint. With a political party this relationship is more complex, as ideology and organisation tend to interact, each influencing the other in often unforeseen ways. The point is captured in a celebrated passage of Marx: 'Men make their own history, but they do not make it just as they please ... The tradition of all the dead generations weighs like a nightmare on the brain of the living.'[10]

For the PCI, that 'nightmare' is its Leninist heritage which, despite the Party's steady abandonment of Leninist theory, has remained cemented into Party practices by virtue of its continuing influence on Party organisation.[11] In this respect a major disparity continues to exist between PCI organisation and ideology. The causes of this disparity lie in the evolution of Party structure, in the blending of the two different political traditions that have shaped Party structure, and in the PCI's slow attempt to overcome its Leninist past by forging a distinctive 'Italian road to socialism'. But this 'contradiction' has other implications, some of them highly positive, for without it Eurocommunism – which entailed a fundamental revision of the PCI's Bolshevik heritage – would not have come into existence. Moreover, that same 'disparity' helped the PCI to make large electoral gains while enabling it to remain ambiguous about what kind of party it really was and what it would do should it ever come to power. The question now, however, is whether the PCI can succeed in winning power democratically, or whether, instead, it is a prisoner of its own past, bound to its own 'dead weight' of history. As Darwin wrote, 'Man still carries in his bodily frame the indelible stamp of his lowly origins.'[12] Perhaps an analogy is to be found here with the PCI and the framework of communism in general.

Sections or Cells: Conflicting Models of Party Organisation

The current form of the territorial section is an adaptation of a model originally devised by the German Social Democratic Party in the late nineteenth century. Following its German counterpart, the Italian Socialist Party, at its third Congress in Parma in 1895, endorsed the switch from associate to individual membership. Thereafter the territorial section became the elementary unit for a party geared primarily to electoral activity and propaganda. The chief function of the section in the Socialist Party model was to promote Party propaganda through rallies, debates, conferences and other 'proselytising' activities, but it also aimed to provide a recreational centre for members. What distinguished the socialist organisational model, above all, was the absence of any intermediate or centralised structure between the constituency parties and the national leadership. Local Party sections enjoyed enormous, if not total, political autonomy, with the result that they often tended to be highly parochial in their outlook and somewhat anarchic in their activities.

Immediately a disparity appears between the socialist and communist organisational models. Whereas the socialist model was loosely based and structured around autonomous territorial units, the Communist Party (i.e. Third International) model stressed subordination, centralisation and an emphasis on workplace cells. Here the focus of political militancy was not in the neighbourhood but in the factories and at the 'point of production' – the so-called 'front line' of revolutionary struggle.[13]

On the surface this difference appears only cosmetic, but, in reality, it reveals a fundamental ideological distinction. Whereas the section is an organ for absorbing, recruiting and 'wooing' the wider public, the cell is an instrument of attack; a sect for waging class warfare which is directed toward industry and economics. This difference has important political as well as social and geographical ramifications. In the political organisation of space, the cell must be located in the workplace, traditionally in factories and, therefore, among the male, manual-labour proletariat. The section, by contrast, is situated in the local piazza, at the very heart of neighbourhood life, alongside other major national institutions including the banks, the *comune* (town hall) and the Church. Situated strategically at the heart of the local community, the section enjoys all the 'prestige of the Piazza' and its patriotic civic monuments. Whereas the cell is by tradition semiclandestine and barely visible, the section vaunts its legitimacy and proudly displays its presence.

Though the PCI eventually favoured the section over the cellular model, the structure of Party organisation today reflects an attempt at mediation between these two traditions, one socialist the other Bolshevik (Massari, 1982: 156). For many years the PCI was effectively two parties: one committed to parliamentary pluralism, the other conspiratorial (Magna, 1983: 180) and still anchored in the defensive Leninist mentality of its pre-war years (Sebastiani, 1983: 81). The question today, however, is, how well has this mediation been carried out and what problems does this conflicting organisational heritage still pose for Italian communism? This also raises the fundamental question, posed by Ostragorski, Weber, Michels and others, of which type of organisation is most appropriate for left-wing parties, and whether ultimately all socialist movements are doomed to become victims of their own bureaucratic and oligarchic tendencies (see Chapter 5).

Bolshevisation of the PCI: 1924–6

At the PSI's Livorno Congress of 1921 the communist delegates split off to form their own party. By all accounts it was a tumultuous occasion. The first communist to speak, the editor of the youth paper, Secondino Tranquilli (subsequently known as Ignazio Silone), implored delegates to 'burn the effigy of unity', and the communist delegates left the conference singing the 'Internationale', to hold their own founding conference in a neighbouring hall (Hoare and Nowell-Smith, 1971: xlvi).

Despite the vehement effect of the ideological schism on the practical structure of party organisation, there was little if any immediate rupture with the socialist model. Throughout the period of Bordiga's leadership (1921–4), the newly formed PCd'I remained fixed in the old Socialist Party mould, its organisation based upon much the same pattern of territorial sections. It was not until the period after 1924 and under Gramsci's leadership (until his arrest in 1926), that the real transformation occurred and the old Bordigan structure was 'Bolshevised'. Several external factors aided this organisational change, foremost among them being pressures from within the Comintern in Moscow. But within Italy, too, the growing state of political instability and industrial unrest, not to mention the rise of Fascism and the increasing number of attacks on working-class and left-wing organisations, helped to prepare the way for Gramsci's reorganisation of the PCd'I into a highly centralised, clandestine and paramilitary organisation.

The spread of Fascism, in particular, strengthened Gramsci's argument against critics – including Bordiga and Serrati – for the full Bolshevisation of the PCd'I. Such a move, he argued, was now a necessity; the Party must go underground or perish. For Gramsci, however, restructuring the PCd'I along Bolshevik lines was not a temporary expedient to be followed only until the storm of organised right-wing violence subsided, but a long-term goal that was both ideologically correct and strategically desirable. Thus he wrote in 1926:

> No one dares say that the Leninist criteria of party organisation [in Italy] are exactly those of the Russian situation, or that their application in Western Europe is purely a mechanical matter. [But] ... to oppose the organisation of the party into cells means to be still tied to the old social democratic conception; it means to find oneself truly in the terrain of the Right, that is, the terrain of those with no will to struggle against social democracy (Gramsci, 1971: 66).

The PCd'I's transformation of 1924–6 was characterised by the adoption of a system of factory, street and village cells coupled with an attempt to strengthen Party recruitment. The Party statutes of 1926, which spoke of a 'new political phase' and a 'new type of party' expressed some ambiguity as to the actual distinction between cells and sections, but the Party Congress at Lyons in 1926 spelt it out categorically: 'The organisation of the Party must be constructed at the base of production and therefore of workplace cells.'[14]

That Gramsci's motives arose less from criteria of political efficiency than from a doctrinaire approach to organisational problems is confirmed in his own writings: 'The cellular type of organisation guarantees the proletarian character of the party better than any other, and better than any other type it guarantees the party against opportunism.'[15]

For Gramsci, it seems, 'opportunism' and Bolshevism were two opposite poles and the only real alternatives set before the Party. Combined with Fascist repression, these reforms meant that after 1926 the territorial section had all but disappeared from the political scene, while the Party network went underground and sectarian. Meanwhile the idea of agitation and proletarian insurrection grew in importance, and the Party began to suffer the effects of clampdown, arrest and persecution. By the end of the 1920s its organisation had been virtually smashed; most of its leaders were in prison or other confinement, while the rest were in hiding or exiled abroad (including Togliatti, Tasca and Longo). Party strategy during these years concentrated on covert propaganda and efforts to instigate labour disturbances. During this period the Party was financed by the Soviet Union, and its tactics were directed from abroad, chiefly by Palmiro Togliatti, the Party's representative in Moscow and subsequent official leader (1944–64).

Up until 1944 the cellular structure was ideally suited to the PCI, which was still an underground coterie inspired by Leninist principles of ideology and organisation. As Gramsci saw it, in a revolutionary situation the workers' movement would have to be led by the proletarian vanguard without 'prior consultation' and without the apparatus of representative assemblies, for revolution was like war; a task requiring discipline, obedience and minute planning under the 'military' command of the party's general staff. Furthermore, as both Gramsci and Lenin saw it, the proletariat was in too wretched a condition to realise its own interests. To raise their consciousness to an awareness of class and revolution was the task of an organised vanguard.[16]

As the tide of war changed in favour of the Allies, more Italians turned to the Resistance, and the Communist Party, which was the largest force in the partisan war, grew in strength and status. Without doubt the communists played the leading role in the struggle for liberation. Of the 300,000 armed partisans enrolled by the end of the fighting an estimated 40–50 per cent were in the communist Garibaldi Brigades, and of the 70,000 partisans killed by the Nazis and Italian Fascists, 42,000 were communists (Sassoon, 1981: 29).

The Party Section in the *Partito Nuovo*

The PCI's return to territorial sections followed Italy's liberation and the return of legal political parties in 1944, but this did not, however, mean a straightforward return to the earlier socialist-style sections. Instead, Togliatti embarked upon the most radical reorganisation the Party had ever witnessed, the result of which was a 'mass party' concept contrary to all previous models of Party organisation in the modern era. The key factor was its size, which was a direct consequence of Togliatti's 'open door' policy. From an estimated 5–6,000 members in 1944, the Party had grown to 1,770,000 by the end of 1945 (Magna, 1983: 180); then to 2,253,000 by 1947 (Ghini, 1982: 269). As a result the Party underwent a radical transformation that at times was disorganised and chaotic – particularly in the South where the Party had to be built virtually from nothing.[17] But this metamorphosis posed formidable practical problems, for not only did it stretch Party manpower and resources to the limit, but it also threatened to swamp the Party in a tidal wave of inexperienced recruits. Rather than bring the Party to the masses, Togliatti's ambitious idea behind this was to bring the masses into the Party, which he likened to a 'great school'. Once inside, they could be educated and trained, or ousted. By uniting the Party and the public in this way he successfully combined ideological considerations with practical expedients, not least because an organised mass membership greatly facilitated the diffusion of Party propaganda.

Togliatti's goal in devising the *Partito Nuovo* was to secure the active participation of all sectors of society so that the task of revolutionary struggle would no longer be restricted to an exclusive minority whose 'raised class consciousness' gave them alone the right to operate within the political process. But the innovation also had immediate practical advantages. From the financial point of view, it would secure a steady flow of funds from the thousands of new contributions – money otherwise difficult to obtain. From the strategic point of view, it would strengthen the Party by creating an organisation with deep and permanent roots in society that would be equipped both to defend itself – should Italy ever again lurch toward authoritarianism – and maintain a state of 'permanent mobilisation' among its membership. Moreover, the *Partito Nuovo* was consistent with Togliatti's idea of transforming Italian society by abolishing the traditional separation between political behaviour and cultural activity.[18]

The idea underlying the *Partito Nuovo* was that in being open to everyone actively interested in politics, the Party would no longer be an association of persons striving to replace one political elite with another. Instead, it would introduce new values and lifestyles with the aim of transforming the Party into a cultural as well as political movement, which would be the forerunner of the new type of society.[19] Like most Marxist parties the PCI shares this ideal of bourgeois society dismantled and reintegrated along Socialist principles, but, unlike others, the PCI has gone a long way toward doing this by establishing itself as a social force to rival that of the dominant culture.

This is how Party militants often perceive the PCI: not simply as a political instrument, but as an instrument, an ideal and a social project fused into one.[20] For the PCI, the *partito di massa* aimed at uniting ends and means in the struggle for communism by becoming the core around which a new social bloc would be forged for unseating bourgeois domination. The mass party symbolises something far deeper than simply Party strength: at the level of 'religion' it is the legitimation of the Party's living faith.

During the PCI's 1945–6 Fifth National Congress the *Partito Nuovo* was officially defined as an 'nonideological party', for which Marxism-Leninism constitutes only a cultural heritage. To join, one did not have to be Leninist or Marxist, but only to agree with the Party's programme and day-to-day policies. Ever since then the PCI has taken pains to emphasise that it has abolished ideological orthodoxy and become a 'secular party' or nonconfessional one (*un partito laico*), open to 'men and women of different ideals; Marxist and non-Marxist, believers and non-believers ... a programmatic party, without discipline of an ideological character'.[21] It is often claimed that the PCI was one of the first communist parties to rid itself of the idea of ideological unity as a prerequisite for membership (Ferrarotti, 1978: 43). This is debatable, however, particularly if the notion of 'ideological unity' is expanded beyond its purely formal definition. Within the PCI, 'unity' itself, the way it is conceptualised and practised, is a fundamental component of Party ideology. Indeed, within the PCI there is what might be called, for lack of a better term, an 'ideology of unity'. Like patriotism in England and other European nation-states, the idea of unity operates as a powerful mobilising force capable of cutting across all other internal Party cleavages. The PCI may not demand that its members profess themselves to be Marxist, but loyalty to the Party is a member's first duty – just as 'defence of the realm' is the first obligation of any patriotic citizen in a nation-state.

The kind of political order the PCI was striving for in the 1940s was ambiguous – a fact reflected in its organisation. Officially, the parliamentary and social-democratic road was repudiated, and liberal democracy with its individual freedoms was considered inadequate (Ferrarotti, 1978: 44). Togliatti instead spoke of 'progressive democracy' and 'structural reforms', suggesting a type of democratic regime that supposedly went beyond abstract legal principles of individual freedom and actually challenged the capitalist system. But with the idea of 'progressive democracy' Togliatti was already advancing a notion of revolution as process rather than violent rupture (Sassoon, 1981: 39). This would inevitably involve a gradualist and evolutionary approach to socialism, rather than insurrection.

However, while the PCI formally accepted the rules of 'bourgeois democracy' and Italy became a constitutional republic, Italian communists still clung proudly to their communist credentials and revolutionary self-image – hence its contradictory self-definition as a 'mass Bolshevik party'. At the level of the section, however, the *Partito Nuovo* fitted neither category, for the idea that Party sections would challenge the parish church in a role it had assumed for centuries was indeed novel.[22] On this, Togliatti wrote:

> The Communist sections in the city boroughs and in the small towns must become centres of popular life, centres where all comrades must go, all sympathisers and those without a party, in the knowledge that they can find there a party that takes an interest in their problems and that will furnish them with guidance; in the knowledge that there they can find someone that can lead them, give them advice and, if need be, the possibility of amusing themselves.[23]

Under the slogan, 'For Every Party Section a House of the People' (*ogni casa del popolo una sezione comunista*), this policy was officially launched at the PCI's Florence Congress in 1947.[24]

Bolshevism or Democratic Socialism: Contradictions in the *Partito Nuovo*

While this new role for the Party section was encouraged, the PCI also placed equal emphasis on developing the role of the cell, which, in effect, meant it was straddling two paths, trying to combine socialist and Bolshevik organisational traditions. This was never an easy task, for while sections were by nature more democratic and open to the outside, cells were quite the opposite, being, in tendency, more closed, inward-looking, authoritarian and military in character (Massari, 1982: 156). Whereas sections recruited their members from a broad range of social categories spanning all social classes, recruitment by cells was limited to workers at the workplace. Furthermore, the two models were incompatible in practical terms, for their spheres of recruitment were bound to coincide, and the success of one usually meant the decline of the other wherever they overlapped. Eventually the cellular model was relegated in favour of the section, but this change came about slowly, with many interesting twists and turns. Significantly, it also paralleled the PCI's disengagement from Soviet communism and its gradual move toward greater internal democracy.

After 1944, however, the two immediate problems facing PCI leaders were, holding together its disorganised horde of recruits, most of them peasants and workers, and providing the Party with a sense of political direction such as it had had during the Resistance. Moreover, the Party also had problems imposing leadership and discipline on its members, for many were calling for a return to class struggle, arguing that the Party should follow the example of the October Revolution. Togliatti's policy of national unity for an anti-Fascist popular front was endured grudgingly by the membership rather than accepted. In June 1944, for example, the Turin Party split, largely over this issue, and an organisation of 2,000 members known as 'Red Star', 'agitated against employers and in favour of revolution after the war' (Clark, 1977: 228).

In the eyes of these members, communism meant the Bolshevik road to socialism; there was no conceivable alternative. Their understanding of Marxism was unsophisticated and often stemmed from gut feeling rather than intellectual analysis. They saw Stalin as the great wartime hero, endowed with mythical qualities: the invincible leader who had defeated the Nazis and saved the Soviet workers' state, and who, they hoped, would send the Red Army to liberate Italy. These attitudes were summed up in two rallying cries that became common among workers in the South: 'Big Moustaches is coming!' and 'We'll do what they did in Russia!' (Sassoon, 1981: 34).

Two different political interpretations of PCI strategy coexisted during the 1940s. One, generally held by the older generation of Party leaders, saw post-war reconstruction in terms of intermediate political goals and structural reforms (Togliatti's 'progressive democracy'); the other held that Togliatti's strategy was nothing but a ploy to trick liberal anti-Fascists into a strategic alliance from whence the secret insurrectionary takeover could be unleashed. The problem was that this was what the PCI's enemies believed, too; that the PCI's professed constitutionalism was merely a trick to pave the way for an eventual seizure of power and repressive one-party state (Sassoon, 1981: 30). For this reason PCI strategy in the early post-war period has been described as 'duplicity' (*dopiezza*) by Italian historians.[25] Indeed, even until the 1950s the PCI continued to maintain a paramilitary underground organisation formed by ex-partisans who had hidden their weapons when the war had ended. Translated literally, *dopiezza* means 'duplicity' or 'double-dealing', but, as Marzani (1980: 102) argues, this is a misleading interpretation of PCI policy. Though the Party had a 'two-track' policy, there was nothing secret about the existence of its armed sector. Given their history, Italian communists had every reason to fear for their fragile democracy and the possible need to resort to arms again.

An interesting question is why the PCI did not organise an insurrection in 1944–5. Certainly, the temptation was there: *then*, if ever, was the moment to strike; the country was in chaos, but the partisans were organised, armed and ready to take action. As many communists saw it, they had defeated the Germans, so why not now carry on the armed struggle against the bourgeoisie? There are two main answers. First, Italy during 1944–5 was still under Allied military occupation. The Allies had already shown their bias by favouring the non-Communist elements in the Resistance. Civil war would have been a bloody affair – plunging Italy back into turmoil, and possibly resulting in dictatorship again. The disastrous civil war in Greece from 1946 to 1949, which resulted in over 5,000 civilian deaths, the defeat of the communists and the execution of over 1,200 Party members, many of them Resistance heroes, shows how dangerous and tragic such a move might have been.[26] In Italy an estimated 150,000 armed partisans might have supported an insurrection, but their strength was concentrated in northern and central Italy. It was unlikely that the peasant masses in the South, untouched by socialist ideology and inexperienced in partisan warfare, would rally to the support of the communists – or that the Soviet Union, following the Yalta and Potsdam agreements, would intervene.

Second, evidence suggests that Togliatti was already developing a new conception of socialism: that the Comintern's temporary popular-front strategy, adopted as an interim expedient to unite anti-Fascist parties in the 1930s, was becoming a permanent strategy. PCI strategy aimed at national unity rather than class war. Reasons for this had already been spelt out on Togliatti's return in 1944 when the PCI's priority was the war of liberation and maintaining anti-Fascist unity. This meant a 'popular alliance' of communists, socialists and Catholics, the three mass groups in Italian society. The 'institutional question' would have to be postponed until later, after a constituent assembly and interim government had been created to conduct the war and guarantee a democratic, anti-Fascist future for Italy. PCI strategy envisaged a staggered process, with the war of liberation and the establishment of a new republic as merely the first phase. However, a great deal of PCI strategy still stems from this period. This also helps explain why Italian communists right from the 1940s became vigorous defenders of the constitution, law and order, the rights of citizenship, individual liberty and parliamentary democracy.

The PCI made something of a 'cult' of the constitution and the Resistance. Its strategy was claimed to be based on Gramscian ideas reinterpreted through the experience of war and the popular front.[27] The essential premise of this was that Italy had not yet completed its bourgeois-democratic revolution, and that to achieve this an interclass alliance was necessary. What began as a temporary strategy ('frontism'), spelt out by the Comintern in 1935, thus became a central element in the interpretation of PCI history and a dominant ideology within it. The constitution became the symbolic embodiment of the progressive goals of the Resistance and a new basis for interclass unity. In Amyot's (1981: 26–7) words,

> The culminating point of this historical account was the Resistance, in which the Communist Party and the working class took up the banner of the national interest. The cult of the Resistance, in which the unity achieved by all anti-fascist forces is constantly stressed, has been assiduously cultivated by the PCI.

PCI strategy aimed primarily at forming alliances with nonproletarian groups, particularly the middle classes. But the creation of a new type of republic also necessitated a revised conception of the role of the party. Many socialist ideas concerning party structure (developed by Karl Kautsky), survived the Second International to acquire a dominant position in the Communist International. One idea was that the Party as an institution should be built separately from the prevailing social order. The contrary view taken by Togliatti conceived of the *Partito Nuovo* as an integrated, *national* party that would actively participate in community life and link factories and villages with democratic institutions at all levels.[28]

Whatever Togliatti's motives,[29] the *dopiezza* of the PCI was manifest in several ways, particularly in Party organisation. The old class model represented by the cell, with its indelible Third Internationalist stamp, posed a problem for the PCI, as the theory of class warfare was inconsistent with the ideology of national unity. This mixed ideological heritage made the task of reconciling organisation with ideology even harder. Just as the early Bolshevik Party had been torn between antagonistic Marxist and Jacobin traditions, so, too, the PCI was torn between seemingly irreconcilable socialist and Leninist traditions – a conflict that some argue has never been satisfactorily resolved by Party theoreticians.

As territorial sections came to replace cells as the principal unit of Party organisation, the function of workplace cells was reduced, in the words of Massari (1982: 158),

> to that of a mere relic testifying to a pretended ideological continuity – that needs to be constantly reaffirmed in the party statute – with the Third International and with the class character of the party (even when it is by now patently clear that the cell exists only on paper, as leaders themselves admit).

For many communists, the switch from cell to section raised the question of whether this signified, as they feared, the end of the PCI's class nature and its evolution toward an 'electoral party', or worse, a 'party of opinion' similar to other Italian parties.

Effects of the Cold War on Party Organisation

Echoing Gramsci some 20 years earlier, PCI leaders defended the retention of workplace cells alongside sections on the grounds that the cell-type organisation 'provides the best conditions for the selection of party cadres'.[30] Under the formula of coexistence, sections became the higher of the two Party organs, responsible for coordinating cells – which performed most of the mundane, daily Party work. But section membership was on a 'group cell' rather than individual basis. In turn, the sections were totally subservient to federal executive committees – which had the statutary right to send representatives to sit on the electoral commission of every section's annual congress.

Despite Togliatti's goal of animating political life in the community via Party sections, the general level of participation at the Party base during the late 1940s and 1950s was disappointingly low, and most Party activity was bureaucratic and inward-looking. But instead of attributing any of this to internal problems inherent in its organisational structure, most PCI leaders blamed lack of discipline, poor ideological preparation and external factors, including the anticommunist offensive and migrations within the country. Though 'excessive centralisation' was sometimes criticised, rarely was any connection made between declining Party activism and the practice of 'democratic centralism' which lay at the heart of Party organisation. The mechanics of democratic centralism will be discussed at length in the following chapters; therefore, only a brief definition will be provided now. Democratic centralism was a doctrine developed originally by Lenin as the organising principle of the CPSU, but which subsequently became a canon of Party organisation in all Marxist-Leninist parties. In principle it allows for the election of leaders and for free and open discussion at all levels of the Party until such time as a formal decision is democratically reached, after which that decision is binding on all members. In practice, however, it has tended to function on the basis of strict hierarchy, rigid discipline over the rank and file, and the subordination of lower bodies to higher ones. Moreover, it has traditionally included the selection of leaders through cooptation from above rather than election from below, which in many communist parties results in the perpetuation of self-selected, unaccountable ruling groups who maintain an effective monopoly over decision-making.[31]

Deprived of any real decision-making power through subordination to higher bodies, and bound to leaders and decisions that were frequently imposed from above, it is hardly surprising that the PCI sections failed to stimulate enthusiasm. Despite the leadership's frequent exhortations to the contrary, the role of the mass membership was largely a passive one of receiving and transmitting Party policies decided on high. What is surprising is the loyalty exhibited by rank-and-file members in accepting this submissive role – which says much about the nature of Party allegiance in that period. That loyalty was fed by a political passion which rested upon a mythical vision of socialism; Manichaean, devotional and grounded on the cult of Stalin (Massari, 1982: 161).

According to Amyot (1981), that loyalty, together with the practice of democratic centralism and the ideology of 'Popular Frontism', combined effectively to eliminate the more progressive, revolutionary Left within the Party. Massari, however, argues the very converse; that rigid centralisation during the 1950s aided rather than hindered progressive developments in PCI strategy, as its leadership – however 'Jacobinist' – was far more progressive than the membership. Without resolving the perceived contradiction between ideology and organisation, PCI leaders were nevertheless able to use the old Leninist traditions of discipline and unity to change the Party and pull it out of the sectarianism into which it was sliding.

However, considerable differences existed within the leadership on the role of the cell, particularly between Togliatti and his vice-secretary, Pietro Secchia, who insisted that the 'cadre' quality of the Party be reinforced to increase the combative capacity of the Party. Unfortunately for Togliatti, the PCI's expulsion from the coalition government and the Cold War meant that his ideas about an 'Italian road to socialism' were suspended for almost a decade, while the PCI was forced into a phase of organisational retrenchment during which the cellular model once again rose to prominence.

Events of the late 1940s had a profound impact on PCI members. Cold War propaganda, Red-scare campaigns, Marshall Plan aid, electoral defeat, the attempted assassination of Togliatti, the 1948 general strike followed by schisms in the trade-union movement, and the creation of NATO in April 1949 – all this struck a terrible blow against communism. The PCI was now compelled to make fundamental organisational changes toward rigidity and sectarianism, bracing itself for the onslaught of the government's anticommunist offensive. Under Secchias direction as head of Party organisation, the membership was streamlined following an organisational model adapted from the Czechoslovak Communist Party (Massari, 1983: 165). Cells were subdivided into small, self-contained units of eight to ten members headed by a collector' (*collettore*) whose duties included maintaining reports and personal profiles of each Party member (see Chapter 7). The new Party statutes of 1948 also introduced other changes symptomatic of a Party closing in on itself. The trend toward decentralisation was heavily criticised, the clause stipulating the use of the secret vote in the election of local executives was dropped, and a new executive tier linking cells and sections was created in the form of factory committees composed of secretaries from a given number of workplace cells. The Party became insular and fragmented, bogged down in its own administration, and increasingly isolated from the public. As a result, internal debate 'lost momentum and required repeated and minute connections among a myriad of small, self-enclosed groups, fixed in their membership' (Ferrarotti, 1978: 49). The psychological impact of this change was considerable, for, as Ferrarotti (ibid.) wrote,

> After the profoundly experienced unity of the people under Fascism and Nazi oppression, especially from 1943 through to 1945, the Italian polity again appeared fragmented and divided. Card-carrying Communists were publicly denounced and officially excommunicated by Pope Pius XII. Rumours that the Red Army would be moving towards the West and invade Italy were widespread. Unemployment was high. The war was not felt to be completely over.

Government policy toward communism became increasingly Draconian and repressive. In July 1947 the DC minister of the interior, Mario Scelba, declared that any assembly within factory gates required prior police permission. The following year he labelled as 'insurrectional acts' the CGIL general strike after the attempt on Togliatti's life, and proceeded – with the help of the judiciary – to arrest hundreds of trade unionists (Sassoon, 1986: 127). Anticommunist witch-hunts compelled the PCI to adopt an increasingly defensive posture, as a result of which it became more bureaucratic, inward-looking and obsessed with centralisation and ideological discipline rather than political initiative.[32]

For Party members these were the 'hard years' (*gli anni duri*). Yet, perhaps, thanks to these organisational manoeuvres the PCI survived attempts to isolate it, and its membership declined only fractionally – from 2,115,327 in 1948 to 2,035,353 in 1956 (Ghini, 1982: 263–4). Unlike other European communist parties, the PCI never lost its social respectability within the parliamentary framework nor its heroic reputation as champion of the Resistance.

Stalinism, the Crisis of 1956 and the Question of Communist Organisation

After 1956 the 'section versus cell' issue was replaced by a more pressing debate concerning the structure of Party organisation and the question of Stalinism. With the eighth Congress (Rome, December 1956), a campaign was launched to renew and democratise the Party – a move which followed Secchia's removal from the offices of organisation and Party vice-secretary. This shake-up was partly stimulated by the easing of De Gaspari's anticommunist offensive and the beginnings of detente between East and West following Stalin's death in 1953. But the real catalyst was Khrushchev's speech to the 20th Soviet Communist Party Congress in February 1956. With unprecedented candour Khrushchev revealed for the first time the atrocities perpetrated by Stalin during his 25 years as ruler of the Soviet Union. Delivered in secret on the morning of 25 February, the full text of the speech was not published outside of the Soviet Union until June.[33]

Returning from Moscow with the PCI delegation in February 1956, Togliatti gave little away to the Italian press or public. The news was withheld even from the PCI Central Committee which met later in March (Pajetta, 1982: 58).[34] Only on 18 March did *L'Unità* mention the existence of a secret report, and until then no other communist newspaper had done so. Despite growing rumours, the issue was successfully avoided throughout the electoral campaign of May 1956 where the communists polled 23.8 per cent of the vote to the PSI's 25 per cent and the Christian Democrats' 34.5 per cent. However, when the news finally broke, its effects throughout the communist world were shattering.[35] In Italy the PCI/PSI Pact of Unity was terminated immediately by Nenni, who, in outrage, turned over his Stalin Peace Prize money to the Red Cross and other charities (Marzani, 1980: 57). Soon after, the socialists began making overtures to the Christian Democratic Party which would eventually lead to their entry into government. For the PCI, instead, as for communist parties everywhere now having to face this trauma, the question was *how* could it have happened? The real issue was whether Stalin's 'violation of Party norms' was an anomaly or whether, in fact, it was the fruit of defects inherent in the theory and organisation of communism itself?

Within the PCI there followed an intensive debate which precipitated the beginnings of a serious 'revisionism' in PCI strategy. Italian communists were not satisfied with Khrushchev's explanation of Stalin's excesses, which Khrushchev attributed to the 'cult of personality' phenomenon. Their analysis went beyond the question of Stalin's personality to the structural factors that had enabled such an abuse of power to occur in the first place. Whatever other lessons there were to be learned, it became evident that the PCI should acquire greater autonomy from its Soviet counterpart. Thus, Togliatti seized upon Khrushchev's assertion of the legitimacy of 'various paths to socialism' as an endorsement of the *actual* policy of the Italian communists, who then proclaimed their own, independent *via italiana al socialismo*. Hereafter the PCI openly asserted the doctrine that the Soviet Union and Soviet Party were no longer the 'leading state' and 'leading Party' for the world communist movement.[36] Every party should be free to follow its own, national course, and there should be unity in diversity. The term Togliatti coined for this was 'polycentrism'.

In the light of the defects inherent in Stalinism, the PCI also set about reviewing the defects in its own organisation. At its eighth PCI Congress in December 1956, General-Secretary Longo attacked a series of factors that he blamed for having weakened Party democracy: excessive centralisation from above, bureaucratisation of executive bodies, lack of political initiative and the overbearing preponderance of 'organisation' over 'politics'. Significantly, he blamed many of these on the practice of democratic centralism, which, he claimed, had 'the tendency to transform itself into bureaucratic centralism, that is, to become mechanical and rigidified in a bureaucracy.'[37] The attempt to 'de-Stalinise' the Party, eradicate sectarianism and animate the sections naturally put decentralisation high on the political agenda. A series of structural reforms was therefore implemented: the groups of ten were dissolved, numerical limits for sections were abandoned, the 'nuclei' disappeared, and membership of factory committees was changed from co-option to election from branch committees. These measures gave greater (though still limited) powers to the rank and file.

However, these were, by and large, changes of secondary significance. The nonaccountability of the Party's high command to its membership, the vertical structure of power and the Leninist principles of discipline and democratic centralism remained largely untouched by these reforms. Furthermore, as if to counterbalance any centripetal forces these reforms might have unleashed, a series of new 'control bodies' was introduced (the federal control commissions and *collegi dei sindaci e dei probiviri*), whose function was to ensure adherence to Party rules and strengthen the disciplinary powers of the leadership.[38]

For the PCI, however, internal problems were overshadowed by yet another traumatic event perhaps even more unsettling than Khrushchev's revelations: the Hungarian uprising. Alarmed by the dissident forces released by the Tito heresy in Yugoslavia and by Khrushchev's speech, the Soviets fought a bitter rearguard action to preserve their domination in Eastern Europe. They threatened Poland, and in November sent tanks to crush the new Hungarian regime in Budapest after its leader, Imry Nagy, had announced in October that Hungary would withdraw from the Warsaw Pact. The uprising ended with the shelling of insurgent centres in the city and the escape of over 200,000 refugees to the West. The Soviet authorities subsequently broke their pledge of safe conduct and executed Nagy and other prominent leaders of what was perhaps the first truly anti-Stalinist communist party.

While the PCI leadership half-heartedly supported the Moscow line that this was a counterrevolution organised by foreign and domestic reactionaries, the communist leadership of the trade-union movement and many communist intellectuals openly sided with the Hungarian insurrectionaries. Like many other communist parties, the PCI suffered a major decline in the wave of disillusionment that ensued. Between 1956 and 1960 some 12 per cent of the membership abandoned the PCI (whose numbers dropped from 2,035,353 to 1,789,269); the number of cells dropped from 56,044 to 39,852 (a fall of 29 per cent), and a 'mortifying inertia' gripped local Party activity everywhere (Massari, 1982: 174).

These events led to the almost complete dismantling of the Leninist cell structure in the early years of the 1960s. PCI leaders had concluded, it seems, that cells were no longer the embodiment of a genuine revolutionary intent, and that 'de-Stalinisation' was in any case a good policy. More importantly, as Tiersky points out (1985: 123), it was generally agreed that 'the Party's "war of position" strategy was ill-served by the cell network', which tended to isolate Party members in small, local groups rather than create points of presence through which the Party could reach the wider public.

Party Organisation during the Period of Capitalist Boom

War and Fascist autarky had held back Italy's economy for 20 years, so that on entering a Europe-wide market, tremendous impetus was given to urbanisation and industrial growth. From 1953 to 1963 Italy witnessed an economic growth unparalleled since the initial phase of industrialisation at the beginning of the century. Average yearly growth of GNP was 5.3 per cent during the period 1951–58; 6.6 per cent 1958–63, and a staggering 8.3% in 1960–1.[39] Within a decade Italy was transformed from an agricultural society to a leading industrial state.[40] This transformation was characterised by a massive internal and external migration, rampant, unplanned, uneven development, rapid urbanisation and a huge exodus from the land and from underdeveloped southern regions to the prosperous North, especially the industrial triangle of Turin, Milan and Genoa. These changes, in turn, had far-reaching social consequences, including the destruction of established communities, the decline of the peasantry, the emergence of a vast new proletariat, changes in work patterns and the status of women, and the spread of mass communications – television, particularly – breaking into established leisure patterns and social habits.

The PCI suffered heavily during this social transformation as the disruption of community life made political organisation difficult. Worse, the social categories disappearing most rapidly (landless peasants and *mezzadri* sharecroppers) were precisely those from which the Party traditionally drew its largest body of support. This also dealt a blow to communist-party theory, for though the proletariat was burgeoning, few were being drawn into its supposed 'vanguard'. The long-awaited crisis of capitalism simply had not occurred. Party leaders accepted this without hiding the fact – they had to, for, in Ferrarotti's (1978: 52) words,

> They could not rely on the model of the Eastern European economy – using the justification that capitalism doesn't work – without jeopardizing their credibility among their working-class followers, who by now were driving around in Fiat 500s all over the country.

Meanwhile, the Party's collateral organisations, including its trade-union confederation (CGIL), were in dangerous decline. High levels of unemployment coupled with an influx of nonunion labour from the countryside presented formidable obstacles for the labour movement. Furthermore, it was the policy of private enterprise to try to deepen the divisions within the labour movement. In 1948, in collusion with the Christian Workers' Association (the ACLI), the Christian Democrat government and the American state department and CIA, the Catholics split away from the CGIL to form a pro-Catholic trade union, the CISL (Marzani, 1980: 140). The following year the Social Democrats and Republicans, organised another union, the UIL. The policy of employers, therefore, was to strengthen the Catholic and social democratic unions against the communist and socialist ones. There was a concerted campaign against left-wing trade unionists, involving the sacking of communist shop stewards, the blacking of known Party members and their assignment to the most demanding jobs in the most enclosed sections of the plants (Sassoon, 1986: 43). Throughout the early 1950s the CGIL suffered major defeats in the elections for shop stewards and a massive decline in its membership, which dropped, in the case of Fiat, from 79 per cent of the workforce in 1948 to just 21 per cent in 1958 (Marzani, 1980: 140).[41] Outside Italy, too, in Budapest, Warsaw and Poznań (June 1956), strikes and riots occurred as a wave of dissatisfaction with the cost of living and Soviet 'exploitation' swept through much of Eastern Europe. Communism was faced with a bewildering paradox: the working class were in revolt, not against the excesses of capitalism, but against socialism. The proletariat were being arrested, silenced, beaten up and killed, not by the reactionary forces of imperialism but by their own 'workers' police' for denouncing their own Workers' State. Nowhere in Marxist-Leninist theory was such an event possible.

Somewhat belatedly the PCI began seriously to question how the Party should react to new social forces. Once again, Party strategy favoured the section as the structure best suited to promoting maximum contact with society.

1968 and after: the Dilemmas of Party Organisation Continue

Surprisingly, the 1970s saw a marked reversal of the PCI's decline – contradicting many of the theories of political sociologists which predicted the inevitable and irreversible decline of the mass party.[42] Rather than wither, the PCI managed to strengthen and expand its ties with society, though more so in areas where the communist presence was already strongly established than in previously unpenetrated zones (hence, the consolidating of PCI hegemony). This was reflected most notably in the large gains made in the administrative elections of 1970, and in 1975 when for the first time communists gained control of most of the major cities north of Naples.

Though sections were now flourishing, the idea of the territorial organisation was again challenged by the New Left. Throughout Italy new movements (women's, students', youth, workers', the unemployed and the homeless) were developing, but *outside* the Party. PCI sections appeared incapable of attracting or articulating these interests. The '*Manifesto* Group', which was subsequently expelled from the Party for factionalism, highlighted the problem:

> The territorial section is perfectly adequate for a type of political struggle, such as that during the 1950s, which runs on a double platform of electoral growth and the prospect of insurrection; that is, for the type of politics that makes propaganda work, the formation of cadres and the defence of basic interests, the primary tasks of the Party ... But when the social and political situation changes, when the task of the Party becomes that of promoting and leading a collection of movements for specific struggles (e.g. workers' or students' struggles) ... the section loses its capacity to represent or lead the real class struggle.[43]

According to the *Il Manifesto* critique (Magri and Maone, 1974), Party sections consistently failed to give priority to the problems of factories and schools, and that is why they were unable to create a real movement and became consumed by routine bureaucratic activities like fund-raising and issuing membership cards. Organisation was thus preventing the PCI from addressing the real points of class conflict and from performing its role as political vanguard. While some PCI members shared these criticisms and abandoned the Party to join protest movements, most PCI leaders dismissed them, arguing that problems of schools and factories all have a territorial dimension and that the section is the best instrument for achieving a broader political unity in pursuit of the goal of forging social alliances. Hence, in effect, the spirit of the popular front continued to shape Party organisation.

Since the 1970s the PCI has continued this policy, and the section has become even more firmly established as *the* basis of Party organisation, while the old-style workplace cell has all but disappeared as a unit of political organisation. The leadership has also encouraged greater links between sections and more expression of the opinions of the base on 'all matters concerning the life of the Party' – from federal budgets and expenditure, to organisational changes, and nominations for posts as Party functionaries. In effect, only in the late 1970s, and with increasing pressure from below, did the Party's Central Committee recommend giving the mass membership more say in Party policy.

Party leaders continue to speak of 'opening up the Party', and to recommend more sections for the South. They also began to research ways of increasing the Party's standing among new social categories – white-collar technicians, clerical workers, computer operators and managerial staff. To these ends, sections were once again urged to increase recruitment in order to close the member-to-voter gap (now approximately 1 to 7) and to further ties with the popular movements. Women's commissions were established to link the Party with the feminist movement. Seminars, courses and study groups were initiated to attract more young people to the Party. These attempts to revitalise local Party organisation proved relatively successful – as shown by the increase in membership (until 1978, when it fell again by 23,000) and in the PCI's electoral growth to 34 per cent of the vote in 1976.

At the 15th PCI Congress in 1979, a new definition of Party sections was coined; they were now 'autonomous bodies of political direction and initiative' having the right to take 'independent positions on all national and international political problems'. The 17th Congress (1989) went further still in its new Party statutes, which declared that 'every Party member has the right to criticise the political conduct of Party leaders and organisations' and, moreover, 'to maintain, even in public, positions different from those of the majority'.[44] However, this apparent invitation to break unity and Party discipline is tempered, if not contradicted, by the statement that 'a decision assumed by the majority must be respected by the minority' (ibid.: 8, Article 6.6).

In the most recent campaign to 'open up' the Party, the 1989 Congress also ratified a new kind of 'thematic' Party section. These were modelled neither on workplace cells nor on territorial organisations, but were intended to be loosely based centres for political initiative, organised around specific themes, including green politics and the battle against drugs, and open to anyone. In the light of this some observers would argue, ironically, that after a span of 65 years the PCI has come full circle, back to its old socialist model of organisation. However, the PCI still carries in its organisational frame the indelible stamp of its Leninist origins, and, though less evident today, the conflict between its socialist and Bolshevik heritages nevertheless continues. The point is summed up by Massari (1982: 183):

> How much, however, the development of democratic life, not in terms of general participation but in terms of the possibility to shape effective decision-making, can reconcile itself with democratic centralism ... is naturally an unresolved question.

5

The PCI–Soviet Rift and the Internal Party Debates of 1983

PCI–Soviet Relations since the 1960s

A bitter dispute flared up between the PCI and the Communist Party of the Soviet Union (CPSU) following the declaration of martial law in Poland in 1980. This row was bound to affect the internal life of the PCI, but its repercussions also overshadowed other developments within the Party. In particular, it coincided with growing demands for more internal democracy and open debate (*trasparenza*). The row dominated internal Party debates throughout 1981 and was still the foremost issue at the 16th national PCI Congress (Milan, March 1983), for it brought to a head one of the most fraught issues in the whole history of Italian communism, questioning the PCI's strained ties with Soviet communism and its identity as a revolutionary Communist Party.

PCI leaders had accepted and endorsed the Soviet suppression of the Hungarian uprising in 1956, even though the issue had provoked heated disagreements within the Party. But the Warsaw Pact-led invasion of Czechoslovakia and suppression of Dubček's attempt to build 'socialism with a human face' it condemned outright. The PCI leadership vowed after 1968 that never again would Soviet military imperialism be condoned, and it renewed its condemnation every year on the anniversary of the Prague Spring invasion. Since 1968 the PCI's stance toward the CPSU had grown increasingly critical and independent.[1] But with the invasion of Afghanistan in 1979 followed by the suppression of the Polish trade union Solidarity this rift developed into an open split marked by an exchange of vigorous denunciations. The culmination of this process was the PCI's conclusion that the Soviet regime was degenerate and that Soviet communism was an historically spent force (see below).

Condemnation of Soviet policy in Afghanistan also came from the Eurocommunist parties of Great Britain, Spain, Belgium, The Netherlands, Sweden and Greece, but none carried their criticism and analysis quite as far as the PCI. In an article carried by *L'Unità* in January 1982, Berlinguer repeated his condemnation of the Soviet Communist Party and set out what was to be a major new perspective, not only on Soviet communism but on the whole history of the socialist movement. Most damning of all was the conclusion that 'the propulsive drive that animated the Bolshevik revolution and the development of Soviet Socialism has now been exhausted.'[2] Berlinguer's article also spoke scathingly about the 'grip of authoritarianism' and 'serious regression' in Eastern Europe.[3] On 21 December 1981 the PCI Central Committee adopted a 17-page resolution which stated, *inter-alia*, that:

1. Trade unions must be independent, even in a socialist society;
2. Democracy and socialism are inextricably linked and that the October Revolution had lost its impetus;
3. The Polish crisis was due to the hierarchical rigidity and dogmatism of the Polish Communist Party;
4. The Soviet model of socialism had proved itself to be inapplicable to Eastern Europe since its unitary character discouraged change;
5. The existence of military power blocs should not be used as a pretext for the suppression of demands for freedom.[4]

This provoked a heated exchange in the official press of the two communist parties.[5] The PCI leadership argued that the Polish crisis called for a thorough analysis and critique of Soviet-style socialism. It accused the CPSU of errors in the economic field; of 'forced development, authoritarian centralisation', and 'bureaucratisation'; of 'the Party-State, the monolithic outlook, the loss of the Party's specifically political function, Marxism distorted into a State ideology' (PCI Central Committee, 1982a: 14). It went even further, claiming that in Soviet practice Marx's critique of ideology had been stood on its head, and ideology had taken the place of reality. The CPSU, it stated,

> has created a sort of 'credo' – Marxism-Leninism, so called, conceived of as an ossified body of doctrine of a near metaphysical type; a set of formulas that are there to provide the reason for and guarantee of a type of political-economic structure, a universally valid model to which real situations and social subjects have to conform, and which the Party – as an iron principle – must bring about or impose (ibid.).

The CPSU counterattacked with a series of scathing articles in *Pravda*. These denounced the PCI's position as nothing short of a 'direct assault against the peoples of the countries of victorious Socialism' and 'those most active in the struggle for world peace'.[6] The charge laid against the PCI leadership was that, by criticising the countries of 'existing socialism' (*i paesi di socialismo reale*), and by siding with the 'right-wing Polish extremists of Solidarność', it had effectively joined the 'class enemy' and the forces of world imperialism. Wittingly or not, the PCI leadership was 'helping anticommunism' and all those forces 'that are hostile to the cause of social progress'. It was the PCI rather than the CPSU that had 'lost its perspective'. According to Soviet leaders, this was because the PCI was gradually abandoning the revolutionary Marxist-Leninist platform:

> Despite what it seems, all the sophisticated theoretical and political 'innovations' used by representatives of the PCI (the 'third way', 'Eurocommunism', 'union of the European Left', 'third phase'), were aimed to conceal this renunciation, to hide the essence of it from the eyes of the working class and Communists in their own country.[7]

The PCI's critique raised a crucial question concerning Marxist-Leninist orthodoxy and, in particular, the notion of the 'leading role' of the Soviet Union and the supremacy of 'Leninist concepts of Socialist democracy'. As Marzani (1980: 3) wrote,

> Within Western mores, these concepts were neither Socialist nor democratic. If to Eurocommunists Socialism meant both political and economic democracy, then a challenge to Soviet authority was inevitable.

The official Soviet line, however, was simply that the concept of Eurocommunism 'is erroneous'. In a review of Santiago Carrillo's book, *Eurocommunism and the State*, the Soviet weekly magazine *Novoe Vremya* ('New Times') put the position bluntly: 'There is only one Communism. Its foundations were laid by Engels, Marx and Lenin and its principles are adhered to by the present-day Communist movement.'[8]

Communist Orthodoxy and the Challenge to Soviet Hegemony

From a comparative and historical perspective there are interesting parallels here with the doctrinal schisms that split the Christian world during the Protestant Reformation four centuries earlier. The pattern of events is similar: Luther leads the revolt against corruption in the doctrine and discipline of the Catholic Church; the Church's claim to exclusive moral and spiritual authority is increasingly challenged by Protestant reformers; the Church tries to reassert its hegemony with the official decree that 'no innovations in religion are permissible'; Luther defies this and nails his famous 'Ninety-five Theses' to the church door at Wittenberg; finally, the Church summons Luther to trial, finds him guilty of heresy and excommunicates him. Luther, however, retaliates by publicly burning the bull of excommunication – a dramatic act that undermines Papal authority still further. Perhaps the Lutheran doctrine of the 'priesthood of all believers'[9] finds its closest analogy in Togliatti's concept of 'polycentrism' – the PCI assertion that each communist party must find its own path to socialism.

The analogy can be pursued further:[10] like the sixteenth-century Roman Catholic clergy, the CPSU tried to reassert its supremacy by dismissing its critics as heretics and traitors. The Diet of Worms convoked by Pope Leo X to put Luther under the Ban of the Empire and reassert discipline finds parallels in the 1969 Moscow conference of communist parties. With Soviet tanks in Czechoslovakia, the CPSU was sharply condemned by the Spanish, French and Italian communist parties. China, Yugoslavia, North Vietnam, North Korea, Albania and The Netherlands refused to attend, and only 60 parties signed the final conference declaration without objections or reservations. The PCI defiantly refused because the Soviet Union would not accept a statement approving 'alternative models' of socialism. Having lost prestige in 1969, the CPSU pushed for another world conference of communist parties, this time in Berlin (July 1976), but again the conference only undermined Soviet influence still further.

The Berlin conference of 1976 was a landmark in communist history, for it marked the official end of Soviet hegemony.[11] A small but nevertheless important sign of this was the conspicuous exclusion of at least four major tenets of Soviet orthodoxy from the conference's final document: for the first time, there was no 'Marxism-Leninism', no 'dictatorship of the proletariat', no 'proletarian internationalism' and no 'struggle against anti-Sovietism'. Instead, the PCI formula of 'International solidarity' was adopted, as was the Eurocommunist thesis that communist parties should develop, 'basing themselves on the great ideas of Marx, Engels, and Lenin, but strictly preserving the equality and sovereign independence of each party: noninterference in each other's internal affairs and freedom to choose their different roads in the struggle for progressive social change and for Socialism' (Marzani, 1980 : 17).

The decline of Soviet hegemony was again highlighted in April 1980, at the Paris meeting of European communist parties still 'loyal' to Moscow, when nearly half the Western communist parties, as well as those of Yugoslavia and Romania, boycotted the meeting. The self-professed 'Eurocommunist' parties now openly disputed Soviet supremacy and rejected the principles espoused in the Brezhnev Doctrine, which stipulated 'communist interdependence' and 'limited sovereignty for Warsaw Pact nations'.[12] The PCI followed this with a major ideological critique, according to which the world socialist movement had now entered a 'new era'. This was what Berlinguer meant by the 'third way' (*la terza via*):

> It is not a case of seeking a middle way between Socialism and capitalism. We are talking about the supersession of capitalism in the stage it has reached here in the industrialised and developed West, by building a Socialism that is achieved in the guarantees of the safeguarding of the democratic freedoms already won and their further development.[13]

Berlinguer's argument was developed within a typical Marxian–historicist perspective. The whole history of socialism was recast into a new analytical framework, according to which the 'first historic phase' began with the development of trade-union and left-wing movements toward the end of the last century. This fell into crisis after the outbreak of World War I and the collapse of the Second International, but the movement was renewed by the October Revolution of 1917. With the successful conquest of power by Lenin's Bolshevik Party, a second phase of history was effectively 'grafted' onto the first. But that, too, is now over, and the dying of the light in the Soviet East has heralded a new dawn in the West, its epicentre being the workers' movement of Western Europe.[14]

Not only did Berlinguer's critique condemn current Soviet foreign policy and the degeneration of the Soviet system, but it also judged Soviet-style communism itself as historically defunct. It had consigned Soviet communism to the famous graveyard or 'scrapheap' of communist history. And having tolled the bell for the death of the Bolshevik era, Berlinguer was, in effect, rewriting history in order to cut all the more decisively the PCI's moorings with Soviet communism.

Moscow's response was to try to ostracise the leadership of the Italian Party from the communist community. Relationships between the two parties reached an all-time low after 1982, yet despite the strain the PCI never sought formally to sever diplomatic links. Instead it insisted that 'normal relations' with the CPSU be maintained 'without ideological preference or prejudice'. What was particularly grating from Moscow's viewpoint was the PCI's assertion that it would seek the same kind of relations with socialist and progressive groups as with other communist parties, and it subsequently called upon the Western European Left to take the lead in the worldwide advance of socialism. That was, to date, the most vivid sign of what appeared to be the PCI's abandonment of the communist world in favour of its growing ties with Western European socialist parties.[15] The PCI appeared to be seeking not simply greater autonomy within the Moscow-centred communist movement, but total disengagement from it. The PCI had, as Urban (1986: 316) wrote, 'thus repudiated once and for all the fundamental Leninist demarcation between communism and social democracy'.[16]

In response to these measures, the Soviet Union tried to stir up dissent within the PCI rank and file, and towards the end of 1980 the pro-Soviet wing of the Party launched an official information bulletin entitled *Interstampa*.[17] The aim of this, beyond publicising the activities of East European regimes, was to establish links with those nuclei of Italian communists 'more faithful to the Kremlin than to Botteghe Oscure'.[18] Significantly, the editor of this magazine was subsequently 'radiated' from the PCI.[19]

Impact of the PCI–Soviet Rift on the Party Rank and File

Severing its ties with the Soviet Union caused problems of internal disruption for the PCI, for though most of the leadership supported the new Party line, it had not yet reconciled this with the Party's mass membership, much of which remained defiantly loyal to the Soviet model of communism.

Since the PCI's publicly critical stand, which began with Berlinguer's speech to the 25th CPSU Congress in 1976, many commentators questioned whether the PCI leadership spoke for the whole Party. Within the PCI many groups disagreed with the leadership, particularly on the issue of the Soviet invasion of Afghanistan. Dissent was minimal, however, among Party cadres. In fact, the January 1982 resolution summarising the official position of the Party was approved overwhelmingly by the Central Committee. But in answer to reports of internal conflicts amongst National Executive (*Direttivo*) members, the Party leader, Emanuele Macaluso, admitted:

> Of course there are conflicts. But how far should we publicise them? The issue arose for us back at the time of the Eleventh Congress and the conclusion we reached then was as follows: open and public debate in the Central Committee and a frank but confidential debate in the National Executive.[20]

Many members opposed this formula for regulating conflict. This was an old bone of contention upon which the Party leadership had always been notoriously rigid, as evidenced, for example, in the expulsion of the *Manifesto* group from the Party in 1969 for contravening these norms. Once again problems of conflict and cohesion were resurfacing under a new guise. Five days before Berlinguer's report to the Central Committee, *L'Unità* (6 July 1983) published an article, 'How I Disagree with the Party Document on Poland', written by Armando Cossutta, lifelong Party official and member of the National Executive. In Cossutta's opinion the PCI's pre-Congress policy document 'failed to reach the necessary unitary conclusions'. He criticised the Party leadership's position in unusually sharp terms. For Cossutta, the document meant:

> Not only a shift, a turning point, but a rupture with our tradition and our history. In effect the resolution 'eliminates' all Socialist Societies hitherto created! ... Does this not mean that what the resolution expresses is not a distancing or criticism of the CPSU and other parties but rather a desire for a real rupture?

Cossutta's question struck a chord of sympathy with a substantial part of the membership. In October he carried criticism further by publishing a book, *Lo Strappo* (translated, 'The Tear', or 'Rip'), which outlined the reasons for his opposition. He then delivered a guarded speech to the Central Committee suggesting that the leadership might use unfair methods to select candidates for the Congress and thus undermine his efforts to rally substantial support. Cossutta knew his views commanded widespread sympathy within the Party membership, particularly amongst the more traditional elements. Since his chances rested mostly on backing at the mass level, his preoccupation with the composition of Congress was justified.

Opinion varied on the extent of dissent among the membership. One clue came from the Soviet paper *New Times* which received large numbers of letters from Italian readers expressing their solidarity with the CPSU and blaming the PCI leadership for the break. An ideological collision was brewing; to many observers it looked as if the PCI might be poised on the brink of a major, perhaps catastrophic, schism.[21] At section-level, my fieldwork revealed hostility between the leadership and the rank and file. Also evident was a widening generation gap between older members and younger cohorts.[22] Ideological divisions often paralleled generational differences and Party leaders were wary of the dangers to Party unity posed by this growing polarisation.[23]

In November and December 1982 a series of pre-Congress debates was held so that members could air their views on the latest Party document and the Cossutta critique. These debates were important not only to those who attended, but to the future of the PCI itself, as it shifted toward a new definition of itself, and as the final defeat of the pro-Soviet wing began.

From 'Historic Compromise' to 'Democratic Alternative': Attitudes of the Membership to Changes in Party Strategy

Between December 1982 and January 1983, in over 12,000 Party sections, Italian communists were attending their local section congresses to elect new executives and nominate delegates for the forthcoming 17th national Party Congress in March 1983. The purpose of these assemblies was also to discuss, amend and ratify the Central Committee's draft policy document.[24]

In Perugia, at Piazza Grimana section,[25] as elsewhere, several pre-Congress meetings had been held throughout November to arouse interest in the PCI's policy statement, but most of these meetings had been poorly attended, and the new document was greeted with little enthusiasm. Even the most highly publicised of these meetings had attracted only 26 members – fewer than a quarter of the section's membership – and instead of enthusiastic support it had aroused mainly animosity. That meeting occurred on 30 November, exactly two days after the publication of the long-awaited Party thesis in *L'Unità*. Since no one had yet fully read the document, the secretary and Mandarini – an 'invited' speaker from the federation[26] – explained its basic contents. The 'Democratic Alternative' was the slogan for the new Party line. This, according to the Party speaker, meant a radical departure from previous policy, particularly the old idea that an alliance with the Christian Democrats was a necessary precondition for the attainment of power. To explain this requires a little background information.

Throughout the 1970s, PCI strategy was that of the 'Historic Compromise' (*compromesso storico*), which was based upon the view that a governmental truce had to be worked out between communists and Catholics (and more specifically the Christian Democrats) if the immobility and instability of the Italian political system were to be overcome. More importantly, the CIA-backed coup in Chile in 1973 was a warning to the PCI, for it demonstrated that imperialism was still aggressive and dangerous. Chile's President Allende, it seemed, had forced the pace of economic and political change without taking prior measures to buttress Chile's fragile democracy against a possible right-wing backlash, which was precisely what had occurred. The implications for Italy were deeply disturbing.[27] Reflecting on the events in Chile and drawing lessons from the Party's own bitter experience in the 1920s, Berlinguer concluded that even if the Left in Italy won 51 per cent of the vote, it would still be unable to hold office in Italy. In his view, open confrontation between the PCI and DC would lead to 'a true and proper division of the country in two, which would be fatal for democracy and would overthrow the very basis for the survival of the democratic State itself' (Berlinguer, 1975: 653). He therefore urged communists to reappraise Christian Democracy and to tease apart its internal contradictions in order to promote its more 'popular, anti-Fascist, democratic and unity-orientated components' and isolate its narrow-minded, sectarian and conservative elements.[28]

A political compromise with the Christian Democrats thus became the core of PCI strategy after 1973. This, however, was always highly controversial, and it created fierce disputes within the Party, not least because many members felt it had been imposed upon them from above with little prior consultation, as indeed it had been. Berlinguer's assessment of the Italian political scene remains a highly contested issue. For some observers it was a lost opportunity, a pitiful strategem whose cowardice and caution were tantamount to a betrayal of the Italian Left.[29] More generous critics argue instead that the climate of political instability, the weakness of the Left and the genuine threat of some form of authoritarian solution to the crisis of power made the Historic Compromise in 1973 both logical and understandable. However, the view of the rank and file in 1983 was distinctly hostile and ungenerous. 'Historic Compromise' almost invariably carried with it pejorative connotations. It had been a gross error of judgement for which the influential Party figures Rodano and Napolitano, rather than Berlinguer, were held responsible. In reply to criticism Napolitano argued that the Historic Compromise had been 'misunderstood' as 'a governmental agreement with the leaders of the DC when it meant in fact something much broader'[30] – namely, a reconciliation in the name of national unity between the polarised forces of Catholicism and communism. But this interpretation was often equally unpopular with the membership. As one local Party veteran expressed it dismissively, 'You can't make socialism with priests.'[31]

Now in 1982 the Party line was changed. 'Democratic Alternative' meant the Party had officially closed the phase of the 'Historic Compromise'.[32] The Christian Democratic Party was once more the enemy. The document spoke of a 'unity of the Left', suggesting an alliance with the Socialist Party in opposition to the Christian Democrats, though, like the Historic Compromise, the precise meaning of the PCI's 'Left-alternative' was ambiguous. For pragmatic leaders, including Reichlin and Napolitano, it meant a piecemeal approach of immediate political reforms, emphasising parliamentary cooperation with the parties of the 'lay Left', particularly the PSI.[33] But, for the left-wing Ingrao current, 'Left-alternative' signified something more radical: cooperation at the level of popular movements and mass mobilisations which would provide the subsequent basis for parliamentary cooperation. This approach was similar to the Comintern's 'popular-front' strategy, but differed in that the new coalition of popular forces was to consist largely of disparate and marginal groups such as pensioners, the unemployed, youth movements, lesbian and gay movements, unskilled migrants from the South and a plethora of popular radical organisations (ecologists, feminists, anti-nuclear campaigners, and pacifists). The aim was to integrate subordinated and oppressed groups into the political process, using this 'social bloc' as a force to stimulate gradual socioeconomic reforms and galvanise other progressive parties into a governmental alliance.[34]

In Perugia, the local Party was excited by the news that Berlinguer, in a television interview given the night before, had announced that the PCI *would* now go into government should the Left win 51 per cent of the vote. Some members felt elated by this reversal of policy, for it signalled an end to the politics of compromise and retreat. Others, however, felt angry about the arbitrary way the decision was reached without any consultation with the membership.

In Piazza Grimana section, therefore, the Party's 'Democratic Alternative' was summarised in vague terms by the local Party secretary as a 'an outline of the strategy for overcoming the electoral impasse'. It was defined as a strategy for winning electoral consensus, for forging new alliances, for coming to terms with the changes in class composition brought about by developments in technology and communications, and for gaining the support of the new and emerging social movements such as feminism, ecology, progressive Catholicism and other nonaligned radical groups. But, above all, it meant uncompromising opposition to the corrupt Christian Democrat system of power.

Older members saw it differently: for them, it meant official repudiation of an unpopular policy imposed on them by the leadership; the final nail in the coffin of the Historic Compromise, which they had always opposed. An attitude of 'we said so all along' prevailed throughout the meeting, eventually precipitating a row between Mandarini and an elderly member of the section's extremely large pro-Soviet wing, who used the occasion to criticise various policies of the Party leadership, which Mandarini, a former secretary of the Perugia federation, represented.[35] Mandarini adopted the hierarchy's position, arguing that, 'historically', the Historic Compromise had been the correct decision in the light of 'concrete conditions' at that time. For this he came under fire from all quarters, and, in a moment of weakness, admitted that he, too, had never really supported the strategy either. As a result of this mistake, the section rounded on him with a mixture of derision, criticism and a barrage of denunciations of the folly of the Party leadership. The result was not what the Party leadership had wanted. For the membership of Piazza Grimana, however, it was a small victory over the bureaucracy, and in the bar afterwards, conversation lingered triumphantly on the theme of how annoyed

Mandarini had been and how hypocritical were Party leaders who denounced past policy only when it was safe and fashionable to do so. By the time of the section congress four weeks later, there were still only a handful of members who had read the Central Committee document; probably no more than ten out of a membership of 150 was the secretary's estimate.

The Section Congresses of 1983: How the Soviet Question was Debated and Resolved

A whole weekend had been timetabled for Piazza Grimana section's congress which, in anticipation of a bigger turnout, was held in a large function room instead of the usual cramped section office. The room was cold and bare of furniture save a desk, an ageing, scratched blackboard and some 40 cheap, rickety wooden chairs. Two naked lightbulbs and a harsh neon strip light highlighted the stark and dingy atmosphere. Forty-one people were present (only five of them women and all but four over the age of 30): they sat huddled in their coats and scarves, hands thrust deep in pockets for warmth or clutching lighted cigarettes. At the front of the room a red PCI flag was draped across the secretary's desk as a makeshift rostrum, and three large painted portraits were mounted in a pyramid behind. At the top was Lenin, clutching his coat lapel and leaning forward from a podium, his hair windswept as he addressed the masses in St Petersburg Square. Below Lenin, a young and boyish-looking Togliatti and to his left, Joseph Stalin, slightly larger than life, smiling majestically, in army uniform with full military decorations. Piazza Grimana was the only section in Umbria, so members boasted, that had refused to remove its portrait of Stalin in the aftermath of 1956 and the PCI's efforts to de-Stalinise the Party. These portraits had been erected partly to placate the traditionalist element in the section, but more to give a sense of dignity and formality to the proceedings. Seated at the rostrum below Togliatti was Mandarini, once again sent to conclude the meeting.

Congress began without ceremony. The first item of business was election of the *presidenza*, the congress 'arrangements committee', whose job is to preside over congress and ensure that procedure is respected. The *presidenza* also nominates two commissions to carry out the assembly's work: an 'electoral commission', which draws up nominations for the new section executive, and a 'political commission', whose task is to summarise the section's collective view on the Central Committee's document and outline the section's plan of work for the coming year. Thus, the *presidenza*, though in theory only a 'caretaker' body until the new executive is elected, in fact, enjoys considerable power, particularly as it is nominated by the outgoing executive rather than elected from the floor. This practice exposes a peculiar flaw in PCI organisation, for it creates potentially ideal conditions for the self-perpetuation of a ruling elite: at all levels of Party organisation, including the Central Committee, new executives have been, in effect, nominated by the outgoing executive. In the past those ruling executives could usually rely on the unquestioning loyalty of the rank and file to ratify their nominees, but since 1985 the issue of who sits on the electoral commissions has become more openly contested from below.

At Piazza Grimana section, however, tradition prevailed, and there was no contestation of the nominations for the commissions, both of which were approved unanimously on a show of hands. The debate opened with the secretary's introductory speech. This commended the section for its achievements over the year before turning to the question of the Democratic Alternative, which was described enthusiastically as the 'clearest' and 'boldest' policy statement for a long time. Compliments were tempered with criticism of previous Party policy, particularly the 1979 'Government of National Unity', which was branded 'an alliance forged solely between Party heads with little regard for the mass following'. The main points of the document were then summarised as follows:

1. The phase initiated by the October Revolution was now finished.
2. European-style social democracy had produced no real solution to the problems of capitalism.
3. The logical synthesis of this was the *terza via* (Third Way) – neither Soviet communism nor social democracy – and the Democratic Alternative was an outline of the strategy for arriving at this road.

Given the numerical majority of the pro-Soviet wing in this section, the secretary made little reference to the controversial issues of Cossutta's amendment, the rift with Moscow or the claim that Soviet communism had exhausted its propulsive drive. Following this, a local government employee in his early 30s gave a long address from the secretary's desk. It consisted of a complex economic analysis of the international scene, commencing with Reagan's 'economic folly', the 'assault of American imperialism' and the implications of the dollar's rising value on Italy's economy. He went on to the national political scene and finally to the present state of affairs in Umbria 'where 33,000 people – 11 per cent of the working population – were currently unemployed. PCI strategy, he concluded, should focus on breaking the US dollar's stranglehold on Italy rather than on criticism of Soviet communism.

The next intervention, by a 50-year-old local-government employee, flatly rejected the Party document in a defiant speech that ended with the statement that 'Democratic Alternative' signifies 'bourgeoise democracy'. His response to Berlinguer's pronouncement on Soviet communism was that 'the phase of history begun by the October Revolution lives on!' The struggle against capitalism, in his view, remained unchanged, and socialism without recognition of the Soviet example was impossible.

Several others, including younger members, felt it necessary to 'defend' the October Revolution. The mood was best expressed by the comment of one member: 'If it wasn't for the Soviet Revolution we wouldn't *be* here today discussing communism or our Party's document.' This was met with nods of agreement from most quarters. Another intervention from a pensioner went further and criticised the leadership for unconcealed 'anti-Sovietism'. He attacked the Party leadership for betraying socialism and for being out of touch with the wishes of the Party rank and file. Mandarini reacted angrily, accusing the speaker of having made a 'photocopy' of the Cossutta amendment. It later transpired that the speech had, in fact, been written for him by the leader of the pro-Soviet wing of the Umbrian Party.

A further seven interventions were made that day, alternatively welcoming and rejecting the Central Committee's document, but a common point was that clarification was needed in order to spell out exactly what it meant in practice. Most members criticised it for being vague and imprecise, which it was. Each intervention was followed by a short silence: some people were thinking, others writing copious notes in preparation for their interventions, and still others reading or rereading the document. The meeting lasted five hours without interval, during which the room grew colder and still smokier. Each intervention followed a predictable, almost standardised format; a long, handwritten speech of several pages, beginning with the state of the world and the state of socialism in the current historical phase before progressing downwards from the state of the nation to that of the local situation in Umbria. The opening lines of each intervention also followed a ritualised pattern, with speaker after speaker announcing 'agreement with the last speaker' or the Party document before proceeding with his or her own points, often in total contradiction to both.[36]

Congress resumed the following day at 8.30 a.m. with more elderly members attacking Berlinguer's verdict on Soviet communism, backed up with condemnation of American imperialism under President Reagan. A total of 20 people spoke from the floor, but significantly only *one* actually formulated a proper amendment, and even that had nothing to do with the Soviet question but instead proposed that the Party adopt a more critical stance toward Israel in the light of the recent massacres in the Lebanese camps of Chatila and Sabra.

Triumph of the Party Leadership

Finally, Mandarini concluded the meeting, skilfully referring, in turn, to each speaker and the issues he or she had raised. He lingered on one member's earlier point about the inadequacy of the section's involvement in the inner city's problems of drugs, housing and the elderly. This, he had suggested, was part of the reason that the section was suffering an 'identity crisis'. According to Mandarini, this part of the city was 'one of the areas most devastated by capitalism in Italy', as he was sure some of the older comrades looking back over the changes in the last 30 years would well realise (a placatory gesture). He refuted the claim that the section had been idle in the neighbourhood, but he developed the theme of the section's 'identity crisis'. He blamed many factors but singled out as the main problem the section's failure to develop an identity consistent with the rest of the Party. The unstated message here was clear: the recalcitrant pro-Soviet old guard (or *filosovietici*) were responsible for the shortcomings of the local Party. He then turned to the criticisms of the Party document, particularly its definition of the 'Democratic Alternative' as a 'new programme, not bound by ideological preconditions'. Several members had objected strongly to the inclusion of this sentence on grounds that they had joined the PCI precisely *because* of its ideological preconditions. Their argument was that the PCI had an ideology; namely, Marxism, and they, at least, were proud to call themselves Marxist-Leninists.

Mandarini explained the Party position diplomatically. What was meant by this definition was 'a Marxist approach based on daily activity and on the situation of the country as we find it; the concrete reality as it *is*, not as some "ideal" would conceive it to be'. He then backed up this argument by producing two books and reading aloud a short passage from each. The first was by Engels, the second by Lenin, and both quotations gave a chapter-and-verse defence of the argument that a 'correct revolutionary strategy arises from the analysis of concrete situations and conditions'. 'This doesn't mean to say that we are denouncing ideology', he continued, 'only a certain type of rigidly dogmatic or inflexible interpretation of it.'

From this, Mandarini launched into more controversial themes. He told the congress that today 'the proletariat are no longer *the* revolutionary class' and that 'we must seek ways to place alongside our old conception the importance of the new emergent classes, those in the tertiary sector, the clerks and technicians.' This was not well received, but Mandarini left no time for interruptions; shifting the discourse to another topic and raising the tone of urgency in his voice, he reminded members of the general strike and the march in Rome that had been called for 18 December. If this congress did not 'reach an agreement and mobilize itself in order to support the trade unions', he warned, 'we will be responsible for the defeat of the working class.'[37]

Urgency was impressed on the audience even further: every day, he said, thousands of workers – women workers, too – are being sacked from their work. Every one of us', Mandarini implored, 'must dedicate our daily work to contributing to the struggle.' The task of the Party, he stressed, was to project the image of itself as the only credible party of government. It was to unify disaffected groups under the Party's banner, to capture the support of the masses – even those formerly aligned with the Christian Democrats. 'Capitalism and the bosses are still the main enemies', he continued, but they had both changed their character, and it was important to distinguish their new forms. Modern capitalism was now interested not in manufacturing, but in the money markets and stock exchanges. Industrial capitalism had been superseded by a new form of nonproductive, parasitical finance capitalism.

Winding to a close, he glossed over the failures of the other Western communist parties, in particular those in Spain and France, whose demise he linked to their inability to carry on the programme of reform they had initiated with the PCI in the late 1970s. 'Outside Russia and China', he stated, 'we are now the only part of the Third International that remains intact.' Finally, he attacked the Cossutta position in a series of angry rhetorical questions: 'What contribution does it make to the struggle in *Italy*? To the complex problems we have here, *now*, in *this situation*?' Mandarini's conclusion was that Cossutta's arguments were archaic and ultimately irrelevant.

After Mandarini sat down, a brief report prepared by the electoral commission was read. Twenty-three names for the new section executive were proposed[38] and then elected by an open show of hands. Only one member was opposed, but only because he thought the list too long. The political commission then read out its statement, which referred to 'impassioned moments' in the debate but failed to specify on which issues these had occurred. It was uninformative and noncommittal on the issue of the PCI–Moscow rift, stating only that the section looked forward to the National Congress and hoped for greater 'refinement' in the Party's international politics and in its judgement on the socialist bloc countries. The only criticism of the Party document to appear in the final record of the section congress concerned not the Soviet Union but a minor, locally sensitive point on the agricultural question.[39] The statement was put to the vote and approved unanimously; and, to sighs of exhaustion and relief, the secretary announced the assembly adjourned. As the older members of the section left, many still speaking of defiance of the Party leadership and congratulating each other on their interventions, one thing was clear: without any substantive amendments to its document, the Party leadership had, in effect, routed its pro-Soviet adversaries.

Part II

Communism and the Question of Democracy

Introduction

The previous chapters looked at the history of Italian communism, its character, its organisation and the way these have developed in relation to its evolving ideology and strategy. The following chapters develop these themes by exploring questions more overtly political and theoretical. In particular, they are concerned with Leninism and the problem all Leninist parties have in reconciling themselves with Western-style pluralist democracy (see Chapter 7).

To understand the problems faced by the Italian Communist Party, it is necessary to highlight some of the structural flaws inherent in communist theory itself and their antecedents in the Bolshevik revolution. Though I have stressed the specificity of Italian communism, the problems that the PCI has had to confront are also endemic to all those parties that are, or were, structured according to those principles of party organisation laid down by Lenin in 1921. These principles, and the ideology of organisation that they embody, represent the core of communist culture but perhaps also the fundamental source of its greatest failure.

From an analysis of the internal Party debates leading up to the 16th PCI Congress in 1983, an attempt is made to tease apart the mechanisms of coercion and control that shape the structure of power relations within communist systems. From here several critical questions are addressed concerning the nature and character of party bureaucracy, internal democracy, and the problem of oligarchy and authoritarianism in communist political culture. At the heart of the issue is the question of Stalinism and its explanation: Was Stalinism the result of a distortion of Party rules and a deviation from Leninist norms, or was it instead a consequence of those norms? This issue has haunted the communist parties of Europe since 1956, and few, if any, have provided a satisfactory answer. The hypothesis examined here is that the root of the problem lies in Leninism, and, in particular, in the communist theory of party organisation and the coercive mechanism of democratic centralism. This appears to be the ineluctable, though as yet unspoken, conclusion that many communists in Italy and elsewhere have been gradually drawn to. Seen in this light, the overriding theme in the post-war history of the PCI has been, in effect, its slow but steady escape from Leninism. The problem, however, is whether 'communism' can theoretically exist *without* Leninism', or, if not, what role there is for any communist party that has renounced its Leninist heritage.

6

Party Democracy and the Structure of Power Relations

The PCI–Soviet Split and the Question of Internal Party Democracy

Party meetings illustrate some of the tensions that exist between local sections and the Party leadership. These often crystallise in disputes over policy, but the tension is also perhaps peculiar to Party structure, particularly as the distance between leadership and base was becoming increasingly apparent in the late 1970s (Barbagli and Corbetta, 1978: 333–7). More importantly, these meetings illustrate the lines of social and political cleavage that continued to divide the PCI throughout the early 1980s.

Though Party rules prohibit factions within the Party, informal ideological currents clearly do exist, though they do not call themselves such.[1] What was noticeable in the early 1980s was the way these currents correlated with class and generational differences, particularly with the increasing polarisation between the Party apparatus and the 'old guard' within the rank and file. This was epitomised at local level by the row between Mandarini and the local Party traditionalists. This was not only a clash between different generations of Party activists, but also a conflict between what for many Italian pundits were two 'irreconcilable political cultures' within the PCI; a conflict of 'old-style Bolshevism' versus modern, democratic Eurocommunism. At another level the conflict reflected deeper historical contradictions in Party organisation and ideology, and it was perhaps another manifestation of PCI's old problem of 'duplicity' (*dopiezza*).[2] This time, however, the day of reckoning on that particular issue appeared to be dawning.

Conflict at section level pivoted largely around ideological differences that were epitomised by contrasting positions on the Soviet issue. But these ideological differences were further complicated by factors of class and status, and by local issues and personality conflicts. The pro-Moscow (*filosovietico*) wing of the Party represented a large body of opinion in the sections, but its strength was not reflected at higher levels. Most of its members were old veterans and former local activists who had joined the Party before 1956; many of them were now pensioners. For the most part they were solidly working-class and had little or no education – outside Party schooling – beyond primary level.[3] Politically, most were unashamedly 'Stalinist' and stuck proudly to what they saw as a firm and uncompromising Marxist-Leninist orthodoxy. Mandarini, in contrast, represented a different 'culture': a man in his early 40s, he had joined the Party in 1960 and had been radicalised through activism in the Young Communists and the trade-union movement. Politically, his was a generation formed after Khrushchev, Hungary, the Sino-Soviet split, the peace movement and the Cuban Missile crisis: a generation that was openly critical of, if not hostile to, Soviet communism.

During the early 1970s there had been a large turnover in Party cadres, which was both cause and consequence of a steady change in attitudes within the PCI. This had gradually shifted the balance of power and opinion in favour of younger, 'post-Stalinist' generations, such as Mandarini's. However, the leadership's declaration on the 'exhaustion' and political bankruptcy of Soviet communism went too far even in the eyes of many younger members. One has only to consider the lasting prestige and symbolic importance of Soviet communism within the Italian Left to understand this. Whereas in Britain the Soviet model of socialism captured and dominated the imagination of most of the Left in the 1930s,[4] in Italy it continued to dominate left-wing politics for at least two decades longer, lasting well into the 1950s and beyond.

For millions of PCI members who joined between 1920 and 1956, Soviet communism meant only one thing; the vanguard of socialism. The CPSU had led the first successful proletarian revolution, and it was the undisputed leader in the world struggle against imperialism and capitalism. However flawed, no one could deny that Soviet communism had created a new epoch in world history and that the principles underlying Lenin's state system, however deviant in practice, were inspired by the quest for peace, progress, emancipation and equality. For the PCI 'old guard', Bolshevism was the only communism they knew or cared to recognise. As one local pensioner put it, 'Why the "third way"? The "first way" was good enough for us.' What PCI leaders like Mandarini appeared to be saying was heresy to them and threatened the cause many had devoted their lives to. They were not likely to take it lightly.

What worried the Party leadership was the precise size of the pro-Soviet wing and the extent of its influence. Opinion polls conducted in 1983 showed that the *filosovietico* hard core amounted to 16 per cent – slightly down from the 18–20 per cent recorded in a similar poll held the previous March.[5] One survey question went to the heart of the matter and asked interviewees to choose one of five formulations describing the Soviet regime. Six per cent took the harshest view that 'the USSR is an expansionist country which is a threat to world peace.' Another 7 per cent went even further and agreed with the proposition that 'the Soviet Union is no longer a socialist country.' Forty-nine per cent agreed that the USSR 'has made great historical contributions, but its socialism is imperfect', which was roughly the Party's official line. However, 32 per cent believed that the Soviet Union 'counterbalances American imperialism and aids the people of the Third World'. The remaining 6 per cent agreed with the extreme pro-Soviet view that the USSR is 'an example of achieved socialism to be imitated'. As far as these polls went, there was little evidence, if any, of a massive rejection of Soviet communism.

Previous studies carried out in 1979 by Barbagli and Corbetta had confirmed the presence of a substantial 'Stalinist tradition' within the PCI, together with a small but growing element diametrically opposed to it.[6] This precarious and potentially explosive balance helps explain the timidity of the leadership's pronouncements on Eastern Europe following the 1968 Czechoslovak invasion. Their caution, according to Barbagli and Corbetta (1978: 938), was born out of a need to 'manoeuvre between two traditions, two political conceptions, two lines absolutely irreconcilable'. The survey showed that the majority of members who had entered the Party before 1956 were 'most certainly Stalinist', but also that this Stalinist tradition had 'left deep traces on a substantial part of those members who entered the Party in the 1970s' (ibid.: 936).

The same pattern emerged in Piazza Grimana section. On the issue of Poland, for example, the predominant viewpoint was totally contrary to the Party leadership's. According to most local members, the Polish dissidents were cowards (*Polacchi, vigliacchi*) who deserved whatever they got. The widely held view was that *Solidarity* was a counterrevolutionary, antisocialist organisation, backed by the CIA and Catholic Church, whose chief aim was to discredit and destablise communism in Eastern Europe, a view which was roughly the official Soviet position too. The PCI, in their view, was falling into a trap well prepared by the forces of capitalism to divide and split the communist movement.

How the Party Leadership Controls the Rank and File

Understanding exactly *how* the pro-Soviet wing came to be defeated in the local sections is equal in importance to, if not of greater importance than, understanding the consequences of their defeat. This raises several key considerations about the structure of power relations and democracy within the Party. In thousands of assemblies throughout Italy patterns similar to those at Piazza Grimana were emerging, as the new Party line was brought to the mass membership. In each local congress I attended during fieldwork, levels of debate were high, if somewhat formal, and a genuine exchange of views occurred. However, what counts in the end are not eloquent speeches from the floor but formalised policy, articulated amendments and the terms of the debate itself. On this latter point several members had tried to extend the debate to issues not included in the draft document, but they were rebuked and told that their task was to 'discuss the facts before them in the document'. This provoked criticisms against the restricted parameters for discussion and the way it militated against the rank and file. The criticism was valid: the leadership's documents effectively define the boundaries of what debates are permitted. Though some additions and subtractions to it are possible, the margins for substantive change are usually extremely small. As Amyot writes (1981: 29), once the leadership has launched a proposal, a fairly broad and open debate is allowed within the lower organs:

> However, this debate is unlikely to fundamentally alter the line pursued by the Party; its real purpose, in the eyes of the leadership, is to make the rank and file aware of the Party's line, to convince them of its correctness and to rebut any possible objections to it by encouraging their expression during the discussion. While the leadership must and often does take into consideration the opinions and humours of the mass membership, and these debates are a useful way of sounding out these opinions, the rank and file has no way of substantially correcting the main lines of Party strategy, which have already been decided.

Yet, despite the fact that ordinary members have little chance of altering proposals from the Central Committee, they devote hours if not days of painstaking work to analysing these proposals. In effect, the whole Party is consumed in the task of debating a document which is not even a general policy statement or draft manifesto, still less a programme for the implementation of actual policies, but merely an exposition of the Party's 'perspectives' on the 'Italian situation' *vis-à-vis* the rest of the world in the current era. It is one of the most fascinating examples of the manipulation of political symbolism to be found anywhere. The 'manipulation' lies in the fact that it fosters the *illusion* among ordinary members that they are active participants in the decision-making process – an illusion which they clearly do believe.[7]

From an anthropological perspective the whole structure of the Party Congress can be understood in terms of manipulated symbols. According to Cohen (1976: 8), symbols are essential for the maintenance of social order, but in order to work efficiently their social function must remain largely unconscious and unintended by the actors. In other words, their power lies largely in their mystique, not in their clarity. Political symbols are simply acts and objects (marches, flags, banners, posters), or concepts and linguistic formations (slogans, shibboleths) that 'stand ambiguously for a multiplicity of disparate meanings' and evoke emotions that impel people to action. Moreover, 'they usually occur in stylised patterns of activities like ceremonial, ritual gift exchange, prescribed forms of joking, taking an oath, eating and drinking together' (Cohen, ibid.: ix).

In short, 'ambiguity' is the hallmark of political symbols and the key to understanding how they work. This applies equally to the PCI Congress and document and the highly 'stylised' way debate is conducted. The

'Democratic Alternative' and 'Historic Compromise' are classic symbols in this sense; they are Italian shibboleths, linguistic formations that stand for a multiplicity of disparate meanings. They are also deliberately opaque. This is perhaps why so many different interpretations of Party policy exist, and are allowed to exist, at any one time. Ambiguity becomes a political tool: like most political parties, the PCI deliberately trades on symbols and avoids being too explicit about policy formulations wherever this might increase its vulnerability or limit its appeal to the maximum number of social groups. This is not as cynical as it seems, given that the PCI is trying to forge a new identity as a non-Bolshevik communist party. Such a task requires breaking new ground and inventing new concepts and labels, the meaning of which the Party itself may be unsure of.

Many rank-and-file members, however, reject the view that their role is passive and subordinate. They claim instead that the influence of local opinion is relative to its size and concentration. If the majority of sections in any given area were strongly critical of a Party proposal, their amendments would be carried to the provincial level where they would be pitched against the majority views of other sections. At this level another majority viewpoint would be reached and then carried to the national Party Congress. Inevitably, minority opinions tend to be crushed by the majority decision. Those who defend this system claim that if a clear majority against Party policy existed it would 'filter through' the committees and congresses to the centre of policy-making, where it would, in theory, be implemented. But the leadership's judgements on China in 1962, the Historic Compromise in 1973 and the Government of National Unity in 1979 are three major examples in which the membership was not consulted either before or after the decision.

Other factors combine to limit rank-and-file influence over Party policy. First, the agenda in Party assemblies is always furnished by higher Party organs. Seldom are motions initiated by the base, and even when they are, the leadership still decides on the parameters of debate. Moreover, the *structure* of Party motions militates against amendment or the expression of dissent. As Amyot (1981: 30) explains:

> They are usually omnibus documents covering everything from the current international situation to the organisational problems of the Party in the locality: they are also vague and imprecise on certain key points. Therefore the debate is often not focussed on particular issues and it is thus all the more difficult for dissent to crystallize.

With such stress on 'unity', open disagreement with a thesis, particularly one that has been approved, goes against both Party custom and the rule of democratic centralism. Dissent is therefore manifest in more circuitous ways; through euphemism, innuendo and veiled talk. Issues therefore often become blurred as minority viewpoints are disguised behind ornate, baroque language that even members themselves find inaccessible.

The leadership's control is also strengthened by the practice of sending Party functionaries to supervise and monitor key section meetings. These officials are usually far more politically astute and adept in persuasion and the machinations of power. The leadership is simply better positioned to dominate the mass membership by its monopoly of mechanisms of political control and consent.

Mechanisms of Control: Oratory and Manipulation of Party Procedure

Another mechanism of control is political oratory. As Seidel (1975: 225) observed while studying language use among the French Left, political discourses are 'symbolic manifestations of ideologies'. The very structure of these discourses often operates as a form of social control. Political speech, especially in formal settings, usually conforms to a set pattern, a kind of predetermined code, or what Bloch (1975: 11) calls a 'linguistic ritual'. Bloch's idea is that the 'formalisation' of oratory transforms certain speech acts into a form of power and coercion. Drawing his argument from tribal politics in Madagascar, Bloch found that certain codes are regarded as politically more significant than others because they draw upon 'customary and accepted sources of legitimacy'.[8] These key symbolic cross-references, which include images, anecdotes, concepts and metaphors, are drawn from a precise set of sources usually restricted to 'a body of suitable illustrations, often proverbs or scriptures', which tends to be orthodox and immutable (Bloch, ibid.: 15). Once a speech shifts into a 'formalized code', the discourse (and the speaker) becomes symbolically imbued with the authority and power of the source. It is as if the speakers, by adopting the correct procedure, had tapped a source of great power and in so doing had appropriated for themselves the symbols of legitimacy. By merging the 'specific into the fixed and eternal', the speakers made their words indisputable and sacrosanct. Communication is thus shifted 'to a level where disagreement is ruled out since one cannot disagree with the right order' (Bloch, ibid.: 16).

This is one way of looking at what happens in Party meetings. Bloch's 'formalised code' principle could be applied to some of the more sectarian and orthodox Marxist-Leninist parties, but it does not quite fit the PCI. Certainly there are formalised procedures and a fixed set of references in PCI discourse that are sometimes used to give legitimacy and authority to the speaker – such as 'class struggle', 'Gramsci' and 'as Togliatti said'. But, generally speaking, PCI discourse is not considered by Party members as either immutable or eternal. In fact, splitting from Soviet communism has meant breaking previously fixed patterns of discourse, defusing key symbols in the Leninist lexicon and inventing a new language – which time has yet to endow with *gravitas*.

However, good oratory is an important and highly esteemed quality in any

Italian political leader, particularly those seeking leadership status in the PCI. A very distinctive style of public speaking has developed within the PCI, particularly among experienced Party cadres, and this tends to be badly imitated by ordinary Party members, as witnessed in the ritualised congress interventions. This is another reason why the base is politically disadvantaged when confronting the leadership; by adopting the style of the Party cadre, ordinary members enter the leadership's frame of reference and use its terms of discourse. This means, in effect, that they are competing in a linguistic game they are less equipped for, whereas the 'other side' wrote the rules and acts as umpire.

In Piazza Grimana, as elsewhere, it was not simply lack of good spokesmen that explained why the pro-Soviet wing was beaten so easily, nor was it always that wing's failure to win the majority; very often it was because of its lack of organisation and ignorance of procedure. The attack on the Party's judgement on Soviet communism, for example, was widely supported in the section but not one of the membership's objections was formalised into an amendment upon which a vote could be taken. Because of the rules of democratic centralism and the prohibition of factions, the pro-Soviet tendency could not form an organised current without risking expulsion for 'factionalism'; therefore they had not organised. No pre-Congress caucus had been arranged, not even to explain the most elementary of procedural tactics, and the idea of the 'Model Resolution' introduced into the British Labour Party rank and file *against* the leadership, was unheard of and would have been treated as anathema. It was precisely here, in the old guard's inability to manipulate procedural rules, that their interventions came to nil.

In other section congresses, the leadership sometimes employed tactics similar to those used in the internecine struggles of the British Labour Party, such as continuing the meeting until many older members had gone home and then taking the vote when the pro-Soviet wing no longer had a majority.

Passive Tendencies of Rank-and-File Activists

The membership's ignorance of procedure manifests itself in other important ways. Analysis of the records (*verbali*) from the other 42 section congresses in the Perugia area showed some surprising results.[9] Attendance at section congresses ranged from as low as six per cent of the membership to as high as 75 per cent in the case of the university section. In one rural section the congress had to be cancelled when only two out of 63 members attended. On average, 20 per cent of the Party membership attended these congresses; that is, 1,503 members out of the total 7,412 in the Perugia area. So, for what is ostensibly the most important event in Party section life (electing its new executive, debating the Central Committee's document, and drafting the section's own policy statement), no more than one-fifth of the membership were actively involved.[10]

The average number of interventions was approximately 10 per section (414 in the 42 congresses). Of these only 25 (6 per cent) were made by women. Surprisingly, only in 8 of the 42 congresses were amendments of any kind made to the Party document: in the remaining 34 sections no alterations or amendments whatsoever were proposed. In most assemblies the only vote recorded was the statutary one approving the section's own statement, which usually 'welcomed' the Party line without commenting on any particular details. This sparsity of amendments indicates either remarkable consensus on the new Party line, or considerable passivity on the part of local Party activists. The impression given by the *verbali* was absolute conformity, but the reality was far from this.

At the next level of Party organisation, Perugia province, the pattern recurred. Out of 190 local Party congresses, 166 approved the Party document without amendment.[11] The remaining 24 congresses proposed between them 119 amendments, 63 of which were defeated. Only 56 amendments were therefore carried forward to the provincial congress. Ironically, virtually all of these were composed by the same few individuals, most of whom were not rank-and-file members but Party cadres and office holders. The usual response from the membership on this point was that leaders are expected to act as representatives or 'tribunes' articulating the membership's interests. But the question remains as to whether the interests of provincial-level cadres are the same as the mass membership, and, if not, whose side do they take when conflict arises between leadership and base?

Evidence from the section and provincial-level congresses suggests their interests are not the same. At the level of the Party base and in the local congresses, the key issues were Soviet communism and ideological 'revisionism', while in the provincial congresses the issue that overshadowed all others was the debate about internal Party democracy. From a class perspective this fact is significant as the PCI's provincial-level leadership is noticeably more middle-class, younger and better educated than its mass membership (Amyot, 1981: 28). According to the historian Covino (1979), there has been a marked '*embourgeoisement*' of the Party apparatus in Umbria since the early 1970s, which perhaps accounts for the disparity between the political concerns of the leadership and the base. In fact, most of the amendments brought to the provincial congress came not from the many sections scattered throughout the countryside, but from a handfall of sections in the *city* of Perugia, where there is a high concentration of middle-class professionals and intellectuals.

At each successive tier of Party organisation beyond the local sections, the defeat of the pro-Soviet wing was heavier. These congresses, in effect, concluded the 'revisionism' that PCI leaders had begun years earlier. Why this happened has already been considered, but *how* the PCI leadership managed such a major policy shift without splitting the Party and without shedding large numbers of members and supporters in a way that most of its European counterparts had been unable to avoid, is another matter.

The PCI leadership has on repeated occasions carried out dramatic and often highly unpopular policy changes without causing internal ruptures – its judgements on the Sino-Soviet split, the Historic Compromise and the Government of National Unity being cases in point. Even more startling was the PCI's reversal over NATO in 1974,[12] which culminated two years later in Berlinguer's conclusion that the Atlantic Alliance is 'a useful shield for building socialism in freedom'.[13] Such an abrupt policy U-turn would probably have provoked pandemonium in any other communist party, but it did not in the PCI, and this is significant.

Party Democracy and the Problem of Bureaucracy

Several factors help explain how the PCI leadership maintains control over its vast and politically heterogeneous membership, some of which have already been discussed:

- The membership's general ignorance of procedure.
- The machinery of discipline and the vertical chain of command inherent in Party structure compared with the weakness of its horizontal links.
- The rule of democratic centralism and the ban on minorities from organising themselves into 'factions'.
- The tactical superiority of the leadership in oratory and political skill, its general monopoly over the terms in which Party policy is debated and its specific control over the political agenda.
- The leadership's command over intellectual resources, particularly the Party media and communications, and its effective appropriation of Party history.
- The tradition of the provincial-level cadres presenting a united front when putting the Party line to the mass membership.
- The ideology of 'unity' and the rank and file's passive acceptance of the commanding role of its 'leadership'.

Ordinary Party members are placed in a subordinate, structurally determined position of weakness when confronting the leadership. To some exent this is common to many, if not all, large parties and bureaucratic organisations, however democratic they profess to be. At a more theoretical level this raises the broader question of whether democracy is compatible with the kind of bureaucracy and centralisation required of any mass party. According to the German sociologist Robert Michels, it is not. In his book *Political Parties* (1911), Michels developed the thesis that all organisations are subject to oligarchic domination; the 'iron law of oligarchy'. This general theory was used in the case of socialist parties to show that the same law applies even to those most committed to democracy, and to demonstrate why all radical parties of the Left become deradicalised as they grow in size.

Michels constructed his thesis from his own intimate knowledge of the

German Social Democratic Party (SPD), to which he had been committed in his youth, though he ended his intellectual career as a supporter of Mussolini. His argument ran as follows. Constitutionally, leaders of socialist party organisations are elected by their members, are accountable to them, and are expected to carry out their policies. But, inevitably, the leadership escapes from these constraints and acts autonomously. Several reasons are given. First, in order to organise a mass movement effectively it is necessary to have full-time leaders and a permanent apparatus of trained officials. Those elected to office acquire specialist knowledge and expertise not available to ordinary members. It becomes impossible for ordinary members to supervise the specialists, who take party decisions on their own initiative. As specialists, the party leaders become indispensable to the organisation. Furthermore, the leaders gradually become divorced from their working-class origins as their lives revolve around the privileged and rarefied environments of parliament or the Party executive. The specialised knowledge necessary for the leadership role confirms the position of the leaders, who end by accumulating influence over the organisation, and the information and procedures necessary for their continued election to executive positions. Added to these factors are external pressures on the organisation that make leadership stability a necessary factor for winning elections and competing in parliament.

Michels also maintained that the masses have a need to be led, partly for psychological reasons, but largely for practical ones, as they tend to be atomised and disorganised. The net result of all this is a self-perpetuating elite, divorced from the control of its members, whose radical goals it eventually substitutes for its own, more conservative ambitions. As Michels put it (1959: 373):

> Thus, from a means, organisation becomes an end. To the institutions and qualities which at the outset were destined simply to ensure the good working of the Party machine (subordination, the harmonious cooperation of individual members, hierarchical relationships, discretion, propriety of conduct), a greater importance comes ultimately to be attached than to the productivity of the machine. Henceforward the sole preoccupation is to avoid anything which may clog the machinery.

Bureaucracy combined with the structural position of leaders and led creates a self-perpetuating oligarchy. Michels's question was whether it was ultimately impossible for *any* democratic or revolutionary party to pursue a democratic or revolutionary policy? Michels's answer was unequivocal: Who says organisation, says oligarchy!' From a necessary tool that serves the party, bureaucracy becomes the master that rules it.

According to Michels, who wrote his seminal work six years before the October Revolution, the 'iron law of oligarchy' applied particularly to revolutionary parties, given the magnitude of their political ambition. To overthrow the centralised power of the bourgeois state, the revolutionary party must build a large organisation and finance a vast warchest, but in the process it ends 'by acquiring a vigorous centralisation of its own, based upon the same cardinal principles of authority and discipline which characterise the organisation of the state' (Michels, 1959: 367). The party's aim of substituting for the existing state a social order of a totally different kind is doomed from the outset by the very organisation necessary for the task. For Michels, therefore, the revolutionary party 'will never succeed in becoming more than an ineffective miniature copy of the state organisation' (Michels, 1959: 369).

Michels's thesis certainly had analytical value when applied to the German Social Democratic Party of 1911, but how relevant is it for understanding Communist Party organisation today? Michels was writing before the Bolshevik Revolution, and though the SPD was a Marxist party it was never organised along Leninist principles. The question is how well, if at all, does Michels's theory help explain political patterns in communist parties organised along Leninist principles? In other words, does democratic centralism provide a solution to those oligarchical tendencies that Michels claimed were inherent in party organisation, or does it, in fact, reinforce them?

One of the few writers to tackle this issue is Grant Amyot (1981: 19 ff.), though he is more concerned with adapting it to explain the 'deradicalisation' of the PCI and the defeat of the Italian Left, than with applying it to address broader questions about the relationship between internal Party democracy and the structure of power. Amyot's thesis is that the PCI failed to become a truly revolutionary party because its leadership allowed an interim strategy to become institutionalised into an official Party ideology. According to Amyot, the 'Popular Front' strategy, adopted as a short-term tactic by those communist parties engaged in anti-Fascist struggle during the 1930s, has remained a central axis of PCI politics ever since. From a temporary expedient, 'frontism' was transformed into a permanent ideology, its central tenet being

> The belief that an alliance between the working class and elements of the petty bourgeoisie and the bourgeoisie proper, leading to an intermediate state of 'progressive democracy' or democratic, anti-monopoly government, is necessary as a first step towards the attainment of Socialism (Amyot, 1981: 25).

Moreover, Amyot maintains that the ascendancy of this subordinate, 'nonrevolutionary' ideology was no accident, but something consciously introduced into the working class by the PCI's revisionist leadership. From this he concludes that PCI 'frontism' is what has effectively 'kept the proletariat within the bounds of reformism' (Amyot, 1981: 18–19).

Stripped to its essentials, this argument amounts to what is perhaps a more complex variation on the familiar 'conspiracy theory', or 'betrayal at the top' thesis – though it must be said that the PCI has not been allowed the corrupting influences of state office. To explain why radicalism was defeated within the PCI, Amyot draws upon Parkin's (1972) contention that sometimes subordinate ideologies, despite their subordinate status, may still manage to raise an effective barrier to revolution, just as the ideology of the ruling class does so at another level.[14] The main flaw in this line of reasoning, however, is that Amyot reifies the categories of 'Left', 'Right', and 'revolutionary', treating them as fixed and unproblematic, and using them as tools of analysis when, in fact, they are highly problematic and should be treated as subjects for investigation in themselves. In other words, the 'deradicalisation' of the PCI is taken as fact rather than as a hypothesis to be substantiated. Everything, therefore, hinges on a rather static and one-dimensional classification of 'revolutionary' and 'reformist', and there is little recognition of the fact that in most communist parties, including the PCI, the 'revolutionaries' of the past often become the most recalcitrant reactionaries of the present.

Whether one agrees with Amyot's conclusion or not, however, what cannot be disputed is that democratic centralism and oligarchy were traditionally united in Communist Party organisation, and the effect of this was invariably to reinforce Party ideology and the dominant position of the leadership. Because of this, organisation and ideology combined to prevent any revision of the fundamentals of the Popular Front strategy adopted by the PCI in the 1930s. As Amyot (1981: 28) put it, 'they have, so to speak, frozen aspects of the Party's fundamental position at the situation of 1935.'

One need not agree with the whole of Michels's theory in order to see its relevance to understanding mechanisms of power and control within the PCI. The PCI has developed a mass membership and a large, stratified and cumbersome bureaucracy. This was inevitable given its aim of organising the masses in all walks of life. As PCI theorists admit, the price paid for this has often been the subordination of political autonomy and initiative to organisational expediency and bureaucratic conservatism. At its peak in the late 1970s, the Party apparatus had become a vast political machine. Its elected local councillors numbered over 28,000,[15] its federal committee members over 8,500[16] and its permanent officials over 3,000 – not to mention the thousands of functionaries employed in PCI-sponsored mass organisations.[17] If one includes those people either directly or indirectly dependent upon the PCI for their jobs in the provinces and *comuni* (town halls) where the PCI holds power, the figure grows to hundreds of thousands.

The expansion of the PCI's political machine, together with those of the other major parties, was given further impetus in 1974 when the Italian parliament passed legislation for the provision of generous public finance to political parties.[18] As a result the PCI received over 10 billion lire in state funds in 1983, in addition to the even larger sum of money it raised through membership subscriptions and campaigns (*sottoscrizioni*).[19]

The need for a constantly expanding warchest, in order to finance the Party's various enterprises, functionaries and technical employees, is therefore another factor that favours conditions for the emergence of oligarchy. Yet another is the class division between the Party's leadership and base. As Amyot (1981: 28) noted:

> The fact that the majority of functionaries are recruited from the middle classes and have superior educational backgrounds, more political experience and greater resources than the ordinary members increases their power. Since the PCI, in keeping with Togliatti's conception of the Partito Nuovo, has become a mass party rather than a cadre party, the differences in political knowledge and skills are much greater than in the Leninist party of the classic type and the need of guarantees of internal democracy is all the greater.

Oligarchy and Democratic Centralism

Michels's work has been widely used in the study of elites and bureaucracy to explain how reformism comes to permeate the labour movement and how new elites rising from the masses eventually become assimilated into established political roles. But, writing before the Bolshevik Revolution, Michels failed to contemplate the possibility that an emergent elite might actually topple and replace the political structure rather than be absorbed into it.[20] However, even if one accepts this argument and rejects Michels's conviction of the inevitable 'deradicalisation' of revolutionary parties, one is still left with the problem of bureaucracy and its effect on democracy. The question is, can the revolutionary party, even if it succeeds in creating a new political order, escape from the oligarchic tendencies that Michels claims are inherent in all mass organisations? To answer this, one must take a closer look at democratic centralism since this has traditionally underpinned the internal organisation of all communist parties, including the PCI.[21]

Empirical and historical evidence suggests that democratic centralism, far from mitigating the perils of oligarchy, reinforces them. In fact, this mixture may explain why so many Soviet-style systems have degenerated into Stalinism.[22] According to its advocates, however, democratic centralism is simply a formula for combining free election of Party leaders and open discussion with strict hierarchical discipline in the execution of democratically reached decisions. Thus, in the conventional terms of Leninist theory, democratic centralism is defined as

> The collection of political principles that define the respective ties between Party and mass, and between the central Party organs and those of the periphery, in relation to the development of the class struggle.[23]

In practice, however, those ties traditionally meant the subordination of lower Party organs to higher ones, since subordination to the 'vanguard group' and to the 'leading party' was integral in Lenin's conception of communism and in the conditions he laid down for parties seeking admission to the Comintern.[24] The notion of 'subordination', however, raises the question of whether true democracy is compatible with the Leninist principles of iron discipline and centralisation?

Democratic centralism has become, in practice if not in theory, a mechanism for the domination of the Party through its central apparatus.

Interestingly, few communist theoreticians accept this, but then few have really called into question the canons of Leninism central to Party organisation. Even the PCI, whose application of the principle was traditionally rather loose and relaxed, has seldom criticised it. The reason for this is that the PCI has traditionally held a rather benign view of democratic centralism, a view which was summed up in the 1983 statutes in the following terms:

> A decision taken by the majority must be respected also by the minority. In order to safeguard the unity of the Party and defend political discipline, fractionalist activities are prohibited.[25]

The consequences of this were described by one former member of the Central Committee as follows:

> There are, if we keep to the essentials, two fundamental rules. First, the existence of a leading group (*gruppo dirigente*) which, historically, is formed by the method of co-optation and functions as the mediator between the immediate experience of the class and the revolutionary tradition. Secondly, the taking of collective decisions through a debate that is real and free, but is carried on principally within the various organs and leads to the achievement of unity successively from the higher to the lower.[26]

The selection of leaders through cooptation was a further factor that strengthened the control of the leadership over the rank and file. Even where leaders were not coopted, the process by which candidates were nominated for election to office tended to be also in the hands of the leadership. For example, in Umbria, the task of drawing up lists for recruitment to Party office theoretically fell to the large regional committee of roughly 100 members. These lists would be drawn from names that had either been put forward or had somehow 'emerged' following discussion within the lower Party organs. In reality, however, most key decisions concerning Party lists were not made by ordinary members at all, but by a small elite at the top of the regional Party, usually comprising no more than five individuals, whose views were accepted unanimously and in good faith by the rest of the Party.[27]

Similar patterns have been reported in other communist parties. As Jensen and Ross (1984) show in their study of the French Communist Party (PCF), for example, ordinary members have little grasp of the machinations at the top of the party. Furthermore, like PCI members, they consider that the free discussion at section level constitutes democracy – but freedom to discuss does not mean freedom to decide.

Generally speaking, the direction of decision-making in the PCI has traditionally been vertical and downward in direction. Furthermore, perhaps because of its preoccupation with unity, the PCI leadership evolved the practice of solidarity among the higher Party organs *vis-à-vis* the lower. This meant that, regardless of whatever doubts or disagreements might have been voiced, the national executive always presented a united front to the Central

Committee, which presented a united front to the federal committees, and so on down the hierarchy (Amyot, 1981: 29). This tradition of not disclosing to the membership differences of opinion within the leadership was part of the whole issue euphemistically described as the problem of 'transparency in the Party' (*trasparenza*) which became the key issue at the 16th national Party Congress of 1983.

Indeed, the most significant result of that Congress was its massive approval of an organisational amendment calling for greater internal Party democracy – something which the Ingrao Left had been campaigning for since the 1960s. Among the provisions of this amendment was the requirement that executive Party organs at all levels reveal to their immediate electors the full substance of their deliberations. This meant that for the first time the Central Committee would be obliged to disclose to the membership the cons as well as the pros of decisions. The opponents as well as the proponents would be made known to lower Party organs, and differences of opinion on Party policy would be aired freely. In short, minority viewpoints would at last be given some recognition. How this amendment develops in practice will be interesting to see. Unfortunately for the pro-Soviet wing, however, the reform came too late to help their cause.

Oligarchy, Control and the Question of Consensus

Michels's thesis on the conservative nature of organisation, combined with democratic centralism and Amyot's 'subordinate Popular Front ideology', goes a long way toward explaining how the PCI leadership maintains Party cohesion and control. But these factors are not, in themselves, sufficient to guarantee stability, as ideological discipline and democratic centralism are also characteristics shared by other communist parties, particularly those of the Fourth International, whose history is rife with schism. There is more to the PCI's cohesion, something that binds its disparate tendencies and prevents them from splintering. In the 'Communist Reformation', to return to our earlier metaphor, Berlinguer challenged the CPSU's monopoly of socialist truth, and the PCI all but formally broke with Soviet orthodoxy. But having repudiated the fundamental canons of Leninism and effectively 'burned the Bull of Excommunication', what prevented the newly unleashed forces of dissent from fragmenting, just as Luther's revolt released a plethora of dissenting sects, from Anabaptists to Calvinists, or just as the Fourth International splintered into a series of small, antagonistic tendencies after Trotsky's death in 1940, with each claiming to be the true heir to the great political philosopher?

The missing ingredient, perhaps, is not so much the subordinate ideology of 'frontism' as the diffuse and dominant ideology of 'unity': a belief in Party solidarity as a prime virtue in itself and as a goal to be achieved at all costs. It is a conception of Party that entails a deep emotional and moral commitment on the part of the membership; something that can be understood only by recognising that the PCI is a social system which has developed its own shared values and a powerful sense of moral community. This is what makes the use of diffuse and informal sanctions so effective.[28] Communist identity and a deeply held sense of solidarity are the backbone of the PCI: from this comes the membership's faith in the role of its leadership and its unquestioning acceptance of Party unity, an acceptance which is what ultimately legitimates the authority of the leaders.

Informal ideological currents and heated political disputes undoubtedly do occur within the Party, but these reveal only one aspect of the PCI. Though the Party is certainly no homogeneous political bloc, its strength is that it can act as one when necessary and when mobilised. This is the argument advanced in favour of strict discipline and democratic centralism; that it enables the Party to act swiftly and effectively, with one voice and without paralysing dissent from within its own ranks. To explain why PCI activists are so committed to their Party, one must look closer at the role of the ideology of unity and the 'meaning' of being communist in Italy.[29]

The Ideology of 'Unity'

'Unity' is the ideology that permeates Party custom. It can be seen in a variety of tangible forms: the name of the Party newspaper (*L'Unità*); the title of the popular Party festivals; the slogan used on banners and leaflets, displayed at marches, demonstrations and mass rallies and seen in all forms of Party propaganda ('Unity of the Left', 'Unity of all Progressive and Democratic Forces', 'Pact of Unity', 'United Front'). From a Bolshevik revolutionary slogan ('Proletarian Unity') connoting class warfare, it has been adapted by the PCI as a rallying call for a very different type of class solidarity. 'Unity' is also one of the cardinal principles enshrined in the Party statutes.[30]

The ideology of 'unity' also operates in more intangible ways, penetrating deeply in popular consciousness and exercising a profound influence over the thought and behaviour of ordinary Party members. It is a value reinforced by social sanctions and one that members have internalised as part of their own code of ethics. The PCI may not have established 'working-class hegemony over civil society', to borrow Gramsci's overworked phrase, but the Party leadership certainly exercises its hegemony over the membership.

Reticence about expressing internal dissent correlates with the sense of exclusiveness and boundary that informs attitudes toward Party membership. Though levels of participation in sections are declining, the sense of belonging remains high. Those who claim that political militancy is on the wane and that the PCI's days as a mass party are numbered often fail to consider such intangibles as these. As Ruscoe (1982: 66) noted,

> Membership of a section no longer means constant attendance – but it still means a sense of belonging, and times innumerable one can meet Party members who very

> rarely go to Party meetings, except at moments of particular importance, but who would be most insulted if their communist credentials were attacked for this dereliction to what they no longer see as their duty.

This new identity does, in fact, call into question the PCI's communist credentials. For the PCI, revolutionary social change will come about not as the result of a sudden radical move, but rather as the cumulative effects of numerous small steps. A novel approach to communist strategy perhaps, but one that poses the question of whether the PCI is still, in any conceivable sense, an embryonic new society developing in the womb of the old social order. Some Italian communists would like to think so.

Although, in practice, the PCI's day-to-day policies are often moderate and indistinguishable from those of social democrats, Italian communists feel passionately that they are not social democrats, for however pragmatic and reformist their policies, they are ostensibly conducted with a view towards a grander scheme of social change. Despite this, many members fear the Party is becoming too integrated into the social order it is trying to oppose and that it is losing its revolutionary credentials. For years the PCI was considered an 'antisystem' party and therefore a threat to political pluralism and parliamentary democracy, but this image is no longer tenable.

As the PCI drew closer to national political power in the late 1970s, much of the political debate in Italy focused on the issue of pluralism and communist ideology. As Ferrarotti (1978: 59) summed it up,

> The PCI has won democratic recognition although democratic practice is not yet one of its basic features as far as Party internal life is concerned ... [it is] still more of a promise than a reality. General instructions still stem from the centre and it is doubtful whether local conventions have an impact on policy decisions.[31]

The challenge for Italian communists was to reconcile inner Party democracy with the demands and practice of democracy 'outside' the Party. Throughout much of its post-war history the PCI operated two codes of democracy: liberal, pluralist democracy within the Italian parliamentary system, and Leninist democratic centralism for its own internal organisation. According to many critics, however, democratic centralism is incompatible with liberal democracy. For the PCI this issue posed an acute problem: how far could the Party go toward 'democratising' itself in a liberal sense without weakening the basis of its own organisation and undermining that which until now has guaranteed internal cohesion? The answer will emerge sooner than most analysts might have anticipated, for at its 18th Party Congress, in March 1989, the PCI finally voted to expunge the term 'democratic centralism' from its statutes. The longer-term and ideological implications of this act are undoubtedly profound, but what political consequences will result from it, we shall have to wait to see.

7

Communist Identity versus Legitimacy: PCI's Awkward Leninist Legacy

'Throughout the debate on hegemony the PCI has left in the dark, I fear, the problem of the internal regime of the party. Until it is confronted in detail ... the whole question of pluralism in society which the PCI has asserted in the past few years will remain incomplete or suspect.

(S. Secchi, 1979, 'L'austero fascino del centralismo democratico', p. 61)

For the first time, perhaps, the 'party' is in question and what used to be an ideological issue is turning into a problem of organisational sociology. At the heart of the issue is the concept of pluralism.

(F. Ferrarotti, 1978, 'The Italian Communist Party and Eurocommunism', p. 30)

'It would be foolish to deny that there is an historic continuity between the ideas and the political practice of the Bolsheviks on the one hand, and the political system of the Stalinist Soviet Union on the other; and this thread of continuity can be found also in the evolution of the idea of democratic centralism.

(M. Waller, 1981, *Democratic Centralism*, p. 7)

Awkward Leninist Legacy

By the mid-1980s the Italian Communist Party had moved a considerable way in distancing itself politically from Soviet communism, but how far it had effectively disengaged from Leninism was, and remains, a problem of a different order. At the heart of the polemic concerning the PCI's legitimacy as a truly democratic and pluralist party was the question of democratic centralism and the Party's Leninist heritage. The problem that critics pointed to, which Italian communists had never answered satisfactorily, was the extent to which Leninism in general – and democratic centralism in particular – has become a blueprint for Party dictatorship and thus a formula for a totalitarian state. Or, alternatively, if Leninist principles do not lead to excessive centralisation, bureaucracy and oligarchy within the party, how do Italian communists explain the development of these characteristics in most, if not all, communist parties currently in power? According to the PCI's harsh judgement, 'the propulsive drive set into motion by the October

Revolution has now been exhausted.' Is the 'degeneration' of Soviet communism, as the PCI sees it, an 'accident of history' or the logical development of a Leninist party in power? The result of 'deviations' from 'Leninist norms', or a consequence of those norms?

So far, Italian communists have avoided carrying the argument to its conclusion and have not, at least publicly, probed deeply into these sensitive issues of theory and ideology. However, in rejecting the Soviet model of communism, the PCI has breached the walls of Leninist doctrine, but it has not yet coupled this with any explicit critique of Leninist theory. Why this has not occurred is a complicated question addressed in the final chapters.

'Leninism' and the Origins of the PCI

From its earliest days, the PCI modelled itself on the Russian Bolshevik Party. Indeed, the Italian Communist Party was created directly in response to Lenin's challenge to the socialist movement, and to the enormous prestige of Bolshevism – as both a strategy and model of organisation. At its foundation in 1921, the PCd'I accepted all 21 of the strict 'Terms for Admission into the Communist International' (the Comintern), formulated by Lenin and laid down before the Comintern's second Congress in 1920. It is worthwhile to reflect on those 'Terms for Admission' for they provide the most succinct statement to be found anywhere in communist literature on Lenin's ideal for a truly Communist Party; how it should organise itself and what its structure and function should be. Amongst these conditions, Lenin stipulated the following.[1]

- Propaganda and agitation must be genuinely communist in character, and all Party press organs must be edited by 'reliable Communists who have given proof of their devotion to the cause of the proletarian revolution'. Furthermore, 'the dictatorship of the proletariat should not be discussed as a simple stock phrase', but 'popularised', systematically dealt with and 'driven home to every rank-and-file working man and working woman, every soldier and peasant'.[1]
- Communist parties must break completely with reformist policy. 'Reformists' and 'centrists' – and Lenin included amongst these the socialist leaders Turati and Modigliani – must be systematically dismissed from positions of responsibility in the working-class movement and replaced by reliable communists.
- Where impossible to conduct communist activities legally, legal and illegal work should be combined. But where class struggle enters a civil-war phase, communists must abandon 'bourgeoise legality' and build up a parallel illegal organisation which, at the decisive moment, will help the Party achieve revolution.
- Persistent propaganda and agitation (agitprop) must be conducted amongst farm labourers, peasants and in the armed forces; failure by

communists to do so 'would be tantamount to betrayal of their revolutionary duty and incompatible with membership'.
- It is every communist's duty to expose the falsehood and hypocrisy of 'social patriotism' and 'social pacifism', and to demonstrate to workers that without the revolutionary overthrow of capitalism 'nothing will save mankind from new imperialist wars'.
- Communists must wage 'systematic and unflagging work in the trade unions, cooperatives and other mass workers' organisations'. Communist cells, which must be subordinate to the Party, should be formed in all of these, their daily task being to 'unmask the treachery of the "centrists"'.
- The composition of communist parliamentary groups should be re-examined to 'eliminate unreliable elements and effectively subordinate these groups to the Party Central Committees. They must demand that every communist proletarian should subordinate all his activities to the interests of a truly revolutionary propaganda and agitation.'
- All publishing enterprises should likewise be subordinate to the Party Central Committee and 'not be allowed to abuse their autonomy'.
- 'Periodic membership purges' must be carried out with the aim of 'systematically ridding the party of petty-bourgeois elements' that inevitably percolate into it.
- It is the duty of all members selflessly to help any Soviet republic in its struggle against counterrevolutionary forces.
- All parties that have kept their social democratic programmes must draw up new communist programmes – subject to the approval of a regular congress of the Communist International or its executive.
- All decisions of the Communist International's congresses and of its executive committee are binding on all affiliated parties: 'the Communist International must be far more centralised than the Second International was.'
- 'Parties wishing to join the Communist International must change their name. Any party seeking affiliation must call itself the *Communist* Party of the country in question (section of the Third Communist International).'[2]
- 'Parties belonging to the Communist International must be organised on the principle of democratic *centralism.* In this period of acute civil war, the communist parties can perform their duty only if they are organised in a most centralised manner, are marked by an iron discipline bordering on military discipline, and have strong and authoritative party centres invested with wide powers and enjoying the unanimous confidence of the membership.'[3]

Accepting these conditions, the PCd'I proclaimed itself Marxist-Leninist, declared war on 'bourgeois democracy' and dedicated itself with pride to the cause of socialist revolution and proletarian dictatorship. But in so doing,

Italian communists also committed their Party to a subordinate, clone-like imitation of the triumphant Bolshevik Party. One reason for this, no doubt, was that conditions in Italy in 1921 – on the eve of Fascism – favoured such an analysis and gave authority to Lenin's model. All the canons of Leninist doctrine were therefore codified into the first Party statutes of 1921–6. These mirrored perfectly the classic Bolshevik positions of the Third International. Interestingly, however, democratic centralism was not introduced until the Lyons Congress, following the PCd'I's 'Bolshevisation' under Gramsci.[4]

These early statutes demonstrate vividly the Italian Communist Party's *image of itself* throughout the 1920s and 1930s: an image not of a national, independent, distinctively 'Italian' party, but of a small branch of the international workers' movement everywhere engaged in the historic struggle for socialism, proletarian unity and world revolution. Italian communists saw themselves as inseparably linked to the Soviet Union, which was the 'leading state' in the van of history and the world's most advanced socialist society.

In statute, deed, and ideology the PCd'I set about constructing its identity totally around Leninist doctrine and Soviet practices. It voluntarily merged and subordinated its identity with that of the Soviet Party. This is confirmed by Martinelli's (1982: 67) conclusion on the 1926 PCd'I statutes:

> It is the document of a party that considers itself, first and foremost, a national section of the Comintern ... of an organ that aims to build a single worldwide communist party.

Up until the 1940s this fusion and deliberate renunciation of a separate role was also reflected in the title the Party gave itself. As the late Professor Lombardo Radice, one of the foremost Party intellectuals, wrote,

> When I joined the party in 1937, there was no 'Italian Communist Party' [PCI]. I became a member of the 'Communist Party of Italy [PCd'I], which was a section of the Comintern, of the Third International. The change from that perspective to the Party as it is today is certainly considerable.[5]

The switch from *Partito Comunista d'Italia* to *Partito Comunista Italiano* was another of the significant changes introduced by Togliatti after 1944. This change in PCI self-definition has other implications, for those 'bonds of fidelity' to the Soviet Union were simultaneously 'chains of command'. Not only was the PCd'I rigorously centralised, disciplined and subordinated through democratic centralism to its own Central Committee, but, in turn, it deferred to the higher authority of the Comintern, and beyond this, to the Comintern's executive in Moscow. The Cold War anticommunist charge levied against the PCI of being an 'instrument of subversion and of Soviet foreign policy' was, therefore, not easily dismissed.

For most of its early, formative history, the PCI defined itself by resemblance to the Soviet model of communism; it drew up its political boundaries around the ideological suppositions of Leninism. This meant above all unity, ideological conformity and discipline. As one PCd'I agitprop circular of 1925 put it,

> We must succeed in instilling in every comrade the precise conviction that the the teachings of Lenin fully corroborate and conform to the political situation that we have to face.[6]

Further evidence of the PCd'I's doctrinal rigidity in this period may be seen in the writings of Party leaders, most notably Gramsci, who declared that 'Leninism, written, is a unitary system of thought and action, in which *everything is simultaneously contained and demonstrated* from the general conception of the world down to the minute practical problems of organisation.'[7] Elements of this ideological stamp were still manifest in the world-view of many older-generation communists – those active in the first two decades after the war. As De Clementi (1982: 925) points out, it was simply not fashionable to adopt a doctrinaire approach to Lenin in the 1920s and 1930s; the codification of a new dogma also

> resolved the double problem of providing an integrated but self-sufficient symbolic universe, capable of strengthening the voluntary segregation of communists from the rest of society, of legitimising Party solidarity, and of establishing a secular mysticism capable of mobilising the emotional recesses of the subaltern masses.

The importance of this Leninist heritage on earlier generations of Party activists is also revealed in archival material dating back to the Stalinist era. One extraordinary set of early, post-war documents from the Perugian PCI Federation archives lucidly illustrates the Party's attitude to Marxist-Leninist ideology and its transmission at local level.

'Ideological Formation': The Role of Local Party Schools

In November 1948 the Central Committee's school commission sent out directives to the Party federations instructing them to establish programmes of mass education in communist doctrine and Party history. Largely at Togliatti's insistence, Party schools were set up throughout Italy, at national, provincial and sectional levels. A Party National Executive letter, dated 3 November 1948, spoke of the 'urgent need to reinforce the work of Marxist-Leninist education in our organisations', with the objective of 'making a militant of every member of the Party, and to prepare tens of thousands of new cadres'.[8]

In addition to studying Party history, organisation and Marxist classics, these courses also aimed at raising general educational standards, since mass education was still undeveloped in Italy, and most members were illiterate peasants and labourers. The influence of these political training courses, which were usually organised in poor, sharecropper villages or working-class neighbourhoods such as Piazza Grimana, is reflected in the political outlook of older members, who frequently justified their views with 'That's what they taught us at Party school.' One of these Party schools was opened in the heart of the Piazza Grimana neighbourhood in Perugia, and was attended by many local section members.[9] These Party courses, their contents and bibliographies, give a vivid insight into PCI ideology and its transmission during this period. The core curriculum in each short course was Leninist ideology and its application to the PCI. Lesson One, for example, was titled, 'Foundations of the PCI: Gramsci and Togliatti's Struggle for a Marxist-Leninist Party: Ideological and Organisational Principles of the Marxist-Leninist Party'.[10]

Similarly, Lesson Four, 'The Struggle for Peace', taught about the rapid social and economic progress achieved in those 'popular democracies liberated by the Red Army'. These courses portrayed the world, in black-and-white terms, as falling into two camps; 'the democratic, socialist bloc of peace, freedom and people's independence, under the direction of the Soviet Union', and 'the imperialist bloc of war, reaction and the subjugation of peoples, under the direction of the United States'.[11] Another lesson began by stating:

> Only the urban industrial proletariat, directed by the communist party, can liberate the rural working masses from the stranglehold of capital and the great property estates, from economic ruin and imperialist wars, forever inevitable as long as the capitalist regime holds out. For the rural working masses there is no other road to salvation than alliance with the communist proletariat.[12]

In yet another course the PCI defined itself as

> the supreme organisational form of the proletariat ... the political vanguard of the working class ... [which] welcomes into its ranks the most conscious, combattive and advanced part of the proletariat ... For that reason the communist party, vanguard organisation of the working class and of the working masses, must never be a creature of the mass, but must always hold itself at the head of the masses.[13]

Ordinary members were ranked in terms of their level of 'Marxist-Leninist ideological preparation'.[14] By the late 1940s the PCI had developed an efficient structure for recruitment and promotion of promising Party cadres. Significantly, the main criterion for selection and promotion rested upon candidates' adduced level of 'class-consciousness', and their formative grounding in Marxist-Leninist orthodoxy. Archives also show that during the particularly rigid years 1948–56, trusted local Party secretaries submitted character profiles and progress reports to federation officers on the behaviour and ideological preparation of section members.[15] One such report gave the following profile:

> Low level of political ideology, has ceased Party work. Element of extremism which leads him to commit thoughtless deeds. Profession, typographer.

Another stated:

> Excellent organiser, works continuously, has the temperament of a man of action. Good ideological/political preparation which is improving through his serious attitude to work and reading of Marxist texts.

Promising young recruits were talent-scouted and sent for training at the national Party schools. On these courses, under the scrutiny of the school, they were vetted for leadership qualities. One local working-class member, for example, who was rapidly promoted in the Perugian Party, was praised, in a federation letter dated June 1953, for being 'endowed with a class instinct, strong attachment to the Party, and a spirit of sacrifice', as well as for having 'good political sensibility and combative ability'. The verdict of the Central Party School on another member in 1952 was less laudatory:

> He has average intelligence, a weak character and little personality or combativity ... At present he appears better suited as a good executive rather than leader.

Local Party secretaries were periodically required to submit autobiographical reports to the federation executive. These 'political curricula vitae' were stylised testimonies written in distinctive PCI language; terse sentences emphasising the good communist qualities and pedigree working-class credentials of the writer, in addition to a standard set of information concerning social background, occupation, reasons for joining the Party, positions held in other organisations, level of education and so forth. One former section secretary, who joined the Party in June 1944, wrote in his testimony:

> My motives for joining the PCI came from discontent; from a sense of rebellion that accumulated in me over many years of Fascism ... To contribute to the rebirth of the country, to give life to a social system that guarantees and makes of Man a human person, not a slave: guarantees that are in the programme the PCI is struggling for and will continue to struggle for until they are realised.

The report continues:

> I am a member of the Federal Committee.
> I have always been a member of the PCI.
> I have no relatives in the police.
> I have never been arrested.
> I have never been sentenced or charged.
> I have been present in all of the struggles conducted by the Party.

> The books I have read are: *The Communist Manifesto*. Joseph Stalin, *Biographical Notes*. *The Collected Works of Lenin*, Vol. 1. 'History of the Bolshevik Party of the USSR'. F. Leone, *History of the Garibaldi Brigades in the Italian Partisan Movement*. Luigi Longo, *Un Popolo alla Macchia*. *Mindszenti* by Ottavo Pastore, and *Ten Days That Shook the World* [by John Reed].

The report concludes: 'My comrades from the Federation can guarantee all that I say.'

Culture and Ideology of Italian Communism after 1956

Details such as these help piece together exactly what Party membership and discipline meant in the early 1950s. But the ramifications for the PCI today are also important. What is shown here is not simply the fact that older Party activists were schooled within a strict framework of classic Marxism-Leninism, but, more importantly, that Leninist ideological purity was a key quality *selected for* in recruiting for leadership roles. What is surprising, therefore, is not the heavy weight of pro-Soviet traditionalists that still dominated many local sections in the early 1980s, but why there were not *more* communists of the orthodox mould within the Party leadership.

One answer to this, perhaps, is the upheaval caused by the crisis of 1956. Khrushchev's speech and the Hungarian uprising severely damaged the PCI's confidence in its ideological heritage and its policy of promoting ideological purity in its cadres. Khrushchev's speech revealed chilling facts that many found unbelievable. It was the most devastating denunciation that had ever been made of the late Marshal Stalin and the 'Stalin Cult'. It disclosed for the first time the horror, the repression and the mass executions that had characterised Stalin's reign. Stalin's concept of 'enemy of the people' had made possible, in Khrushchev's words, 'the cruellest repression against anyone who in any way disagreed with Stalin'.[16] 'Barbaric tortures' had been used to extract false confessions, and tens of thousands of innocent victims had been sent to their deaths on the basis of trumped-up charges. He held Stalin personally responsible for the ruthless deportation of minorities in the USSR during the 1930s and 1940s. Stalin's 'despotism', 'megalomania' and 'self-glorification' were blamed for the numerous military catastrophes the USSR suffered during the war. Particularly devastating were Khrushchev's figures for the purges of 1937–8:

> It has been determined that of the one hundred and thirty-nine members and candidates of the Party's Central Committee who were elected at the 17th Congress, ninety-eight were arrested and shot mostly in 1937–8 ... The same fate was met not only by the Central Committee members, but also by the majority of delegates with either voting or advisory rights; one thousand one hundred and eight were arrested on charges of anti-revolutionary crime ... The delegates to that Congress

were active participants in the building of our Socialist State ... How can we believe that such people could prove to be 'two-faced' and had joined the camp of the enemies of Socialism?[17]

'Deviation from Leninist Norms': the Soviet Theory of Stalinism

The official Soviet line was that the cause of Stalin's excesses lay in a grave degeneration of socialist legal norms resulting from the 'cult of the individual' and from Stalin's deviant personality. The final lines of Khrushchev's epic speech called for the 'cult of the individual' to be decisively condemned as 'alien to Marxism-Leninism', and for a complete restoration of 'Leninist principles of Soviet Socialist democracy'.[18] But many PCI leaders had already begun to ask how one individual had been able to abuse power in such an arbitrary way. An awkward problem presented itself: was Stalinism the result of a structural fault in communism itself rather than simply a psychological deviation in the individual? If so, it called into question the whole foundation of the Soviet system.

Togliatti was prudent in articulating his views on the matter. In an interview given to the journal *Nuovi Argomenti* in 1956, he deflected questions concerning Khrushchev's disclosures by adamantly defending the legitimacy of the Soviet regime and criticising the hypocrisy of democracy in the West.[19] Only later did he speak of the suffocation of Soviet democracy by 'bureaucratic and authoritarian leadership and by the violation of the legal norms of the regime'.[20] But this, he added, is a risk any socialist society in transition is prone to, and the issue of the one-party state was never seriously called into question.

Slightly more explicit was Togliatti's so-called 'Yalta Memorandum'. This document, drafted by Togliatti in August 1964, is often cited, somewhat spuriously and overoptimistically, as the beginning of Eurocommunism and of Togliatti's conception of pluralism. It was intended as a long reflection to be presented to Khrushchev as the basis for discussion at their forthcoming meeting at Yalta (21 August 1964). Unfortunately, only hours after its completion, Togliatti was struck down by a massive cerebral haemorrhage, from which he died. A copy of the memorandum had been sent to Rome, and despite Soviet objections it was published. Though not overtly critical of the Soviet model, it did reject as unsatisfactory the 'cult of personality' thesis, and it proposed that the return of democratic and personal liberties suppressed by Stalin could be hastier: 'The general impression', Togliatti wrote, 'is that there is a slowness and resistance to return to the *Leninist norms that used to guarantee freedom of expression and debate* both inside the Party and outside, in the field of culture, art and politics.'[21] This sentence is revealing, for it suggests that Togliatti, even until his death, still held 'Leninist norms' as inviolable. He clearly failed to carry the analysis a step further and examine the roots of a problem that perhaps lay in Leninism itself.

The PCI's reluctance to broach this question of Leninism in depth had major consequences, for, having used 'deviation from Leninist norms' to explain Stalin, the Party had once again reaffirmed the legitimacy of Lenin, making it all the more difficult for the Party to examine objectively and critically the basis of such assumptions. 'Leninist norms' were used as the vehicle for analysing the causes of Stalinism, but rarely did any communist party dare suggest that perhaps the origins of Stalinism lay in those norms themselves.

How far has the PCI gone since Togliatti, or how far is it prepared to go, in its theoretical 'correction' of Marxism-Leninism? Though it has carried out substantial practical revisions, these have not yet been complemented by any comprehensive, official restatement. As many critics argue, PCI theory still leaves many questions unanswered, for example, those of private property, the functioning of the free market and the principle of profit as an indicator of sound management. Similarly, though there are very few Italian communists today who still take guidance from Lenin's theory of imperialism, the Party has made no explicit renunciation or denunciation of Leninist theory.[22] Up until the early 1980s the PCI was, in fact, quite adamant that it would not renounce its ideological heritage. The reason was summed up by Berlinguer in 1978:

> [They tell us that] if you do not renounce Lenin from A to Z, if you don't break with the CPSU, you are Asians not Westerners. Do you think it would stop there? No, because from the repudiation of Lenin, Marx would be next. From the break with the CPSU, one would have to recognise the October Proletarian Revolution as an error! [23]

Yet only two years later Berlinguer delivered a definitive repudiation of the CPSU following the crisis in Poland. Despite this, the PCI broke no diplomatic ties with Moscow, nor was its new international perspective backed by any thoroughgoing theoretical critique of Leninism. The PCI was playing its familiar game of waiting, doing nothing and hoping for events themselves to resolve any outstanding ideological problems. But until these and other related questions are satisfactorily resolved, major problems will continue to face the PCI when dealing with issues concerning NATO, the EEC, defence policy, the role of public ownership and the nature of the state. The problem for the PCI is that it is torn between what Lange (1979) has called its struggle for identity and its quest for legitimacy within the Italian parliamentary system. It is faced with both an identity crisis and a dilemma, for it cannot carry its critique of Soviet communism and Leninism too far without raising some awkward questions about its own history and theory of organisation.

Pluralism or Leninism? Communist and Bourgeois Theories of Democracy

Central to the debate about the PCI's internal organisation and communism's legitimacy is the concept of pluralism. Pluralism has several meanings, not always clearly distinguished. It can mean institutional arrangements for the distribution of political power among a multiplicity of autonomous groups, or it can stand for the doctrine that such arrangements ought to exist. Alternatively, the term denotes a political situation in which no particular political, cultural, ideological or ethnic group is dominant. The general sense of the term is fairly clear, usually referring to a situation in which various rival political parties compete for power.[24]

Western European democracies are usually defined as pluralist because there is more than one party at work, and there is an alternation of government. Most Eastern European or 'socialist' states were not pluralist in this sense since there was either a single party in power or a variety of parties under the supreme leadership of the Communist Party exercising a monopoly of power (the party-state). So long as the leading role of the Communist Party is assured this is consistent with Leninist theory.

During the mid-1970s an animated debate developed in Italian politics over the issue of 'Leninism versus pluralism', and numerous PCI positions on Gramsci and hegemony were challenged.[25] The attack was led, in the main, by socialist intellectuals of the PSI. Their argument, which caused considerable discomfort amongst PCI leaders, was that Leninist norms, and hegemony, are incompatible with pluralist democracy.[26] Leninism and pluralism are reputedly irreconcilable, opposed and antagonistic systems of government. Yet both claim to be 'democratic'. The difference between them lies in the divergent liberal and Marxist-Leninist conceptions of democracy, and how each defines the 'will of the people'. Democracy in its classic sense means simply 'rule of the citizen body', as in a state having government by all the people, whether by direct or by representative government. It is also generally taken to mean popular participation at all levels of decision-making by the 'unbridled commonality', rather than 'the insolence of a despot'.[27]

In the Western tradition the conception of democracy in its ideal form stresses the equality of all citizens before the law; a government responsible to the majority and obliged to obey laws expressing the will of the majority, provided that there is 'universal' suffrage by free, secret ballot; regular elections with more than one political party; freedom of speech, press, and religion; and the other civil liberties. According to Marxist-Leninist analysis (formulated over 80 years ago), the Western liberal democratic tradition is utterly false and corrupt because of the structures of capitalism: civil-libertarian elements are simply bourgeois ideological trappings masking the reality of class struggle, of the inequality and exploitation inherent in capitalist relations of property and production, and of the repressive nature of the state apparatus. In Lenin's view, democracy in bourgeois society was a sham:

> Democracy for an insignificant minority, democracy for the rich – that is the democracy of capitalist society ... Marx grasped the essence of capitalist democracy splendidly when, in analysing the experience of the [Paris] Commune, he said that the oppressed are allowed once every few years to decide which particular representatives of the oppressing class shall represent and repress them in Parliament.[28]

Similar views were expressed at the first Congress of the Communist International in Moscow two years later, when Lenin put forward his theses on 'bourgeois democracy' and the 'dictatorship of the proletariat'. He asserted that

> the most democratic bourgeois republic is no more than a machine for the suppression of the working class by the bourgeoisie, for the suppression of the working people by a handful of capitalists.[29]

For Lenin, true democracy was impossible under capitalism. Workers' democracy was the only true form of democracy, and this could only be achieved following the violent overthrow of the capitalist class, the suppression of the bourgeoisie, the dictatorship of the proletariat, and the 'withering away of the state'.[30] In the post-war period the series of communist regimes that came into existence in Eastern Europe distinguished themselves from 'bourgeois democracy' by giving themselves the title of 'people's democracies'.

As the PCI draws closer to winning national power, the question of its democratic legitimacy becomes crucial. The Marxist theory of the state[31] and the Leninist conception of Party[32] are hardly tenable propositions for winning electoral credibility in the arena of Italian politics. Italian communists are vague on their conception of a future socialist society in Italy, and they refrain from full-scale discussion of the nature of the democratic state. In the words of Italian sociologist Franco Ferrarotti (1978: 64),

> they assert that they accept the rules of 'bourgeois democracy' because they do not see anything better at hand. At the same time they cling to a distinction between 'formal' and real democracy and hope for a polity in which formal rights will be given economic substance.

From the point of view of policy, Ferrarotti (ibid.) adds, 'It would be difficult to distinguish them from social democrats.' Italian communists dispute any such claim and argue that they have not given up their ideology. This is why the issues of democracy, Leninism and democratic centralism are such polemics. What kind of democracy and what kind of communism does the PCI now profess? What remains of its Leninist legacy? If the Leninist concept of 'Party' is, as historians often claim, 'despotic', containing 'in embryo the whole hierarchical totalitarian structure in which the socialist system was subsequently embodied',[33] what implications does this have for the PCI today?

The events of 1956 opened up previously sacrosanct and inviolable issues of communist ideology and orthodoxy (hitherto, ideas such as the 'leading role of the party', 'democratic centralism', and 'dictatorship of the proletariat' were simply not negotiable).[34] But despite genuine debate, the PCI failed to grasp the Leninist nettle, and recoiled from the suggestion that, in order to explain Stalin, one must go back to Lenin. Only recently has the PCI begun to make theoretical inroads into Leninism, but much of the Leninist legacy remains, giving rise to major contradictions in Party ideology and identity. To clarify this, we require closer examination of 'Leninism'.

Key Tenets of Leninist Philosophy

There are few revolutionaries in the world who are not, or who do not consider themselves to be, in some sense, Leninist. Few philosophies have had such an influence in shaping the political and cultural landscape of the modern world. After Marx and Engels, the chief architect of modern communism and dialectical materialism is Lenin. His single most important contribution to Marxism was the creation of, and theoretical justification for, the centralised Party machine. It was Lenin who devised the strategy for the revolutionary seizure of power, who led the first socialist state, and who inspired communists throughout the world. Thanks to Lenin, Russian Marxism, which until World War I had been little more than a backwater, became Marxism *par excellence*, an exemplar that was totally to dominate the revolutionary socialist movement.

'Leninism', as distinct from Marxism, refers specifically to those theories and doctrines based on the central beliefs of V.I. Lenin (1870–1924) on the politics, organisation and strategy of revolutionary struggle.[35] Lenin's amendments did not simply furnish Marxist philosophy with a practical theory of organisation to take it one step forward; they profoundly altered the whole course of Marxist thought by grafting onto Marxism, as if by some immutable hyphen, the concept of 'Leninism'. 'Marxism-Leninism', not 'Marxism', subsequently became *the* theory and praxis of all communist revolutionary action.[36]

Lenin's core 'amendment' to Marx lay in a new organisational plan for the 'Party', one differing fundamentally from all previous Marxist parties.[37] Ideas for this were developed in two pamphlets, *What is to be Done*? and *One Step Forward, Two Steps Back*, as well as in numerous articles written between 1902 and 1904. Reduced to bare outlines, these were the propositions advanced. First, unlike more fatalistic and evolutionary Marxists, Lenin argued that the objective laws of history in no way destroy the role of the active individual in history; the conscious revolutionary can, by correct political action, stimulate revolution 'and speed up what was historically inevitable according to the laws of historical materialism'. Theoretical rationalisation for this claim was summed up in the slogan, 'There can be no revolutionary action without revolutionary theory.'

Second, Lenin drew an analytical distinction between 'trade unionist' and 'socialist consciousness'. Few passages from Marx have been more quoted than the famous sentence, 'The emancipation of the working class is the work of the working class itself,' which summed up the essence of economic materialism; that is, that relations of production create the revolutionary proletarian ideology from which effective social revolution must spring. Upon this principle Marx and Engels distinguished their 'Scientific Socialism' from the Utopianism and 'made' revolutions of idealist dreamers.[38] Aware of this, Lenin knew that his conception of party organisation was logically untenable without the most major change in Marxist theory ever made by someone claiming to be an 'orthodox Marxist'. Marxism, he argued, confused the mentality of trade unionism with that of socialism, hence, 'The history of all countries shows that the working class, exclusively by its own effort, is able to develop only trade union consciousness.'[39] Spontaneous development of the workers' movement, he added, leads 'precisely to its subordination to bourgeois ideology ... the ideological enslavement of the workers to the bourgeoisie'.[40] So, according to Lenin, 'socialist consciousness' or 'class political consciousness' can be 'brought to the workers only from without', from theories worked out by 'educated representatives of the possessing classes'.[41]

This is what theoretically justifies the 'leading role' of the Party, for unless guided by a socialist vanguard the working class becomes subordinated to the bourgeoisie. Lenin's reasoning about the trade-union and labour movement – like Marx's reasoning about the petty bourgeoisie and peasantry – was that, unable to create its own ideology, it is politically impotent and can merely follow (or be captured by) either the revolutionary proletariat or the bourgeoisie. For Lenin, the choice was crude and simple:

> There is no middle course (for mankind has not created a 'third' ideology, and, moreover, in a society torn by class antagonisms there can never be a non-class or above class ideology).[42]

In Leninism, it is the Party intellectual who creates the ideology upon which the revolution depends. Such a view, with its implicit elitism, prefigured very accurately the meaning of the 'dictatorship of the proletariat' over society.[43] The theory is also profoundly un-Marxist; as Sabine writes:

> Few political theories have given to intellectuals a role as world-shaking, and none has assigned to the proletariat so small a share in the proletarian revolution.[44]

Leninism undoubtedly explains much of the appeal of communism to intellectuals. To be in the vanguard of the most 'advanced class', leading the oppressed forward in an historic struggle for 'progress' and a new social order is an exquisitely romantic and satisfying – if immensely arrogant – image of one's role. But such a conception is anti-Marxist. Moreover, it is a dialectical refutation of Marxism itself, for if socialist ideology must be produced and disseminated by middle-class intellectuals, what remains of the principle, theoretically accepted by all Marxists, that new relations of production arise in society not as the result of deliberate and conscious activity of men, but spontaneously and independently of the will of men? Where in Marx is such an historic role attributed to an ideology provided through the Party? In Sabine's words:

> By what nicety of economic materialism does a productive system that has created bourgeois and proletarian classes and made them irreconcilably antagonistic to each other, also produce out of the middle class an intelligentsia whose social function is the making of an ideology to destroy the middle class?[45]

Stripped of Marxian technicalities, Lenin's view of working-class people was that they do not naturally have much inclination for revolution, but since revolution is inevitable, this is tantamount to saying that they have little capacity to think for themselves, govern themselves, or know what is good for themselves. The role of the Party, as a body of Marxist professionals, is therefore to educate them for socialism and for proletarian dictatorship.

Leninism and the Vanguard Party Model

According to Leninist theory, the working class needs a party made up not of the working class itself, but of self-appointed guardians; a vanguard elite of *déclassé* revolutionary intellectuals carefully selected for their outstanding 'moral and political' qualites; an elite that has made the revolution its profession, and whose rigorous Marxist scholarship guarantees the right of leadership and the purity of the revolutionary doctrine. The role of the Party is to lead and guide the working class, inject its doctrine into the workers, infiltrate their organisations and struggles, and seek to use them for its purposes. Only 'bourgeois politicians', wrote Lenin, can believe that the task of a socialist is to serve the workers in *their* struggles. The task of the socialist politician is 'Not to assist the economic struggle of the proletariat, but to make the economic struggle assist the Socialist movement and the victory of the revolutionary party.'[46]

Central to the identity that Leninists traditionally accorded themselves was this myth of the revolutionary socialist vanguard. In what was later used as the basis for a description of the Party in its charter of 1934, Lenin wrote, in one of the resolutions of the Communist International in 1920:

> The Communist Party is part of the working class, namely, its most advanced, class-conscious and therefore most revolutionary part. The Communist Party is formed of the best, most intelligent, self-sacrificing and far-seeing workers.[47]

Whereas Leninists accept this as plain truth, for non-Leninists such self-complimentary aggrandisment appears to be a fallacy that is difficult to substantiate. Words such as 'unity', 'organisation', 'discipline', 'combat', 'command', 'centralism', and 'army' were the terms most frequently employed by Lenin when writing about the structure and role of the Party. Secrecy and centralisation would increase and enhance, rather than diminish, the quality of activity in other more open organisations.[48]

It followed as a matter of course that such a party had to be highly centralised and hierarchical to fulfil its tasks. Operating clandestinely in despotic

Tsarist Russia, the Bolsheviks had little room for free criticism or open democracy within the Party. Lenin's conception of the Party demanded united leadership, rule from the top, and strict, almost military discipline – a model of Party organisation derived in part from the Communist League and from the Russian terrorist organisation, Narodnaia Volya.

Centralised authority and the Party's 'leading role' were therefore made linchpins of Leninism long before the October Revolution. These have since become central canons of all communist parties, each modelled on Leninist ideas of the 'revolutionary vanguard' and the principle of 'democratic centralism'.[49] For Lenin, democracy in Party organisation was a 'useless and harmful toy'; serious revolutionaries, he insisted, needed iron Party discipline.[50]

The 'Vanguard Party' identity – which really set communism apart from other varieties of socialism – fitted comfortably with Lenin's broader philosophical outlook. Despite his numerous adaptations of Marx, Lenin's views remained rigidly couched within a framework of professed Marxian orthodoxy. Dialectical materialism, which Marx and Engels described as merely a 'working hypothesis', became in Lenin a universal method applicable in every field of science and the only safe guide for obtaining true knowledge.[51] Philosophy and social science, so the argument went, are inevitably partisan, and the most that any scientific theory of society can achieve is a general outline of the objective logic of economic and historical evolution.

Within the framework of dialectical materialism there are two systems of social science: one produced in the interests of the bourgeoisie (reactionary, 'backward' and 'historically doomed'), the other ('progressive' and superior) in the interests of the proletariat. In a similar vein the bourgeois/proletarian division exists for all art and literature. The conclusion of this is simply that ineradicable class struggle becomes the prime factor, over and above scientific evidence, in determining the truth of scientific conclusions. It follows that objectivity in social and humanistic studies is impossible and, furthermore, pointless since the criterion for 'truth' becomes ultimately the Party line.

Lenin's last works were all concerned with questions of historical materialism, particularly the transition from capitalism to communism. His *Imperialism: The Highest Stage of Capitalism* proposed that capitalism had reached its final monopolistic phase and was now 'ripe' for overthrow.[52] It asserted that war was an inevitable social phenomenon brought about at a particular stage of capitalist evolution by predictable crises in the expanding capitalist economies. Such a theory restored Marxism as a philosophy of inevitable social revolution and

> took it out of the hands of cowards and sentimentalists, of pacifists, reformists, conciliationists, and democrats. The class struggle was once more clearly inevitable, the 'reality' behind the false appearance of peace, of freedom for the working class within the framework of parliamentary liberalism.[53]

Finally, in *State and Revolution,* Lenin expanded upon the Marxist theory of the state as an instrument of class domination, emphasising points that Marx and Engels had not elaborated: the 'need to smash the bourgeois State machinery', the establishment of the proletarian state, 'proletarian dictatorship', and a distinction between a 'lower' phase of communism, where reward is proportional to work and the state is still needed, and a 'higher stage', in which reward is proportional to need and the state will 'wither away' completely.[54]

Leninism or Marxism? Trotsky and Luxemburg on Lenin

Despite the prestige Lenin gained from the October Revolution, a prestige which dwarfed that of all his Marxist opponents, his theories were not without their critics. Trotsky, Plekhanov, Axelrod, Martov and Rosa Luxemburg at different times all published criticisms of Lenin's propositions – particularly those concerning 'centralism' and 'dictatorship', so crucial to the whole Leninist approach. In a penetrating critique of Leninism in 1904, Rosa Luxemburg spared nothing in denouncing Lenin's proposals as 'un-Marxist' and 'highly dangerous' to the autonomy of the workers' movement. She scathingly condemned the authoritarianism and elitism she foresaw in Lenin's model:

> The ultra-centralism asked by Lenin is full of the sterile spirit of the overseer. It is not a positive and creative spirit. Lenin's concern is not so much to make the activity of the party more fruitful as to control the party – to narrow the movement rather than to develop it, to bind rather than to unify it.[55]

She also attacked the dangers inherent in Lenin's mistrust and contempt of working-class spontaneity, pointing out the absurd contradiction in this:

> If we assume the viewpoint claimed as his own by Lenin and we fear the influence of intellectuals in the proletarian movement, we can conceive of no greater danger to the Russian Party than Lenin's plan of organisation. Nothing will more surely enslave a young labour movement to an intellectual elite hungry for power than this bureaucratic straightjacket, which will immobilize the movement and turn it into an automaton manipulated by a Central Committee.[56]

These were shrewd insights given that Luxemburg was writing as early as 1904. For her, only the decentralisation and autonomy of the working class could provide effective guarantees against opportunism, intrigue and personal ambition. The working class, she concluded, 'demands the right to make its mistakes and learn in the dialectic of history', and not even the 'infallibility of the cleverest Central Committee' can legitimately substitute the role of the Party for that of the working class.[57]

Legitimately or not, this is what happened in Russia, and subsequently in each of the Soviet-style states. On the theme of 'substitution', however, Trotsky in 1904 wrote one of the most brilliant and remarkable documents ever published by a Marxist supposedly in the 'Leninist' tradition.[58] It was, as Trotsky's biographer put it, 'the most strident bill of impeachment that any Socialist had ever drawn up against Lenin'.[59] Significantly, however, Trotsky wrote it before joining the Bolsheviks and while still a Menshevik opposed to Lenin's faction of the Russian Social Democrats.

Trotsky accused Lenin of bullying the revolutionary intelligentsia into a Marxist orthodoxy in order to train them as leaders of an immature and timid working class, and of trying to force the pace of history. To be in possession of a proletarian doctrine, such as Marxism, he warned, 'was no substitute for a politically developed proletariat'. Lenin's distrust of the masses and his theory that workers by themselves could not rise from trade unionism to revolutionary socialism was, Trotsky wrote, 'the theory of an orthodox theocracy'. The conception of a party acting as the leading instrument in place of the proletariat would end, in Trotsky's view, as follows:

> The party organisation [the caucus] at first substitutes itself for the party as a whole; then the Central Committee substitutes itself for the party as a whole; and finally a single 'dictator' substitutes himself for the Central Committee.[60]

With his characteristically savage but devastating irony Trotsky ridiculed Lenin's style and his attempt to impose discipline on the Party, as 'hideous, dissolute and demagogical'. In the same passage he described Lenin, in damning epithets, as 'morally repulsive', an 'adroit statistician' and a 'slovenly attorney' whose suspiciousness was 'a flat caricature' of Robespierre and the 'tragic Jacobin intolerance'.[61]

Trotsky ended his critique with a plea against conformity and the optimistic assertion that 'A proletariat capable of exercising its dictatorship over society will not tolerate any dictatorship over itself.'[62] Nor can the tasks of the working class be solved, he finished, 'by placing above the proletariat a few well-picked people ... or one person invested with the power to liquidate and degrade'.[63] But almost as if Trotsky's critique were a mirror of the future, this is exactly what occurred – though it was not Lenin but his successor who was to become the Russian 'Robespierre'. Trotsky's analysis practically foresaw the Stalinist dictatorship and the course through which the Party and revolution would move. According to this critique, Stalin was there all along, latent in the Leninist party structure and in the logic of its 'substitution' of the caucus for the party, the Central Committee for the caucus, and finally the dictator for the Central Committee.

The tragedy of this contained all the more pathos for the fact that Trotsky's writings bore clear omens pointing to his own eventual fate. 'Trotsky could have no inkling', writes Deutscher, 'that one day he himself would go much further than Lenin in preaching and glorifying that "substitutionism", before he would shrink in horror from its consumation.'[64]

Yet even when expelled by Stalin and writing, from exile, *The Revolution Betrayed*, Trotsky still felt compelled to defend the Soviet regime against 'bourgeois critics'. Stalin's triumph was explained not as a structural inevitability but as the result of the bureaucratic growth of the state, stagnation of the Party and the abandonment of the theory of permanent revolution.[65] Corrupt and bureaucratic leadership and Stalin's manipulation of the Party machine had exploited the bewilderment and passivity of the workers.[66] Above all, democratic centralism was acquitted of any 'leading role'; only its abuse under Stalin was condemned, for it was then used by the Central Committee to strangle the inner life of the Party. The theory, in Trotsky's view, was blameless:

> The combination of these two concepts, democracy and centralism, is not in the least contradictory. The present doctrine that Bolshevism does not tolerate factions is a myth of the epoch of decline. In reality the history of Bolshevism is a history of the struggle of factions.[67]

But the doctrine that fails to equate democratic centralism with the success of Stalinism is equally a myth of an epoch of communist decline.[68] To anyone but Leninists – who refuse to admit it – the thread of continuity is indisputable. However, this is something that even the most orthodox communists are now having to face up to. The PCI has tried to confront this issue, as we shall see in the following chapter, but how far the other communist parties have done so, or can do so, is debatable. Any serious critique of Leninism has potentially devastating implications and would probably undermine the whole theoretical basis upon which communism is founded. That, at least, is one reason why any challenge to democratic centralism is so threatening to communist parties.

8

Democratic or Bureaucratic Centralism? Ideology, Organisation and Crisis in Communism

> The internal life of the Italian Communist Party is regulated according to the method of democratic centralism, so as to ensure necessary unity of address in Party action, clarity in terms of political debate, assumption of responsibility on the part of each militant and leader, the maximum participation of militants in political decisions and struggle, and the rigorous protection of rights.
>
> (*Statuto del PCI*, 1983)[1]

By the mid-1980s, the PCI had gone a long way in extricating itself politically and constitutionally from its Leninist legacy. Only democratic centralism, the traditional Leninist formula for regulating internal Party democracy and, at least in the past, for guaranteeing ideological subservience to the Soviet Union, remained enshrined in its 1983 statutes. But at the March 1989 Congress, delegates finally voted to drop this, too, from the Party statutes. Without any great fanfare the 1989 Congress brought to a close an entire era in Italian Communist Party history.

The decision to abolish democratic centralism in many ways marked the definitive break with communist orthodoxy.[2] This move also coincided with President Gorbachev's policies of reform and the increasing abandonment by the Soviet Union of the old notion of its 'leading role' in the communist world – though whether this greatly influenced the PCI's decision or merely confirmed a trend already well established in PCI politics is debatable. Yet, surprisingly, this dramatic step was not accompanied by any real critique or repudiation of Leninism *per se*: if anything, the PCI was silent and somewhat surreptitious on the issue. This is perhaps understandable given the importance the PCI attaches to history: having effectively broken with its own history and severed the ideological fetters that had guided and shaped it for over 60 years, the Party found that its once proud Leninist legacy had become an uncomfortable skeleton in the cupboard. In this respect, the PCI's reluctance to publicise this apparently small, but, in effect, highly significant constitutional change is entirely logical. If it were to admit that the failure of Eastern European-style 'achieved socialism' was the result of the failure of Leninist orthodoxy (as it now appeared to be saying, at least tacitly), then it would also have to accept another damning indictment: namely, that had it won power before its acceptance of parliamentary pluralism when, by its own definition, it was still a Leninist Party, then it might have committed errors of authoritarianism like those of its Eastern European counterparts.

Reading between the lines, we find that this is precisely the conclusion reached by the Communist Party of Great Britain (CPGB) in its 'Manifesto for New Times'. Reflecting on why the Labour Party had, in the past, repeatedly rejected its application for affiliation, and banned communists from individual membership, the CPGB admits (1989: 20) that a major reason for this was

> the party's membership of the Communist International and the acceptance by the party of the decisions and theories of the International, many of whose decisions were determined by Stalinist thinking and practice and were wrong and harmful to the work of the British and other communist parties.

Just how wrong and harmful they would have been for the British political system is not dwelt upon here. Neither is the issue of the CPGB's critique of Stalinism, or whether that critique extends into Leninism. Nor is much said about why it has taken the CPGB so long to move out of the shadow of Stalinism. All that it does say on this is that 'in the 1980s, the break with Stalinism led to a rupture in the party', and that the Communist Party has 'emerged from these traumatic years ... with a commitment to a more democratic identity: to political pluralism' (ibid.: 20–1). This may be encouraging news for Eurocommunists and those seeking to change the face of communism, but the implicit message is that before the early 1980s British communism was still essentially Stalinist in its organisation and in its basic world-view.

Given that political parties rarely repudiate their own past, particularly communist parties, who have a special relationship with history and a heavy investment in its construction, the symbolic implications of the PCI's formal abandonment of democratic centralism should not be underestimated. To appreciate the full significance of this, one needs to understand something of the theory of democratic centralism, its differing interpretations, and the history of its development.

'Functional' Significance of Democratic Centralism

With the notable exceptions of Tiersky (1985) and Waller (1981), few Western analysts have given serious consideration to democratic centralism, and this is surprising for it is, as Waller claims, 'one of the most important political concepts to emerge in the twentieth century' (ibid.: 5). The reason for this, according to Waller, is that the meaning of democratic centralism has generally been assumed to be that imparted by Soviet political practice; namely, 'a verbal acknowledgement of the value of democracy which serves only to conceal a reality of centralism – that is, autocracy, dictatorship, totalitarianism' (ibid). Similarly, in Soviet-bloc countries, with the exception of a few dissidents, whose views have generally been dismissed as heretical, communist theoreticians have been characteristically weak and defensive in their justification of the principle, and muted in its critique.[3] The reason for this, perhaps, is that Party organisation is a highly sensitive and conservative realm of communist theory. While some communist intellectuals recognise that there are flaws in the Leninist theory of Party organisation and would be hard-pressed to defend democratic centralism in terms of democratic or Marxist ideals, most would also agree that it would be almost impossible to abandon its practice without also damaging other aspects of communist theory and organisation – an effect which, in turn, would threaten to destabilise the Party leadership and undermine its legitimacy.[4]

However much communist parties may differ in their application of the principle, democratic centralism remains fundamental to communist identity, for it is the organisational ideology and practice that distinguishes communist parties world-wide from all other types of politics.[5] Its influence covers *all* aspects of Party life, from the character of internal Party debates to the formation of the Party's strategy and the recruitment of its leaders. Above all, it is the mechanism that perpetuates ruling communist elites.[6] As Tiersky (1985:17) writes,

> Far from being merely an ideological slogan and a brief set of essentially hypocritical rules of order, democratic centralism in the Stalinist period became the real political culture and practical ideology of Communist orthodoxy, as it still is today wherever communism remains essentially Stalinist.

Most communist parties see democratic centralism differently. For them it is simply a device that provides a link between revolutionary theory and proletarian organisation. According to conventional Leninist theory, it is supposed to be the 'synthesis of freedom and order' that reconciles the divergent views of individuals with the 'united will of the Communist Party', and balances 'democratic participation with the need for leadership and central planning'. In theory, it admits of no contradiction between democracy and centralisation. Its 'centralism' lies in the Party programme, to which all members owe undivided allegiance, and in the united Party leadership, which can demand the subordination of lower Party organs and enforce iron discipline on all members. Its 'democracy' lies in the membership's eligibility for election to all Party organs and in every member's active participation in Party work. In principle, therefore, free discussion and criticism of every proposal by Party members are built into the decision-making process.

In reality, however, there has always been a large gulf between theory and practice, as well as flaws in the theory itself. If we examine the internal functioning of most communist parties, whether in Eastern or Western Europe, it is quite clear that 'free discussion and criticism' have not been guaranteed by democratic centralism, but have been crushed by it. As Chapter 6 illustrated, various factors intervene to prevent the accountability of the leadership to the mass membership or the latter's active participation in the decision-making process. Most notable among these factors is the power inherent in the Party bureaucracy and in its hierarchical structure of command, which inhibits a proper two-way exchange between Party leadership and base.[7] This is not simply a problem of 'bureaucratisation'; it follows logically from the Leninist conception of the Party – the function of which is to decide questions of policy and pass judgements on the 'correctness' of opinions in the light of Marxist-Leninist theory.

In theory, Marxism-Leninism enables the communist party to find the right orientation in any situation and to see the innerconnection between past and current events – and it is upon this supposition that it proclaims its 'leading role'. From this function follows the peculiar combination of free discussion and closed decision that characterises democratic centralism. Some issues remain open for discussion (the leadership usually decides which), and these may become legitimate matters for 'self-criticism'. Other issues have been decided upon 'and have taken their place among the dogmas closed to discussion' (Sabine, 1948: 676). This combination of fixed principles and free controversy within set limits has no equivalent in Western European thought except perhaps, as Sabine claims, in the medieval distinction between revelation and reason. For Sabine, therefore, orthodox communism

> is a kind of political clericalism, and its philosophy is a kind of secular scholasticism. However much it may change, the changes must always be derived by a complicated reinterpretation from the unchanging principles of Marxism. The Party, when it speaks *ex cathedra*, also speaks infallibly.
>
> (Sabine, ibid.)

Advocates of democratic centralism reject this, arguing that it is not Lenin's theory of Party organisation itself, but its *distortion* that results in dogmatism and authoritarianism (cf. Marzani, 1980; Waller, 1981). In principle, democratic centralism provides as near perfect a model of Party democracy as can be found anywhere. Since higher organs are elected from below, all directives of a higher body are absolutely binding, and the authority of the Party leadership – elected from one congress to the next – is indisputable. According to Marzani (1981: 45), there is nothing in this that even the most sensitive liberal or social democrat would find abhorrent. Indeed, he adds that,

> Intermittently, many Socialist parties have had democratic centralism. Democratic trade unions, of whatever ideology, operate on a basis of democratic centralism – that is, after a free discussion and a free vote the majority decision is binding on the minority. This principle gives muscle to consensus.

But, against this, critics would argue that most socialist parties and trade unions are hardly 'paragons of achieved democracy'. Such examples, far from strengthening the case for democratic centralism, actually weaken its credibility.

The case of the 1984–5 miners' strike in Britain provides an illustration of some of the conflicts between leadership and democracy that are inherent in democratic centralism. The decision-making process of the National Union of Mineworkers (NUM) also operated according to a type of democratic centralism: once a decision had been taken by the (democratically elected) national leadership, ordinary members were expected to fall into line and obediently carry out the leadership's policy. Those who did not were branded 'scabs', or 'scabby bastards' and 'traitors' to their union and their class, who 'deserved' to be ostracised and condemned.[8] The organising principle of the union and its ideological stance required that, ballot or no ballot, the leadership's decision was binding on all union members – and, as if by logical extension, on the rest of the British Left.[9]

The argument used to stifle dissent within the NUM and the British Left was similar to the coercive argument used by Stalin and other Soviet leaders to bring about the unquestioning loyalty and obedience of other communist parties. This argument had three essential elements: firstly, that in situations of 'class war' democracy was a luxury that had to take second place to revolutionary struggle; secondly, that where the class struggle had reached a 'critical phase', the state of emergency demanded a system of command that would give total authority to the organisation leading and directing that struggle; and thirdly, that, given the political stakes involved, all those who were not seen to be 'with us' were classified as being 'against us' and, therefore, as aiding the class enemy and the forces of reaction.[10]

The effect of this kind of discourse, like the effect of the Cold War on communist parties that felt deeply threatened by powerful external forces, was effectively to rule out dissent (which became classified as 'treachery'), and to shift the argument onto a Manichaean plane where only questions of 'right and wrong', or 'good and evil' were permitted. The consequence of this was a climate of moral coercion where doubt or disagreement with the fundamental choices of the leadership were effectively 'disallowed', and where nonconformity was steamrollered under the moral issue of loyalty and betrayal. Thus, in the case of the NUM, democratic centralism worked extremely well in strengthening the position of the leadership, in deflecting internal criticism, and in enlarging its sphere of influence and command not only over its own membership, but over all those people who felt morally obliged to lend their support and defend the strike. Interestingly, the British Communist Party, in its 'Manifesto for New Times' (1989: 11), now accepts that the lack of democracy in the NUM was a prime factor in the failure of the strike:

> The concentration on picketing as a major tactic and the refusal to have a national ballot limited its ability to maximise public opinion in its favour. In ways it was a struggle bred from the politics of the past. It was seen by many as the apogee of militant, male, machismo trade unionism.

What is hinted at here, but not said explicitly, is that this struggle was bred not only from 'the politics of the past', but equally from an organisational ideology of the past. It is not made explicit because, at the time of writing, democratic centralism is still central to the organisation and ideology of the CPGB and its principles are still enshrined in the Party's published programme, *The British Road to Socialism*. Indeed, if doubts about Leninist principles of Party organisation existed at all among the communist parties of Europe in the early 1980s, none of them were voiced publicly, and all the parties reaffirmed their commitment to democratic centralism. The 1979 and 1983 PCI statutes, therefore, paralleled closely those of the CPSU and other communist parties, and they were almost identical in their respective clauses concerning internal Party democracy:[11]

> Decisions taken in conformity with the statute are binding upon all those belonging to those respective organisations and, if taken by the leading national organs, upon the entire Party. A decision assumed by the majority must be respected also by the minority. To safeguard the unity of the Party and defend its political discipline, 'fractionalist' activities are prohibited (*Statuto del PCI*, 1983, Article 8: 19–20).

In practice, this meant that resolutions passed by a majority (or passed by the Party leadership) were obligatory: all members had uniformly to carry them out, and minorities had to abandon their views. This rule sanctioned more than just the subordination of minorities to the majority, for an outvoted minority was now forbidden – under threat of expulsion – to form factions or agitate for rejected proposals. The result was a statutory ban preventing any defeated minority from organising itself or promoting its views in such a way that it might one day become the majority. This rule thus guaranteed by statute the leadership's continued domination over the Party mass membership.

It is easy to see from this how democratic centralism can become, as it so often has become, a legal formula for 'bureaucratic centralisation' and the perpetuation of an oligarchical elite at the top of the Party apparatus. Indeed, it is hard to see how the result should ever be otherwise. The question that must surely have haunted all serious communists since Khrushchev's secret speech of 1956 is, what role did *structural* features of the Soviet system play in Stalin's rise to power? Most communists rejected, and continue to reject, the argument that the seeds of Stalinism were contained in the Leninist vanguard-party model. In a similar fashion, most parties of the Fourth International continue to reject the argument, once proposed by Trotsky himself, though subsequently retracted, that Lenin's organisational blueprint contained the 'Dictator' from the very outset. The orthodox communists' view was that Stalinism arose from a 'degeneration' or 'distortion' of the Soviet system. Even today, most communist intellectuals, including those in the CPGB, refuse to accept the structural implications of Stalinism. Instead, it is euphemistically referred to as 'the problem of stagnation', yet in most instances, the euphemism is not intentional; it betrays an implicit assumption that Lenin's party model was blameless, and that the regimes of 'achieved socialism' could be saved if they would return to the 'correct' Leninist formula that had once guaranteed socialist freedom and democracy. Thus, the 'stagnation' hypothesis carries with it suggestions of a kind of 'Paradise Lost'; of nostalgia for the 'Golden Age' of communism before it had been corrupted under Stalin and Brezhnev.

For those who follow such a line of reasoning, particularly the parties of the Fourth International, the collapse of 'achieved socialism' in Eastern Europe is not a reflection of any crisis in *communism*; it is, instead, merely a reflection of the inevitable 'crisis in Stalinism'.[12] Hence, the 'solution' to the problem is summed up in the slogan 'Reform, but not Reformism!' (i.e. piecemeal improvement to the Leninist system rather than radical re- or deconstruction of that system). Another consequence of this 'stagnation' approach is that serious debate about Stalinism, within communism, has frequently been sidetracked into an analytically sterile Marxist historicism which examines exactly *when*, or at what *precise* historical moment after the October Revolution, stagnation began, rather than examining what might have been wrong with Bolshevism in the first place.

Few communist parties have seriously addressed the question of what role democratic centralism played, within the one-party state, in the 'stagnation' of Soviet-style communism. The evidence suggests that these two principles of communist organisation are not only faulty and inadequate, but, worse still, that they appear to have led everywhere to repressive forms of authoritarianism and dictatorship. The question therefore arises, is Leninism in power a formula for despotism?

Variations on the argument have been articulated both inside and outside the PCI (cf. Magri and Maone, 1974; Elleinsteine, 1976; Sechi, 1979; Gill, 1980; Waller, 1981, and Tiersky, 1985). The two most recent of these studies are also, by far, the most interesting and detailed. Waller and Tiersky both focus on democratic centralism as a crucial element in the failure of Leninism, but they draw rather different conclusions. While Tiersky condemns democratic centralism outright, and asserts that Leninism is hopelessly and irretrievably flawed, Waller tries to defend the principle of democratic centralism against what Soviet practice has made of it. Yet even Waller concedes that there is 'an historical continuity' between the Bolshevik concept of democratic centralism and the political system of the Stalinist Soviet Union (ibid.: 7). However, according to Waller, this system arose not from any logical development of Lenin's ideas but from an *historic break* with Leninism which led to a major distortion of the theory: a break brought about by specific historical events and pressures in the early days of the Bolshevik Revolution when the USSR was struggling for survival against the onslaught of the Western imperial powers.

History of Democratic Centralism after the Bolshevik Revolution

Undoubtedly, there is some truth in Waller's claims about the evolution of Lenin's ideas. In the history of Bolshevism a key shift *did* occur in the context in which Lenin's Bolshevik Party operated before the October Revolution and after it. The term 'democratic centralism' was first adopted by the second Congress of the Russian Social Democratic Party as early as 1903, and the concept was subsequently employed by both Bolshevik and Menshevik factions of the Party in late 1906 (Tiersky, 1985: 17). At this point, however, democratic centralism was little more than an ambiguous slogan; that is, 'a vague and contradictory set of notions which could alternately imply more centralism or more democracy as circumstances demanded' (ibid.). It was adopted primarily for convenience, and 'more as a "weapon" than an autonomous rule', since it provided the best mechanism for regulating decision-making in an insurrectionary party (ibid.). For a clandestine organisation struggling for survival against a repressive police state and a tsarist autocracy, democratic centralism provided an ideal instrument. It was only after Russia became a single-party dictatorship dominated by the Communist Party that democratic centralism became enshrined as a constitutional doctrine, one that would eventually serve to legitimise and sustain a Stalinist political order.[13]

As Waller claims, a major turning point in the development of democratic centralism occurred during the state of emergency in the revolutionary period. Faced with the pressures of civil war, economic chaos and military crisis, the Bolshevik Party Congress of 1921 passed an unprecedented ordinance to ban factional activity within the Party. This prohibition did not simply put severe limits on the rights of opposition; it challenged its very right to exist. Henceforth, any organised opposition to the Party was outlawed. The result was that, as Marcel Leibman put it in *Leninism under Lenin* (1975: 299),

> Those mechanisms of control and criticism, serving as antidotes to the features of authoritarianism that were already present in Party life, suffered in March 1921 a definitive and maiming blow.

That maiming blow left the opposition, and the principle of opposition, permanently crippled. It was precisely in that ban that seeds were sown for the degeneration of the revolutionary dictatorship of a class into the dictatorship of a person. This is also the view of Lenin's biographer, Robert Conquest (1972: 10):

> But for his [Lenin's] survival to introduce the surprise resolution at the Tenth Congress [May 1921] suppressing organised opposition in the Party, Russia might not have been thrown into the hands of Stalin and the Party apparatus.

The Bolshevik ban on factions, introduced in emergency conditions and intended as a *temporary* measure, thus became ossified into a organisational law of Soviet communism, and thereafter was reproduced and reified as a constitutional principle at the level of the state. The problem for the Soviet Union – which it shares with those parties organised according to democratic centralism – was that after the Bolshevik seizure of power, the distinction between the Party and the state became progressively blurred as the identity of the Communist Party, its function and its personnel, were merged with those of the state. This convergence of Party and state into the 'party-state' led ineluctably to a situation where disloyalty to the former was indistinguishable from disloyalty to the latter. As E.H. Carr (1959: 219–20) wrote, liberal democracy had established a distinction between loyalty to party and loyalty to the state, and had found a place for both, but

> This distinction disappeared in the one-party state with significant consequences. On the one hand, loyalty to the state came to require acceptance of specific doctrinal conformities hitherto associated with party. On the other hand, dissent from party doctrine or prescriptions incurred the moral stigma and later the physical sanctions, hitherto reserved for disloyalty to the state ... The mere existence of an efficient machinery of repression invited the use of it. Opposition became a crime because the means were now available to track it down and punish it.

The Bolshevik Party's 'interim' prohibition on organised opposition, far from being relaxed after the emergency situation had subsided, was 'preserved and even strengthened in the parties which owe their origins to the Third International' (Amyot 1981: 29). This prohibition was subsequently adopted by all parties of the Communist International. Indeed, Lenin's 'Twenty-one Articles of Admission' into the Comintern effectively demanded this of them. The result was that virtually every communist party came to incorporate this into its statutes, thus enshrining within its political culture a monopolistic party practice that Lenin never intended as a long-term measure.

The argument posed by advocates of Marxism-Leninism is that since Soviet communism was corrupted by Stalin, the type of internal democracy practised by most existing communist parties is a 'far cry' from the true Leninist principles of democratic centralism.[14]

However, controversy exists as to whether or not the Bolshevik prohibition was intended to be temporary. Far from being a 'deviation from Leninist norms', such a prohibition was arguably an inevitable development of them – particularly in the light of Lenin's general conception of class, party, and state. By 1919, all the essentials of Lenin's ideas had been made explicit, and it is clear from his writings that 'centralism' in the revolutionary Party commanded the highest priority. It was the first and essential component; the 'democratic' element was always dependent upon centralism since the centre could virtually dictate the composition and representation of the peripheries.

Lenin could not have been unaware of this, particularly as other revolutionaries who criticised his party model – from Martov to Axelrod, and from Luxemburg to Trotsky – had all argued that democratic centralism would lead to autocracy. As Conquest (1972: 46) argues, the truth would seem to be that, 'Though Lenin was prepared to argue that this was not the case, he also made it clear that he did not mind even if it was.'

Generally speaking, Lenin was contemptuous and dismissive of democratic organisations. Like his view of morality, his conception of democracy was defined almost exclusively in terms of the value democracy it served to the revolutionary struggle and to the proletarian dictatorship. Jacobinist opportunism and revolutionary expediency were his guiding principles and what this demanded, in organisational terms, was a rigidly centralised and disciplined party. For Lenin, only the *principle* of communism really mattered; that is, 'progress' in the dialectics of history, the seizure of power, and scientific socialism. The means for communism's attainment were, logically speaking, morally indifferent. In other words, the revolutionary ends justified any means.

Whether Lenin intended it or not, the ban on 'factionalist activity' was nevertheless consistent with his other propositions and represented merely another step forward in the direction of centralisation and subordination to the Party's 'most class-conscious and self-sacrificing vanguard' (cf. Conquest, 1972: 46). This is not to say that the continued suppression of democracy in the USSR was desired by Lenin or foreseen by him: it was simply expedient in the circumstances. Whether it could have been different, or whether it was possible to make a revolution any other way in 1917, these are unresolved issues that are continually debated. However, since Lenin's death, attempts to challenge or reform this fundamental principle of communist organisation have been systematically opposed by the leadership of the CPSU and other communist parties, who have used the principle itself as their chief weapon for eliminating any would-be reformers or internal dissidents. None of these parties has provided a convincing answer to the Stalinist puzzle. Following the example of the PCI, many Western European communist parties have turned to Gramsci's writings in search of an answer. But does Gramsci's Marxism provide a satisfactory critique of Stalinism, and does it offer any escape from the apparently damning consequences of Leninism?

Gramsci's Critique of 'Bureaucratic Centralism': the Answer to Stalinism?

Ever conscious of the problem of 'bureaucracy' in Party organisation, Gramsci drew a distinction between what might be termed a 'functional' and a 'nonfunctional' democratic centralism. To explain functional democratic centralism, he accorded prominence to the concept of *organicità* ('organicity'), which, in his view, expressed the 'unity and cohesion' of the revolutionary movement and that movement's 'forward drive'. The idea behind this was that legitimacy comes from below rather than is imposed from above. As Gramsci (1971b: 188–9) wrote,

> 'Organicità' can only be found in democratic centralism, which is, so to speak, 'centralism' in movement – i.e. a continual adaptation of the organisation to the real movement, a matching of thrusts from below with orders from above, a continuous insertion of elements thrown up from the depths of the rank and file into a solid framework of the leadership apparatus which ensures continuity and the regular accumulation of experience.

Gramsci's idea was that there should be an organic harmony between the Party and the masses, and where this relationship breaks down, 'bureaucratic centralism' results:

> The prevalence of bureaucratic centralism in the State indicates that the leading group is saturated, that it is turning into a narrow clique which tends to perpetuate its selfish privileges by controlling or even stifling the birth of oppositional forces (Gramsci, ibid.: 189).

Gramsci was well aware of the argument that Marxism is 'merely an ideology of the discontented intelligentsia, trying to replace the old privileged groups with a "New Class" which would oppress the proletariat in its turn' (Clark, 1977: 3). This was a common theme in anarchist thought, and one that found echoes in the writings of Mosca, Pareto and Michels, whose work Gramsci would have been familiar with. Much of his intellectual attention was, therefore, directed to precisely this problem concerning the relationship between Party, state and masses, and the dangers of the Communist Party becoming 'mummified and anachronistic' in moments of crisis (Gramsci, 1971: 211). Gramsci's argument was that bureaucratic centralism ultimately arises from 'a lack of initiative and responsibility at the bottom' (ibid.: 189), rather than from anything intrinsically rigid or suffocating in the principle of democratic centralism itself. In his view, democratic centralism was inherently flexible and therefore blameless. Thus, in a celebrated passage of *The Modern Prince*, he wrote (ibid.) that 'Democratic centralism offers an elastic formula, which can be embodied in many diverse forms: it comes alive only insofar as it is interpreted and continually adapted to necessity.'

In order to maintain such elasticity, there needs to be, according to Gramsci, 'an organic unity between theory and practice, between intellectual strata and popular masses, between governors and governed' (ibid.). This type of approach was consistent with Gramsci's general attitude toward theory and history; an attitude that was practical, innovative, and far from dogmatic. In his view, a 'healthy' political party was one that knew how to relate to a constantly changing reality. Gramsci insisted, therefore, on the need to adapt Bolshevism to local conditions, and he had little concern for abstract and deductive formal rules – indeed, he was nearly expelled from the Party for his nonconformism during his imprisonment in 1926. Gramsci's political views, like those of Lenin, were steeped in a culture of revolutionary action rather than governmental procedure. However, the consequence of this was that he, as Tiersky (1985: 110) writes, 'underestimated or perhaps simply neglected the needs of large organisations for procedures and institutions'.

Significantly, Gramsci's concerns about bureaucratic centralism were not so much anti-Stalinist as antiliberal, and the examples he cited of bureaucratic stagnation were, curiously, the League of Nations and the Piedmont administration in the first decades after Italian unity.[15] But Gramsci's conclusion on the problem of 'bureaucratic centralism' appears to be unclear, and, to say the least, somewhat simplistic and idealistic, as can be seen in the following passage from *The Modern Prince* (1971b: 155):

> When the Party is progressive it functions 'democratically' (democratic centralism); when the Party is regressive it functions 'bureaucratically' (bureaucratic centralism). The Party in this second case is a simple, unthinking executor. It is then technically a policing organism, and its name of 'political party' is simply a metaphor of a mythological character.

Advocates of Gramscian Marxism often overrate the quality of this analysis and portray Gramsci as a kind of Marxian prophet whose insights into internal Party democracy have paved the way forward in the escape from Soviet-style communism to the 'Promised Land' of a new communism. For example, Gramsci's meditations about the need to overcome the divisions between leaders and led in 'bourgeois society', and create a new state where this relationship is 'functional' rather than 'technical' or 'static', are acclaimed by Showstack Sassoon (1980: 168), as 'a criticism of the bourgeois mode of politics and ... a critique of Stalinism'. Yet, in reality, Gramsci's only remedy for oligarchy appears to be 'a correct theoretical understanding of the way in which a party should function', a remedy which, in turn, depends upon the party fulfilling its 'historical function' in abolishing class divisions (ibid.).[16] To any but the most partisan observer, such an argument appears to be confused or, worse still, to be jargon based more on a Utopian belief than on reason. If the 'historical function' of the Party is to bring about the classless, communist society, then to argue that a 'functional' relationship between state and society will be realised only when the Party has 'fulfilled its historical function' is merely to reiterate an old article of Marxist faith that the communist society lies somewhere in the distant future when the state has 'withered away', at the 'end of history'.

Similarly, Carl Marzani (1980: 46) enthusiastically declares that Gramsci 'saw clearly' the problem of oligarchy over 50 years ago:

> When the Party is progressive it functions 'democratically'; when the Party is regressive it functions 'bureaucratically'... . What a succinct insight into a Stalinist

party. And is this insight to be given up because a Bettino Craxi or a Sir Harold Wilson bays at the moon? Eurocommunists find resonance in this thinker and cherish his meditations.

But Gramsci's distinction between 'bureaucratic' and 'democratic' centralism is neither clear nor succinct. It is a tautology to claim that when the Party is 'progressive' it functions democratically, and when it is not, it becomes 'bureaucratic'. This is tantamount to saying that when the formula works, let us call it 'democratic centralism', but when it does not, call it something else. In the same passage Gramsci argues (1971: 155) that all political parties 'carry out a policing function' (i.e. 'safeguarding a certain political and legal order'), and this can be either repressive or progressive. This, too, is questionable, as many would argue that 'policing', in the literal sense, is the prerogative of the state, or of an independent police force and judiciary sanctioned by the state. To sanction a policing role for parties carries with it the potential for a dangerous confusion of roles, and an inadequate separation of powers between party and state. Certainly a function of all parties is to *reconcile* people to a political and legal order, but whether this is quite what Gramsci meant by 'policing' is uncertain.

Similarly, Gramsci's notion of *organicità* is far from clear. The idea that a functional relationship between leaders and led can be achieved through democratic centralism by 'matching thrusts from below with orders from above', rests firmly on this concept of 'organicity'. This, in a sense, was Gramsci's answer to the classic communist problem of reconciling spontaneity and internal Party dissent with the need for unity and discipline. For Gramsci, there was no abstract, rationalistic formula for guaranteeing the correct relationship; it depended instead upon a method of politics, a certain sensitivity in political orientation, and the Party's ability continually to adapt itself to changing circumstances. All of this was summed up in the concept of *organicità*. The problem with this concept, however, is defining what is meant by an 'organic' relationship. Presumably Gramsci intended it to mean the obverse of a 'mechanistic' relationship, but what makes a relationship 'mechanistic', as opposed to 'organic', appears to be intangible, and the structural basis of such relationships is far from clear.[17]

Stripped of its sentimental overtones, the Gramscian notion of an 'organic' relationship appears to be almost meaningless: a disembodied abstraction with no material foundation. The word 'organic' suggests a relationship that is natural and deep-rooted, dynamic and evolving, yet also somehow unknowable. Such a conception is vague to the point of being almost 'mystical'. Furthermore, the biological analogy implicit in the notion of 'organic harmony' recalls some of the most conservative ideas in functionalist social science, from Herbert Spencer and the so-called 'organistic school of sociology' to Talcott Parsons and beyond. It is surprising that communist theoreticians, normally so scathing on the biological determinism and Social Darwinism implicit in the organic analogy in social science, should so readily accept these concepts when applied to their own theory of organisation.

Finally, just where in the communist world has the problem of internal Party democracy actually been resolved 'progressively'? Certainly not in any of the countries of 'achieved socialism', all of which adhere strictly to democratic centralism. Of all communist parties the PCI has perhaps come closest to confronting the problem, but it still has some way to go in developing a coherent theoretical critique of Leninism. In this respect, I fear that Gramsci's so-called 'correct theoretical understanding' of how the Party should function progressively offers little comfort or solution to the problem of bureaucratic centralism and Stalinism. The roots of Stalinism lie not only in a dogmatic or schematic interpretation of Lenin, as many communists still claim, but also in democratic centralism itself and in Lenin's theory of the one-party state. No tinkering with these fundamentals, and no amount of 'organic harmony' can ever abolish the dangers of authoritarianism that inhere in the structure of Lenin's Party model and in the political culture that arises from Leninist ideology and organisation.

Whether any Leninist party in power can escape from this dilemma and achieve sufficient intraparty democracy to prevent despotism has yet to be demonstrated. This is precisely the issue being tested in the Soviet Union today. Gorbachev's attempt to reform the Soviet system has met with considerable resistance from conservatives within the Central Committee. But pressures from the Soviet republics, combined with the Party's inability to reform itself, have prompted him to announce that the Party intends to renounce its monopoly on power.[18] Having resisted the move toward 'bourgeois' multiparty pluralism, Gorbachev has now all but admitted that his reforms cannot succeed within the framework of democratic centralism and the one-party state. But whether they will fare better in a multiparty system or satisfy the growing demands for regional autonomy within the USSR has yet to be seen.

Democratic Centralism and Communist Identity

During the mid-1980s the PCI showed all the signs of a party going through an 'identity crisis'. As one local Party activist from Perugia remarked, 'the PCI has shifted from being a Leninist Party to something different – not social democracy, but something as yet still undefined.' The PCI is trying to formulate a new identity, one that plays down many of the traditional symbols of communism, including the clenched-fist salute, the hammer and sickle of communist internationalism, the proletarian vanguard depicted as male manual workers united in industrial conflict, and the Leninist language of class war. Instead, it now extols respectable, characteristically middle-class values, including honesty, efficiency, good administration, civil liberties and the rule of law.

In the construction of this identity ('neither social democracy nor

Marxism-Leninism'), the PCI's Leninist legacy has posed major problems. Relics of that legacy have continued to permeate the organisation and the culture of Italian communism. Thus, the PCI's identity crisis was bound up with the crisis in communism itself. Perhaps the core of this problem hinges around the issue of democracy and the principle of democratic centralism: once this principle is challenged, so, too, are the ideological and organisational bases of leadership, authority and legitimacy – in other words, the entire nexus of power relations and decision-making that has hitherto given structure and coherence to communist parties everywhere.

Within the PCI, the principle of democratic centralism, like the ideology of 'unity', traditionally served to bind the Party together into an effective, disciplined political force. That reason alone was enough for the PCI leadership to defend and to justify its continued use. The PCI's argument rested largely on the observation that factions in other political parties have become a major and continuing source of corruption and political clientelism. Thus, as the PCI sees it, Party 'factionalism' is ultimately responsible for much of the general malaise and corruption that has continued to plague the Italian political system. PCI leaders, therefore, have typically contrasted the positive aspects of democratic centralism with the internecine warfare, clientelism and power-brokerage characteristic of the Christian Democrats and other parties.[19]

However, the history of democratic centralism in the PCI over the past two decades is essentially that of a secularised dogma being allowed to fall into progressive disuse. This occurred *pari passu* with a general policy of 'secularisation' in the Party, a policy carried out in a steady but piecemeal fashion. Thus, by 1979 the PCI leadership could finally declare itself officially a 'lay party' – which, in Italian politics, means a party no longer bound to a traditional, communist ideological world-view. At the same Congress the PCI also abolished the statutory obligation of all Party members to 'study' Marxism-Leninism. At one level this might appear irrelevant, as few ordinary members still took the obligation seriously anyway, but the significance went beyond the mass membership. As Tiersky (1985: 113) writes,

> What counted here was more the effect this had on the habits and mentality of party cadres and militants as opposed to the simple card-carrier. They were being, in effect, told two things: (1) that party policy is not a function of a scientific application of scientific doctrine; and (2) that it is no longer necessary to explain or to defend PCI policy as a function of the world political development scenario worked up in Moscow and ratified in international communist documents and meetings.

From here, the PCI leadership moved swiftly to the constitutional position that it was no longer necessary even to be a 'Marxist' in order to hold office in the Party, yet it remained defensive about democratic centralism and Lenin.[20] Berlinguer continued to defend democratic centralism even at the

1983 Congress – when the main issue of debate was internal Party democracy. He did so, quite cleverly, by arguing that since democratic centralism was no longer an ideological totem, those calling for an official abolition of democratic centralism were themselves 'being ideological' and, therefore, against the ethos of secularisation. The Congress accepted the leadership's line, which now designated democratic centralism as a 'method' rather than a set of 'principles'. The result, in effect, was the demotion of democratic centralism from, as Tiersky (1985: 112) put it, 'an ideological essence and "an emblem on a flag" to a set of clearly parliamentary rules, with increased rights and guarantees especially for local party instances and individual members *vis-à-vis* the the party's central authority'.

These internal changes are some of the most visible signs of the PCI's protracted retreat from a Leninist world-view, but the pressure for change came from outside the Party as well as inside.

Faced with increasing criticism of its internal democracy, PCI leaders had difficulty in justifying the practice to themselves, let alone to the Party's mass membership. As Giorgio Napolitano declared, in a characteristically oblique understatement: 'We have still to find a way for a better compromise between unity and open debate in our Party. We cannot say a completely satisfactory solution has been found.'[21]

Internal Party Criticisms of Democratic Centralism: Acceptance of Multiparty Pluralism

Within the PCI, democratic centralism was challenged for the first time in the late 1960s by leaders of the Manifesto group, who were subsequently expelled from the Party as a result. But it was the historian and PCI intellectual, Salvatore Sechi, who carried the debate into a more public and controversial arena. Writing in the sociological review *Il Mulino*, Sechi stated (1978: 62), that 'in Italy there exists a real danger of an involution towards an authoritarian mass society.' That danger, he added, 'could also arise from the missing solution to the problem of the internal regime of the PCI'.

In the typically ambiguous and veiled style Italian communists adopt when discussing internal Party matters in public, Sechi (1978: 63) suggested that with a 'certain' use of democratic centralism there was the risk, not only of authoritarianism, but also of 'Bonapartism, Jacobinism, bureaucratic oligarchy and the absorption of the autonomy of the working class and its organisations into the state'. The argument caused considerable embarrassment for the PCI, despite Sechi's rejoinders that this risk lay not so much in a party of opposition, as in a party of government and in the 'merging' of functions between party and state that may occur when a party has the resources of the state at its disposal.

Sechi's message was ambiguous. On the one hand, he seemed to be saying that the PCI posed a threat to Italian democracy, but, on the other hand, that the threat of authoritarianism lay not in democratic centralism *per se*, but only in its application under conditions of a one-party state. The latter case would not apply to the PCI since it has emphatically rejected the idea of a communist monopoly of power, and has long ago renounced the theory of the one-party state. This was announced officially in 1975 when the Italian and French communist parties issued a joint declaration which stressed their intention to achieve power through parliamentary means, and their acceptance of a multi-party system.[22] This was underlined with even greater clarity the following year at the conference of European communist parties held in East Berlin. Here Berlinguer told delegates that

> In Italy, where the working class and our Party have been, and are, protagonists in the fight to restore, defend and develop democracy, we are fighting for a Socialist society which has at its foundation the value of individual and collective liberties and their guarantee, the principles of the secular, non-ideological nature of the state and its democratic organization, the plurality of political parties and the possibility of alternation of government majorities, the autonomy of the trade unions, religious freedom, freedom of expression, culture, arts and the sciences.[23]

The sinister side of Sechi's argument was that the PCI was, in effect, operating two types of democracy: pluralism outside the Party and democratic centralism inside. For Sechi, this represented a dangerous contradiction. The lack of pluralism within the Party might, he suggested, threaten to influence Italian democracy at large were the PCI to form a government.

The PCI leadership dismissed Sechi's hypothesis outright, though it did accept, in its 1982 draft theses, that 'new terms on which to pose the relationship between democracy and unity', had to be found.[24] Once again, though, it defended democratic centralism on the grounds that this method guarantees unity, and unity guarantees 'the political autonomy of the Party' and its ability to command a credible consensus for an alternative government.[25] However, the PCI leadership appeared uncertain on the issue of reforming the Party's internal regime. For example, while it recognised the negative consequences of an overemphasis on 'unity' which at times had 'been practised in such a way as to dull the specific characteristics and autonomous initiative of the party', it also insisted that 'not always has defence of our historical patrimony and political line against distortions and massive attacks conducted from various sides been sufficiently prompt and firm.'[26]

Though freedom of discussion and dissent are principles openly proclaimed in PCI speeches and official documents, 'disunity' is considered a major crime against the Party, and is vehemently condemned and penalised. Threats to Party unity have always been severely dealt with. Among the crimes perceived to be a threat to unity are 'instrumentalism', 'personalism', and 'the aggregation of groups practising factionalism'.[27] For many people, however, the last named of these is the essence of pluralist democracy; namely, formal currents of opinion and factions crystallising around competing ideas. For the PCI, the dilemma was obvious: to 'secularise' the Party meant abandoning democratic centralism, but to abandon democratic centralism would both threaten 'Party unity' and undermine the position of the leadership. Democratic centralism has always been the most important 'centripetal' force guaranteeing order and internal Party discipline. Would removing it not, therefore, unleash all the Party's 'centrifugal' tendencies, which, like Pandora's box, would spread chaos into the communist world? This was a gamble that few communist leaders have hitherto been prepared to take.

Once again, the PCI leadership has found a way round the problem: it has abolished democratic centralism, but retained the ban on internal Party factions. Yet there is a major contradiction in all this. The new Party statutes, approved at the Congress in March 1989, have substituted the old formulas about Party discipline and unity with a novel set of clauses. Thus, it is now the 'right and duty' of each member not only 'to criticise the political work of the leadership at any level of party organisation' (Article 3, Clause [e]), but also, from time to time, to 'maintain and sustain, also publicly, differing positions to those of the majority' (Article 3, Clause [f]). Yet this is immediately contradicted by Article 6.6, which states:

> Deliberations adopted in conformity with the Statute are binding on all those who belong to the respective organisations and, if adopted by the national leadership, on the whole party. A decision taken by the majority must be respected by the minority barring the rights of members indicated in clauses 'e' and 'f' of Article 3.[28]

Democratic Centralism outside the Party

Even before being officially dropped, democratic centralism had been reworked from 'a political culture of totalitarian discipline into a constitutional set of rules' (Tiersky, 1985: 116). But in other spheres of Party life it had also been steadily eroded over a period of some 20 years. This can be seen throughout the Italian communist world. For example, PCI parliamentary candidates and prospective Party candidates are no longer imposed from above by a central Party committee operating secretly and using the infamous political 'biographies' – 'which are a standard Stalinist operational tool' (Tiersky, ibid.). This contrasts with the French Communist Party which still produces 'correct' candidates: the PCI committee that vetted such candidates was abolished years ago (Tiersky, 1985: 122).

Since the creation of the regional tier of government in 1970, there has been a marked degree of decentralisation of authority in the PCI, and many local Party organisations now choose their own candidates. No longer is there an expectation of monolithic or unanimous voting in the PCI parliamentary group, though the ban on factions still tends to result in a certain homogeneity and unity in voting patterns. Gone, too, is the traditional 'transmission belt' relationship between the PCI and the largely communist-dominated trade-union movement (CGIL). Ever since the 1960s the CGIL has been heavily engaged in autonomous, and traditional, trade-union activities, and not for several decades has it seen its role primarily as that of a propaganda and recruitment wing of the Party.

The PCI still supports a host of auxiliary or 'flanking' organisations for women, youth, sport, culture and so on, but it no longer holds a purely instrumental view of these organisations. Nor does it demand their unwavering obedience or loyalty. None of these bodies can seriously be considered Party 'front organisations'; they would attract few members if they were. Neither do members of these organisations see their own role as subservient to the interests of the Party. In short, the process of secularisation has been conducted outside as well as inside the Party, and the ties of democratic centralism that once bound all these organisations under the umbrella of Party discipline have been irrevocably severed.

If democratic centralism was a formula for tyranny – and it certainly has been a recipe for totalitarianism in those socialist states where it is practised at government level – why has a crisis of authoritarianism *not* occurred in the PCI? The answer Sechi (1978: 62) gave was that

> This contradiction has never become explosive because of the ability of the Communist leadership to find a series of corrections, adaptations and abrogations in the concrete application of the Statute. It is because of such adjustments that great ruptures and lacerations have been avoided.

This is not a very comforting thought: what Sechi is saying, in effect, is that authoritarianism was avoided in the PCI only because of the leadership's 'mis-application' of democratic centralism. In other words, the oligarchic and despotic tendencies inherent in democratic centralism were not brought to fruition simply because the PCI 'deviated' from Leninist norms and carried out 'a series of corrections, adaptations and abrogations' of the proper rules. Similar conclusions were drawn by the *Manifesto* group. The PCI leadership, they argued, had long recognised the problems inherent in applying Leninist principles to the Italian system. But rather than define new organising principles, it had attempted instead to ameliorate the difficulties by piecemeal and partial alterations, 'allowing a few rules to fall into disuse, suspending the application of others, providing a flexible and tolerant approach to the rest'.[29]

Sechi and the *Manifesto* group provided good descriptions of the problem of Communist Party organisation, but their solutions were inadequate and unconvincing. For Sechi (1978: 66), the answer lay not in any 'rigid formula (calls for discipline, votes, respect for Politburo decisions, etc.), but in a *custom* and in a *method* of work'. What this means in practical terms is unclear and becomes increasingly confused as Sechi tries to explain or, perhaps, to conceal through jargon, something that is logically incoherent. His solution (ibid.), echoing Gramsci, is found in

> A dynamic process which sees the moment of centralisation and discipline ... as a synthesis of the result of maximum participation ... overcoming the custom of uncritical and ritual acceptance of the political proposals of the speaker.

Like other communist intellectuals, Sechi poked at flaws in communist theory only to draw away from their logical conclusions, as if recoiling from the brink of some frightening abyss. In this case the metaphorical 'abyss' was the prospect of dismantling those canons of Leninist orthodoxy still enshrined in PCI ideology and organisation. The PCI itself has still not fully grasped the Leninist nettle, at least not in name, though it has abandoned virtually every major aspect of Leninist theory.

Is democratic centralism a formula for tyranny? The answer seems to be 'no', or, at least, not by itself. In a one-party state where the functions and identity of party and state fuse, it is highly likely to be so, but in a multiparty, pluralist system the risk is obviously diminished, though it is perhaps never completely extinguished. However, democratic centralism is not the only type of political organisation that facilitates dictatorship and tyranny; it merely allows dictators to rule more systematically. Democratic centralism helps to concentrate and perpetuate power at the apex of any large organisation, and therefore the potential for authoritarian rule is always present. It creates a structure for internal control and command which can easily be dominated and manipulated by a Central Committee or a First Secretary – and as Trotsky and E.H. Carr both pointed out, the very existence of such a mechanism invites its use.

The French Communist Party offers a vivid case in point. Having embarked upon the Eurocommunist road of liberalisation in the mid-1970s, the PCF subsequently lost ground to Mitterrand's newly resurrected Socialist Party. As a result, the PCF leadership concluded that Eurocommunism was a source of dissension and weakness. The minority within the Party who had favoured a PCI-type stance now fell silent, or they got out. PCF strategy was tendentially that of the old Popular Front policy, but this rested on the belief that the Communist Party would always be the dominant party of the Left, and did not need to change much to maintain this position. But once this premise was cast into doubt, the PCF leadership ordained changes from above which, according to J. Friend (1986: 64), were 'promulgated, not discussed, [and] easily rejected once their instant usefulness became questionable'. The Eurocommunist element could not convincingly argue that the Party must accept an inferior position. Thus, 'they were vanquished by the myth of the united, infallible party' and 'with the sword of democratic centralism in its hand, the leadership equated all criticism with subversion' (ibid.).

Why, then, have the excesses of authoritarianism not occurred within the PCI? In contrast to other communist parties, the PCI chose long ago to follow the path of democratic reform and Western-style parliamentary constitutionalism. But this happened in *spite of*, rather than *because of*, democratic centralism. With few exceptions, the progressive changes in Party strategy and organisation have been orchestrated by PCI leaders themselves, typically acting as a 'radical vanguard' against the more orthodox and conservative mass membership. It is unmistakably a story of reform from above, or, as Tiersky (1985: 101) put it, a policy of 'decommunisation' which 'has dared not speak its name ... a sort of protracted tacit leadership "conspiracy" to transform the political culture of the hierarchy and the mass membership'. The liberalisation of Italian communism since the 1960s has been a highly self-conscious policy, which, according to Tiersky (ibid.), has four goals:

> (1) to achieve legitimacy in Italian political life, thus moving the PCI off an historical dead-end strategy by making it an acceptable ally and, ultimately, government partner; (2) to justify disengaging Italian communism from the Soviet-controlled international communist movement ... ; (3) to re-educate the party bureaucracy and rank-and-file to accept the Italian Republic, and liberal parliamentary democracy generally speaking, as intrinsically desirable and permanent rather than temporary and instrumental ... ; and (4) to preserve internal equilibria inside the party during this period of deep change, in order to avoid a party split.

From the old, orthodox communist perspective, this policy would undoubtedly confirm the betrayal-at-the-top thesis. On the other hand, paradoxically, it could be argued that the PCI leadership is perhaps the only true 'communist vanguard' amongst the parties of the Third International. Unlike its more regressive counterparts in France, the Soviet Union and Eastern Europe, the radical and progressive PCI leadership has brought about an extraordinarily successful set of changes to their Party. In this respect the PCI, ironically, could claim to be one of the few communist parties that have remained true to the ideals of Marxism, rather than to what Lenin and Soviet practice has made of it. No other communist party has made or encouraged greater intellectual advances in Marxist theory, or gained such a popular footing in a democratic society. If Leninism entails 'vanguard leadership' and the 'leading role of the Party', then, on that score at least, the PCI is more 'Leninist' than the rest. The paradox in this, however, is that the PCI leadership has used Lenin's democratic centralism not only to disengage from the Soviet Union, but also to escape from the structures and ideology developed by Lenin himself and from the very principles upon which the PCI was first created.

Conclusion: End of the Road for Leninism?

The Italian Road to Socialism under Occhetto

The PCI Congress in March 1989 marked another turning point in the development of Italian communism. Occhetto's two-and-a-half-hour speech was a powerful illustration of how far he had brought the Party along its 'new course'. In it, he paid homage to the mechanism of the market – described as 'the measure of efficiency for the whole economy' – and he reaffirmed the PCI's commitment to democratic reform in the Western democratic socialist tradition.[1] This was the first Party Congress since Occhetto was appointed PCI general-secretary in 1987, and it served as a powerful confirmation of his position as undisputed Party leader. The Congress also ratified Occhetto's new political strategy, one that sought finally to banish from the Party the last remnants of Stalinism.

Under Occhetto's leadership the PCI has undergone a transformation in both its policies and public image. Whereas previous leaders emphasised the continuity of their policies with those of the past, Occhetto deliberately stressed the opposite; the *discontinuità* of his 'new course' and its rupture with the past. Significantly, he sought legitimacy for this reformist stance not from Lenin, but from the tradition of the French Revolution, and of European, rather than Russian, intellectuals. In an interview given to the journal *Espresso* in January 1989, Occhetto declared that the PCI was 'neither the child of the revolution of October 1917, nor of Jacobinism, but of the principles of 1789'.[2]

The theses for the 18th Congress represented a bold synthesis of Occhetto's ideas; even the language in which they were cast was radically different. Instead of the traditional language of Italian Marxism, they were, according to Salvatore Veca, the philosopher whose ideas have reputedly inspired Occhetto, 'full of echoes of American democrats, German social democrats, and liberal thinkers such as Ralf Dahrendorf'.[3] However, for much of the Party rank and file, Occhetto's prose appeared 'muddled' and 'excessively academic'. Yet despite considerable suspicion and resistance from the more traditional elements within the Party, Occhetto also succeeded in promoting a younger generation of Party leaders and in rallying round him both the Ingrao Left and the Party's Right and Centre. This left the pro-

Moscow old guard, led by Armando Cossuta, increasingly isolated and anachronistic. Ironically, however, PCI–Soviet relations have improved considerably since Gorbachev's premiership, and Occhetto's visit to Moscow in February 1989 marked a new phase of friendly dialogue between the leadership of the PCI and the CPSU. How far the 'Gorbachev effect' has influenced the internal dynamics of the PCI is difficult to gauge. Virtually every current within the Party, including the pro-Soviet old guard, see Gorbachev's reforms as highly positive, but draw different lessons. For the latter group, Gorbachev's policies are seen as a vindication of the Bolshevik Revolution and proof that the Soviet system is capable of reforming itself – contrary to Berlinguer's argument that the Soviet model represents a spent force and a closed chapter in the history of socialism. Elsewhere the attitude is that the CPSU is coming round to positions adopted years ago by the PCI, though there is fear that the obstacles before Gorbachev may eventually defeat him.[4] In terms of PCI policy, however, Gorbachev's honesty in admitting the political and economic shortcomings of the Soviet model has provided a spur to Occhetto's 'new course' and has helped convince the Party of the need to take a new initiative in Italian politics (see below).

If the 18th Congress set out to emphasise the PCI's break with tradition, it nevertheless also highlighted the membership's continuing emotional ties with Soviet communism. This was vividly demonstrated at the 1989 Congress – which critics described as a 'show biz spectacle'. Out of the 3 billion lire (£1.5 million) spent in staging the Congress, a huge screen was erected behind the podium, upon which was beamed the giant face of Gorbachev, who delivered a message of greeting to the delegates as they sat below, spellbound. It was Occhetto's idea that Gorbachev should send a video-recorded address to the Congress.[5] Drawing a parallel between the PCI's search for 'new solutions to the new problems of our times' and the 'revolutionary restructuring' underway in the Soviet Union, Gorbachev remarked to his attentive and enthusiastic listeners that he felt 'as though I am participating in your work'.[6]

In less conciliatory tones, Occhetto's keynote was a defiant challenge to the PSI and to Craxi's claim to leadership of the Italian Left. Dismissing the PSI's claim to be the only credible reformist alternative, Occhetto accused the socialists of opportunism in allying themselves with the ruling coalition parties, and of blocking any possibility of a progressive, Left-alternative in Italy. This brought enthusiastic applause from the delegates. Craxi, on the other hand, walked out during Occhetto's standing ovation, visibly angered by the speech, which he later dismissed as 'full of old stuff', little different from the old-style communism. However, the changes were real, as Craxi undoubtedly realised, and the new social-democratic direction laid down by Occhetto represented a serious threat to the PSI's goal of leading the Left-alternative in Italy.

As if to consecrate this new direction and the Party's new sense of unity, delegates approved Occhetto's strategy with a massive majority of 95 per cent. Ingrao, however – who received perhaps the longest and loudest applause of any speaker – gave a veiled challenge to Occhetto when he told the Congress that the PCI would never abandon its name, nor the hope of changing the capitalist system.[7]

The Italian Road to Socialism: What Remains of Leninism?

With hindsight, a clear pattern emerges in the development of PCI policy over the past 25 years, culminating in Occhetto's 'new course'. However else one might define it, the 'Italian road to socialism' has undoubtedly been part of a long march from the Soviet Union and Leninism, toward the European socialist tradition – though the PCI still differentiates itself from existing models of social democracy, neoliberalism and 'statism'.[8] Little now remains of that Leninist heritage that for almost seven decades gave Italian communism its meaning, its identity and its political culture. Almost every aspect of Soviet-style communism has been challenged by the PCI leadership and purged from the Party. The old-style Party organised around a cell structure with a covert strategy for insurrection has long been abandoned. Only a tiny minority of members still holds to the notion that the Soviet Union and its Party play a vanguard or 'leading role' in the world communist movement. The concept of one-party rule and the Leninist theory that justified it are rejected not only as 'anachronistic', but also as politically and morally unacceptable.

In their place the PCI advocates the need for power-sharing, political pluralism and the rotation of parties in government. In economic affairs it advocates planning but rejects nationalisation, with economic solutions to be based loosely around Keynesian policies buttressed by condemnations of the excesses of market forces, but with no objection to markets *per se*. Indeed, the PCI openly advocates a mixed economy and eclectic 'managerialism', both of which were once widely denounced as bourgeois. All the major concepts in the lexicon of Leninism have similarly been 'consigned to the attic' (Abse, 1986: 92); class war, proletarian internationalism and the dictatorship of the proletariat are now relics of a dying language found perhaps only in Albania, North Korea and China. Finally, the Italian communists have also taken steps toward a formal burial of the coercive mechanism of democratic centralism. In short, the PCI has, in characteristically unspoken fashion, consigned its Stalinist remnant to the mausoleum.[9]

What, therefore, remains of 'communism' in the PCI, and has it, in reality, ceased to be a communist party? A quarter of a century ago the political scientist Giorgio Bocca remarked that one of the PCI's most enduring features was its ability to disguise a very revisionist practice in a most orthodox language, but that language, too, has now changed, though the repudiation of Lenin has yet to be made official. For many observers, the PCI is no longer a communist party and it neither wants nor is capable of making a revolution (Tiersky, 1985: 99). Its declarations concerning a *terza via* or third way between capitalism and communism have not materialised into anything concrete as regards a new model for the management of the economy. While the PCI continues to make exciting contributions to political theory, its greatest weakness is finding viable economic solutions to the problems of modern capitalism.

In defence of the 'revisionist' PCI, however, it may be said that no communist party or communist regime anywhere has come up with a satisfactory economic policy, and the PCI's lack of faith in nationalisation and the command economy is justified. But Italian communism has to be understood in the context of Italian politics and its specific problems. Over half the Italian economy is already in the hands of the state, yet the state sector is riddled with corruption and notoriously inefficient. The problem, as the PCI sees it, is to overhaul the state system and make it work; to rewrite the constitution and bring about major structural changes in the system of government and its institutions. Reform of the tax system, for example, is seen as major avenue of attack, since the burden of taxation falls mainly on wage earners and salaried employees, while tax evasion is rife among the self-employed and the rich – a system on which the DC is reputed to thrive. From the PCI perspective, modern Italian capitalism has become increasingly parasitical; the welfare state has been corrupted into a system for buying votes in return for jobs, pensions and benefits, and vast amounts of government money have been wasted on development projects that have benefited speculators and politicians rather than the public in whose name they are justified. To the charge that the PCI wants to 'manage capitalism better than the Christian Democrats', some delegates to the 1989 Congress responded with an unequivocal 'yes'.

Is the PCI still a 'Communist' Party?

The historic dilemma for the PCI – and most other European communist parties – lies in reconciling Leninism with liberal pluralist democracy. With the collapse of the old communist regimes in Eastern Europe, the questions of Leninism and democracy and the legitimacy of one-party communist rule are again brought to the fore. Throughout the former Soviet bloc, including Yugoslavia and Lithuania, the very concept of a one-party state and of a communist monopoly on power has been rejected. By the end of 1989, only the USSR still retained its constitutional defence of the one-party state and the communist monopoly on power – but even here changes were afoot. Haunted by rampant nationalism in the Baltic and elsewhere, Gorbachev began to hint that major political reforms were needed in order to prevent the break-up of the Soviet Union. On 13 January 1990, he went a step further when he told Lithuanian communists and nationalist leaders that the USSR 'shouldn't be afraid of a multiparty system the way the devil fears incense'. He went on to say that he saw 'no tragedy in a multiparty system if, and I can tell you this straightforwardly, it arises as a result of a normal historical process and answers the needs of society' – though he warned that allowing more than one party was 'no panacea' for the ills of the USSR.[10] A few weeks later, on 5 February, in a speech to the CPSU, he pushed the reform process still further when he proposed a formal end to the Party's monopoly on power, and the introduction of a multiparty system. In an historic statement to the opening session of an extraordinary meeting of the Central Committee, Gorbachev declared that the Communist Party henceforth intended

> to struggle for the status of ruling party but will do that strictly within the framework of the democratic process, giving up any legal or political advantages ... The Party in a democratic society under renewal can exist and play its role as vanguard only as a democratically recognised force. This means that its status should not be imposed through constitutional endorsement.[11]

This meant, among other things, abolition of Article Six of the Soviet constitution, which enshrines the Communist Party's monopoly on power. Equally important, it also represented a fundamental inroad into hitherto sacrosanct communist ideology and a major departure from the Leninist theory of the vanguard party. Once the Party's 'leading role' is rejected as a constitutional principle, little remains of the theoretical justification that once sustained communist parties in power. Gorbachev's speech was tantamount to a repudiation of the Communist Party's old self-image: the Leninist definition of the Party as the vanguard of progress upon whom history has bestowed a special right to rule. Like the PCI before it, the CPSU has embarked upon its own road to revisionism, but it has yet to confront fully the problem of Lenin. The further it moves toward a pluralistic, multiparty system, the more its Leninist heritage is likely to become both a source of embarassment and an electoral liability.

Conservatives and anticommunists have naturally made much political capital from all this, citing the breakdown of communist regimes in Eastern Europe as 'evidence' of the failure of socialism in general, and the 'imminent worldwide triumph of liberal democracy', as Francis Fukuyama would have it.[12] In a similar vein, *The Economist*, in derisory tones, claims that Occhetto's goal is to take his 'pinker-than-red-communists' into Europe's 'social democratic camp', pointing out triumphantly that 'even Cossutta' has accused the PCI leader of creating a party 'which is communist only in name'.[13] However, the issue is not so black-and-white as this, for, as the PCI has shown, the term 'communism' is neither monolithic nor fixed, and its meaning is both complex and open to interpretation. Moreover, to conflate the words 'communism', 'socialism', and 'Marxism' as though they were all one and the same thing is a false and analytically sterile exercise. As both Bestor (1948) and Williams (1976) have argued, the meaning of 'communism' fluctuated considerably up until the October Revolution of 1917, when the term was appropriated by the All-Russian Communist Party (Bolsheviks). Thereafter its meaning became almost synonymous with Marxism-Leninism and the Soviet model of society. Marx and Engels called their manifesto 'Communist' rather than 'Socialist' because, as Engels described it: 'Socialism in 1847 signified a bourgeois movement, communism a working-class movement. Socialism was, on the Continent at least, quite respectable, whereas communism was the very opposite.'[14] But elsewhere, particularly in England, 'communism' was generally associated with 'community' and with localised experiments in common property, while 'socialism' was the harsher word as it was linked to atheism, militancy, and the reorganisation of society as a whole. In fact, socialism remained the predominant term used to describe most Marxist and left-wing movements until the Russian Revolution.

The post-1918 renaming of 'communism' by the Bolsheviks was, in the words of Raymond Williams (1976: 74), 'an act of historical reconstitution of the word, rather than of steady continuity'. Following Lenin's interpretation, 'communism' became a higher stage beyond socialism, through which, however, it must inevitably pass. It also acquired a more universal definition with Lenin's 21 articles for admission to the Comintern, and was subsequently transformed into an orthodoxy ('Marxism-Leninism') by Stalin in his book, *The Foundations of Leninism.*

In rejecting the 'leading role' of the Soviet Party, the dictatorship of the proletariat, the Bolshevik model for the seizure of power, and Marxism-Leninism as an ideological orthodoxy, the PCI has abandoned communism in its classic, ideal-typical sense. To a lesser extent, so have most other Western European communist parties, but this does not mean they have abandoned Marxism. According to the PCI, its critique of the 'exhaustion' of the Soviet model of communism was derived firmly from a Marxist analysis – 'an analysis of reality that is critical, historical and scientific, but at the same time follows values derived from the tradition of workers' movements of Marxist inspiration'.[15] In the view of the PCI, it was the Soviet communists, not the Italians, who had abandoned Marxist principles: both parties were claiming to represent the true spirit of Marxism.

Ironically perhaps, it was Marx who said of himself that he was not a Marxist, a comment that reflected his relative indifference to doctrinal rigidity and the completeness of his social philosophy. It also reflected the misgivings that both Engels and Marx in later life had about the dogmatism of some of their followers. Lenin was, without doubt, the greatest disciple of Marx and Engels, yet his ideas represented a radical departure from the Marxist tradition of Western Europe. Lenin's Marxism followed a tradition set by other Russian revolutionaries in being thoroughly dogmatic, to be supported in all contingencies by what Sabine (1948: 665) calls 'a kind of scholastic exegesis of the master's *ipsissima verba*'. At the same time, however, Lenin insisted that theory was only a guide to action – a set of suggestive ideas to be used in assessing concrete situations rather than a static body of doctrine. In reality, Lenin combined intellectual rigidity with extreme suppleness wherever he found it expedient to do so. His ability to unite opportunism with what he regarded as strict adherence to principle was one reason why he was so successful. But this set a pattern in Communist Party practice whereby it was possible to 'prove' that no policy, however unexpected, was really a departure from Marxism, but that it was only a better understanding of what Marxism had always really meant (ibid.).

The official definition of Lenin's philosophy, as laid down in Stalin's *Foundations of Leninism* (1924), is that 'Leninism is Marxism in the epoch of imperialism and of the proletarian revolution'. Lenin's work reputedly brought Marxism 'up to date' with developments in the capitalist society of which Marx and Engels saw only the beginning. But if the present epoch is no longer that of 'the proletarian revolution', as most communist parties would themselves agree, then it is logical to argue that a post-Leninist form of Marxism is now long overdue.

The PCI is no longer a communist party in the classic sense; indeed, its departure from the canons of Leninism is one of the chief reasons why it has been so successful. As Occhetto himself recently admitted,

> The strength of the PCI derives very much from the fact that it has been the party that moved furthest away from the basic principles on which the Comintern parties were founded.[16]

But what kind of a party is it? According to many members, the PCI is a 'mass Marxist party', very different from any political party hitherto created. Others define it instead as 'a mass party characterised by a strong reformist tendency, whose political culture is fundamentally Marxist, but open to contributions from all democratic political thought'.[17] It is misleading, therefore, to describe Italian communism as 'half-way between Leninism and social democracy', as some authors suggest.[18] In establishing itself as a mass party of Marxist inspiration, the PCI has developed a political culture that goes beyond the traditional Leninist Party. Hegemony, which is essentially an 'evolutionary' (but novel) approach to winning power, has replaced 'proletarian dictatorship' as the strategic core of Party theory. Furthermore, the PCI has developed a very diffferent conception of the state from that of Lenin. As Mancini (1977: 6), writing for the Party school expressed it: 'It is no longer just the Bosses' State, the State of the ruling class, but a State which the masses can enter into and change the relations of power.' From the PCI's perspective, the working class have not only become firmly integrated into the Italian state and political systems, but also have fundamentally changed them in the process. Similar arguments are advanced by Ingrao (1978: 101–4), who rejects the view held by Althusser and others that the state is an oppressive apparatus that must be rejected completely by the working class and 'conquered from the outside'.

The PCI's attempt to define an Italian road to socialism with its elusive 'third way' between capitalism and the socialist command economy is still bedeviled by problems, but, at the theoretical level at least, this has undoubtedly been one of the most exciting innovations in Marxist thought since Lenin. In setting out upon the Italian road to socialism back in 1956, the PCI took what was to become the first step toward redefining communism, though this was not a conscious aim at the time. The Party's formal acceptance of multiparty pluralism in the 1970s and its renunciation of democratic centralism in 1989 represented two further landmarks in that process. By the close of 1989, all that remained of Leninism within the PCI was the name 'communist' and the Party old guard – but here, too, changes were imminent.

The Debate about Changing the Party's Name

On 14 November Occhetto let it be known that the PCI was considering dropping the term 'communist' from its name and the hammer and sickle from its logo.[19] The announcement, made at a press conference at the Party headquarters in Rome, came as a surprise to both the Party membership and the press, and brought a flurry of attention and speculation from the Italian media. Even in Britain it was the topic of a *Guardian* editorial and front-page news in *The Independent*, which ran the story under the eye-catching heading 'Italy's Communists give up Communism'. As it transpired, this was a premature verdict, as the 56-member PCI executive had merely begun an animated discussion on the change-of-name issue, and no decision had yet been reached. The main issue discussed was the need to call a meeting of the Central Committee, which, in turn, would convoke a special Congress in 1990 to decide whether to 'refound' the Party under a new name with the aim of uniting the Left in Italy under a new identity.

This was not the first time the PCI had debated changing its name. At its Florence Congress in 1985, a communist deputy had proposed that the Party should change its name to the *Partito Democratico del Lavoro* (the 'Democratic Party of Work'), but the move was roundly rejected. However, in a speech given just before the 1989 Party Congress, Occhetto raised the issue again, making it clear that neither he, nor the group of 40-year-olds that he has promoted, found the idea heretical. The decision to put the change-of-name issue back on the agenda was Occhetto's idea, inspired largely by the dismantling of the Berlin Wall, but also by domestic considerations. Occhetto seized upon the turbulent events in Eastern Europe to push for the changes he believed would lead his Party out of the political isolation into which it had been sliding.

Significantly, a week before the announcement, Occhetto had met Neil Kinnock in Brussels to solicit his support, in what was the first meeting between an Italian Communist Party leader and a leader of the British Labour Party. The PCI had for some time been lobbying for recognition among European socialists and had formed extremely close relationships with the

German SPD. These moves fuelled rumours that the PCI was preparing to seek readmission to the Second International – which it had left in 1921. What PCI leaders feared, it was said, was that with the collapse of the communist regimes in Eastern Europe, the PCI itself would now be damned by its identification with the word 'communist'. As Occhetto said,

> We in Italy have borne this name with honour. It has been dishonoured by those who built totalitarian systems in their countries. The collapse of the Berlin Wall has changed the European Left; we must change too.[20]

After the massacre at Tienanmen Square, which was the Chinese Communist Party's military solution to its moral disintegration, many observers had predicted the PCI's complete electoral eclipse, yet this did not happen: the PCI vote recovered from its low of 25.8 per cent in the 1987 general election, to receive 28 per cent in the June 1989 European elections, and its vote held at 26.6 per cent in the Rome city-council elections of October 1989. But despite this halt in its electoral decline, the PCI was still facing the same predicaments as before, though the need for a new initiative was now given a new urgency by the rapidly changing political map of Europe.

Occhetto's announcement that the PCI intended to give up the name 'communist' and to relaunch itself under a new banner was a calculated risk designed to elicit what commentators described as a 'controlled explosion' in Italy. But that explosion may yet backfire on him, as the attempt to persuade the Party to accept a new identity stunned many ordinary members and threatened to provoke a long and divisive quarrel. Indeed, it so inflamed passions within the Party that a spontaneous and angry protest developed outside the PCI's Rome headquarters on 20 November, which, according to reports, 'posed a physical threat to known Occhetto supporters when they arrived for a Central Committee meeting' that evening.[21]

The Central Committee none the less voted by 219 to 73, with 34 abstentions, to back Occhetto's plan to change the Party name, despite fierce opposition from both the Party's hard Left and pro-Soviet old guard. Supporting the decision, Occhetto said: 'We offer something that goes beyond a name change. We propose to create a new force, to unfreeze the Italian political system.'[22]

Similar winds of change were blowing through the Communist Party of Great Britain (CPGB), which held its Congress in London on 25 November 1989. Here, too, changing the Party's name was debated, but a motion to drop the title 'Communist' was heavily defeated. However, in his keynote speech, Martin Jacques, editor of *Marxism Today* and a member of the Party's executive committee, told delegates, in no uncertain terms, that events in Eastern Europe had given a new urgency to the question of the Party's future. He added:

> It is the end of the road for the communist system as we have known it: the central plan, the authoritarian state, the single-party system, the subjugated civil society. Stalinism is dead, and Leninism – its theory of the state, the concept of the party, the absence of civil society, its notion of revolution – has also had its day.[23]

Like the PCI, the CPGB was searching for a new identity and, though many had not yet realised it, an escape from Leninism. If the PCI special Congress called for 1990 approves Occhetto's move – as it probably will – the question will be not so much what name will replace 'Communist', as what kind of ideology and organisation will replace that of the old Party? The answer will emerge more clearly over the next few years, but it seems likely that the new Party will continue along the path set by Occhetto at the 1989 Congress when the PCI took the final step toward becoming a fully 'secular' and democratic, mass-socialist Party.

For many PCI members, however, the name change will come as a psychological blow. However much the leadership tries to persuade people of the correctness of the decision, it will still be interpreted as a renunciation of the past – and therefore all that the older generation of Party activists struggled for. Furthermore, as this study has tried to show, communism in Italy has come to acquire a rather particular and positive set of meanings; it is *sui generis*, something peculiarly 'Italian' rather than Bolshevik or Soviet, and it still commands a great deal of loyalty and respect from the Italian people. While the PCI leadership hopes that dropping the name 'Communist' will be acknowledged as a public confirmation of the Party's formal and definitive repudiation of Leninism, some members will, no doubt, see the name change as a defeat. To some extent this is correct: it does represent a defeat for communism. It is a symbolic statement that Marxism-Leninism, at least in the view of Europe's largest communist party and heir of the Third International, is irredeemable.

But this does not represent a defeat for Marxism or for socialism. On the contrary, the PCI's attempt to redefine communism and to give it a new identity has not been a failure. Even before Occhetto's move to abandon the 'communist' label, the PCI had already succeeded in becoming the first 'post-Leninist' communist party. But the real lesson of the PCI is that communism with a 'human face' is not feasible until Leninism has been dismantled, and the Party freed from the grip of its authoritarian strictures and structures. In some respects the name change will be a disappointment to those who had hoped to rescue the name of communism from its exclusive associations with Lenin and Soviet practice. This may all be, in the end, a point of semantic rather than substantive importance, but for the many Party and ex-Party members in Italy who still identify – emotionally if not intellectually – with the old Party symbols, the label 'communist' is no arbitrary matter, and its removal is likely to lose the Party many supporters. The gamble is that these will be offset by the new supporters and members that the refounded Party will gather.

The Future of the (Ex-) Italian Communist Party?

The Italian Communist Party has set out on uncharted waters on a course that will steer it toward either division and decline or further political success and the leadership of a realigned Italian Left. Its avowed objective is to break the pattern of post-war politics that has enabled successive Christian Democrat-led governments to dominate state and society in Italy for over 42 years. That in itself, according to many PCI members, would precipitate changes of a revolutionary order in Italy. The PCI's problem, however, is that to unite the Italian Left round a common platform requires an alliance with the Socialist Party. Herein lies one of the major weaknesses of Occhetto's strategy, for the socialists have repeatedly refused to enter into a coalition dominated, as they see it, by the PCI. Indeed, for over two decades the PSI has served as a junior but indispensable partner in government, and it has enjoyed, more than almost any other party, the privileges and rewards of state patronage which come from being in government. Whether it would give up these privileges in order to join a reformist government whose programme would threaten the very system of political clientelism upon which the PSI has for so long flourished is questionable. Furthermore, the conditions for an alliance acceptable to Craxi are unlikely to be acceptable to the PCI – unless it renounced its campaign to combat the abuse of the state system and the whole problem associated with Italy's continuing *sottogoverno* (system of political patronage). Changing the Party's name resolves none of these domestic problems.

The success of the PCI as one of Europe's largest and most influential parties of the Left has been contingent upon its unity and internal solidarity, but whether this will remain intact is uncertain. An opinion poll published in November 1989 suggested that six out of ten Italians favour a change of Party name[24] – a poll which might augur well for the electoral success of the new Party, but the views of the mass membership have yet to be canvassed. Occhetto's strategy will undoubtedly meet fierce opposition from supporters of Cossutta and Ingrao, and from members of the old *Manifesto* group and the CGIL. Some of these dissidents may unite in opposition and eventually form their own breakaway party. With the abolition of democratic centralism and a progressive weakening of the ideology of unity, which was traditionally based on a powerful and collective sense of communist identity, the fabric that has held the Party together so well in the past may well disintegrate in the future. If that scenario is correct, then Occhetto's gamble may well prove to have failed. If the gamble succeeds, however, Occhetto could see his Party emerge triumphantly from the ghetto of permanent opposition into which it has been confined ever since the first Cold War. Whatever the outcome, the PCI provides valuable lessons for other communist parties, and it remains a source of inspiration for all those European socialists – Marxist and non-Marxist – who have rejected Lenin.

Notes and References

Introduction

1. Further discussion of the name-change issue is contained in the Conclusion to this book.
2. For further analysis of this, see Chapter 2.
3. For an analysis of the origins and character of Italy's marked political geography, see Chapter 3.
4. Staar, 1980, *International Yearbook on Communist Affairs*, p. xxi.
5. See Carrillo, 1977, *Eurocommunism and the State*. For a good account of Eurocommunism, see Tokes (ed), 1978, *Eurocommunism and Detente*; Boggs and Plotke (eds) 1980, *The Politics of Eurocommunism*; Claudin, 1978, *Eurocommunism and Socialism*; Filo della Torre et al. (eds), 1979, *Eurocommunism: Myth or Reality?*.
6. For the most pessimistic view and an argument constructed along these lines, see Godson and Haseler, 1978, *Eurocommunism: Implications for East and West*. See also Hodgson, 1979, 'The US Response'.
7. For further discussion of the Cold War and its impact on the PCI, see Chapters 1, 2 and 4.
8. For an analysis of this, see Juan Botella (1989), 'Spanish Communism in Crisis' in Waller and Fennema (eds). Unlike the PCF or PCI, the Spanish Party after 1975 was either unwilling or unable to build on the anti-Fascist resistance in order to create a more permanent basis for Party allegiance. As Botella writes (p. 80), internal strife prevented it from strengthening its position by building 'a sub-cultural setting that might become a shelter for hard times'.
9. This is also the conclusion reached by Pacheco Pereira (1989), 'A Case of Orthodoxy: The Communist Party of Portugal', in Waller and Fennema (eds), p. 93.
10. John Bloomfield, 1989, 'Communism, Crisis and Change', *7 Days: Communist Party Weekly*, 28 Oct, p. 7.
11. Gareth Steadman Jones, 1989, p. 231.
12. Reported in Keesing's, June 1989, p. 36746.
13. Keesing's, Aug 1989, p. 36856.
14. Anne Tomforde, 1989, 'SED Corruption Revelations Decisive', *The Guardian Weekly*, Vol. 141, No. 23, (10 Dec), p. 7.
15. This is illustrated most vividly by D. Kertzer (1980).
16. For further discussion of hegemony, see Chapter 3.
17. PCI Statuto, 1983, p. 3.
18. The idea of a Marxist culture (or 'sub-culture'), is discussed by Lovett (1980),

and by Kertzer (1980). Though some writers have long argued that the PCI is no longer a threat to NATO or Western democracy (cf. Kogan, 1962: 48), many conservative journals – including *Encounter*, *Foreign Affairs*, and *Foreign Policy* – disagree. According to Hodgson (1979), the view that 'Eurocommunism is simply the old Stalinist enemy in a new guise' still permeates much of the thinking behind US foreign policy.

19. Leading writers in this tradition include Almond (1954), Banfield (1958), Selznik (1960), Almond and Verba (1963), and La Polombara (1963; 1964; 1974). Their method involved an attempt to construct pseudoscientific models of political behaviour that were then used to explain communism as the consequence of a backward political culture. Borrowing heavily from the ideas of clinical psychology, some interpreted communism in terms of social pathology, personality disorder and deviancy. The result was the 'communist as fanatic' stereotype. This is discussed further in Chapter 2.
20. This approach characterised numerous anthropological studies, including those of Weingrod (1968), Silverman (1967; 1967; 1975), Davis (1973), Kertzer (1980) and White (1980) – all of which analyse politics within a specific local context. These studies generated valuable insights, but, being limited to the microworld of local village politics, they often failed to engage wider problems or else made generalisations based on very limited community-study data. With the exception of White, few give much consideration to ideology, history or the influence of macroevents on local political patterns.
21. This school is represented by the works of political scientists and historians, including Tarrow (1967), Allum (1973), Amyot (1981), Sassoon (1981), Ruscoe (1982) and Urban (1986). Most of these authors focus on specific aspects of the PCI (i.e. PCI political strategy, PCI–Soviet relations, or specific historical periods). Though these get nearer to understanding the PCI's success, they often ignore the local, the cultural, and the subjective dimensions of PCI politics; that is, the way the PCI sees itself and the way that Party history and strategy are received and experienced by ordinary Party members. Much has also been written on the PCI by Italian sociologists, including Poggi (1968), Galli and Prandi (1970), Barbagli and Corbetta (1978), and Sechi (1979), as well as by Bologna University academics and contributors to the review *Il Mulino*. The PCI has also commissioned its own sociological investigations (cf. Ilardi and Accornero [1982]; and Aris [1984]).
22. Many of the findings come from first-hand experience based on 18 months' intensive fieldwork in the communist-controlled city of Perugia in Umbria – the smallest of the three regions which comprise Italy's 'Red-Belt' zone. My initial period of fieldwork in Perugia was from July 1982 to January 1984. This included regular attendance at local-, provincial-, and national-level Party meetings; participation in local Party work and PCI rallies and festivals; and attendance at Party congresses at local and national level. Throughout the period of fieldwork, informal conversations and formal interviews with local activists, Party functionaries and national Party leaders were recorded. Other sources included uncollated and unpublished archival data from local sections, the Perugia Federation, and the national Party school in Rome (the 'Frattocchie'), where I attended a training course for Party cadres in 1983.
23. For useful anthropological studies of political symbolism and ritual, see Kertzer, 1988, *Ritual, Politics and Power*; Bocock, 1974, *Ritual in Industrial*

Society; Douglas, 1966, *Purity and Danger*; Lukes, 1975, 'Political Ritual and Social Integration'. For interesting case-studies, see Lane, 1981, *The Rites of Rulers*, and Abélès, 1988, 'Modern Political Ritual: Ethnography of an Inauguration and a Pilgrimage by President Mitterrand'.

24. A good example of the latter is the EEC's 1973 'Declaration on the European Identity'. Useful anthropological treatment of the concept of identity can be found in Epstein, 1978, *Ethos and Identity*; and MacDonald (ed), 1990, *Inside Identities: Ethnography in Western Europe*. For detailed treatment of the concept applied to psychology, see Erikson, 1968, *Identity, Youth and Crisis*.
25. For illustrations of this in the evolution of PCI identity, see Chapter 2.
26. For an excellent study of identity from this kind of perspective, see Epstein, 1977, *Ethos and Identity*, and Sword, 1983, 'Ethnic Identity and Association Among Polish Émigrés in a British Town'.
27. For a more detailed exposition of this, see Shore, 1990, 'Ethnicity as Revolutionary Strategy'.
28. Cf. Poliakov, 1971, *The Aryan Myth*.
29. For a good ethnographic study that illustrates how this process works, see W. Christian, 1972, *Person and God in a Spanish Valley*.
30. PCI Electoral Propaganda Leaflet, 1981, 'Veniamo da lontano e andiamo lontano'.
31. For ethnographic studies of *campanilismo*, see Pratt, 1981, 'A Sense of Place'; and Silverman, 1975, *Three Bells of Civilisation: The Life of an Italian Hill-Town*.
32. For excellent insight into this, see Anderson, 1983, *Imagined Communities: Reflections on the Origin and Spread of Nationalism*.
33. The comments of J. Bloomfield on this theme are illuminating. Reviewing David Forgacs and Geoffrey Nowell-Smith's book on *The Cultural Conditions for Political Transformation*, she writes: 'One of the underlying concerns that emerges from this book is the role of culture in the creation of collective identity, both as a nation and as a class, which is a precondition of revolution. This collective identity enables the subject to rise up, and intervene in history as a protagonist' *Marxism Today*, Vol. 29, No. 6 June 1985: 40.
34. *Lo Statuto del PCI*, 1983, p. 71.
35. This is a working definition adapted from Gould, 1964, p. 16. For discussion of definitions, see Christensen et al., 1972; Abercrombie, 1980; Bottomore (ed), 1983. I reject the ambiguous early Marxist definition of ideology as 'false consciousness', or distorted views based on illusion that serve only to buttress class rule – though some ideologies may well have this function, (see, for example, Guizzardi, 1976, 'The Rural Civilisation: Structure of an Ideology For Consent': see also Marx and Engels, 1968, *The German Ideology*, pp. 23 ff.; Marx and Engels, 1957, 'Contribution to the Critique of Hegel's Philosophy of Law', pp. 38–52).

    I also reject the definition, once popular amongst Western social scientists, of ideology as 'secular religion', or a 'closed conceptual system' characteristic of totalitarian political movements (cf. Mannheim, 1936, *Ideology and Utopia;* Arendt, 1953, 'Ideology and Terror: A Novel Form of Government'; Bell, 1960, *The End of Ideology*; and Shils, 1955, 'The End of Ideology?'). Both Marxists and liberals have distinguished ideology from 'true consciousness', or 'social science', thus drawing an analytical separation between falsehood and facts; between dogma and scientific truth or whatever. This is a false distinction. Ideologies are phenomena common to all groups and all societies, though they vary in form. As Bell (1977, pp. 298–9) himself was later to admit, ideologies may be regarded as 'social formulas', or belief systems which can be used to mobilise people to action. Ideologies are interpretative schemes used by social groups to make the world intelligible to themselves; they are just one kind of symbol system amongst many others, such as the religious or the scientific, (cf. Geertz 1975, 'Ideology as a Cultural System' pp. 193–233). The latter definition is the one closest to the conception of ideology employed in the present study – though some writers prefer the broader term 'conceptual system' instead.

36. Gramsci (1971) contrasted what he called 'common sense' with systematic thought. Common sense is practical, organic and uncritical, but fragmentary and incoherent. This was identified with the masses. Theoretical thought was identified with an elite. Either a dominant class can impose a theoretical consciousness on the masses (hence their possible subjugation to bourgeois ideology), or an intellectual stratum can develop common sense into a revolutionary consciousness (hence the vanguard role of Party intellectuals, as ideas become transformed into material force).
37. Marx, 1968, 'Preface to a Contribution to the Critique of Political Economy', p. 181. This point is reiterated in the *German Ideology* and forms one of the fundamental premises of the materialist conception of history.
38. As Gramsci wrote:

> To the extent that ideologies are historically necessary they have a validity which is 'psychological'; they 'organise' human masses, and create the terrain on which men move, acquire consciousness of their position, struggle, etc. ... The analysis of these propositions tends, I think, to reinforce the conception of historic bloc in which precisely material forces are the content and ideologies are the form, though this distinction between form and content has purely didactic value, since the material forces would be inconceivable historically without form and the ideologies would be individual fancies without the material forces.

(Gramsci, 1971, 'The Study of Philosophy', in *Selections from the Prison Notebooks*, pp. 376–7).

39. These points are dealt with in greater detail in Chapter 7.
40. Foremost amongst those who shared this view were Karl Liebknecht and the Polish/German revolutionary, Rosa Luxemburg (1871–1919), both founder members of the *Spartakusbund* ('Sparticists') – a left-wing, revolutionary splinter group which broke from the German Social Democratic Party in 1917. Though both supported the Bolshevik Revolution, they ardently criticised Lenin's tactics, organisation and Party discipline. (See R. Luxemburg, 1961, *The Russian Revolution, and Leninism or Marxism)*.
41. This view also prevails in Gramsci's conception of the political party: 'Thus, since every party is only the nomenclature for a class, it is obvious that the party which proposes to put an end to class divisions will only achieve complete self-fulfilment when it ceases to exist because classes, and therefore their expressions, no longer exist' (1971, *Selections from the Prison*

Notebooks: 152). This theory presupposes that classes will disappear with the 'withering away of the state'. In a classless society the role of 'parties' is rendered obsolete, for all interests can be represented in the one single party, the party of the working class: the Communist Party.

42. The question of legitimacy and succession is particularly fraught with difficulty in communist states. Since most were created by revolutionary seizure of power involving a break with previous political traditions, the usual elements of political authority – the precedent of legal norms, tradition, continuity, and the theoretical right of the state to govern – are absent (cf. M. McCauley and S. Carter [eds], 1985, *Leadership and Succession in the Soviet Union, Eastern Europe and China*; see also N. Harding [ed], 1984, *The State in Socialist Society*; and Schapiro, 1970, *The Communist Party of the Soviet Union*).
43. Indication of this comes from the spate of writings attempting to tease Gramsci apart from Lenin. See De Giovanni, 1976, 'La questione del partito'; and Mancini, 1977, 'A proposito di alcuni temi Gramsciani'. For a collection of writings in English on this theme, see Mouffe (ed), 1979, *Gramsci and Marxist Theory*.
44. Marx and Engels, 1968, *The Communist Manifesto*, p. 35.

Chapter 1

1. The notion of 'historical epoch' adopted here is close to that used by the Brazilian Marxist and educationalist, Paolo Freire: 'An historical epoch is characterised by a series of aspirations, concerns, and values in search of fulfilment; by ways of being and behaving; by more or less generalised attitudes. The concrete representations of many of these ... constitute the themes of that epoch' (Freire, 1973, *Education for Critical Consciousness*, p. 5).
2. For an interesting analysis which identifies only six distinct political generations, see Accornero et al., 1983, *L'identità comunista*. Strangely, three of these are located in the decade between 1970 and 1980.
3. On the heuristic use of the concept of 'political generation', cf. K. Mannheim, 1959, *Essays in the Sociology of Knowledge*, London, Routledge and Kegan Paul, pp. 276–322.
4. These have been incorporated into the text. Some of the original autobiographies transcribed into English can be found in Shore, 1985, 'The Italian Communist Party: Ideology, Identity, Organisation' (unpublished D. Phil. thesis).
5. The initial impetus for compiling a PCI history from the Italian Communist perspective came from recording the oral testimonies and personal histories of Party members during fieldwork in Perugia (and in Party meetings attended in Rome, Milan, Pisa and Reggio Emilia). These autobiographies provided a framework which was then developed, using mainly official, popular PCI historical sources. These included: Sezione centrale scuole di partito del PCI (no date), *Quaderni di Storia Del PCI*; PCI, 1980, *PCI '81: Almanacco del Sessantesimo*; E.P. Amendola, P. Spriano, and R. Giannotti (eds), 1981 ; G. D'Alo and F. Lazzari (no date), *Il Partito Comunista Italiano: Alcune linee di storia e di politica*; Sezione centrale di stampa e propaganda, 1976, *Almanacco PCI '76*; L. Gruppi, 1981. In addition *Keesing's Contemporary Archives* was consulted for specific dates and facts. Other sources on general twentieth-century Italian history included Kogan (1983), Cammett (1967), Hoare and Smith (1971), Marzani (1980), Seton-Watson (1967) and Sassoon (1981).

6. Figures cited in Cammett, 1967: 65.
7. But it was not until summer 1920, at the Communist International's second Congress, that Lenin's 21 Articles for membership to the Third International were put forward. Among these were demands that the PSI expel its reformists and change its name from *Partito Socialista Italiano* to *Sezione Italiana dell' Internazionale Comunista.* For further discussion of Lenin and the Comintern, see Chapter 7.
8. For further discussion of this, see Chapter 4.
9. Nenni, quoted in Cammett, 1967, *Antonio Gramsci and the Origins of Italian Communism*, p. 66.
10. Cf. Hoare and Nowell-Smith, 1971, 'Introduction', *Antonio Gramsci: Selections from Prison Notebooks*, p. xxviii.
11. Sambuccari, 1983, 'Interviews'. All of the fieldwork 'interviews' cited throughout this book are contained in Shore, 1985, 'The Italian Communist Party'.
12. Hence their receptivity 'to political expedients of quite a different order' (Cammett, 1967: 121).
13. Hoare and Nowell-Smith, 1971, p. lxiii.
14. This is discussed further in Chapter 4. For a detailed analysis of this, see Bates, 1976, 'Antonio Gramsci and the Bolshevisation of the PCI'.
15. Zinoviev, cited in Hoare and Nowell-Smith, 1971, p. lxx.
16. In Italy, fractionalism within the Russian Party was identified with the struggle in the PCd'I with Bordiga (who sided with Trotsky on a number of major issues). Hence, Stalin put pressure on Scoccimarro to include an attack on Trotsky in his prepared speech on Bolshevisation and the struggle against Bordiga (Hoare and Smith, 1971, p. lxxvii).
17. Rasimelli, 1983, 'Interviews', in Shore, 1985.
18. For a good analysis of the character of PCI militants, see the essays by Accornero, Magna, Hellman and Pasquini in Accornero et al., 1983, *L'identità comunista*; also useful is Pridham, 1981, *The Nature of the Italian Party System.*
19. A comment by Bordiga expressed this attitude succinctly: 'The bourgeois counterrevolution for us is the proof of the inevitability of the revolution' (cited in Hoare and Smith, 1971, p. lxxv).
20. This anti-Fascist reputation was particularly helpful to the PCI during the first Cold War and later in 1960 (see below in this chapter and Chapter 4).
21. For an interesting survey of Italy during this period, see Galli and Prandi, 1970, *Patterns of Political Participation in Italy*. As these authors point out, the principal division in post-war Italian society was not geographical or generational but 'a division between a moderate Italy and a revolutionary Italy' – made deeper by international stresses – and one between rival conceptions of Italy's future as a socialist 'people's democracy' or a capitalist 'liberal democracy' (ibid., p. 12).
22. In addition, 40 per cent of all school buildings had been severely damaged; so had 20 per cent of hospital buildings and 8,327 bridges. In agriculture the damage amounted to an estimated cost of 550 billion lire, and 825 billion in industry. Against an inflationary rise in the cost of living to 750 per cent, wages increased by only 30 per cent (cf. Amendola et al., 1981, *Storia fotografica del partito comunista*, p. 2).

23. What Togliatti's motives were, and why the Italian communists did not organise an insurrection at this point are two questions explored in Chapter 4.
24. For an analysis of the background to and theory behind the *Partito Nuovo* see Chapters 2, 3 and 4.
25. Caponi, 1983, 'Interviews'.
26. Cannavota, 1983, 'Interviews'.
27. Many of the PCI's top leadership during the Berlinguer era, including Berlinguer himself, were recruited during the period spanning 1941–7.
28. This metaphor actually first appeared, in February 1945, in a propaganda article written by Goebbels, but its popular usage as a term to describe ideological restraint and the absence of freedom of movement after Yalta and Potsdam in the Soviet-bloc countries of Eastern Europe is owing to Churchill (Palmer, 1983: 203).
29. Following the victory of the Christian Democrat Party, De Gasperi was also put under considerable pressure from the United States – which he resisted – actually to outlaw both the Communist and Socialist Parties (Kogan, 1983, *Political History of Italy*, p. 41).
30. The provisions of this pact included: (1) the liquidation of every remnant of the Fascist regime; (2) industrial reform and reconstruction based on the nationlisation of monopoly industries, the big banks, and public services; (3) agrarian reform based on the liquidation of the *latifundia* (the large estates) and on an increase in co-operative forms of agricultural production; (4) improvement in workers' conditions through wage increases, pensions, and cost-of-living subsidies; (5) social legislation guaranteeing work with minimum-wage rates, medical assistance, sickness provision and old-age pensions; (6) rigorous taxation on the incomes of the wealthy, a capital levy, and other measures of fiscal reform to benefit the workers and small investors; and (7) a foreign policy enabling Italy to regain as quickly as possible her political and economic independence (*Keesing's*, 1946, p. 8261).
31. For a detailed account of this incident, see Giorgio Bocca, 1973, *Palmiro Togliatti*.
32. Cannavota, 1983, 'Interviews'.
33. The basic assumption made by US foreign-policy advisers after 1947 was that communist influence should be contained within existing territorial limits, either by armed intervention (Vietnam) or by economic aid and technical assistance (the Colombo Plan and Marshall Plan aid).
34. For an analysis of PCI organisational manoeuvres during this period, see Chapter 4.
35. One of the best accounts of this is Tarrow, 1967, *Peasant Communism in Southern Italy*; a good analysis of the traditional *latifundia* system of land tenure is contained in Blok, 1974, *The Mafia of a Sicilian Village*.
36. For a detailed account of Communist and Socialist Party reactions to Khrushchev's denunciation of Stalin, see *Keesing's*, (1956, pp. 15020–1). The impact of Khrushchev's speech on the PCI is explored further in Chapter 7.
37. For an informative study of the construction of this myth, see Gill, 1980, 'Political Myth and Stalin's Quest for Authority in the Party'.
38. The evolution of the idea of 'Eurocommunism' and its treatment by various authors is succinctly explained by P. Elliot and P. Schlesinger (1979). Cf. McInnes (1979: 35–68) and Filo della Torre et al. (1979: 318–329).

39. OECD figures, cited in Sassoon, 1986, *Contemporary Italy*, p. 31.
40. Forini, 1983, 'Interviews'.
41. In 1962 the Cuban missile crisis dominated international politics. It was in this tense political climate that the peace movement developed throughout Europe: the CND in Britain, and in Italy the first Peace March took place in Perugia (1961), organised by Aldo Capitini.
42. *Pacem in terris* (1963) was followed by a seemingly more liberal and progressive encyclical, *Populorum progrssio*, or 'The Great Social Problem' 1(1967), written by John XXIII's successor, Paul VI.
43. Keesing's, 1968, pp. 22885–7 and pp. 22993–6 *passim.*
44. Lenin was perhaps the single most influential philosopher of the *movimento.* Beginning in Pisa with *Potere Operaia*, Marxist-Leninist (and later Maoist and Trotskyist) groupings spread throughout Italy. For a comprehensive account of this general movement, see G. Pansa (1980).
45. Cf. Franca Rama's caricature of the student militant in *La Madre* in Fo and Rama (1983).
46. These soon spread throughout Italy. Between 1970 and 1971 major clashes erupted in Reggio Calabria and Aquila, and in both instances riots were orchestrated by the MSI and other neo-Fascists (see Keesing's, 1971: 24031–3).
47. In an attempt to rob a Milan bank on 12 December 1969, 16 people were killed. An anarchist, Pietro Valpreda, was arrested and charged for this, but on weak evidence. The Left accused neo-Fascists of engineering the attack and cover-up, suggesting there had been major involvement by the Ministry of the Interior and the secret service. Ten years later, in February 1979, two neo-Fascists were arrested, and, after a lengthy trial in which several leading Christian Democrat ministers were implicated, were found guilty and sentenced to life imprisonment.
48. This was not the first time that Italy had come close to an attempted coup. In 1967 two leading socialist journalists charged that General Giovanni De Lorenzo had been plotting a coup in the summer of 1964. As Kogan (1983: 219) concluded, 'Although the courts finally exonerated De Lorenzo, certain aspects of the issue remain a mystery.'
49. See Berlinguer, 1973, 'Reflessioni sull' Italia dopo i fatti del Cile', *Rinascita*, 28 Sept; *Rinascita*, 5 and 9 Oct; these articles are also reprinted in Berlinguer, 1975, *La questione comunista*, 609–39.
50. These points are considered in Chapter 5.
51. For an analysis of this exchange see Chapter 5.
52. Though in fact many later returned to the PCI after the 1983 elections when the Party of Proletarian Unity (PdUP) presented a joint list with the PCI. Shortly after, it merged with the PCI altogether.
53. According to Ministry of the Interior figures, there were 2,366 individual 'terrorist' incidents in 1979 (causing 22 deaths), 1,264 in 1980 (causing 120 deaths) and 848 in 1981 (causing 26 deaths). A total of 113 different organisations claimed responsibility for the 1981 incidents, 91 of them extreme Left (the Red Brigades accounting for 61 incidents) and the rest extreme Right. A police report on 22 June 1982 stated that between March 1969 and March 1982 a total of 364 people were killed, and 1,075 injured in acts of terrorism, and that 1,414 members of armed extreme-Left groups and 432 of armed

extreme-Right groups were imprisoned (*Keesing's*, 1984, p. 32755). At the same time, internal security continued to be undermined by an almost uninterrupted spate of Mafia killings and corruption.

54. The repercussions of this conflict and its ideological implications are explored further in Chapters 5 and 6.
55. Forini, 1983, 'Interviews'.
56. Macaluso quoted in Pridham (1981: 93)
57. Quoted in Sani (1983: 450).
58. Figures taken from PCI (1989), *Organizzazione, dati, statistiche*, pp. 13, 23 and 32.
59. PCI (1988), '18 Congresso del PCI', *L'Unità*, 4 Dec 1988, 10–12 *passim*. For an English translation of the Congress theses, see *The Italian Communists: Foreign Bulletin of the PCI*, No. 4, Oct–Dec 1988: 21–89.
60. It was Marx, according to Engels, who first discovered this law, 'according to which all historical struggles, whether they proceed in the political, religious, philosophical or some other ideological domain, are in fact only the more or less clear expression of struggles of social classes ... which has the same significance for history as the law of the transformation of energy has for natural science' (Engels, 1968: 95).
61. Sebastiani, 'Tra vecchio e nuovo: i comunisti dopo gli anni settanta' (1983: 33); cf. G. Are, 'Il PCI come organismo politico' in R. Mieli (ed), (1983: 38–42).
62. Cf. Enzo Trapanese, 1983, 'Relazione di ricerca' in R. Mieli (ed), *ibid.*, pp. 48–173.
63. For example, a strong sense of solidarity with fellow Party members and a commitment to maintaining ties with the masses. For further reading on this, see Sebastiani (1983).
64. This, according to Pridham (ibid.), 'has inspired the description of them as "the generation of the historic compromise"'.
65. Cf. G. Berlinguer, 1977, 'Perchè meno quadrioperai e contadini?' *Rinascita*, 10 June: 7–8.
66. For an interesting though highly critical verdict on the 'Historic Compromise', see Abse (1986). For the reply to this and the sometimes heated debate it provoked in the pages of the British journal, *New Left Review*, see Tobias (1987) and Abse (1987).
67. This thesis was used to explain the decline in working-class support for radical working-class movements – typically seen as a result of affluence causing workers (or their leaders) to adopt middle-class attitudes and values. This idea was supported by the Bell/Lipset 'End of Ideology' theory in the 1950s, but was rejected by Goldthorpe et al.'s (1969) empirical 'affluent worker' study.

Chapter 2

1. The work of Allum (1979) and Kertzer (1980) tends to corroborate this.
2. 'La Proposta di alternativa', Central Committee of the PCI, *L'Unità*, 28 Nov, 1982: 15.
3. This statement was made in the previous pre-Congress document (1978), 'Draft Thesis for the 15th National Congress of the PCI' in *The Italian Communists: Foreign Bulletin*, p. 118.
4. Ibid., p. 119. Similar criticisms were also voiced by the dissident pro-Soviet editorial group associated with the review *Interstampa* (see editorial, No. 1,

Jan 1983: 23). What the PCI calls 'an organic cadre policy' refers to a centralised process of selective recruitment, or positive vetting.

5. For some useful studies of this, see Kish (1969); Galli and Prandi (1970); Allum (1973); Tarrow (1967); Poggi et al. (1968).
6. This official inquiry, undertaken by Stefano Jacini in 1877, resulted in the publication in 1885 of a 15-volume report (cf. Mack-Smith, 1969, pp. 148–57. See also Procacci, 1973, pp. 342–3).
7. Evans's (1976) ethnographic account of life in a small Venetian community demonstrates this most clearly; see also Stern's (1975: 221–58) study of the PCI in northeastern Italy.
8. In Umbria, for example, blasphemy has become part of everyday speech. The targets of these expletives are usually the Virgin Mary and God, and in each case the blasphemy consists in equating the holy and sacred with the profane and vulgar. For example, among the common expressions are *porca Madonna* (pig-Madonna), *Madonna putana* (Virgin-whore), *Dio cane*, (God-dog), *Dio maiale*, (God-swine).
9. See Galli and Prandi (1970) and Kish (1969). For a detailed analysis of the political geography of Umbria, see Galli (1981).
10. Cf. Kertzer (1980); White (1980); Wade (1971).
11. Quoted in Amyot, 1980: 132.
12. A.L. Epstein, 1977, *Ethos and Identity* (pp. xiv–v), describes almost identical processes in the formation of ethnic groups.
13. The leadership, by contrast, is overwhelmingly dominated by intellectuals and the professional middle classes (cf. Ferrarotti, 1978; Covino, 1979).
14. See Tarrow (1967: 109). After 1948 the PCI expelled many of its more sectarian members.
15. Cf. Blackmer, 1968; Hellman, 1975; and Lange, 1979; See also the discussion of 'hegemony' in Chapter 3.
16. The difference between these two conceptions is elaborated in Duverger, pp. 62–8.
17. Duverger, ibid.: 2–3. However, later in the book Duverger adds, confusingly, that the concept of a 'devotee party' is 'too vague to constitute a separate category, but it corresponds to an undeniable fact' (p. 71).
18. Significantly, in January 1953, only the year before the publication of Almond's book, McCarthy had become chairman of the Senate Sub-Committee on Investigations, and for the following twelve months he conducted a campaign against the alleged 'Leftist' doctrines encouraged by the US Information Service libraries abroad. McCarthy's campaign against the 'Red menace' extended into the universities and was particularly directed against what he called 'twisted-thinking eggheads'.
19. These periodicals include *Encounter, Foreign Affairs Commentary, Foreign Policy*, and *The World Today*.
20. This is illustrated in the ethnographic literature on Italian communism; cf. White (1980); Shore (1985).
21. Cf. Shore, 1985 – see Interviews, Appendices in particular; White, 1980; Kertzer, 1980.
22. H.K. Smith (1950), *The State of Europe*, cited in Higgins, 1974, *The Cold War*: 43.
23. For an interesting study of McCarthyism which uses anthropological insights

and the witch-hunt model, see Cardozo, 1982, 'A Modern American Witch Craze', in A. Marwick (ed), *Witchcraft and Sorcery*, pp. 469–76.

24. As depicted, for example, in the novels of Zola and Conrad.
25. These included Catholic Action – which between 1945 and 1953 rose from 1,772,265 to 2,578,288 members – the Catholic Women's Union, Men's Union, and Teachers' Movement; the *Centro sportivo italiano*; the *Fronta della Famiglia* and *Fronta della Moralità*; representatives from the Diocese Missionary Works; the Apostles of Prayer; the Children of Mary; and the Italian Artisan Association, not to mention the various confraternities and numerous other Catholic organisations (Gallerano, 1975: 9).
26. A collection of these posters may be found in Romano and Scabello. For an analysis of these posters and other themes in Christian Democrat ideology, see Pratt (1984).
27. See Guizzardi for an interesting study of the way 'Christian Civilisation' has been used as an ideology for consent.
28. According to the communists, the campaign amounted to a form of 'psychological terrorism', and it terrified people into not voting for the popular front (Gallerano, 1975: 10).
29. Togliatti, 1948, quoted in *Keesing's*, May 1948: 9259.
30. For a structural study of the recurrent themes in modern horror and science fiction, see Twitchell (1986).
31. For example, Article 49 of the 1948 Constitution states that 'all citizens have the right to associate freely in political parties in order to contribute through democratic procedure to the determination of national policy.'
32. For different views on this, see Galli and Prandi (1970: Chapter 5), Nichols (1973: 113–27); Pridham (1981: 249–50); Allum (1973: 22–3, 138).
33. For discussions of Italian political culture and patron–client relations, see Almond and Verba (1963); Galli and Prandi (1970); Allum (1973); Sartori (1966); Graziano (1977); Pridham (1981). The classic statement on political culture in southern Italy is found in Banfield's evocative though much criticised account of the 'moral basis of backward society' (1957). For more recent anthropological studies of patronage and political behaviour, see White (1980), Chubb (1983) and Shore (1989). See also Blok's study of the Mafia (1974); Schneider and Schneider's study of Sicilian politics and economics (1976), Weingrod's study of Sardinia (1968), and Wade's study of political behaviour and world-view in a central Italian village (1971, 1975).
34. Cf. Page, 1983, 'When the Partitocrazia has to Stop', *Guardian*, 21 May 1983: 9; for an ethnographic study of clientelist politics within modern state bureaucracies, see Shore (1989).
35. The organisation and strategy behind the PCI's *Partito Nuovo* model is discussed in Chapters 3 and 4.

Chapter 3

1. See Gramsci, 1971, *Prison Notebooks*: 106–13, 245–63. For some of the earlier analyses of this concept, see Bates, 1975; Boggs, 1976; Williams, 1960.
2. According to Showstack Sassoon's definition (1980: 471), 'the hegemony of a dominant class is created and re-created in a web of institutions, social relations and ideas ... woven by the intellectuals who, according to Gramsci, are all those who have an organisational role in society.' For interpretations of

Gramsci's political theory, see Anderson (1976), Boggs (1976) and the essays in the volume edited by Mouffe (1979).

3. For the PCI, the issue of 'hegemony of the working class' is linked to the debate over pluralism and democracy. Some authors, including H. Stuart Hughes, see hegemony as 'totalitarian thought in liberal guise' (quoted in Williams, 1960: 586). For the French philosopher Althusser (1978), Gramsci's use of the notion 'hegemony of the working class' was little more than a euphemism to escape the strictures of prison censorship; what he really meant was dictatorship of the proletariat'. For other writers, including Mouffe, Ferrarotti and Gruppi (1981), hegemony is a profoundly new conception providing a basis for the democratic transition to socialism: 'a "possible" euro-communism which avoids both the perils of Stalinism and of social democracy' (Mouffe, 1979: 15).
4. See Showstack Sassoon (1980) for a more exhaustive treatment of these points.
5. Gramsci uses this concept of 'passive revolution' in partially conflicting ways (1971b: 46, 206–7): as revolution without mass participation and as 'a "molecular" social transformation which takes place as it were beneath the surface of society'. See also Buci-Glucksman (1979).
6. For more detail on PCI strategy, see Donald Sassoon, 1981, *The Strategy of the Italian Communist Party*. Useful though now somewhat dated is Percy Allum's *The Italian Communist Party since 1945* (1970).
7. According to the *The Communist Manifesto* (1968: 41), 'The bourgeoisie forged the weapons that bring death to itself; it has also called into existence the men who are to wield those weapons – the working class.' Michels (1959: 368) was more sceptical but nevertheless echoes this point: 'The revolutionary party is a state within the state, pursuing the avowed aim of destroying the existing state in order to substitute for it a social order of a fundamentally different character.'
8. These figures are taken from Ghelli (1982), 'La fiducia che viene da quello straordinario cantiere rosso', *L'Unità* (Supplement to No. 187), 29 Aug 1982.
9. For the response to these and the argument that Gramscian thought is inseparable from the Leninist tradition, see Salvadori in Mouffe (ed) (1979).
10. According to the old PCI statutes (1983: 16–18), Party members' duties included proselytising, defending the Party against any attack, participating in meetings, contributing to organisational work and implementing Party decisions.
11. This is illustrated in the internal Party conflicts outlined in Chapter 5. Party schools are discussed further in Chapter 7.
12. See 'Interviews' (Tenca) in Shore (1985).
13. White (1980), makes similar points about communist political socialisation in the southern Italian village of Luco.
14. Interview with I. Rasimelli (Shore, 1985, 'Appendices').
15. 'Myth' in Sorel's view (1950: 184) is opposed to 'Utopia', which he dismisses as a 'deceptive mirage of the future'. For further discussion of the relationship between ideology and myth, see Tudor (1972).
16. Sorel, quoted in Sabine (1951: 725).
17. A similar argument is made by Pitt-Rivers (1977: 140–1), who contrasts 'history' – meaning past activity connected diachronically with the present – and 'myth', which refers only to 'not now', to 'once upon a time', or to what certain Australian Aborigines call 'dream time'.

18. Mussolini adds (1935: 847): 'For this reason the Fascist conception of life is serious, austere, religious: poised totally upon a world upheld by moral force and responsibilities of the spirit. The Fascist disdains the "easy" life.'
19. Mussolini, quoted in Sabine (1951: 724).
20. The relationship between Nazi myth and Nordic paganism is an interesting case in point here (see Eliade, 1968: 26).
21. See Shore, 'Interviews: Forini' (1985).
22. Sechi was publicly condemned by the PCI leadership in 1980 for his views on democratic centralism, the Soviet Union and his interpretation of the history of the Italian workers' movement; then, in 1983, for his heretical interpretation of the Party's 'democratic alternative' strategy. Significantly, however, he was not expelled from the Party.
23. For the PCI's explanation of this incident, see the editorial in *L'Unità*, 26 Oct 1982.
24. Statuto del PCI, 1983, pp. 15–18.
25. Reported in *L'Unità*, 11 Dec 1974, pp. 13–14.
26. For a good study of Bacon's ideas, particularly his conception of the 'man of science', see Prior (1954).
27. Unlike individuals, societies have no organic memory, yet societies need history in order to have knowledge of themselves and to understand their relationship with the past and with other societies. As Marwick (1970: 13) argues, every society must therefore have 'some priest, bard or keeper of the Public Records responsible for preserving and communicating such knowledge'.
28. For details on Bacon's idea of a 'scientific priesthood', see the description of Bensalem, Bacon's Utopia portrayed in *New Atlantis* (in Ellis et al., eds, 1864). For an analysis of these ideas and their impact on modern European thought, see Zellinsky (1975).
29. Cf. Engels, 1892 (1968: 411), 'Socialism: Utopian and Scientific'. Commenting on Marx's materialist conception of history and theory of surplus-value, he states that 'with these discoveries socialism became a science'.
30. Cf. Gramsci's conception of the Party as the 'organic intellectual' of the proletariat. In this context communist intellectuals are portrayed as the 'General Staff' of the workers' movement; i.e. the strategists coordinating the revolutionary war from a detached overseer's perspective. To quote Gramsci: 'Hence the intellectual General Staff of the organic party often does not belong to any of these factions, but operates as if it were a directive force standing on its own, above the parties.' (Gramsci, 1971, *Prison Notebooks*, p. 148); see also Gramsci's notes on the role of the intellectuals and the political party, ibid., pp. 5–23, 147–56.
31. The subject of internal Party control is explored at length in Chapters 6 and 7.
32. See Marwick (1970) for an interesting discussion on the 'uses of history'.
33. The British Communist Party provides a case in point. Much of the internecine struggle between its pro- and anti-Eurocommunist factions has focused precisely on rival interpretations of history. This reached a head at the Party's contested 1985 Congress when General-Secretary Gordon McLennon (1985: 6) bitterly attacked as 'contemptible' the activities of the pro-Soviet wing of the Party in using the Party's 'proud heritage ... against the Party'.
34. Orwell (1938) 1984, *Homage to Catalonia*, p. 234. Orwell's conclusion was that 'the concept of objective truth is fading out of the world.' In defence of

liberal history he adds, 'Nazi theory indeed specifically denies that such a thing as "the truth" exists. There is, for instance, no such thing as "Science". There is only "German Science", "Jewish Science", etc. The implied objective of this line of thought is a nightmare world in which the Leader, or some ruling clique, controls not only the future but *the past.*' Lenin also rejected the notion of 'objectivity' in history: for him, there are only 'class histories' – bourgeois history and proletarian history.

35. For further reference to 'invented traditions', see the contributions to Hobsbawm and Ranger, eds (1983). For an analysis of 'traditional authority' as a form of power, see Max Weber (1946), in Gerth and Mills (eds).
36. Cf. Clark (1975), 'Gramsci: The Patron-Saint of the Left, *Times Literary Supplement*, 31 Oct.
37. Berlinguer (1981), 'Per aprire una fase nuova nella lotta per il socialismo'. For an English translation, see *The Italian Communists: Foreign Bulletin of the PCI*, No. 1, Jan–March 1982, pp. 3–45.

Chapter 4

1. For observations on the internal life of Party sections, see Argilli (1970); Kertzer (1980); Marzani (1980); Amyot (1981); and Ruscoe (1982).
2. PCI, *Organizzazione, dati, statistiche* (1989: 41).
3. Massari (1982: 178)
4. See Chapter 3.
5. Cf. Lenin (1961), *What is to be Done?* However, even the Bolshevik model under Lenin was not as rigid as this ideal-type suggests.
6. It is unlikely that in 1945 PCI leaders had formulated so elaborate a theory since few would have read the works of Gramsci. More likely Togliatti's decisions were guided by immediate political conditions and his own particular interpretation of Stalin's popular-front strategy.
7. This was the view adopted, in particular, by many socialist parties. In Britain, for example, the Labour Party concluded that the Czech coup 'brought to a close a whole era in post-war history', and Herbert Morrison described it as 'horribly similar to the Hitler technique'. For documentary material on how Western nations reacted, see Keesing's, 1948: 9147–8.
8. In a recent interview by a journalist from *Espresso*, the former PSI general-secretary, Giacomo Mancini, admits that large sums of money were regularly paid to the PCI and PSI through the Soviet embassy. After 1956, the PSI found a more lucrative source of income from private industry (including Agnelli and Fiat), and from the giant state industries ENI and IRI, which were obliged to pay, as Mancini practically boasts, in order to obtain 'political protection' (cf. Forcello, E., 1989, 'Le confessioni di Mancini', *La Repubblica*, 22 Aug: 8).
9. This definition can be found in Togliatti's *Instructions for the Provincial Organisation Congresses* (Togliatti, 1946:112 – cited in Massari, 1982: 156).
10. Marx and Engels, 1968: 98 ('The Eighteenth Brumaire of Louis Bonaparte').
11. Most significant in this respect is the practice of 'democratic centralism', which is discussed in Chapters 6, 7 and 8.
12. Charles Darwin, 1887, *The Descent of Man*, Vol. II, Part. iii, Chapter 21, Last Words.
13. Similar attitudes – sometimes called 'workerism' – are found in many of the Trotskyist parties in Britain; for example, see Taafe (1981), *Militant: What We*

Stand For, London, Cambridge Heath Press. For an analysis of these parties, see Baker (1981) and Tomlinson (1981).

14. PCI (1981), 'Le Tesi del Congresso di Lione (1926)', in *Almanacco del PCI 1981*, p. 252; the document continues: 'This principle is essential for the creation of a "Bolshevik" Party. It stems from the fact that the Party must be equipped to lead the working-class masses, which naturally have become unified by the capitalist process of production. Placing its organisational base at the point of production, the Party chooses the class upon which it is based. It proclaims itself a class party, and a party of one class only, the working class.'
15. 'L'organizzazione base del partito' in Gramsci (1971a: 271), also cited in Massari (1982: 155). Further evidence for this is found in the Lyons Congress theses. For example, thesis 24 states that 'The organisation of the proletarian vanguard in the communist party is the essential part of our organisational activity.' Furthermore, it declares: 'Complete ideological unity is necessary for the Party to fulfil at each moment its function as leader of the working class. Ideological unity is the essence of the Party's power and its political capacity, it is indispensable for transforming it into a Bolshevik Party. The basis of that ideological unity is the doctrine of Marxism and of Leninism, the latter of which is understood as Marxist doctrine adapted to problems of the period of imperialism and the beginnings of the proletarian revolution.' ('Le Tesi del Congresso di Lione', 1981: 250).
16. On this point, cf. the discussion of Gramsci's letters directed against the Anarchists in Joll (1977: 53).
17. This is documented in 'Il balzo nel Mezzogiorno, 1943–1953' in G. Amendola (1976).
18. Cf. Baldassarre (1983: 41–3).
19. See the discussion of 'hegemony' in Chapter 3. These points are also discussed by Baldassari (1983).
20. Cf. Mannheimer and Sebastiani, 'Concezione del partito nei quadri del PCI: ideale, progetto e strumento' in Ilardi and Accornero, eds (1982: 693–720). For a comprehensive survey of the attitudes of Party leaders and militants, see the essay by Peter Lange in Accornero et al. (eds), *L'identità Comunista* (1983: 299–365).
21. *L'Alternativa Democratica – draft document for the XVIth Congress* , (1983: 14).
22. For an interesting account of how the local parish church dominates community life in northeastern Italy, see Evans (1976), *Life and Politics in a Venetian Community*.
23. 'I compiti nuovi nella situazione attuale' in Togliatti, *Opere Scelte* (1974: 37).
24. Cf. Secchia, 'Migliorare il lavoro del partito. Rapporto d'organizzazione tenuto al V congresso nazionale del PCI' (1946).
25. For an account of this, see Giorgio Bocca's study of Palmiro Togliatti (1973).
26. It also led to the death of over 21,000 soldiers. See *Keesing's* (1949).
27. Amyot (1981: 26 ff).
28. Cf. Togliatti, 'Che cosa e il partito nuovo' (1944).
29. This controversy has continued to the present day and was particularly debated on the occasion of the 25th anniversary of Togliatti's death (see for example, P. Branca, 'Rileggere Togliatti', L'Unità, 22 Aug 1989: 2; E. Macaluso, 'Il Togliatti italiano per me è quello vero', *L 'Unità*, 3 Sept 1989: 2).
30. 'La Risoluzione della conferenza di organizzazione della Federazione

Comunista napolitana, giugno 1944', cited in Massari (1981: 158).
31. Cf. Lenin (1947), *What is to be Done?* for the context in which democratic centralism was justified. Two of the most thorough historical surveys of democratic centralism to date are Waller, M. (1981), *Democratic Centralism*, and Tiersky, R. (1985), *Ordinary Stalinism*. Points raised by these authors are discussed in Chapters 6, 7 and 8.
32. Cf. Secchia, 'Piu forti i quadri migliore l'organizzazione' (speech to the sixth Congress, Rome, 1948), cited in Massari (ibid.).
33. For further discussion of Khrushchev's speech and its aftermath, see Chapter 7.
34. Only one member of the National Executive, Terracini, even alluded to the question of the 'cult of personality' – an indiscretion that was immediately picked up by the press, to the Party's embarrassment.
35. For a summary of the reactions of various political leaders to Khrushchev's speech and the statements of Togliatti and Nenni, see *Keesing's*, 4–11 Aug (1956: 15020–1).
36. The sense of bewilderment and disillusionment with Soviet communism is reflected in the diary of Vittorio Vidali, a PCI delegate to the 20th CPSU Congress. On the way back from Moscow, after the Congress, he wrote, 'Raijk? Slansky? Kostov? Gomulka: And so many others? Here and now we see passing out of history the concept of a leading nation, a model party, and guiding individuals. It is as well that all this should end. At least this much will be of use: we shall begin to think with our own heads, to say what we really believe, to learn to say no' (cited in Marzani, 1980: 8).
37. Longo, 'Rapporto sullo Stato' in *PCI VIII Congresso: atti e risoluzioni* (1957: 554). For further discussion of democratic centralism, see Chapters 6–9.
38. See PCI, *IX congresso. Rapporto di attivita del Comitato Centrale* (1959: 93).
39. Ferrarotti (1978: 52). Compared with Britain's growth rate of below 0.5 per cent per annum during much of the 1980s, the magnitude of this growth is all the more apparent.
40. For an analysis of Italy's economic performance during this period, see Zarisky (1972), *Italy: The Politics of Uneven Development*.
41. The most devastating blow for the PCI came in the 1954 Fiat elections when the CGIL lost control of the shop-floor 'internal commissions' to the DC-aligned CISL (Sassoon, 1986, p. 126).
42. For example, Barbagli and Corbetta and other contributors to the sociological review *Inchiesta*.
43. L. Magri and F. Maone (1969), 'L' Organizzazione comunista' in *Il Manifesto*, No. 4 (Sept).
44. 'Statuto del partito comunista approvato del XVIII Congresso Nazionale', 22 March 1989, Article 3, (e) and (f).

Chapter 5

1. For a good analysis of PCI–Soviet relations, see Urban, 1980, 'Moscow and the PCI in the 1970s: Kto Dovo?'; see also Urban, 1986, *Moscow and the Italian Communist Party*. Useful studies of the CPSU's reaction to Eurocommunism are also contained in R. Tokes (ed), 1978, *Eurocommunism and Detente*.
2. Berlinguer repeated the phrase in an article in *L'Unità*, January 1982: 'The propulsive drive provided by the phase of the development of Socialism which

began with the October Revolution has been exhausted.' For an English translation of the speech, see Berlinguer (1982), 'A New Phase in the Struggle for Socialism', in *The Italian Communists: Foreign Bulletin of the PCI*, No. 1, p. 11. The full text of this and the exchange between Moscow and the PCI can be found in the PCI's 'Un'idea nuova del socialismo: La posizione dei comunisti sui fatti di Polonia. L'articolo della *Pravda* e la risposta de *L'Unità*' (1982).

3. Berlinguer, 'Un'idea nouva del socialismo ...' (ibid.).
4. Reported in *Keesing's Contemporary Archives*, 30 April 1982, p. 31456.
5. All the quotations cited here are from the PCI's reprint ('Un idea nuovo del socialismo ...', ibid.), which gives the complete text of the CPSU article published in *Pravda* on 20 January 1982.
6. Ibid., pp. 14–15. Prior to the PCI's condemnatory resolution, the Soviet response had focused on quiet diplomacy and confidential letters of disapproval – some of which the PCI published openly – (see, for example, L'Unità, 17 March 1982, p. 16).
7. Ibid. The PCI resolution was also bitterly attacked by the French Communist Party and by the presses of most of the Warsaw Pact states for what the Hungarian communists termed 'joining the bourgeois press' and 'completely ignoring the activities of counterrevolutionary forces' in Poland (*Keesing's*, 1982, p. 31456).
8. Cited in Ferrarotti, 1978, p. 60. An Italian edition of *Novoe Vremya* began publication in October 1980, evidently stimulated by an awareness of this substantial pro-Soviet minority within the PCI.
9. For a study of Luther's political philosophy, see the article by J. Porter (1981), 'Luther and Political Millenarianism', in *Journal of the History of Ideas*, XLII, No. 3, pp. 389–406.
10. Good accounts of the Reformation can be found in either W. Edwards, 1952, *Notes on European History* (Vol. II) or *The Cambridge Modern History* (Vol. I, Chapter 19).
11. This point is argued by Marzani, 1980, p. 14, and in Chapter 1, 'The End of Soviet Hegemony', pp. 3–22.
12. The 'Brezhnev Doctrine' is the Western term given to the Soviet principle of international law used to justify the Czechoslovakian invasion of 1968 and the suppression of the Dubček government by armed intervention. In essence, it was the doctrine that the Soviet Union and her allies had the right to intervene in the affairs of any member country whenever socialism in that country appeared threatened by or vulnerable to 'hostile forces' attempting to restore a capitalist regime.
13. Berlinguer, 1982, 'A New Phase in the Struggle for Socialism', *Foreign Bulletin of the PCI*, p. 23.
14. Berlinguer, ibid., pp. 32–3.
15. In March 1980 the PCI held important talks with SPD chairman Willy Brandt and French Socialist leader François Mitterrand – acclaimed as something of a breakthrough in relations between the PCI and the European Left, (cf. *L'Unità*, 14 and 25 March 1980).
16. Joan Barth Urban, 1986, *Moscow and the Italian Communist Party*, p. 316.
17. Full title, *Interstampa: Monthly Bulletin of Information and Documents on Peace and Socialism*. Significantly, too, the Soviet review *New Times* had started publishing an Italian edition in October 1980.

18. 'Botteghe Oscure' is journalist shorthand for the Rome headquarters of the PCI (it is, in fact, the name of the street where PCI headquarters is located).
19. Also significant in the period following the Polish crisis and the PCI–CPSU rift was the sudden increase in the number of branch offices of the 'Italia–URSS' cultural association for promoting better Italian–Soviet relations through tourism, seminars and exchanges.
20. Quoted in G. Sani, 1983, p. 450.
21. Most of the Italian daily newspapers – particularly *La Republicca*, *Corriere della Sera*, and *La Stampa* – carried numerous articles and leaders speculating about possible splits in the PCI in the run-up to the National Congress in March 1983.
22. Cf. the comments of the former national secretary of the FGCI, Marco Fumagalli (Chapter 1).
23. Significantly, the 'instructions' for congress procedure emphasise that one of the primary aims when electing section executives is to achieve a maximum 'welding' (*saldatura*) between generations. For this reason, too, local FGCI officers are entitled by statutory right to sit in on executive meetings (*Statuto del PCI*, 1983, 'V: I congressi e le conferenze di partito', pp. 27–38).
24. 'La proposta per l'alternativa'. The PCI's draft pre-Congress document was published in *L'Unità*, 28 Nov 1982.
25. Sezione Piazza Grimana (officially named 'Sezione Primo Ciabatti') is a section of roughly 150 members located in an old inner-city quarter of Perugia. I carried out fieldwork in this section from 1982 to 1984.
26. Here the procedural instructions say only that 'the Federal Committee will ensure that one of its representatives is present at all section congresses' (ibid., p. 3). In effect, federations have a statutory *right* to send Party cadres to sit in on section assemblies, and these have the right both to speak *and* to be a member of the all-important electoral commission which draws up lists for the new section executive.
27. See Berlinguer, 'Riflessioni sull'Italia dopo i fatti del Cile', Rinascita, 28 Sept 1973 and 5 and 9 Oct 1973. These articles are reprinted in A. Tato (ed), *La Questione Comunista, 1969–75* (1975: 698 ff.).
28. Berlinguer, 1974, 'Report to the Central Committee in Preparation for the 14th Congress of the PCI', quoted in Sassoon (ed) 1978, *The Italian Communists Speak for Themselves*, p. 149.
29. Cf. the two articles in *New Left Review* by Abse, 'The PCI Congress' (1986) and 'A Reply to Gundle' (1987).
30. Giorgio Napolitano, Interview, Camera de Deputati, Rome 4 Jan 1983.
31. In fact, as Barbagli and Corbetta's analysis showed (1978: 938–56), much confusion surrounded the interpretation of the 'Historic Compromise' at the Party base. Only 13 per cent of their sample shared an interpretation similar to that of the leadership in regarding the 'Historic Compromise' as a proper 'strategy': the majority (59 per cent) were in favour of it, but saw it merely as a 'tactic' for attaining a government of the Left, and 8 per cent regarded it as a tactic for obtaining a government with the PCI alone in power (Barbagli and Corbetta, *ibid.*, pp. 952–3).
32. In fact, from a different point of view, many argue that it effectively ended with the death of Aldo Moro in 1978.

33. Cf. Reichlin's speech to the 16th PCI Congress, reprinted in *L'Unità*, 3 March 1983: 5–9.
34. For a good explanation of this strategy, see Amyot (1981), pp. 57–67. See also Ingrao, *Masse e potere* (1977); and Ingrao, *Crisi e la terza via* (1978).
35. Mandarini was subsequently elected to the Central Committee of the PCI and later became president of the Umbrian regional government.
36. The formalised and ritual nature of PCI interventions does not seem to have changed much since the 1960s when it was criticised by the 'Il Manifesto' group (cf. Gagliardi, 1983).
37. The national strike did take place that day and again one month later when over 6 million workers downed tools in protest against government attempts to de-index wages (the *scala mobile*).
38. At all levels of Party organisation there is a tendency to try to resolve the need to represent all social categories and generations simply by enlarging the number of committee members. The result is usually that real decision-making is merely pushed up to a higher level of Party organisation. Of these 23, only 2 were women. There were no 'workers' (*operai*) or agricultural labourers of any kind, no teachers, professionals, intellectuals, or small traders. Instead, there were 3 artisans, 11 clerks and technicians, 2 students, 1 housewife and 3 pensioners (Source: *Verbali, congresso della sexione Primo Ciabatti*, Perugia, Dec 1982).
39. 'Documento Della Commissione Politica Approvato Alla Unanimità Del Congresso di Sezione "Primo Ciabatti"', Perugia, Dec 1982.

Chapter 6

1. Italian political pundits have characterised these ideological strands somewhat falsely as competing 'political cultures'. Thus, according to Fausto de Luca and other journalists, Napolitano and Ingrao represent 'the two cultures of the PCI; the culture of "movements" and the culture of "government"' (*La Repubblica*, 5 March 1983, p. 1).
2. See Chapter 5.
3. During the 1940s and 1950s a network of local and provincial Party schools was established throughout Italy (see Chapter 7 for further discussion of these).
4. Cf. Ben Pimlott, 1977, *Labour and the Left in the 1930s*, Cambridge University Press.
5. See, for example, Di Rienzo, 1983, *L'Espresso*, pp. 12–16. This poll was conducted by the Makno Institute at the time of the congresses and published in January 1983. Sixteen per cent of those polled agreed with the proposition (similar to Cossutta's amendment) that 'The PCI must follow a form of Socialism of Marxist-Leninist stamp and must remain a revolutionary party.' Nine per cent favoured the European social-democratic form of socialism, whilst 66 per cent supported the Berlinguer/Ingrao position that socialism in Italy requires its own specific road, which should 'take into consideration' the lessons of reformist European social democracy.
6. Cf. Barbagli and Corbetta, 1978, *Una tattica e due strategie: inchiesta sulla base del PCI*, *Il Mulino*, pp. 922–66.
7. This was one of the appeals of communism and 'communist identity' discussed earlier (cf. Chapter 3).

8. This theme was developed originally in Max Weber's notion of 'traditional authority' (see Gerth and Mills [eds], *From Max Weber*).
9. These notes were collated from the section congress records of the 42 congresses held in the Perugia *Comprensorio*, PCI Federation of Perugia Archives.
10. Furthermore, only 10 per cent (151) of those 1,503 were women (out of an estimated 2,700 women members in the Perugian Party).
11. Source: Verbali Della Commissione Verifica Dei Poteri, 18th Congress of the Federation of Perugia, 13 Feb 1983. PCI Federation Archives, Perugia.
12. Up until 1969 the PCI was resolved that Italy should withdraw from NATO; a few years later in 1974 the line was that it was no longer 'realistic' to think of unilateral withdrawal (Barbagli and Corbetta, 1978 p. 930).
13. Berlinguer (1976), *La Politica internazionale dei comunisti italiani*, pp. 149–60. The PCI argued for the simultaneous dissolution of both NATO and the Warsaw Pact, but accepted that 'unilateral action would disturb the balance of forces' in a 'potentially dangerous fashion'.
14. F. Parkin, 1972, *Class Inequality and Political Order*, pp. 128–36. Parkin analyses the deradicalisation of working-class parties in terms of 'the "political acculturation" of underclass party leaders', which is explained in terms of the 'normative pressure imposed on those who assume positions of authority in the state' (*ibid*., p. 133). This seems to be much the same thing as organisational conservatism.
15. Belligni, 1982, 'Gli amministratori comunisti', in Ilardi and Accornero (eds), p. 538.
16. Ghirelli, 1983, *Organizzazione dati statistiche*, pp. 113–14. Note that this figure combines the 1979 total for *both* federal committee and federal control commission totals.
17. This is Amyot's conservative estimate. The precise figure for 1978 was 2,349 (Lanchester, 1978: 660).
18. 'Legge 2 maggio 1974, n. 195 sul contributo dello Stato allo finanziamento dei partiti politici'. This law was amended in 1981 by another ('Legge 18 novembre 1981, n. 659'), which raised the yearly state contribution to political parties to 82,886 million lire, i.e. nearly £40 million (see, Article 3). A further 15,000 million lire was donated for electoral expenses incurred during the 1983 European Parliament elections to those parties who obtained at least one seat (source: Gazzetta ufficiale della Repubblica italiana, Rome, No. 323, 24 Nov 1981 – reprinted in J. Masclet and P. Mutignon (eds), 1986, 'Le Financement public des Partis et la reglementation de leurs ressources et dépenses', *Problems politiques et social: La Documentation Française*, No. 527 (10 Jan), Nancy, France, p. 35.
19. In 1982 the amount raised was 21.3 billion lire (Ghirelli, 1983, ibid., p. 121). See Chapter 2 for further reference to PCI finance.
20. Cf. Beetham, D. (1981), 'Michels and His Critics', *European Journal of Sociology*, 22, pp. 81–99. For a concise summary of these points see D. Beetham (1986), 'Roberto Michels' in V. Bogdanor (ed), *The Blackwell Encyclopaedia of Political Institutions*, pp. 364–6.
21. For further analysis of democratic centralism, see Chapters 7 and 8.
22. This argument is developed in Chapters 7 and 8.
23. *Dizionario dei termini marxisti*, 1977, p. 46.
24. Lenin's 21 conditions for membership of the Comintern are analysed in Chapter 7.

25. *Statuto del PCI*, 1983, Article 8, Clauses (d) and (e), p. 20.
26. L. Magri and F. Maone, 1974, 'Problemi di organizzazione nell'esperienza del PCI', p. 188.
27. The Umbrian power-elite at the time of writing comprised the regional party secretary, the president of the regional government, a leading regional government officer, the former president of the Perugian provincial government and the secretary of the PCI Perugian federation. Most of these officers were also current or former PCI Central Committee members.
28. Galli and Prandi (1970, p. 87) comment on this 'sense of belonging to an integrated community' as one of the factors explaining Party strength and unity despite growing disillusionment with the prospect of imminent revolution. The way informal mechanisms of social control are used to impose sanctions in small communities is a theme explored in much of the anthropological literature of the Mediterranean (cf. Du Bouley, 1975; Bailey, 1971; Pitt-Rivers, 1954).
29. See Chapters 1, 2 and 3.
30. See, for example, Article 12 of the 1983 statutes covering the rules concerning 'Unity and Discipline of the Party'.
31. Ferrarotti, 1978, p. 59.

Chapter 7

1. V.I. Lenin, 1920, 'The Terms of Admission into the Communist International', in *Collected Works*, Vol. 31, p. 207. All the following citations from these 'Terms of Admission' are from the same source.
2. Ibid., p. 211. Lenin's emphasis.
3. Ibid., p. 210.
4. For an analysis of early PCI statutes, see Martinelli (1982); 'Gli statuti del PCI, 1921–1970'. See also the essay by Andreina De Clementi (1982), 'Radiografia del partito 1921/1926'.
5. Lombardo Radice, 1978, interviewed in Urban (ed), *Eurocommunism: Its Roots and Future in Italy and Elsewhere*, p. 32.
6. 'Campagna di Lenin', circolare Agitprop, 19 Dec 1925, cited in A. De Clementi, 1982, p. 925.
7. Gramsci, 'L'Organizzazione base del partito' in *L'Unità* 15 Aug 1925, cited in A. De Clementi, 1982, p. 925 f.). Significantly, it was in this period (April 1925) that the first Marxist-Leninist Party school was founded.
8. Letter from Luigi Amadesi, Direzione del PCI, Commissione Scuola del Partito ai Comitati Regionali e alle Federazione Comunisti, 3 Nov 1948, PCI, Perugia Federation Archives.
9. This was the Scuola Provinciale del PCI 'Primo Ciabatti', Perugia.
10. 'Per le scuole del partito', 1948, *Lezione* 1, p. 1 (PCI, Perugia Federation Archives).
11. 'Per le scuole del partito: Teoria e Tattica Marxista-Leninista Sulle Questioni della Guerra e della Pace', 1948, *Quarta Lezione: La Lotta per la pace; comitato centrale del PCI*, p. 1.
12. Scuola Provinciale del PCI 'Primo Ciabatti', *Introductory Remarks on Party School Courses*, Federation of Perugia Archives, p. 1.
13. 'deve sempre tenersi alla testa delle masse', in 'Che cosa e il partito comunista nella dottrina marxista-leninista' (undated circular), *Come e organizzato il PCI*, PCI, Perugia Federation Archives, p. 1.

14. Traditionally referred to in PCI discourse as 'the ideological formation of Party cadres' (*formazione ideologica dei quadri*).
15. These were the *'collettore'* referred to in Chapter 5.
16. The full text of Khrushchev's speech is reported in *Keesing's Contemporary Archives*, 1956, pp. 14992–5.
17. Khrushchev, 1956, p. 14993.
18. Ibid.
19. Togliatti, 1956, Interview in *Nuovi Argomenti*, reprinted in 'Democrazia Socialismo, Autonomia e Internazionalismo', PCI, *Allegato all'Almanacco PCI*, 1976, p. 6.
20. Ibid., p. 7.
21. Togliatti, 1964, Il memoriale di Yalta', reprinted in *Democrazia e Socialismo, Autonomia e internazionalismo*, p. 30 (my emphasis).
22. Lenin's 'economic theory of imperialism' holds that imperialism is the last stage of capitalism. Imperialism leads inevitably to conflict and war which becomes the catalyst for revolution and the final overthrow of capitalism. Cf. V.I. Lenin, 1915, *Imperialism: The Highest Stage of Capitalism*.
23. Berlinguer, *L'Unità*, 18 Sept 1978 (cited in Tiersky, 1985: 113).
24. Alternatively, where the interests of some competing groups dominate others, 'pluralism' may also be an ideology used to describe a social organisation as 'pluralist' when in reality it is not. For further analysis on pluralism, see R.A. Dahl (ed), 1966, *Political Opposition in Western Democracies*. See also R. Miliband, 1969, *The State in Capitalist Society*.
25. Cf. Accardi (ed), 1978, *Pluralismo o Leninismo: Il dibattito ideologico nella sinistra italiano e gli interventi*; B. Craxi, 1979, 'Leninism and Pluralism', *Socialist Affairs*.
26. According to Craxi, Marxism-Leninism belongs to the 'Jacobin tradition' and socialism to 'the pluralist tradition of Western civilization. On the one hand the authoritarian and centralistic, and on the other hand the libertarian and pluralistic'. (Craxi, 1979, p. 59). For Craxi, communism is a 'Stone Age absurdity' which, had it prevailed, would have 'Asianised Western civilisation'.
27. R. Williams, 1967, *Keywords*, pp. 82–7.
28. V.I. Lenin, 1917 (1968), *The State and Revolution*, pp. 326–7. It should be noted, however, that Marx and Engels were writing before the introduction of universal suffrage – when women and the propertyless were still disenfranchised – hence, capitalist democracy, at least in Marx's day, was a case of 'democracy for the rich'.
29. Lenin, 1919, 'Theses and Report on Bourgeois Democracy and the Dictatorship of the Proletariat', in *Selected Works in Three Volumes* (1975 edn), p. 99.
30. For a full description of Lenin's views on this, see Lenin, *State and Revolution*, pp. 319–37. The arguments propounded here are all derived from Engels's work on 'Scientific Socialism' and the problem of the state (cf. Engels, 1968, 'Socialism: Utopian and Scientific', in *Marx and Engels: Collected Works in One Volume*, pp. 394–460).
31. Cf. Marx and Engels, *The Communist Manifesto*, which defined the state as 'but a committee for managing the common affairs of the whole bourgeoisie' (1968, p. 37).
32. Cf. Lenin, 'State and Revolution', p. 267.
33. Kolokowski, 1978, *Main Currents in Marxism*, p. 388.

34. In most of the 21 Soviet-style communist political systems, these ideas and most of Lenin's original propositions are still treated as immutable articles of faith. (Cf. A. Brown and J. Gray [eds], 1977, *Political Culture and Political Change in Communist States*.)
35. Leninism as a rigid doctrine *per se* dates from the period after Lenin's death, and was largely created from selected passages of Lenin, Marx and Engels, plagiarised and first expounded as a theory to be communicated to all Party cadres by Stalin. See J. Stalin, 1934 (1973), *Foundations of Leninism*. For an analysis of Stalin himself, see B. Franklin (ed), 1973, *The Essential Stalin*.
36. On the differences between 'Marxism' 'Leninism' and 'Marxism-Leninism', see Sabine, 1948, pp. 628–708; Bertram D. Wolfe, 1961, introduction to Rosa Luxemburg's *The Russian Revolution* and *Leninism or Marxism*. See also L. Schapiro, 1970, *The Communist Party of the Soviet Union*, and J.P. Plamenatz, 1954, *German Marxism and Russian Communism*.
37. For further analysis of this, see B. Wolfe's brief account in the introduction to Rosa Luxemburg's essays, 1961, pp. 11–17.
38. See Chapters 2 and 3 of *The Communist Manifesto*. Marx and Engels also insisted that 'The Communists do not form a separate party opposed to other working-class parties. They have no interests separate and apart from those of the proletariat as a whole. They do not set up any sectarian principles of their own, by which to shape and mould the proletarian movement' (1968, p. 46).
39. V.I. Lenin, 1902 (1947), *What is to be Done?*, p. 31.
40. Ibid.
41. Ibid, p. 78.
42. Ibid. pp. 41–2.
43. This point is one that is also shared by several historians, including Sabine (1948) and Wolfe (1961, p. 13).
44. Sabine, 1948, p. 671.
45. Ibid., p. 672.
46. V.I. Lenin, *Collected Works*, Vol. 4, p. 273.
47. Ibid., Vol. 2, p. 466.
48. Ibid., Vol. 5, p. 375.
49. Sabine (1948, p. 676) adds the dry comment, 'though no one but Lenin was able to perceive its democracy'.
50. As Lenin himself expressed it, 'Bureaucracy versus democracy is the same thing as centralism versus automatism, it is the organising principle of revolutionary political democracy as opposed to the organisational principle of the opportunists of Social Democracy. The latter want to proceed from the bottom upward and consequently, wherever possible and to the extent that it is possible, it supports automatism and "democracy" ... The former proceed from the top, and advocate the extension of the rights and powers of the centre in respect of the parts' (Lenin, *Selected Works*, Vol. 2, p. 447).
51. Lenin's chief philosophical work was devoted to an attack on 'subjective idealism' and a defence of Marxism and dialectical materialism as 'scientific' and therefore 'true' socialism. His *Materialism and Empirio-Criticism* (1909) is still regarded as a basic philosophical text in the Soviet Union.
52. But because of uneven development, socialism would not triumph in all countries simultaneously as Marx had expected, so Lenin reasoned.
53. Sabine, 1948, p. 686.

54. One loophole in this theory that Leninists fail to answer satisfactorily is, what happens to the Party in the rationale of dialectical materialism? Presumably, like the state, its function will have been superseded when history progresses to communist society; therefore it, too, should 'wither away'.
55. Rosa Luxemburg, 1961, p. 94.
56. Ibid., p. 102.
57. Ibid., p. 108.
58. This pamphlet, 'Our Political Tasks', first appeared in Geneva in 1904.
59. Isaac Deutscher, 1956, *The Prophet Armed: Trotsky 1921–1929*, p. 89.
60. L. Trotsky, in Deutscher, 1954, p. 90.
61. Ibid.
62. Ibid., p. 93.
63. Ibid.
64. Deutscher, 1956, p. 96.
65. Trotsky, 1937 (1965), *The Revolution Betrayed*, pp. 89–90.
66. Ibid., p. 92.
67. Ibid., pp. 94–5.
68. Even Waller (1981, p. 7), who defends democratic centralism, accepts that there is an uncomfortably strong connection. This point is analysed further in Chapter 8.

Chapter 8

1. PCI Statute, 1983, Article 8, pp. 18–19.
2. For an outline of what is meant by orthodox communism, see Lenin (1947), *What is to Be Done?* A good analysis of this is contained in Sabine (1948), Conquest (1972), and Chapter 7.
3. Serious challenges to democratic centralism came most notably in Czechoslovakia in 1968 and Poland in 1980 (cf. Timmermann, 1985, 'A che serve il centralismo democratico?', *MondOperaio*, pp. 84–7). For theoretical writings on democratic centralism by PCI and other intellectuals, see Palmiro Togliatti Institute (ed), 1982, *Dossier: Centralismo Democratico Nell'Elaborazione di Lenin, Luxemburg, Stalin, Gramsci*, Rome; see also contributions to De Giovanni, Gerratana and Paggi (eds), 1977, *Egemonia, Stato, Partito in Gramsci*.
4. For example, Dubček's reforms to democratic centralism alone, 'provided a more than sufficient motive for Soviet repression in Czechoslovakia in 1968' (Timmermann, ibid., p. 86).
5. Cf. Waller (1988), 'Democratic Centralism: The Costs of Discipline', in Waller and Fennema (eds), *Communist Parties in Western Europe*, p. 23. For a comparative analysis of Communist Party organisation, see the other essays in this volume.
6. According to the statutes of the CPSU, it is the 'force that guides and shapes Soviet society ... the nucleus of the political system' (from the 'Soviet Constitution', reprinted in *Tempi Moderni*, No. 41, 1977, p. 18).
7. See Chapter 6, 'How the Party Leadership Controls the Rank and File'.
8. See, for example, the excellent account given in Adeney and Lloyd, 1986, *The Miners' Strike* (especially pp. 70–128).
9. In fact, many miners argued that the NUM leadership was in breach of its own rules. The attempt to get an all-out strike without a ballot has been described

as 'one of the most fateful decisions made within the Labour movement this century' (Adeney and Lloyd, 1986, p. 81). By sending thousands of flying pickets to areas such as Nottinghamshire where the miners had held their own ballot and voted against supporting the strike, the NUM not only alienated many of its potential supporters and split the entire British trade-union movement, but it also handed the government the ideal weapon it needed to defeat the strike (cf. Goodman, 1985, *The Miners' Strike*, pp. 75–7).

10. For example, at his first mass rally in October 1982, the NUM president, Arthur Scargill, told the Welsh miners that they had to choose between loyalty to the union on the one hand and 'the Tory government's philosophy' on the other. As Adeney and Lloyd (1986, p. 81), described the speech: 'Its hidden message was a command that they be bound to him as he was to them, a Bruderbund down through time. There was no half-way house: if not for, you were against, lost in the snare of Tory philosophy.'
11. For an English translation of past and current CPSU statutes, see G. Gill, 1988, *The Rules of the Communist Party of the Soviet Union.*
12. Copious examples of this can be found in the publications of parties of the Fourth International in Britain. 'Stalinism in Crisis' was the title of a rally and conference on the future of Europe, organised by 'Socialist Outlook' in December 1989, and addressed by Ernest Mandel and other leading Trotskyist writers.
13. This point is developed most cogently by Tiersky (1985, pp. 17 ff.).
14. For example, this is what Amyot (1981: 29–30) argues in the case of the PCI.
15. This point is argued by Tiersky (1985: 110). Showstack Sassoon, however (1980: 162), suggests that 'Stalinisation' was also a possible target of his critique – though there is no evidence for this.
16. According to Gramsci (1971, p. 15), the basic function of the party is 'directive and organisational'. Like the state, its function is to weld together its own group of 'organic intellectuals', with the aim of 'turning them into qualified political intellectuals, leaders (*dirigente*) and organisers of all the activities and functions inherent in the organic development of an integral society' (ibid., pp. 15–16).
17. The problem here is compounded by the fact that Gramsci uses the term 'organic' in so many contradictory ways. The vague notion of an 'organic relationship' contrasts significantly with the more precise and materialist definition given to the concept of 'organic intellectuals' (cf. Gramsci, 1971, pp. 6–20). It also contrasts with the concept of 'organic centralism' (ibid., pp. 186–8), which, for Gramsci, denotes absolute monarchy and enlightened despotism. More confusing still, Gramsci (ibid.: 189) states that democratic centralism is also '"organic" because, on the one hand, it takes account of movement, which is the organic mode in which historical reality reveals itself, and does not solidify mechanically into bureaucracy; and because, on the other hand, it takes into account that which is relatively stable and permanent.'
18. Cf. Helen Womack, 1990, 'Countdown to the death of Article Six', *The Independent*, 9 Feb, p. 10. This point is examined further in the concluding Chapter.
19. Cf. Napolitano and Berlinguer, 1981, pp. 14–15. Also cited in Tiersky (1985: 111).
20. Cf. Note 23, Chapter 7.

21. Napolitano, address given to the ASMI Conference, 'The Italian Communist Party's Strategy for Socialism in the 1980s', Cambridge, 12 May 1984. See also Napolitano, 1981, 'Programma, Unità e centralismo democratico' in *Critica Marxista*, 19 (Feb), pp. 45–56. For the traditional approach of other PCI leaders, see Alessandro Natta and Gian Carlo Pajetta, 1963, 'Il centralismo democratico nell'elaborazione e nell'esperienza dei comunisti', *Critica Marxista*, 1, No. 5–6 (Sept–Dec), pp. 103–130.
22. Berlinguer, interviewed in *La Stampa* in February 1976, summarised the PCI's policy as follows: 'The accession of the working classes to political power can and must be achieved in Italy in a manner fully consistent with democratic institutions, the principles of freedom and the procedures for change embodied in our constitution ... We consider various forms of economic management necessary, allowing wide scope for private enterprise within a national public programme that is democratically prepared and democratically carried out. The surest way to avoid the temptation to authoritarianism is to base political power in the broadest possible foundations of agreement and participation by the people forging an alliance of all popular anti-Fascist parties.' (Berlinguer, 1976, reported in *Keesing's Contemporary Archives*, p. 27693).
23. Berlinguer, June 1976, reported in *Keesing's Contemporary Archives*, 24 Sept 1976, p. 27953.
24. PCI Central Committee, 1982, 'La Proposta per il cambiamento', p.1 5.
25. Ibid.
26. PCI Central Committee, 1978, 'Draft Thesis for the Fifteenth Congress', English translation in *The Italian Communists: Foreign Bulletin of the PCI*, p. 111.
27. PCI Central Committee, 1982, ibid.
28. *Statuto del partito comunista italiano* (approvato dal XVIII Congresso Nazionale), 22 March 1989, p. 8. Whether this contraction is deliberate or not is unclear, though, according to Valentini (*Espresso*, 19 March 1989, p. 12), at the same time as the PCI was drawing up plans for the abolition of democratic centralism, various experts were also working 'to stitch together a collection of norms that would prohibit the formation of currents'.
29. Magri and Maone, 1969, p. 189.

Conclusion

1. Occhetto, 'conclusion at the 18th Congress of the PCI', *The Italian Communists: Foreign Bulletin of the PCI*, No. 1 (Jan–March) 1989, p. 73. See also Occhetto's interview published in *L'Unità*, 4 Sept 1989. For a statement in English on 'the reform of the Party for the PCI's "new course"', see *The Italian Communists*, No. 4, Oct–Nov 1988, pp. 74–89.
2. Cited in Valentini, C., 'Compagni, movimento', *Espresso*, 19 March 1989, p. 9.
3. Ibid., p. 11.
4. This lingering uncertainty is captured in the title of a recent PCI publication, *'Se vince Gorbaciov'* ('If Gorbachev wins' – Supplemento al numero 259 dell'Unità, 1987), an edited collection in commemoration of the 70th anniversary of the Bolshevik Revolution.
5. Cf. Wyles, J., *Financial Times*, Wednesday, 22 March 1989.
6. 'Il Saluto di Gorbaciov al congresso', L'Unità', 22 March 1989, p. 18.
7. For a summary of Ingrao's speech, see B. Ugolini, 'E per l'eretico Ingrao l'abbraccio di Occhetto', *L'Unità*, 21 March 1989, p. 3.

8. '18 Congresso del PCI: documento politico', *supplemento a L'Unità*, No. 272, 4 Dec 1988, p. 3.
9. M. Sheridan (1989) 'Italian Communists Move on Party Reform', *The Independent*, 22 March, p. 10.
10. Speech reported in J. Blitz, 'Gorbachev Hints at Multiparty Soviet Union', *Sunday Times* (14 Jan 1990, p. 1).
11. Reported in Quentin Peel, 'Party Monopoly Likely to Go', *Financial Times*, 6 Feb, 1990, p. 1.
12. Francis Fukuyama's thesis on the decline of competing ideologies and the consequent 'end of history' first appeared in June 1989, in the American conservative journal, *The National Interest*. A shortened form of this article subsequently appeared in two essays, 'The End of History' and 'Marxism's Failure', *The Independent*, 20 and 21 Sept 1989.
13. *The Economist*, 11 March 1989, p. 49.
14. Engels, 1968 (1890), 'Preface to the German Edition of *The Communist Manifesto*', in *Selected Works in One Volume*, p. 34.
15. PCI Central Committee, 1982, 'Draft Document for the XVIth Congress', p. 14.
16. Achille Occhetto, interviewed by Eric Hobsbawm, 1990, *Marxism Today*, Feb, p. 15.
17. This was the definition given by several delegates to the 1989 Party Congress.
18. See, for example, Clark and Hine, 1980, 'The Italian Communist Party: Between Leninism and Social Democracy?' in Childs (ed), *The Changing Face of Western Communism*, pp. 112–46.
19. As Occhetto later explained it (1990, *Marxism Today*, ibid.), 'Left culture and the very manner of being a party needs redefining. We need to find a new form for a party capable of drawing into action and struggle the subjects of *today's* contradictions ... not of the nineteenth century. For instance, our traditional idea of the social alliance of workers and peasants is meaningless today, even if it is still represented by the emblem of the hammer and sickle.'
20. Sheridan, M., 'Italy's Communists Give up Communism', *The Independent*, 15 Nov 1989, p. 1.
21. Wyles, J., 'Italy's Communists Search for a Future', *Financial Times*, 22 Nov 1989, p. 3.
22. Reported in *The Independent*, 25 Nov 1989, p. 12.
23. Jacques, M., 'It's the End of the Road for Communism', *The Sunday Times*, 26 Nov 1989, p. B9.
24. Cf. Wyles, J., 'Italy's Communists Plan New Party of Left', *Financial Times*, 27 Nov 1989, p. 2.

Bibliography

Abélès, Marc (1988) 'Modern Political Ritual: Ethnography of an Inauguration and a Pilgrimage by President Mitterrand', *Current Anthropology*, Vol. 29, No. 3 (June), pp. 391–404.

Abercrombie, Nicholas (1980) *Class Structure and Knowledge*, Oxford, Blackwell.

Abse, Tobias (1986) 'The PCI Congress', *New Left Review*, No. 158, pp. 91–7.

Abse, Tobias (1987) 'A Reply to Gundle', *New Left Review*, No. 163, pp. 36–9

Accardi, Claudio (ed) (1978) *Pluralismo o Leninismo: il dibattito ideologica nella sinistra italiana e gli interventi/Bettino Craxi*, Milan, Sugar Co.

Accornero, Aris, et al. (1983) *L'identità comunista: I militanti, le strutture, la cultura del PCI*, Roma, Riuniti.

Adamson, Walter (1980) 'Gramsci's Interpretation of Fascism', *Journal of the History of Ideas*, Vol. 41, No. 4, pp. 615–34.

Adeney, M. and Lloyd, J. (1986) *The Miners' Strike, 1984/5: Loss Without Limit*, London, Routledge and Kegan Paul.

Alberoni, F. et al. (1967) *L'attivista di partito*, Bologna, *Il Mulino*.

Allum, Percy (1970) *The Italian Communist Party since 1945: Grandeurs and Servitudes of a European Socialist Strategy*, Occasional Publication No. 2, Reading Graduate School of Contemporary European Studies.

Allum, Percy (1973) *Italy – Republic without Government?*, London, Weidenfeld and Nicolson.

Allum, Percy (1978) 'Italy', in J. Clark (ed), *Encyclopaedia of Modern History*, London, Hamlyn.

Allum, Percy (1979) 'Italy', in S. Henig (ed), *Political Parties in the European Community*, London, Allen and Unwin.

Almond, Gabriel (1954) *The Appeals of Communism*, Princeton, New Jersey, Princeton University Press.

Almond, G. and Verba, S. (1963) *The Civic Culture: Political Attitudes and Democracy in Five Nations*, Princeton, New Jersey, Princeton University Press.

Althusser, Louis (1977) *For Marx*, London, New Left Books.

Althusser, Louis (1978) 'Due, tre parole (brutali) su Marx e Lenin', *L'Espresso*, 29 Jan, pp. 46–51.

Amendola, E., Spriano, P. and Gionnotti, R. (eds) (1981) *Storia fotografica del partito comunista*, Rome, Riuniti.

Amendola, G. (1976) 'Il balzo nel Mezzogiorno, 1943–1953' in G. Amendola (ed), *Gli Anni della Repubblica*, Rome, Riuniti.

Amyot, Grant (1981) *The Italian Communist Party: The Crisis of the Popular Front Strategy*, London, Croom Helm.

Anderlini, Fausto (1982) 'La cellula', in Ilardi and Accornero (eds), *Il partito comunista italiano: Struttura e storia dell'organizzazione 1921–1979*, Milan, Feltrinelli, pp. 185–226.
Anderson, Benedict (1983) *Imagined Communities: Reflections on the Origin and Spread of Nationalism*, London, Verso.
Anderson, Perry (1976) 'The Antinomies of Antonio Gramsci', *New Left Review*, No. 100, Nov 1976–7 (Jan), pp. 5–77.
Anderson, Perry (1976) *Considerations on Western Marxism*, London, New Left Books.
Angius, G., Berlinguer, L., et al. (1983) 'Come siamo, come vogliamo essere', *Rinascita*, XL, No. 3 (Jan) pp. 3–6.
Apter, David and Eckstein, H. (eds) (1963) *Comparative Politics*, New York.
Ardener, Shirley (ed) (1981) *Women and Space: Ground Rules and Social Maps*, London, Croom Helm.
Arendt, Hanna (1953) 'Ideology and Terror: A Novel Form of Government' *Review of Politics*, Vol. XI.
Argilli, M. (1970) *Un anno in sezione: vita di base del PCI*, Milano, Edizione della Libreria.
Bacon, Francis (1864) 'New Atlantis' in Ellis, R., Spedding, J. and Heath, D. (eds), *The Works of Francis Bacon*, Boston, Warne.
Bailey, F.G. (1969) *Stratagems and Spoils: a Social Anthropology of Politics*, Oxford, Blackwell.
Bailey, F.G. (1971) 'Gifts and Poison' in Bailey (ed), *Gifts and Poison: The Politics of Reputation*, Oxford, Blackwell, pp. 1–26.
Bailey, F.G. (1973) 'Losa' in *Debate and Compromise: The Politics of Innovation*, Oxford, Blackwell, pp. 164–99.
Baker, Blake (1981) *The Far Left. An Exposé of the Extreme Left in Britain*, London, Weidenfeld and Nicolson.
Baldasarre, Antonio (1983) 'Un nuovo partito di massa?' *Democrazia e Diritto*, No. XXIII (Jan–Feb) pp. 41–64.
Banfield, Edward (1958) *The Moral Basis of Backward Society*, New York, Free Press.
Barbagli, M. and Corbetta, P. (1978) 'Una tattica e due strategie: inchiesta sulla base del PCI' *Il Mulino*, No. 3, pp. 922–67.
Barbagli, M. and Corbetta, P. (1978) 'Partito e movimento: aspetti e rinnovamento del PCI', *Inchiesta*, VIII, No. 31 (Jan–Feb).
Barnes, Samuel H. (1967) *Party Democracy: Politics in an Italian Socialist Federation*, London, Yale University Press.
Barnes, S. and Sani, G. (1974) 'Mediterranean Political Culture and Italian Politics: An Interpretation' *British Journal of Political Science*, Vol. 4, pp. 289–303.
Barth, Frederick (1969) *Ethnic Groups and Boundaries*, London, Allen & Unwin.
Barthes, Roland (1972) *Mythologies*, London, Jonathan Cape.
Bates, Thomas (1975) 'Gramsci and the Theory of Hegemony', *Journal of the History of Ideas*, Vol. XXXVI, pp. 351–66.
Bates, Thomas (1976) 'Antonio Gramsci and the Bolshevisation of the PCI', *Journal of the History of Ideas*, Vol. XXXVI, pp. 351–66.
Bell, Andrew, (1986) *Against Racism and Fascism in Europe*, Pamphlet produced by the Socialist Group, European Parliament, Brussels.
Bell, Daniel (1960) *The End of Ideology: On the Exhaustion of Political Ideas in the Fifties*, New York, Free Press.

Bell, Daniel (1977) 'Ideology' in A. Bullock and O. Stallybrass (eds), *Fontana Dictionary of Modern Thought*, Glasgow, Fontana pp. 298–9.

Bellini, Luigi (1966) *L'evoluzione demografica dell'Umbria dal 1861 al 1961*, Perugia, Centro Regionale.

Belmonte, Thomas (1979) *The Broken Fountain*, New York, Columbia University Press.

Berlinguer, Enrico (1973) 'Reflessioni sull'Italia dopo i fatti del Cile' *Rinascita*, 28 Sept, 5 Oct, and 9 Oct.

Berlinguer, Enrico (1975) *La Questione Comunista: 1969–1975*, Roma, Riuniti.

Berlinguer, Enrico (1976) *La Politica Internazionale dei Comunisti Italiani*, Roma, Riuniti.

Berlinguer, Enrico (1977) *Austerità occasione per trasformare l'Italia*, Roma, Riuniti.

Berlinguer, Enrico (1981) 'For the Democratic Alternative', in *The Italian Communists. Foreign Bulletin of the PCI*, No. 3 (July–Sept), pp. 32–40.

Berlinguer, Enrico (1981) 'The PCI's Documents on Poland' in *The Italian Communists. Foreign Bulletin of the PCI*, No. 4 (Oct–Dec), pp. 66–149.

Berlinguer, Enrico (1982) 'A New Phase in the Struggle for Socialism', in *The Italian Communists: Foreign Bulletin of the PCI*, No. 1 Jan–March, pp. 3–45.

Berlinguer, Enrico (1983) 'Una proposta all'Italia civile e moderna: il rapporto del segretario del partito al XVI congresso', *L'Unità*, 3 March, pp. 1–9.

Bestor, A.E. (1948) 'The Evolution of the Socialist Vocabulary', *Journal of the History of Ideas*, Vol. IX, No. 3, pp. 259–302.

Blackmer, Donald (1968) *Unity in Diversity: Italian Communism and the Communist World*, Cambridge, Mass., MIT Press.

Blackmer, Donald (1972) 'Italian Communism: Strategy for the 1970s', *Problems in Communism*, 21, No. 3, (May–June) pp. 41–56.

Blackmer, Donald (1975) 'Continuity and Change in Postwar Italian Communism', in Blackmer and Tarrow (eds), *Communism in Italy and France*, Princeton, New Jersey, Princeton University Press, pp. 21–68.

Bloch, Marc (1961) *Feudal Society* (2 volumes), London, Routledge and Kegan Paul.

Bloch, Maurice (1975) 'Introduction' in M. Bloch (ed), *Political Language and Oratory in Traditional Society*, London and New York, Academic Press, pp. 1–28.

Blok, Anton (1974) *The Mafia of a Sicilian Village: A Study of Violent Peasant Entrepreneurs*, Oxford, Blackwell.

Blondel, Jean (1978) *Political Parties: A Genuine Case for Discontent?*, Harmondsworth, Penguin.

Bloomfield, Jude (1985) 'Review of D. Forgacs and G. Nowell-Smith (eds), 'The Cultural Conditions for Political Transformation', *Marxism Today*, Vol. 29, No. 6, p. 40.

Bocca, Giorgio (1973), *Palmiro Togliatti*, Bari, La Terza.

Bocock, Robert (1974) *Ritual in Industrial Society*, London, Allen and Unwin.

Boggs, Carl (1976) *Gramsci's Marxism*, London, Pluto Press.

Boggs, Carl and David Plotke (eds) (1980) *The Politics of Eurocommunism: A Comparative Study*, London, Macmillan.

Bogliari, P. (1979) *Il movimento contadino in Umbria dal 1900 al fascismo*, Milan, Franco Angeli.

Boissevain, Jeremy (1966) 'Patronage in Sicily', *Man*, No. 2, pp. 18–33.

Boissevain, Jeremy (1974) *Friends of Friends: Networks, Manipulators and Coalitions*, Oxford, Blackwell.

Boissevain, Jeremy and Friedl, John (eds) (1975) *Beyond the Community: Social Processes in Europe*, The Hague, Department of Educational Science of The Netherlands.

Botella, Juan (1989) 'Spanish Communism in Crisis', in M. Waller and M. Fennema (eds), *Communist Parties in Western Europe*, Oxford, Blackwell, pp. 69–85.

Boothman, Derek (1983) 'Problems of Translating Political Italian', *The Incorporated Linguist*, Vol 22, No. 4 (Autumn), pp. 179–82.

Bottomore, Tom (ed) (1983) *A Dictionary of Marxist Thought*, Oxford, Blackwell.

Brown, Archie and Gray, Jack (eds) (1977) *Political Culture and Political Change in Communist States*, London, Macmillan.

Buci-Glucksmann, Christine (1979) 'State, Transition and Passive revolution' in C. Mouffe (ed), *Gramsci and Marxist Theory*, London, Routledge and Kegan Paul.

Bullock, Alan and Stallybrass, Oliver (eds) (1977) *Fontana Dictionary of Modern Thought*, Glasgow, Fontana.

Cammett, John (1976) *Antonio Gramsci and the Origins of Italian Communism*, Stanford, Calif., Stanford University Press.

Cammett, John (1980) 'Introduction', in Marzani, *The Promise of Eurocommunism*, Westport, Conn., Lawrence Hill, pp. ix-xvii.

Campbell, John (1964) *Honour, Family and Patronage: A Study of Institutions and Moral Values in a Greek Community*, Oxford, Clarendon.

Capucelli, Luciano (ed) (1975) *Antifascismo e resistenza nella provincia di Perugia (documenti e Testimonianze)*, Perugia, Urbani SAS.

Cardozo, R. (1982) 'A Modern American Witch Craze', in A. Marwick (ed), *Witchcraft and Sorcery*, Harmondsworth, Penguin.

Carnieri, Claudio, et al. (1976) 'Cattolici e comunisti in Umbria' in *Cronache Umbre: riviste mensile di politica e cultura*, 1, No. 1 (Jan–Feb) pp. 14–52.

Carr, Edward H. (1959) *A History of Soviet Russia: Socialism in One Country 1924–1926* (3 volumes), London, Macmillan.

Carr, Edward H. (1961) *What is History?*, Harmondsworth, Penguin.

Carrillo, Santiago (1977) *Eurocommunism and the State*, London, Lawrence and Wishart.

Carrillo, Santiago (1977b), 'Genuine Democratisation of Society and its Institutions', *Marxism Today*, 21, No. 10 (Oct) pp. 306–13.

Christian, William (1972) *Person and God in a Spanish Valley*, New York, Seminar Press.

Christensen, R.M., et al. (1972) *Ideologies and Modern Politics*, London, Nelson & Sons.

Chubb, Judith (1983) *Patronage, Power and Poverty in Southern Italy: A Tale of Two Cities*, Cambridge, Cambridge University Press.

Clark, Martin (1975) 'Gramsci: Patron-Saint of the Left' *Times Literary Supplement*, 31 October.

Clark, Martin (1977) *Antonio Gramsci and the Revolution that Failed*, New Haven and London, Yale University Press.

Clark, Martin and Hine, David (1980) 'The Italian Communist Party: Between Leninism and Social Democracy?', in David Childs (ed), *The Changing Face of Western Communism*, London, Croom Helm, pp. 112–46.

Claudin, Fernando (1978) *Eurocommunism and Socialism*, London, New Left Books.

Cohen, Abner (1969) 'Political Anthropology: The Analysis of the Symbolism of Power Relations', *Man*, Vol. 4, pp. 215–35

Cohen, Abner (1976) *Two-Dimensional Man: An Essay on the Anthropology of Power and Symbolism in Complex Society*, London, Routledge and Kegan Paul.
Cohen, Anthony (ed) (1982) *Belonging: Identity and Social Organisation in British Rural Communities*, Manchester, Manchester University Press.
Cohen, Ronald (1973) 'Political Anthropology', in J.J. Honigmann (ed), *Handbook of Social and Cultural Anthropology*, Chicago, McNally, pp. 861–81.
Conquest, Robert (1972) *Lenin*, Glasgow, Fontana.
Covino, Renato (1979) 'Il PCI umbro negli anni '70: composizione sociale del gruppo dirigente in Umbria', *Segno Critico*, I, No. 1, pp. 19–54.
Covino, Renato (1980) 'Il '68 in Umbria. Limiti del movimento fallimento delle avanguardie', *Segno Critico*, II, No. 5, pp. 17–56.
CPSU (1977) *Rules of the Communist Party of the Soviet Union: Endorsed by the 22nd CPSU Congress*, Moscow, Progess Publishers.
Craxi, Bettino (1979) 'Leninism or Pluralism', *Socialist Affairs*, May–June, No. 3, pp. 59–61.
Crimi, Bruno et al. (1984) 'Enrico Berlinguer, un idea: L'uomo, le battaglie, le vittorie, le sconfitte' *Panorama*, No. 949, 25 June, Milan, Arnoldo Mondadori.
Crockatt, Richard (1987) 'The Cold War, Past and Present', in R. Crockatt and S. Smith (eds) *The Cold War, Past and Present*, London, Allen and Unwin, pp. 3–23.
Crossman, R.H.S. (ed) (1950) *The God that Failed: Six Studies in Communism*, London, Hamish Hamilton.
Dahl, R.A. (ed) (1966) *Political Opposition in Western Democracies*, London and New Haven, Yale University Press.
D'Alo, Giuseppe and Lazzari, F. (undated) *Il partito comunista italiano: alcune linee di storia e di politica*, Rome, Sezione di organizzazione del PCI.
Daniels, Robert V. (ed) (1960) *A Documentary History of Communism*, Vol. 1, Vintage Books, New York.
Darwin, Charles R. (1887) *The Descent of Man, and Selection in Relation to Sex*, London, Murray.
Davis, John (1970) 'Morals and Backwardness: A Comment on the Moral Basis of Backward Society', *Comparative Studies in Society and History*, Vol. 12, 340–53.
Davis, John (1973) *Land and Family in Pisticci*, New York, Athlone.
Davis, John (1977) *People of the Mediterranean: An Essay in Comparative Social Anthropology*, London, Routledge and Kegan Paul.
De Clementi, Andreina (1982) 'Radiografia del partito dopo la scissione di Livorno 1921/1926', in Ilardi and Accornero (eds), *Il Partito Comunista Italiano*, Milan, Feltrinelli pp. 899–934.
De Giovanni, Biagio (1976) 'Lenin, Gramsci e la base del pluralismo' *Critica Marxista*, No. 3–4.
De Giovanni, Bagio et al. (eds) (1977) *Egemonia, stato, partito in Gramsci*, Rome, Riuniti.
De Giovanni, Biagio (1978) 'La questione del partito: laicità e critica della "dopiezza"' *Critica Marxista*, 16, No. 6 (Nov–Dec) pp. 45–68.
Deutscher, Isaac (1954) *The Prophet Armed: Trotsky 1921–1929*, London and New York, Oxford University Press.
Drucker, H.M. (1979) *Doctrine and Ethos in the Labour Party*, London, Allen and Unwin.
Du Bouley, Juliet (1976) 'Lies, Mockery and Family Integrity' in J. Peristiany (ed), *Mediterranean Family Structures*, Cambridge, Cambridge University Press, pp. 389–407.

Duverger, Maurice (1951; 1954) *Political Parties: Their Organisation and Activity in the Modern State*, London, Methuen.
Eco, Umberto (1973) 'Il linguaggio politico', in G. L. Beccaria (ed), *I linguaggi settoriali in Italia*, Milan, Bompiani.
Edwards, W. (1952) *Notes on European History*, (Vol. II) London, Harrap.
Eliade, Mircea (1968) *Myths, Dreams and Mysteries: The Encounter Between Contemporary Faiths and Archaic Realities*, London, Collins.
Elleinstein, Jean (1976) *The Stalin Phenomenon*, London, Lawrence and Wishart.
Elliot, Philip and Schlesinger, P. (1979) 'On the Stratification of Political Knowledge: Studying Eurocommunism, an Unfolding Ideology', *Sociological Review*, 27 (Feb), pp. 55–81.
Engels, Friedrich (1870; 1968) 'Preface to the German Edition of *The Communist Manifesto*', in *Marx and Engels: Selected Works in One Volume*, London, Lawrence and Wishart, pp. 32–4.
Engels, Friedrich (1884; 1968) 'Socialism: Utopian and Scientific' in *Marx and Engels's Selected Works in One Volume*, London, Lawrence and Wishart, pp. 394–460.
Epstein, A.L. (1978) *Ethos and Identity: Three Studies in Ethnicity*, London, Tavistock; New York, Aldine.
Erikson, E. (1968) *Identity, Youth and Crisis*, London, Faber and Faber.
Espresso (1983) 'Lottizzati di tutta Italia', *L'Espresso*, 13 Feb, pp. 6–11.
Evans, Robert (1976) *Life and Politics in a Venetian Community*, Notre Dame (Indiana), Notre Dame Press.
Evans-Pritchard, E.E. (1940) *The Nuer*, Oxford, Oxford University Press.
European Communities (1973) 'Declaration of the European Identity', *Bulletin of the European Communities*, No. 12, point 2501, pp. 118–27.
Fedele, Marcello (1978) 'Oltre il Partito Nuovo? Alla ricerca di una terza via', in *Democrazia e Diritto*, 5–6; No. xviii, Sept/Dec, pp. 752–8.
Fedele, Marcello (1979) *Classi e partiti negli anni '70*, Roma, Riuniti.
Fedele, Marcello (1982) 'La dinamica elettorale del PCI 1946/1979', in Ilardi and Accornero (eds), *Il Partito Comunista Italiano*, Milan, Feltrinelli, pp. 293–312.
Fedeli, Armando (1944) 'Per una giusta politica di quadri' *L'Unità* (reprinted in *Chronache Umbre* 1977, II, No. 1, (Jan) pp. 85–7.
Femia, Joseph (1975) 'Hegemony and Consciousness in the Thought of Antonio Gramsci', *Political Studies*, Vol. XXIII, No. 3, pp. 325–88.
Femia, Joseph (1979) 'Gramsci, the Via Italiana, and the Classical Marxist-Leninist Approach to Revolution', *Government and Opposition*, 14 (Winter), pp. 69–95.
Ferrara, Giovanni (1983) 'Il partito padre-padrone', *La Repubblica*, 8 February, p. 8.
Ferrara, Giovanni (1983) 'Ma quanti soldi per quei partiti', *La Repubblica*, 9 April, p. 6.
Ferrarotti, Franco (1976) 'Some reflections on the Idea of Dynastic Capitalism', *Social Compass*, XXIII, No. 2–3, pp. 107–19.
Ferrarotti, Franco (1978) 'The Italian Communist Party and Eurocommunism', in Morton A. Kaplan (ed), *The Many Faces of Communism*, New York and London, Free Press, pp. 30–71.
Filo della Torre, Paolo, et al. (eds) (1979) *Eurocommunism: Myth or Reality?*, Harmondsworth, Penguin.
Flores, M. (1976) 'Quaderno dell'attivista', *Ideologia, organizzazione e propaganda nel PCI degli anni cinquanta*, Milano, Mazzota.

Fo, Dario and Rame, F. (1983) *Theatre Workshops at Riverside Studios*, London, Red Notes.

Foster, George M. (1965) 'Peasant Society and the Image of Limited Good', *American Anthropologist*, Vol. 67, No. 2, pp. 293–316

Franklin, Bruce (ed) (1973) *The Essential Stalin: Major Theoretical Writings, 1905–52*, London, Croom Helm.

Franklin, S.H. (1961) 'Social Structure and Land Reform in Southern Italy', *Sociological Review*, Vol. 9, pp. 323–49.

Freire, Paolo (1973) *Education for Critical Consciousness*, New York, Seabury.

Friend, J. W. (1986) 'After Eurocommunism', *Studies in Comparative Communism*, Vol. XIX, No. 1 (Spring), pp. 55–65.

Gagliardi, Rino (1983) 'PCI: il vero "strappo" del Congresso e sulla democrazia nel partito', *Il Manifesto*, 16 Feb, p. 1.

Gallerano, N. (1975) 'La DC Nel Periodo Gasperiano', in L. Romano and P. Scabello (eds), *C'era una volta la DC*, Rome, Savelli Editore.

Galli, Gino (1956) 'La condizione dei contadini umbri, 1860–1900', *Cronache Umbre*, 1, No. 3.

Galli, Gino (1976) 'I rischi del partito dove governiamo', *Cronache Umbre*, No. 8 (Nov), pp. 92–5.

Galli, Gino (1982) 'Il partito e l'amministrazione locale. Il caso dell' Umbria', in Ilardi and Accornero (eds), *Il Partito Comunista Italiano*, Milan, Feltrinelli, pp. 553–80.

Galli, Giorgio (1966) *Il bipartismo imperfetto. Comunisti e democristiani in Italia*, Bologna, Il Mulino.

Galli, G. and Prandi, A. (1970) *Patterns of Political Participation in Italy*, New Haven, Conn. and London, Yale University Press.

Gambuli, Settimio (1976) 'A 30 anni dal 1946: come hanno votati gli umbri', *Cronache Umbre*, No. 8 (Nov), pp. 18–36.

Geertz, Clifford (1966) 'Religion as a Cultural System', in Michael Banton (ed), *Anthropological Approaches to the Study of Religion* (ASA Monograph No. 3), London, Tavistock, pp. 1–46.

Geertz, Clifford (1975) 'Ideology as a Cultural System', in Geertz (ed), *The Interpretation of Cultures*, London, Hutchinson and Co., pp. 193–233.

Gellner, Ernest (1977) 'Patrons and Clients', in E. Gellner and J. Waterbury (eds), *Patrons and Clients*, London, Duckworth, pp. 1–16.

Gerth, H.H. and Mills, C. Wright (eds) (1948) *From Max Weber: Essays in Sociology*, London, Routledge and Kegan Paul.

Ghelli, Luciano (1982) 'La fiducia che viene da quello straordinario "cantiere rosso"' *L'Unità* (Supplement to No. 187), 29 August.

Ghini, Celso (1982) 'Gli iscritti al partito e alla FGCI 1943/1979', in Ilardi e Accornero (eds), *Il Partito Comunista Italiano*, Milan, Feltrinelli, pp. 227–92.

Ghirelli, Francesco (1983) *Assise dei segretari di sezione. Organizzazione dati statistiche*, Perugia, PCI Federation Archives.

Gill, Graeme (1980) 'Political Myth and Stalin's Quest for Authority in the Party', in T.H. Rigby, Archie Brown and Peter Reddaway (eds), *Authority, Power and Policy in the USSR*, London, Macmillan, pp. 98–117.

Godson, Roy and Haseler, Steven (1978) *Eurocommunism: Implications for East and West*, London, Macmillan.

Goldthorpe, John, et al. (1968) *The Affluent Worker: Political Attitudes and Behaviour*, Cambridge, Cambridge University Press.

Goodman, Geoffrey (1985) *The Miners' Strike*, London, Pluto Press.
Gould J. and Kolb, W. (1964) *A Dictionary of the Social Sciences*, London, Tavistock.
Gramsci, Antonio (1971a) 'Legalismo e "Carbonismo" nel PCd'I', in *La costruzione del partito comunista 1923–1926*, Turin, Einaldi.
Gramsci, Antonio (1971b) *Selections from the Prison Notebooks*, Q. Hoare and G. Nowell-Smith (eds), London, Lawrence and Wishart.
Graziano, Luigi (1977) 'Patron–Client Relations in Southern Italy', in S.W. Schmidt et al. (eds), *Friends, Followers and Factions*, University of California Press, Berkeley, Los Angeles and London, pp. 360–78.
Grillo, Ralph (ed) (1981) *State and Nation in Europe*, New York, Academic Press.
Gruppi, Luciano (1981) *Il Partito comunista italiano: Le fonti e gli sviluppi storici, teorici e culturali della politica comunista*, Roma, Sezione Centrale Scuola di Partito.
Guizzardi, Gustavo (1976) 'The "Rural Civilization": Structure of an Ideology for Consent', *Social Compass*, Vol. 23, No. 2–3, pp. 197–220.
Gundle, S. (1987) 'The PCI and the Historic Compromise', *New Left Review*, No. 163, pp. 27–35.
Harding, Neil (ed) (1984) *The State in Socialist Society*, London, Macmillan.
Hansen, James (1981) 'Not So Red Bologna', *New Society*, Vol. 55, No. 950 (29 Jan), pp. 181–2.
Heiberg, Marianne (1980) 'Basques, Anti-Basques and the Moral Community', in R. Grillo (ed), *State and Nation in Europe*, Academic Press, New York, pp. 45–59.
Hellman, Stephen (1975) 'The PCI's Alliance Strategy and the Case of the Middle Classes', in Blackmer and Tarrow (eds), *Communism in Italy and France*, Princeton, New Jersey, Princeton University Press, pp. 373–419.
Hellman, Stephen (1977) 'The Longest Campaign: Communist Party Strategy and the Elections of 1976', in H.R. Penniman (ed), *Italy at the Polls: The Parliamentary Elections of 1976*, Washington, DC, American Enterprise Institute for Public Policy Research.
Higgins, Hugh (1974) *The Cold War*, London, Heinemann.
Hitler, Adolf (1933; 1972) *Mein Kampf*, London, Hutchinson.
Hoare, Quentin and Nowell-Smith, G. (1971) *Gramsci: Selections from the Prison Notebooks*, London, Lawrence and Wishart.
Hobbes, Thomas (1885; 1972) *Leviathan, or, the Matter, Form and Power of a Commonwealth, Ecclesiastical and Civil*, (ed and abridged by J. Plamenatz), London, Fontana.
Hoffer, Eric (1951) *The True Believer*, New York, Harper and Row.
Hobsbawm, Eric J. (1959) *Primitive Rebels: Studies in Archaic Forms of Social Movement in the Nineteenth and Twentieth Centuries*, Manchester, Manchester University Press.
Hobsbawm, Eric J. (1977) *The Italian Road to Socialism: An Interview with Giorgio Napolitano*, London, Journeyman Press; Westport, Conn., Lawrence Hill.
Hodgson, Geoffrey (1979) 'The US Response', in P. Filo della Torre et al. (eds), *Eurocommunism: Myth or Reality*, Harmondsworth, Penguin, pp. 277–306.
Hodson, H.V. and Hoffman, V. (eds) (1983) *The Annual Register: A Record of World Events*, Bath, Longman.
Howe, Erving (ed) (1976) *The Basic Writings of Trotsky*, New York, Schocken Books.

Hymes, Edward (1973) *A Dictionary of Modern Revolution*, London, Allen Lane.

Ibba, Fausto (1983) 'Se me lo proponessero, penso che accetterei di iscrivermi', *L'Unità-Speciale* (PCI 1984 recruitment campaign), p. 7.

Ilardi, Massimo (1982) 'Sistema di potere e ideologia nel PCI: le conferenze nazionale d'organizzazione', in Ilardi and Accornero (eds), *Il Partito Comunista Italiano*, Milan, Feltrinelli, pp. 3–34.

Ingrao, Pietro (1977) *Masse e potere*, Rome, Riuniti

Ingrao, Pietro (1978) *Crisi e la Terza Via*, Rome, Riuniti.

Ingrao, Pietro (1981) 'Crisis of the Parties and Crisis of the State', *The Italian Communists. Foreign Bulletin of the PCI*, No. 3 (July–Sept), 123–34.

'Italy' (1980) *The Europa Yearbook 1980: A World Survey*, Europa, London, pp. 847–91.

Italy, Constitution, (1981) *Costituzione della Repubblica Italiana: Statuto dei Diritti dei Lavoratori*, Rome, ITER.

Jenson, Jane and Ross, George (1984) *The View from Inside*, Berkeley, University of California Press.

Joll, James (1977) *Gramsci*, Glasgow, Fontana.

Keesing's (1934–90) *Keesing's Contemporary Archives*; since 1988 called *Keesing's Record of World Events*, Circa (ed), Harlow, Longman.

Kenny, Michael and Kertzer, David (eds) (1983) *Urban Life in Mediterranean Europe: Anthropological Perspectives*, Chicago and London, University of Illinois Press.

Kernig, C.D. (ed) (1972) *Marxism, Communism and Western Society: A Comparative Encyclopaedia*, New York, Herder and Herder.

Kertzer, David (1980) *Comrades and Christians: Religion and Political Struggle in Communist Italy*, Cambridge, Cambridge University Press.

Kertzer, David (1981) Review of Caroline White's 'Patrons and Partisans', in *Anthropology Quarterly*, Vol. 54, No. 1, pp. 44–6.

Kertzer, David (1988) *Ritual, Politics and Power*, New Haven, Conn., Yale University Press.

Khrushchev, Nikita S. (1956) *The secret speech delivered to the closed session of the Twentieth Congress of the Communist Party of the Soviet Union*, Nottingham, Spokesman (also published in *Keesing's*, (July 21–28) 1956, Harlow, Longman, pp. 14992–7.

Kirchheimer, Otto (1958) 'The Party in Mass Society', in *World Politics*, Oct 1957–July 1958, pp. 289–94.

Kish, George (1969) *Italy*, New York, Van Nostrand Reinhold.

Kogan, Norman (1962) *The Government of Italy*, New York, Thomas Crowell.

Kogan, Norman (1966) *A Political History of Postwar Italy*, London, Pall Mall Press.

Kogan, Norman (1983) *Political History of Italy: The Postwar Years*, New York, Praeger.

Kriegel, Annie (1972) *The French Communists: Profile of a People*, Chicago, University of Chicago Press.

Kriegel, Annie (1978) *Eurocommunism: A new kind of Communism?*, Stanford, Calif., Hoover Institute Press.

Kolakowski, Leszek (1978) *Main Currents in Marxism 2: The Golden Age, Its Origins, Growth and Dissolution*, Oxford and New York, Oxford University Press.

Kundera, Milan (1980) *The Book of Laughter and Forgetting*, Harmondsworth, Penguin.

Kuniholm, Bruce (1987) 'The Origins of the First Cold War', in Crockett and Smith (eds), *The Cold War Past and Present*, London, Allen and Unwin, pp. 37–57.

La Malfa, Ugo (1978) 'Communism and Democracy in Italy', *Foreign Affairs*, 56 (April), pp. 476–88.
Lane, Christel (1981) *The Rites of Rulers*, Cambridge, Cambridge University Press.
Lange, Peter (1975) 'The PCI at the Local Level: A Study of Strategic Performance', in Blackmer and Tarrow (eds), *Communism in Italy and France*, Princeton, New Jersey, Princeton University Press, pp. 259–304.
Lange, Peter (1979) 'Crisis and Consent, Change and Compromise: Dilemmas of Italian Communism in the 1970s', *Journal of West European Politics* (Oct), pp. 110–32.
Lange, Peter and Tarrow, Sydney (eds.) (1980) *Italy in Transition: Conflict and Consensus*, London, Frank Cass.
La Palombara, Joseph (1963) *Interest Groups in Italian Politics*, Princeton, New Jersey, Princeton University Press.
La Palombara, Joseph (1965) 'Italy: Fragmentation, Isolation, Alienation', in Lucian W. Pye and Sidney Verba (eds), *Political Culture and Political Development*, Princeton, New Jersey, Princeton University Press, pp. 282–329.
La Palombara, Joseph (1974) *Politics within Nations*, Englewood Cliffs, New Jersey, Prentice-Hall.
Leduc, Victor (1978) 'The French Communist Party Between Stalinism and Eurocommunism', *Political Quarterly*, 49 (Oct–Dec), pp. 400–10.
Leibman, Marcel (1975) *Leninism Under Lenin* (trans. Brian Pearce), London, Jonathan Cape.
Lenin, V.I. (1902; 1947) *What is to be Done?*, Moscow, Progress Publishers.
Lenin, V. I. (1909; 1970) *Materialism and Empirio-Criticism: Critical Comments on a Reactionary Philosophy*, Moscow, Progress.
Lenin, V. I. (1915; 1978) *Imperialism: The Highest Stage of Capitalism*, Moscow, Progress.
Lenin V. I. (1917; 1968) 'The State and Revolution', in *Lenin: Selected Works*, London, Lawrence & Wishart, pp. 264–351.
Lenin, V. I. (1919; 1975) 'Theses and Report on Bourgeois Democracy and the Dictatorship of the Proletariat', *Selected Works in Three Volumes*, Moscow, Progress, pp. 98–111.
Lenin, V. I. (1920; 1966) 'The Terms of Admission into the Communist International', *Collected Works* (47 volumes), Vol. 31 (April–Dec 1920), Moscow, Progress, pp. 206–11.
Levi, Carlo (1945; 1981) *Cristo si e fermato a Eboli*, Turin, Einaldi.
Lévi-Strauss, C. (1978) *Myth and Meaning*, London, Routledge and Kegan Paul.
Li-Causi, Luciano (1975) 'Anthropology and Ideology: The Case of Patronage in Mediterranean Societies', *Critique of Anthropology*, 4–5 (Autumn), pp. 90–110.
Lipset, Seymour M. (1963) *Political Man: The Social Bases of Politics*, London, Heinemann.
Lombardo Radici, L. (1978) 'Communism with an Italian Face' (interview), in G. Urban (ed), *Eurocommunism: Its Roots and Future in Italy and Elsewhere*, London, Temple Smith, pp. 32–57.
Longo, Luigi (1957) 'Rapporto sullo Stato', in *PCI: VIII Congresso, atti e risoluzioni*, Rome, Riuniti.
Lovett, Clara M. (1980) 'Marxism and Culture in Italy', in *Problems in Communism*, (Nov–Dec), pp. 77–80.
Lovin, Clifford R. (1967) '*Blut und Boden*: The Ideological Basis of the Nazi

Agricultural Programme', *Journal of the History of Ideas*, Vol. XXVIII, No. 3, pp. 3–22.
Low-Beer, John (1978) *Protest and Participation: The New Working Class in Italy*, Cambridge, Cambridge University Press.
Lukes, Steven (1975) 'Political Ritual and Social Integration', *Sociology*, Vol. 9, pp. 289–308.
Luxemburg, Rosa (1961) *The Russian Revolution and Leninism or Marxism* (ed B. Wolfe), Ann Arbor, Michigan, University of Michigan Press.
Mack-Smith, Denis (1969) *Italy, A Modern History*, Ann Arbor, Michigan, University of Michigan Press.
Mack-Smith, Denis (1983) *Mussolini: A Biography*, New York, Vintage.
Magna, Nino (1983) 'Dirigenza e base', in Accornero et al. (eds) *L'Identità Comunista*, Rome, Riuniti, pp. 179–222.
Magri, L. and Maone, F. (1974) 'Problemi di organizzazione nell'esperienza del PCI', in *Classe, Consigili, Partito* (Il Manifesto, Quaderno No. 2), Rome, Alfani.
Malinowski, Bronislaw (1963) 'Myth as a Dramatic Development of Dogma', in *Sex, Culture and Myth*, London, Rupert Hart-Davis, pp. 245–55.
Mancini, Claudia (1977) *A Proposito di alcuni temi Gramsciani; riflessioni sul seminario 'Egemonia, Stato, Partito in Gramsci'*, Scuola Centrale del PCI, Rome (Frattocchie).
Mancini, G. and Galli, G. (1968) 'Gramsci's Presence', *Government and Opposition*, III, pp. 325–38.
Mandel, Ernest (1978) *From Stalinism to Eurocommunism, The Bitter Fruits of 'Socialism in one Country'*, London, New Left Books.
Mannheim, Karl (1936; 1979) *Ideology and Utopia: An Introduction to the Sociology of Knowledge*, London, Routledge and Kegan Paul.
Martinelli, R. (1982) 'Gli statuti del PCI, 1921–1970', in Ilardi and Accornero (eds), *Il Partito Comunista Italiano*, pp. 63–82.
Marwick, Arthur (1970) *The Nature of History*, London, Macmillan.
Marx, Karl (1852; 1968) 'The Eighteenth Brumaire of Louis Bonaparte', in Marx and Engels, *Selected Works in One Volume*, London, Lawrence and Wishart, pp. 94–179.
Marx, Karl (1859; 1968) 'Preface to a Contribution to the Critique of Political Economy', in Marx and Engels, *Selected Works in One Volume*, London, Lawrence and Wishart, pp. 180–4.
Marx, K. and Engels, F (1968) 'Manifesto of the Communist Party', in *Selected Works in One Volume*, London, Lawrence and Wishart, pp. 35–63.
Marx, K. and Engels, F. (1975) 'Contribution to the Critique of Hegel's Philosophy of Law', in Marx and Engels, *On Religion*, Moscow, Progress, pp. 38–52.
Marx, K. and Engels, F. (1846; 1976) 'The German Ideology', in *Collected Works* (40 Volumes), Vol. 5, London, Lawrence and Wishart, pp. 19–539.
Marzani, Carl (1980) *The Promise of Eurocommunism*, Westport, Conn., Lawrence Hill.
Marzo, Enzo (1983) 'Lo storico Sechi rischia la radiazione dal PCI', *Corriere della Sera*, 5 July, p. 4.
Massari, Oreste (1982) 'La Sezione', in Ilardi and Accornero (eds), *Il Partito Comunista Italiano*, Milan, Feltrinelli, pp. 153–84.
Massari, Oreste (1982b) 'L'anticipazione del partito comunista umbro', *Laboratoria Politica*, 2, No. 2–3 (March-June), pp. 273–89.

Massari, Oreste (1982c) 'La Federazione', in Ilardi and Accornero (eds), *Il Partito Comunista Italiano*, Milan, Feltrinelli, pp. 127–52.

McCauley, Martin and Carter, Stephen (eds) (1985) *Leadership and Succession in the Soviet Union, Eastern Europe and China*, London, Macmillan.

McKenzie, Robert T. (1955) *British Political Parties: The Distribution of Power within the Conservative and Labour Parties*, London, Heinemann.

McKenzie, W.J.M. (1978) *Political Identity*, Manchester, Manchester University Press.

McLennon, Gordon (1985) 'What Kind of Party Do We Want?' (speech to the 1985 Congress of the CPGB), reprinted in *Focus: The Communist Party Weekly, Congress Special*, 23 May, pp. 16–18.

Michels, Robert (1915; 1959) *Political Parties: A Sociological Study of the Oligarchical Tendencies of Modern Democracy*, New York, Dover.

Mieli, Renato (ed) (1983) *Il PCI allo specchio*, Milan, Rizzoli.

Miliband, Ralph (1969) *The State in Capitalist Society*, London, Weidenfeld and Nicolson.

Mouffe, Chantal (ed) (1979) *Gramsci and Marxist Theory*, London and Boston, Routledge and Kegan Paul.

Mussolini, Benito (1935) 'Fascism', in *Enciclopedia Italiana* (35 volumes), Rome, Instituto della Enciclopedia Italiana, Vol. XIV, pp. 847–78.

Napolitano, Giorgio (1981) 'Programma, unità e centralismo democratico', in *Critica Marxista*, 19 (Feb), pp. 45–56.

Napolitano, Giorgio (1981b), 'Il Problem del partito nell'attuale fase politica' (speech to Central Committee, 7 Jan), published in *L' Unità*, LVIII, 8 Jan, pp. 8–9.

Napolitano, Giorgio (1983) (interview with G. Napolitano, 4 Jan), Rome, Camera dei Deputati.

Napolitano, Giorgio (1984) Address given to ASMI Conference, 'The Italian Communist Party's Strategy for Socialism in the 1980s' (12 May), Cambridge.

Narkiewicz, Olga (1987) *Eurocommunism 1968–1986: A Select Bibliography*, London, Mansell.

Natta, Alessando and Pajetta, Gian Carlo (1963) 'Il Centralismo democratico nell'esperienza dei comunista italiani', *Critica Marxista*, No. 5–6 (Sept–Dec), pp. 103–17.

Nicchi, B. 1964 'Problemi di organizzazione, Relazione di B. Nicchi al comitato federale di Perugia dell febraio, 1964', in *I comunisti umbri: scritti e documenti*, Perugia, Edizione di Cronache Umbre, pp. 391–3.

Nichols, Peter (1973) *Italia, Italia*, Glasgow, Fontana.

Nichols, Peter (1982) 'Berlinguer Expels Dissident Leader', *The Times*, 26 Oct

Orwell, George (1949; 1984) *Nineteen Eighty-Four*, Harmondsworth, Penguin.

Orwell, George (1938; 1984) *Homage to Catalonia*, Harmondsworth, Penguin.

Ostrogorski, M (1902) *Democracy and the Organisation of Political Parties* (2 Vols) London, Macmillan.

Pacheco Pereira, José (1989) 'A Case of Orthodoxy: The Communist Party of Portugal', in M. Waller and M Fennema (eds), *Communist Parties in Western Europe*, Oxford, Blackwell, pp. 86–95.

Page, Campbell (1983) 'When the Partitocrazia has to stop', *The Guardian*, 21 April, p. 5.

Pajetta, Gian Carlo (1982) *Le Crisi che ho vissuto: Budapest, Praga, Varsavia*, Rome, Riuniti.

Palmer, Alan (1979) *The Penguin Dictionary of Twentieth-Century History*, Harmondsworth, Penguin.

Pansa, Giampaolo (1980) *Storie italiane di violenza e terrorismo*, Bari, Laterza.

Parkin, Frank (1972) *Class, Inequality and Political Order. Social Stratification in Capitalist and Communist Societies*, London, Paladin.

Pasquino, Giordano (1982) 'Il PCI nel sistema politico Italiano degli anni'70', *Il Mulino*, XXXI, No. 6, Nov/Dec, pp. 857–97.

PCI Publications

PCI Congress (1959) *IX Congresso. Rapporto di attivita del Comitato Centrale per il IX Congresso Nazionale del PCI*, Rome, SETT.

PCI (1926; 1980) 'Le Tesi del Congresso di Lione', in *Almanacco del 60'*, Rome, Dipartimento stampa, propaganda e informazione, pp. 243–55.

PCI (1983) *Statuto del Partito Comunista Italiano* (Approvato al XVI Congresso del PCI), Milan, 2–6 March 1983, Rome, ITER.

PCI Central Committee (1978) 'Draft Thesis for the 15th National Congress of the PCI', in *The Italian Communists: Foreign Bulletin of the PCI*, (special edn), Rome, Botteghe Oscure.

PCI Central Committee (1981) 'Joint Declaration by the Italian Communist Party and the Communist Party of Spain', in *The Italian Communists. Foreign Bulletin of the PCI*, No. 2 (April–June), pp. 68–73.

PCI Central Committee (1982a) *Un idea nuova del socialismo: la posizione dei comunisti sui fatti di Polonia. L'articola della Pravda e la risposta de l'Unità* (PCI pamphlet, special edn), Rome, Botteghe Oscure.

PCI Central Committee (1982b) 'A Reply to *Pravda*: Our Position Arises from the Facts' (Extracts from the article appearing in *L'Unità*, of 28 Jan 1982), *The Guardian*, 8 Feb, p. 9.

PCI Central Committee (1982c) 'La Proposta di Alternativa per il Cambiamento' (documento approvato dal CC e dalla CCC per il XVI Congresso del PCI), *Supplemento a L'Unità*, No. 265, 28 Nov, Rome, GATE.

PCI Dipartimento stampa, propaganda e informazione (1980) *PCI '81: Almanacco del Sessantesimo*, Rome, Fratelli Spada APA.

PCI Scuola Centrale (undated) 'Che cosa e il partito comunista nella dottrina marxista-leninista', *Come è Organissato il PCI*, Perugia, Perugia Federation Archives.

PCI, Scuola Centrale (1948) 'Teoria e tattica marxist-leninista sulle questione della guerra e della pace' (in 4 lezioni), *Per la scuola del partito: corsi e lezione*, Rome, Botteghe Oscure (Perugia Federation Archives).

PCI, Scuola Centrale (1948) *Direttive sul lavoro di educazione comunista*, (3 Nov) Rome, Botteghe Oscure (Perugia Federation Archives).

PCI, Scuola Centrale (1978) *Formazione dei quadri e sviluppo del partito*, Rome, Salemi.

PCI Scuola Centrale (undated) *Quaderni di Storia del PCI*, Rome, Botteghe Oscure.

PCI, Scuola Centrale (1981) *La scuola di partito negli anni '80: problemi e prospettive*, Rome, Salemi.

PCI, Scuola Centrale (1982) *Dossier: centralismo democratico nell'elaborazione di Lenin, Luxemburg, Stalin, Gramsci*, Rome (Fratocchie).

PCI Perugia Federation Publications

PCI (1961; 1976) 'Come nacque e si svillupo il PCI in Umbria', *L'Unità* article reprinted in *Cronache Umbre*, No. 8.

PCI (1977) *I comunisti Umbri: scritti e documenti (1944–1970)*, Perugia, Edizione di 'Cronache Umbre'.

PCI (1982) *Indicazioni del comitato federale per lo svolgimento dei congressi di sezione e di cellula*, Perugia, 4 Dec, Perugia, Federation Archives.

PCI (1983) *Verbali: congressi di sezione, comprensorio Perugino*, Perugia, Federation Archives.

PCI (1983) *Verbale dalla Commissione Verifica dei Poteri*, (XVIII Congress of the PCI Federation of Perugia, 13 Feb), Perugia, Federation Archives.

PCI Section Primo Ciabatti (Piazza Grimana) Documents

PCI (undated) *Autobiografia del compagno Rosini, Otello alla segretaria della Federazione Provinciale del PCI*, Perugia, Section Archives.

PCI (1982) *Verbale: congresso della sezione Primo Ciabatti*, Dec 1982, Perugia, Section Archives.

PCI (1982) *Documento della commissione politica approvato alla unanimità dal congresso di sezione Primo Ciabatti*, Dec 1982, Perugia, Section Archives.

PCI, Scuola Provinciale del PCI (undated) La fondazione del PCI e la lotta di Gramsci e Togliatti per un partito marxista-leninista. I principi ideologici ed organizzativi del partito marxista-leninista', Perugia, Piazza Grimana Archives.

Peristiany, J.G. (ed) (1965) *Honour and Shame: the Values of Mediterranean Society*, London, Weidenfeld and Nicolson.

Pierucci, Francesco (1978) *Le lotte contadine in Umbria (1900–1950)*, (Quaderni Regione dell'Umbria), Umbertide, Caldari SD.

Pierucci, Francesco (1983) *Il movimento operaio in Umbria (1850–1950)*, Citta di Castello, La Nuova Stampa.

Pimlott, Ben (1977) *Labour and the Left in the 1930s*, Cambridge, Cambridge University Press.

Pinzani, Carlo (1982) 'Il partito nella clandestinità: problemi di organizzazione 1926/1932', in Ilardi and Accornero (eds), *Il Partito Comunista Italiano*, Milan, Feltrinelli, pp. 975–1006.

Pitt-Rivers, Julian (1954) *The People of the Sierra*, London, Weidenfeld and Nicolson.

Pitt-Rivers, Julian (1977) *The Fate of Shechem: Or the Politics of Sex*, Cambridge, Cambridge University Press.

Plamenatz, J.P. (1954) *German Marxism and Russian Communism*, London, New York and Toronto, Longmans, Green and Co.

Poggi, Gianfranco, et al. (eds) (1968) *L'organizzazione partitica del PCI e della DC*, Istituto di Studi e Ricerche 'Carlo Cattaneo', Bologna, Il Mulino.

Poliakov, Leon (1971) *The Aryan Myth. A History of Racist and Nationalist Ideas in Europe*, New York, Meridian.

Pope John XXIII (1963) *Pacem in terris*, Encyclical letter, 'Peace on Earth', London, Catholic Truth Society.

Porter J.M. (1981) 'Luther and Political Millenarianism', in *Journal of the History of Ideas*, Vol. XLII, No. 3, pp. 389–406.

Pratt, Jeff (1981) 'A Sense of Place', in R. Grillo (ed), *Nation and State in Europe*, London, Academic Press, pp. 31–43.

Pratt, Jeff, (1984) 'Christian-Democrat Ideology in the Cold War', in E. Wolf (ed), *Religion, Power and Protest in Local Communities*, Berlin, New York, Amsterdam, Mouton, pp. 213–38.

Pratt, Jeff (1986) *The Walled City: A Study of Social Change and Conservative Ideologies in Tuscany*, Göttingen, Herodot.

Pridham, Geoffrey (1981) *The Nature of the Italian Party System: A Regional Case Study*, London, Croom-Helm.

Prior, M. (1956) 'Bacon's Man of Science', *Journal of the History of Ideas*, XV, pp. 41–54.

Procacci, Giuliano (1973) *History of the Italian People*, Harmondsworth, Penguin.

Pye, Lucian and Verba, Sydney (1965) *Political Culture and Political Development* (Studies in Political Development, 5), Princeton, New Jersey, Princeton University Press.

Ranger, Terry and Hobsbawm, Eric (eds) (1983) *The Invention of Tradition*, Cambridge, Cambridge University Press.

Redfield, Robert (1956) *Peasant Society and Culture: An Anthropological Approach to Civilization*, Chicago, Chicago University Press.

Riccamboni, G. (1976) 'The Italian Communist Party and the Catholic World', *Social Compass*, Vol. 23, No. 2–3, pp. 141–69.

Di Rienzo, R. (1982) 'À chi i ceti medi? À me', *L'Espresso*, No. 31, (8 August), pp. 6–9.

Di Rienzo, R. (1983) 'Fu vero strappo? Sondaggio: il PCI à congresso', *L'Espresso*, 16 Jan, pp. 12–16.

Rivington-Edwards, P. (ed) (1967) *The Encyclopaedia of Philosophy*, London, Macmillan; New York, Free Press.

Rizzo, A. (1977) *La frontiera dell'eurocommunismo*, Bari, La Terza.

Romano L. and Scabello, P. (eds) (1975) *C'era una volta la DC*, Rome, Savelli Editore.

Rossi, Raffaele (1976) 'La storia dell'ultimo trentennio in Umbria: proposta per una periodizzazione', *Cronache Umbre*, No. 8 (Nov), pp. 7–17 and No. 9 (Jan 1977), pp. 63–76.

Rossi, Raffaele (1977) 'Il PCI in una regione rossa', (interview by Renzo Massareli), Perugia, Grafica.

Ruscoe, James (1982) *The Italian Communist Party, 1976–81: On the Threshold of Government*, London, Macmillan.

Russell, Bertrand (1946; 1984) *A History of Western Philosophy*, London, Unwin.

Russo, Giovanni (1979) 'Il compromesso storico: The Italian Communist Party from 1968 to 1978', in P. Filo della Torre et al. (eds), *Eurocommunism: Myth or Reality?*, Harmondsworth, Penguin, pp. 69–111.

Sabine, George H. (1948) *A History of Political Theory*, London and Toronto, George Harrap.

Samuel, Raffael (1984) 'Mr Benn Consults Some Household Gods', *The Guardian*, 4 Oct, p. 16.

Sani, Giacomo (1979) 'The Changing Face of the PCI', in D.E. Albright (ed), *Communism and Political Systems in Western Europe*, Boulder, Colorado, Westview Press, pp. 43–94.

Sani, Giacomo (1983) 'Italy', in Robert Wesson (ed), *Yearbook on International Communist Affairs*, Stanford University, Stanford, Calif., Hoover Institution Press, pp. 449–55.

Sassoon, Donald (ed) (1978) *The Italian Communists Speak for Themselves*, Nottingham, Spokesman.

Sassoon, Donald (1981) *The Strategy of the Italian Communist Party: From the Resistance to the Historic Compromise*, London, Frances Pinter.

Sassoon, Donald (1986) *Contemporary Italy*, New York and London, Longman.

Schapiro, Leonard (1970) *The Communist Party of the Soviet Union*, London, Eyre and Spottiswoode.

Schneider, Jane and Schneider, Peter (1976) *Culture and Political Economy in Western Sicily*, London and New York, Academic Press.

Sebastiani, Chiara (1983) 'I Funzionari', in Accornero et al. (eds), *L'Identità Comunista*, Rome, Riuniti, pp. 79–178.

Secchia, Pietro (1946) 'Migliorare il lavoro del partito', *Rapporto d'organizzazione tenuto al V congress nazionale del PCI*, 24 Dec, Rome, Riuniti

Secchia, Pietro (1948) *Piu forti i quadri migliorare l'organizzazione. Intervento al VI congresso nazionale del PCI*, gennaio 1948, Rome, La Stampa Moderna.

Sechi, Salvatore (1979) 'L'austero fascino del centralismo democratico', in Barbagli, Corbetta and Sechi (eds), *Dentro Il PCI*, Bologna (Istituto 'Carlo Cattaneo'), Il Mulino, pp. 61–111.

Seidel, Gill (1975) 'Ambiguity in Political Discourse', in Bloch (ed), *Political Language and Oratory in Traditional Society*, London, Academic Press, pp. 205–26.

Selznick, Phillip (1960) *The Organisational Weapon: A Study of Bolshevik Strategy and Tactics*, New York, McGraw Hill.

Seton-Watson, Christopher (1967) *Italy From Liberalism to Fascism, 1860–1925*, London, Methuen.

Shakespeare, William (1951) *As You Like It, The Complete Works of Shakespeare* (Edited by Peter Alexander), London and Glasgow, Collins.

Shils, Edward (1955) 'The End of Ideology?', *Encounter*, Vol. V.

Shore, Cris (1985) 'Organisation, Ideology, Identity: Social Anthropology of Italian Communism', Unpublished D.Phil. Thesis, Sussex University.

Shore, Cris (1989) 'Patronage and Bureaucracy in Complex Societies: Social Rules and Social Relations in an Italian University', *JASO*, Vol. XX, No. 1.

Shore, Cris (1990) 'Ethnicity as Revolutionary Strategy: Communist Identity in Italy', in S. MacDonald (ed), *Inside Identities: Ethnography in Western Europe*, Berg Press (in press).

Showstack Sassoon, Ann (1980) *Gramsci's Politics*, London, Hutchinson.

Silone, Ignazio (1950) (autobiographical account), in R.H.S. Crossman (ed), *The God that Failed: Six Studies in Communism*, London, Hamish Hamilton.

Silverman, Sydel (1966) 'An Ethnographic Approach to Social Stratification: Prestige in a Central Italian Community' *American Anthropologist*, Vol. 68, pp. 899–921.

Silverman, Sydel (1967) 'The Community–Nation Mediator in Traditional Central Italy', in Potter, Diaz and Foster (eds), *Peasant Society: A Reader*, Boston, Mass., Little, Brown and Co.

Silverman, Sydel (1968) 'Agricultural Organisation, Social Structure, and Values in Italy: Amoral Familism Reconsidered' *American Anthropologist*, Vol. 70, pp. 1–20.

Silverman, Sydel (1975) *Three Bells of Civilization: The Life of an Italian Hill Town*, New York, Columbia University Press.

Sivini, Giordano (ed) (1979) *Sociologia dei partiti politici*, Bologna, Il Mulino.

Sorel, Georges (1908; 1950) *Reflections on Violence*, London, Allen and Unwin; London, Collier Books.

Sorge, Bartolomeo, S.J. (1978) 'Will Eurocommunists and Eurocatholics Converge?', in G.R. Urban (ed), *Eurocommunism*, London, Temple Smith, pp. 255–77.

Spesso, Ruggero, et al. (1982) 'Non sono comunisti "euro" e perciò sono poco gradito', *Interstampa. Mensile di documenti e informazione sulla pace e il socialismo*, 2, No. 11 (Nov), p. 4.
Spesso, Ruggero, et al. (1983) 'Preoccupante caduta della componente operaia', *Interstampa*, No. 1, (Jan), p. 23.
Spinelli, Altiero (1978) 'How European are the Italian Eurocommunists?', in G.R. Urban (ed), *Eurocommunism*, London, Temple Smith, pp. 179–210.
Spriano, Paolo (1975) *Storia del partito comunista italiano (V: La Resistenza, Togliatti e il partito nuovo)*, Turin, Einaldi.
Stalin, Joseph (1924; 1940) 'The Foundations of Leninism' and 'On the Problems of Leninism', in *Leninism*, London, Lawrence and Wishart, pp. 1–85; 118–74.
Staar, Richard (ed) (1980) *Yearbook on International Communist Affairs*, Stanford University, Stanford, Calif., Hoover Institute Press.
Staar, Richard (ed) (1988) *Yearbook on International Communist Affairs*, Stanford University, Stanford, Calif., Hoover Institute Press.
Steadman Jones, Gareth (1989) 'The Crisis of Communism', in S. Hall and M. Jacques (eds), *New Times: The Changing Face of Politics in the 1990s*, Lawrence and Wishart, London, pp. 230–5.
Sword, Keith (1983) 'Ethnic Identity and Association among Polish Émigrés in a British Town', Unpublished D.Phil. Thesis, University of Sussex.
Tarrow, Sydney (1967) *Peasant Communism in Southern Italy*, New Haven, Conn., and London, Yale University Press.
Tiersky, Ronald (1985) *Ordinary Stalinism: Democratic Centralism and the Question of Communist Political Development*, Boston, Allen and Unwin.
Timmermann, Heinz (1985) 'A che serve il centralismo democratico?', *Mond-Operaio* (Dec), pp. 81–7.
Thomson David (1966) *Europe since Napoleon*, Harmondsworth, Penguin.
Togliatti, Palmiro (1944) 'Che cosa è il partito nuovo', *Rinascita*, No. 4 (Oct–Dec).
Togliatti, Palmiro (1945) 'I compiti del partito nella situazione attuale', in *Togliatti, politica comunista*, Rome, Soc. ed. *L'Unità*, reprinted in *Critica Marxista*, I, Nos. 5–6 (Sept–Dec 1963).
Togliatti, Palmiro (1946) 'Istruzione per le conferenze provinciale di organizzazione', in Ufficio Segretaria (ed), *PCI, V–VI Congresso: Risoluzioni*, Rome, PCI.
Togliatti, Palmiro (1956; 1976) 'Intervista a "Nuovi Argomenti" 1956', in *Democrazia e socialismo, autonomia e internazionalismo (allegato all'Almanacco PCI '76)*, Rome, PCI.
Togliati, Palmiro (1964; 1976) 'Memoriale di Yalta 1964', in *Democrazia e socialismo, autonomia e internazionalismo (allegato all'Almanacco PCI '76)*, Rome, PCI.
Togliatti, Palmiro (1979) *On Gramsci and Other Writings*, (ed D. Sassoon), London, Lawrence and Wishart.
Tokes, Rudolf (ed) (1978) *Eurocommunism and Detente*, New York, New York University Press.
Tomlinson, John (1981) *Left–Right: The March of Political Extremism in Britain*, London, John Calder.
Trotsky, Leon (1937; 1965) *The Revolution Betrayed. What is the Soviet Union and Where is it Going?*, New York, Ment Publishers.
Trotsky, Leon (1954) *The Prophet Armed. Trotsky 1921–1929*, ed Isaac Deutscher, London and New York, Oxford University Press.

Tudor, Henry (1972) *Political Myth*, London, Pall Mall Press.
Turner, Victor (1968) 'Myth and Symbol', *Encyclopaedia of the Social Sciences*, London and New York, Macmillan and Free Press.
Twitchell, James (1986) *Dreadful Pleasures: Anatomy of Modern Horror*, Oxford, Oxford University Press.
Vidotto, V. (1975) *Il partito comunista italiano dalle origine al 1946*, Bologna, Cappelli.
Urban, George (1978) 'Introduction', in Urban (ed), *Eurocommunism: Its Roots and Future in Italy and Elsewhere*, London, Temple Smith, pp. 7–12.
Urban, Joan Barth (1981) 'Review of Kertzer's book *Comrades and Christians*' *Anthropological Quarterly*, Vol. 54, No. 1 (Jan), pp. 51–2.
Urban, Joan Barth (1980) 'Moscow and the PCI in the 1970s: Ktto Kovo?', *Studies in Comparative Communism*, Vol. XIII, Nos. 2 and 3, (Summer/Autumn), pp. 99–167.
Urban, Joan Barth (1986) *Moscow and the Italian Communist Party: From Togliatti to Berlinguer*, London, I.B. Taurus.
Urban, Joan Barth (1988) 'Italy', in R.F. Staar (ed), *Yearbook on International Communist Affairs*, Stanford University, Stanford, Calif., Hoover Institute Press.
Wade, Robert (1971) 'Political Behaviour and World-View in a Central Italian Village' in F.G. Bailey (ed), *Gifts and Poison: The Politics of Reputation*, Oxford, Blackwell, pp. 252–80.
Wade, Robert (1975) 'The Base of a "Centrifugal Democracy": Party Allegiance in Rural Central Italy' in J. Boissevain and J. Friedl (eds), *Beyond the Community: Social Processes in Europe*, The Hague, Department of Science of The Netherlands, pp. 29–55.
Waller, Michael (1981) *Democratic Centralism: An Historical Commentary*, Manchester, Manchester University Press.
Waller, Michael (1988) 'Democratic Centralism: The Costs of Discipline', in Waller and Fennema (eds), *Communist Parties in Western Europe. Decline or Adaptation?*, Oxford, Blackwell, pp. 7–26.
Watson, Jack (1974) *Twentieth-Century World Affairs*, London, John Murray.
Webster, David (1981) 'The Labour Party and the New Left' *Fabian Tract 477*, London, Blackross Press.
Weingrod, Alex (1968) 'Patrons, Patronage and Political Parties', in *Comparative Studies in Society and History*, Vol. 10, pp. 377–400.
White, Caroline (1980) *Patrons and Partisans: A Study of Two Southern Italian Comuni*, Cambridge, Cambridge University Press.
Wice, Hilary (1984) 'History Should Make Pupils Proud – Sir Keith', *Times Educational Supplement*, 24 Aug, No. 2557, p. 8.
Williams, Gwyn A. (1960) 'The Concept of 'Egemonia' in the Thought of Antonio Gramsci', *Journal of the History of Ideas*, XXI, pp. 586–99.
Williams, Raymond (1976) *Keywords: A Vocabulary of Culture and Society*, London, Flamingo.
Wiskemann, Elizabeth (1971) *Italy since 1945*, London, Macmillan.
Wolf, Eric (1966) 'Kinship, Friendship and Patron–Client Relationships in Complex Societies', in M. Banton (ed), *The Social Anthropology of Complex Societies*, ASA Monograph 4, London, Tavistock, pp. 1–22.
Wolfe, Bertram D. (1961) 'Introduction', in Rosa Luxemburg, *The Russian Revolution, and Leninism or Marxism*, Ann Arbor, Michigan, University of Michigan Press.

Zarisky, Raphael 1972, *Italy: The Politics of Uneven Development*, Hinsdale, Ill., Dryden Press.

Zelinsky, Wilbur (1975) 'The Demigod's Dilemma', *Annals of the Association of American Geographers*, Vol. 65, No. 2, pp. 123–43.

Zingarelli, Nicola (1970) *Vocabolario della lingua italiana* (10th ed), Milan, OFSA-Casaril.

Index

Abse, Tobias, 187
ACLI, 107
Action Party, 33
Afghanistan, Soviet invasion of, 5, 45, 47, 110
Allende, Salvador, 43, 116
Allum, Percy, 33, 34, 39, 41, 66
Almond, Gabriel, 56, 59, 60
Althusser, Louis, 191
Amendola, E., 34
Amendola, Giorgio, 36, 89
Amyot, Grant, 41, 44, 50, 51, 57, 100, 102, 131, 135, 138, 142, 172
Andreotti, Giulio, 2, 45
Andropov, Yuri, 7
anticlericism, 55
anticommunism, 60–6, 90
Arlacchi, Pino, 46
Avanguardia Operaio, 42
Avanti, 29
Axelrod, 161

Bacon, Francis, 85
Banco Ambrosiano, 45
Barbagli, Marzio, 128, 130
Barnes, Samuel, 52
Belgian Communist Party, 6
Berlin, blockade, 37; conference, 113; Wall, 9, 10
Berlinguer, Enrico; on Eurocommunism, 5, 43, 45, 84, 87, 180; on Lenin, 154; NATO, 136; on Soviet communism, 111; and the *terza via*, 45, 113–14, 180; *see also* Historic Compromise
Bestor, A. E., 189
Blackmer, Donald, 35, 58, 70
Bloch, Maurice, 133
Bocca, Giorgio, 187
Boggs, Carl, 12
Bordiga, Amadeo, 29, 31, 94
Borghese, Valerio, 42
Brezhnev, Leonid, 7; Doctrine, 113
British Communist Party (CPGB), 6, 165, 168–9, 193
Bukharin, Nikolai, 31, 86
Bulgaria, 6, 9
bureaucratic centralism, 164, 169, 173–84, *see also* democratic centralism

Burgess, Guy, 62
Buxton, James, 46

Cammett, John, 4, 30
Cantril, Hadley, 60
Caponi, Alfio, 35
cargo cults, 82
Carr, E. H., 49, 86, 172, 183
Carrillo, Santago, 4, 5, 112
Catholic Church, 10, 38, 52–4; political ideology, 55; and Christian Democrat Party, 64; trade unions, 107
Catholic-world (*mondo catolico*), 52–3
Catholicism, 10, 52–5; dialogue with Marxism, 41, 43
Ceausescu, Nikolai, 9
CGIL, *see* Confederation of Italian Workers
CGL, *see* General Workers' Confederation
Che Guevara, 42
Chernenko, Konstantin, 7
Chile, 43, 116
Chinese Communist Party (CCP), 7
Christian Democrat Party (DC), 2, 34, 36; clientelism, 41, 48–9, 67–9; ideology, 65; domination of state, 66
Churchill, Winston, 36
CIA, 43, 107, 116
CISL, *see* Italian Confederation of Workers
Clark, Martin, 98, 174
clientelism, *see* patronage
Cohen, Abner, 131
Cold War, 4, 36, 38, 40, 46, 49, 90; and communist identity, 59–66; effect on PCI, 50, 101–3
Comintern, *see* Communist International
communism, *see* democratic centralism, ideology, Italian Communist Party, Leninism, Marxism
Communist International, 29–30; on social democracy, 31–2; terms for admission into, 146–7, *see also* organisation
Communist Party of Italy (PCd'I), 29–32, 36, 94, 148–9
Communist-world (*mondo comunista*), 52–3, 75, 80
community, 15

Confederation of Italian Workers (CGIL), 12, 103, 107, 195
Congress, (PCI); 1926, 94; 1946, 97; 1956, 103; 1979, 109; 1983, 110, 142; 1987, 47, 192; 1989, 48, 109, 181, 186–7; federation-level, 49; section-level, 119–23, 134–5
Conquest, Robert, 171, 173
Constituent Assembly, 2
constitution, Italian, 66
containment, US policy of, 37, 39, 49
Corbetta, Piergiogio, 128, 130
Cornwell, Rupert, 84
corruption, 178
Cossutta, Armando, 115, 116, 120, 186, 195
Covino, Renato, 50, 135
Craxi, Bettino, 48, 186, 195
Crockatt, Richard, 62, 63
culture; communist, 10, 12, 27, 47, 127; Marxist, 13, 73; Catholic, 52
Cypriot Communist Party, 3, 6
Czechoslovakia, 6, 9, 36; 1948 coup, 90–1; communist party, 41, 102; 1968 Soviet invasion of, 44, 110

D'Annunzio, Gabriele, 29
Dahrendorf, Ralf, 185
Dalla Chiesa, General Carlo Alberto, 46
Daniels, Robert, 60
Darwin, Charles, 92
DC, *see* Christian Democrat Party
De Clementi, Andreina, 149
De Gasperi, Alcide, 33, 36, 64, 90
democracy; Marxist critique of, 19–20, 33; and pluralism, 144, 154–5, 180; Lenin's critique of, 155–6
Democratic Alternative, 117–18, 120, 122, 132
democratic centralism, 20, 41, 127, 145, 147; definitions of, 101–2, 140; development of, 171–3; and the NUM, 167; and oligarchy, 140–2; in PCI section congress, 119–20; PCI's abandonment of, 164; theory of, 166–7; *see also* bureaucratic centralism, democracy, Leninism, oligarchy
Deutscher, Isaac, 162, 163
dialectical materialism, 160
discourse, 132–4
dopiezza, 99–100, 128
Douglas, Mary, 64
Dubcek, Alexander, 41, 86, 110
Duverger, Maurice, 59

East–West relations, 4, 10
Eastern Europe; communist parties of, 4; 8–10, 20, 193; and Eurocommunism, 6–7; and iron-curtain, 36; and Soviet Union, 10
economic miracle, 106
EEC, 19
elections; Italy, 48; European Parliament, 47, 193 (*see also* table of elections)
Eliade, Mircea, 81
Ellensteine, Jean, 170
Elliot, Phillip, 61
embourgeoisement thesis, 50, 135
Engels, Frederich, 49, 191
Epstein, A. L., 15
Eurocommunism, 3–6, 48; and concept of hegemony, 71; conflict between Euro-communists and conservatives, 50, 128–9; joint declaration on, 43; origins of term, 68–9; in the PCF, 183–4; Soviet response to, 112
European Left, 3–4, 47
Eurosocialism, 48
Evans-Pritchard, E. E., 15

Fascism, 30–3, 35, 58–9; Mussolini's definition of, 81–2
Federazione Giovanile Comunista Italiana (FGCI), 11, 16, 44, 47
Femia, Joseph, 12
feminism, 118
Ferrara, Giovanni, 67
Ferrarotti, Franco, 40, 65, 71, 103, 106, 144, 156
Fiat, 107
fieldwork, 13, 26, 28
Finnish Communist Party, 3
fission–fusion principle, 15
Forini, Enzo, 40, 46
Fourth International, 142, 169
France, 39
Franco, General, 4, 39, 86
French Communist Party (PCF), 3, 5, 6, 183–4
Friend, J., 5, 183
Frontism, 102, 138, 142
Fuchs, Klaus, 62
Fukuyama, Francis, 189
Fumagalli, Marco, 47
funeral ritual, communist, 74

Gallerano, N., 64
Galli, Giorgio, 34, 62, 79
Garibaldi Brigades, 35, 95
Gellago, Ignacio, 5
General Workers' Confederation (CGL), 29, 31, 37, 39
generations, political, 27–8
German Democratic Republic, 9
German Social Democratic Party (SPD), 92, 137, 192
Ghini, Celso, 37, 44, 96, 103
Gill, Graeme, 170
Gorbachev, Mikhail, 177, 186, 188, 189
Government of National Unity, 33
Gramsci, Antonio, 10, 31–2, 94; on bureaucratic centralism, 173–7; on hegemony, ideology, 17–18, 71–5, 81; on Italian bourgeoisie, 54; on Lenin, 94–5; on state, society and the role of the party; 11, 71–2, 81, 85, 174–5

Greek Communist Party, 3, 6, 99
Guizzardi, Gustavo, 55

hegemony; concept of, 10–11, 50, 71–8, 85–6, 191; over party membership, 143; *see also* Gramsci, history
Higgins, Hugh, 63
Historic Compromise; origins of, 43, 116–17; criticism of, 45, 50, 51; as political symbol, 132
history, concept of; communist party view of, 83–7; Marx on, 49; as power, 84; re-writing of, 85–6, 114
Hitler, Adolph, 35
Hoare, Quentin, 30
Hobsbawm, Eric, 59
Hoffer, Eric, 60
Honecker, Erich, 9
Hot Autumn, 42
Hungarian Socialist Workers' Party, 8
Hungary, 6, 8, 39, 105
Husak, Gustav, 86

Icelandic Communist Party, 3
Identity, communist; concept of, 14–17, 36, 50; construction, 52–69, 70–1; and democratic centralism, 177–9; and political patronage, 67; and United States, 63–4
ideology, 17–19; Catholic, 55–6, Leninist, 18–20; and myth, 81–3; in social science, 60–3; *see also* Frontism, Italian Communist Party, Leninism, Stalinism
ideology of unity, 17, 97, 136, 142, 143–4, 195
Ingrao, Pietro, 51, 89, 117, 195
Interstampa, 114
Italian Communist Party (PCI); allied organisations, 12; and Church, 52–6, 89; class composition, 50, 53; definitions of, 11, 89; identity, 14–16, 36, 50, 52–69; intellectuals, 35, 50, 75, 84–5; and Marxism–Leninism, 18–20, 57, 75, 78, 80, 90, 97–8, 111, 153–4, 187–91; party schools, 77, 149–52; relations with Soviet Union, 44–6, 70, 87, 91, 110–23; *see also* membership; organisation
Italian Constitution, 2
Italian Road to Socialism (*via italiana al socialismo*), 10, 20, 39, 102, 104, 185–8
Italian Confederation of Workers (CISL), 107
Italian Socialist Party (PSI), 29–31, 36, 38, 48–9, 56, 92, 94, 186

Jacques, Martin, 193–4
Jakes, Milos, 9
Jaruzelski, General, 6, 9
Jensen, Jane, 141
John XXII, pope, 40
John Paul II, pope, 45

Kamenev, Rosenfeld, 31
Kautsky, Karl, 100
Kennedy, Robert, 41
Kertzer, 13, 60, 68, 75, 77
KGB, 7
Khruschev, 38–9, 85–6, 105, 152–3
Kinnock, Neil, 192
Kogan, Norman, 36, 61, 64, 88
Kohl, Helmut, 4
Korea, 37
Kundera, Milan, 86
Kuniholm, 63, 64

L'Unità, 12, 74, 104
La Torre, Pio, 46
Labour Party, 134
land tenure, *see mezzadria* and *latifundia*
Lange, Peter, 154
latifundia, 37
Leibman, Marcel, 171
Leninism, 11, 18–21, 127; and democracy, 155–61, 173; formative influence on PCI, 148–52; influence on New Left, 42; and party organisation, 145–8, 153–63, 184; and Stalinism, 80, 84, 153–4, 194; Trotsky and Luxemburg, critique of, 161–3; *see also* democratic centralism
Leo X, pope, 112
Liberalism, 34
Lombardo Radice, Lucio, 148
Longo, Luigi, 42, 105
Lotta Continua, 42
Luther, Martin, 112, 142
Luxemburg, Rosa, 161–2

Macaluso, Emanuele, 47, 115
Maclean, Donald, 62
Mafia, 46
Magna, Nino, 93
Magri, Lucio, 108, 170
Mancini, Claudia, 191
Mandarini, Francesco, 116, 118–19, 121, 123, 129
Manifesto group, 42, 107, 179, 182, 195
Mao Tse-tung, 42
Maone, Filippo, 108, 170
March on Rome, 30
Marchais, Georges, 5, 43
Marinelli, Renzo, 148
Marshall Plan, 36
Martov, Julius, 161
Marx, Karl; on class and bourgeois democracy, 19, 157–8; on history, 49, 92; on ideology, 17–18; on Marxism, 190
Marxism Today, 193
Marxism; analysis of in American social science, 60–3; distinction between Leninism and, 157–9, 189–91, 194; myth of, 82–3
Marzani, Carl, 37, 99, 104, 107, 112, 113, 167, 175
Masaryk, Jan, 90
Massari, Oreste, 93, 98, 101, 102, 106, 109
Matteotti, Giacomo, 31

Mazowiecki, Tadeuz, 9
McKenzie, W. J. M., 14
membership (PCI), 11–12; character during early years, 30–1; under Fascism, 32–3, 57–9; immediate post-war, 35–6; during Cold War, 38–9, 103; after 1956, 41, 44, 105–6; from Berlinguer to Occhetto, 48–9, 109; attitude toward Soviet Union, 98, 114–15, 129–30; belonging to the Party, 73, 78–9, 143; *see also* culture, hegemony, subculture, world-view
mezzadria, 38, 56
Michels, Robert, 92, 136–8, 140
Mitterrand, 4, 183
monarchism, 34
Morning Star, 6
Moro, Aldo, 39, 41, 44
Mouffe, Chantal, 12
movimento, 42, 45, 46
Movimento Sociale Italiano (MSI), 40
MSI *see* Movimento Sociale Italiano
Mussolini, 30–1, 33, 66, 81
myth, 47; political, 80–3; Nazi, 15

Nagy, Imre, 8, 105
Napoleone, Roberto, 84
Napolitano, 47, 58, 89, 117, 179
National Union of Mineworkers (NUM), 168
nationalism, 16, 55, 58
NATO, 12, 19, 37, 84, 136
Natta, Alessandro, 5, 47
Nenni, Pietro, 33, 104
new course, 185–6
New Forum, 9
New Left, 40–2, 107
New Times, 168
Nixon, Richard, 42
Nowell-Smith, Geoffrey, 30

Occhetto, Achile, 47, 185–7, 192–5
OECD, 36
oligarchy, 136–43
OPEC, 44
Ordine Nuovo, 29
organisation; of Italian political parties, 68; of PCI, 88–109, 139; Third International model of, 93
Orwell, George, 86
Ostrogorski, M., 92

P2 Masonic Lodge, 45
Pact of Unity, 36, 39, 104
Pajetta, Gian-Carlo, 104
Parkin, Frank, 138
Parsons, Talcott, 176
Partito Nuovo, 34, 58, 70–1, 89–91, 95–101
partitocrazia, 67
party system, 2, 52, 66–9
patronage, 12, 44, 48, 67–9, 195, *see also* corruption, *partitocrazia*

Paul I, pope, 45
PCd'I, *see* Communist Party of Italy
peasants, 34, 54, 78, 106
Peng, Li, 7, 8
Philby, Kim, 62
Piazza Fontana incident, 42
Pius XII, pope, 38, 103
Plekhanov, Georgi, 161
Poggi, Gianfranco, 66
Poland, 6, 7, 9, 45, 110, 115
Polish Communist Party (PUWP), 6
political socialisation, 25–51, 54, 76–7; and 'deviancy', 60–1
polycentrism, 104, 112
popular front, 32, 65, 98–9, 118, 138; *see also* Frontism
Portuguese Communist Party (PCP), 3
Prague Spring, 41
Prandi, Alfonso, 62, 66, 79
Pratt, Jeff, 65
Pridham, Geoffrey, 50, 66, 67
Prior, M., 85
Procacci, Giuliano, 54
proletarian dictatorship, 19, 43, 161
PSI, *see* Italian Socialist Party

Rasimelli, Ilvano, 32
Reagan, Ronald, 4, 61
recruitment (PCI), 25, 27, 74
Red Army, 30
Red Belt, 2, 41, 53, 77
Red Brigades, 42
Resistance, 2, 32–3, 54, 95
Riccamboni, G., 52, 53
Risorgimento, 54, 55
rites of passage, 25
ritual, 25, 133
Rocco, Alfredo, 82
Romania, 6, 8, 9
Romano, L., 64
Ross, George, 141
Ruscoe, James, 143–4
Russell, Bertrand, 91

Sabine, George, 158, 159, 167, 190
Salazar, Antonio de Oliveira, 4
Sambuccari, Mario, 31
Sassoon, Donald, 25, 97, 98, 99
Scabello, P., 64
Scalfari, Eugeneo, 67
Scelba, Mario, 47
Schlesinger, Philip, 61
Sebastiani, Chiara, 33, 74, 93
Secchia, Pietro, 102
Sechi, Salvatore, 84, 170, 179–80, 182–3
Second International, 29
Seidel, Gill, 133
Selznik, Philip, 59
Sereni, Marina, 46
Serrati, Giacinto, 29

sessantottini, 44
Seton-Watson, Christopher, 54
Shangkun, Yang, 7, 8
Showstack Sassoon, Ann, 175
Silone, Ignazio, 57, 94
Sino-Soviet summit, 7
social anthropology, 13, 26–7
social democracy, 34
socialism, 3, 54, 55, 189–90, 194
socialist parties, European, 29
Socialist Unity Party (SED), 9
Solidarnosc, 9, 110, 130
Sorel, Georges, 80–2
Soviet Communist Party (CSPU), history of, 171–3; *see also* Gorbachev, Italian Communist Party, Leninism, membership, Stalinism
Soviet Union; and Eastern Europe, 10; and PCI membership, 32, 35, 44, 46
Spanish Civil War, 6, 86
Spanish Communist Party (PCE), 3, 5, 6
Spencer, Herbert, 176
Spriano, Paolo, 84
SS-20 missiles, 5
Stalin, Joseph, 31, 32, 85, 103–6, 152–3
Stalinism, analysis of, 80, 84, 104–5, 140, 165, 169–70, 173–7, 194; Trotsky's interpretation of, 162–3
Starr, Richard, 4
state, in communist theory, 11
statutes of the PCI; on democratic centralism, 141, 148, 181; on history, 84
Steadman Jones, Gareth, 8
stereotypes, 64
Stern, Alan, 55
strappo, 115
sub-culture, 2, 53, 67, 74–5
Swedish Communist Party, 3
symbols, political, 13, 14, 16, 52, 131–2; communist party, 71, 83, 177

Tambroni, Fernando, 39
Terracini, Umberto, 2
terrorism, 42, 44, 45
Thatcher, Margaret, 4
third way (*terza via*), 4, 45, 47, 113, 120, 129, 192
Tienanmen Square massacre, 8, 193
Tiersky, Ronald, 106, 165, 166, 170, 179, 181, 184, 188
Togliatti, Palmiro, 33, 34, 37, 50, 65, 153; and *Partito Nuovo*, 58, 95–101
Trotsky, Leon, 11, 31, 86, 142
Truman Doctrine, 36, 62–3
Tuscany, 37

UIL, 107
Umbria, 28, 37, 119
United States, 36, 39; foreign policy, 63–4; *see also* containment, Cold War, identity
Urban, George, 4
Urban, Joan Barth, 12, 114
USSR, *see* Soviet Union

Van Gennep, Arnold, 25
Veca, Salvatore, 185
Verba, Sidney, 56
via italiana al socialism, *see* Italian Road to Socialism

Walesa, Lech, 9
Waller, Michael, 165, 167, 170
Warsaw Pact, 8, 41
Weber, Max, 92
White, Caroline, 54
Williams, Gwyn, 72, 73
Williams, Raymond, 189–90
World War I, 29
world-view, communist; 14, 26, 31, 34–5, 38, 40, 43–4, 46–8, 50; and hegemony, 77–8; and identity, 78–9, 79–81; Marxist, 73; proletarian, 72

Xiaoping, Deng, 7

Yabang, Hu, 7
Yalta Memorandum, 153

Zhivkov, Todor, 9
Zinoviev, 31
Ziyang, Zhao, 7, 8